WITHDRAWN
HARVARD LIBRARY
WITHDRAWN

RELIGION AND HUMAN PURPOSE

STUDIES IN PHILOSOPHY AND RELIGION

1. FREUND, E.R. *Franz Rosenzweig's Philosophy of Existence: An Analysis of* The Star of Redemption. 1979. ISBN 90 247 2091 5.

2. OLSON, A.M. *Transcendence and Hermeneutics: An Interpretation of the Philosophy of Karl Jaspers.* 1979. ISBN 90 247 2092 3.

3. VERDU, A. *The Philosophy of Buddhism.* 1981. ISBN 90 247 2224 1.

4. OLIVER, H.H. *A Relational Metaphysic.* 1981. ISBN 90 247 2457 0.

5. ARAPURA, J.G. *Gnosis and the Question of Thought in Vedānta.* 1985. ISBN 90 247 3061 9.

6. HOROSZ, W. and CLEMENTS, T. (eds.) *Religion and Human Purpose.* 1987. ISBN 90 247 3000 7.

7. SIA, S. *God in Process Thought.* 1985. ISBN 90 247 3103 8.

8. KOBLER, J.F. *Vatican II and Phenomenology.* 1985. ISBN 90 247 3193 3.

9. GODFREY, J.J. *A Philosophy of Human Hope.* 1986. ISBN 90 247 3353 7.

10. PERRETT, R.W. *Death and Immortality.* 1987. ISBN 90 247 3440 1.

RELIGION AND HUMAN PURPOSE
A Cross Disciplinary Approach

edited by

WILLIAM HOROSZ and TAD CLEMENTS

1987 **MARTINUS NIJHOFF PUBLISHERS**
a member of the KLUWER ACADEMIC PUBLISHERS GROUP
DORDRECHT / BOSTON / LANCASTER

Distributors

for the United States and Canada: Kluwer Academic Publishers, P.O. Box 358, Accord Station, Hingham, MA 02018-0358, USA
for the UK and Ireland: Kluwer Academic Publishers, MTP Press Limited, Falcon House, Queen Square, Lancaster LA1 1RN, UK
for all other countries: Kluwer Academic Publishers Group, Distribution Center, P.O. Box 322, 3300 AH Dordrecht, The Netherlands

Library of Congress Cataloging in Publication Data

```
Religion and human purpose.
  (Studies in philosophy and religion ; 6)
  Includes index.
  1. Religion--Philosophy--Addresses, essays,
lectures. 2. Intentionality (Philosophy)--Addresses,
essays, lectures. I. Horosz, William. II. Clements,
Tad S.  III. Series: Studies in philosophy and religion
(Martinus Nijhoff Publishers) ; v. 6.
BL51.R346  1985       200'.1             84-14826
```

ISBN 90-247-3000-7 (this volume)
ISBN 90-247-2346-9 (series)

Copyright

© 1987 by Martinus Nijhoff Publishers, Dordrecht.

All rights reserved. No part of this publication may be reproduced, stored in a retrieval system, or transmitted in any form or by any means, mechanical, photocopying, recording, or otherwise, without the prior written permission of the publishers,
Martinus Nijhoff Publishers, P.O. Box 163, 3300 AD Dordrecht,
The Netherlands.

PRINTED IN THE NETHERLANDS

TABLE OF CONTENTS

Preface VII

List of Contributors IX

PART I
FROM THE PHILOSOPHICAL PERSPECTIVE

1. Linguistic Philosophy and 'The Meaning of Life', Kai Nielsen — 3
2. Phenomenology of Religion and Human Purpose, J.N. Mohanty — 31
3. The Concept of Purpose in a Naturalistic Humanist Perspective, Tad S. Clements — 49
4. The Recovery of Human Purpose in the Religious Life, William Horosz — 69

PART II
FROM THE RELIGIOUS PERSPECTIVE

5. Orthodox Judaism and Human Purpose, Walter S. Wurtzburger — 105
6. Liberal Judaism and the Human Purpose, Jacob B. Agus — 123
7. Human Purposiveness in St. Thomas Aquinas, Francis J. Kovach — 143
8. The Concept of Purpose in Reformation Thought, Robert Bretall — 165
9. The Liberal Commitment to Divine Immanence, William Horosz — 197

PART III
FROM THE PERSPECTIVE OF INDIAN RELIGION

10. Purpose of Man in the Tradition of Indian Orthodoxy, S.P. Banerjee — 235
11. The Concepts of Man and Human Purpose in Contemporary Indian Thought, D.P. Chattopadhyaya — 271

PREFACE

The cross-disciplinary studies in this volume are of special interest because they link human purpose to the present debate between religion and the process of secularization. If that debate is to be a creative one, the notion of the 'human orderer' must be related significantly both to the sacred and secular realms. In fact, if man were not a purposive being, he would have neither religious nor secular problems. Questions about origins and destiny, divine purposiveness and the order of human development, would not arise as topics of human concern. It would appear, then, that few would deny the fact of man's purposiveness in existence, that the pursuit of these purposes constitutes the dramas of history and culture. Yet the case is otherwise. For, concerning 'purposes' itself, widely divergent, even antithetical, views have been held. The common man has mistrusted its guidance for purpose, much too often, 'changes its mind'. Its fluctuations and whimsical nature are too much even for common sense. The sciences have identified purpose with the personal life and viewed it as a function of the subject self. Consequently they had no need for it in scientific method and objective knowledge. The religions of the world have used purpose in its holistic sense, for purposes of establishing grandious systems of religious totality and for stating the ultimate goals in man's destiny. Yet even in this domain, religion has denied the designing powers of purpose in fashioning such systems of totality and mistrusted its guidance for the final purposes for life.

Other questionings, too, have driven man away from the reliance on the directives of his purposive nature. Is purpose simply a human phenomenon? Or does it have analogues in the sub and supra realms beyond the human dimension? What is the source and justification, if any, for purpose, whether human or otherwise? How does it relate to the process of symbolization or to man's elemental modes of response to existence? Can human purpose be causally explained, that is to say, can teleological explanations be translated into deterministic patterns? Is the concept of purpose applicable to human action or to the 'behaviour' of machines of certain sorts, such as servomechanisms?

In the present encounter between religion and secularization, the issue of purpose comes to the fore with renewed vigor. Can religion have other uses for purpose than its construction of systems of totality and man's ultimate goals? Are such totalistic religious schemes prior to purposive being? In this exchange between the sacred and secular widely divergent views also prevail. When religions absolutize their schemes of totality, do they have any other recourse out of the problem of pluralism and relativism (of the many systems of totality) other than the path of making claims of ultimacy for the system of totality to which one is committed and which one views as somehow being prior to purposive being? Can the present dialogue between the sacred and secular be creative without a new look at human purpose and its relevance to both spheres of influence?

Questions such as these have occupied many thinkers, past as well as present, in diverse fields. But these questionings have a new urgency about them in the timely debate between religion and secularization. This volume is a modest cooperative effort along cross-disciplinary lines to link human purpose to the dialogue between the sacred and the secular, faithfully and critically assessing the relation of purpose to man and his religions. The distinction between orthodoxy and liberalism should display marked differences on purpose and man's relation to the eternal. Philosophers from many schools of thought, just as religionists from divergent traditions, will here speak their minds in the current debate. This renewed concern with 'purpose' is significant in the debate between religion and secularization because it attempts to state the case for the 'human orderer' in existence and of his participation in both processes.

William Horosz and Tad Clements

LIST OF CONTRIBUTORS

Jacob B. Agus, Rabbi at Beth El Congregation, Baltimore, Adj. Professor of Jewish Thought at Temple University and the Reconstructionist Rabbinical College.

S.P. Banerjee, Professor of Philosophy, University of Calcutta, India.

Robert W. Bretall, Professor of Philosophy, University of Arizona, Tucson, Arizona.

Debi Prasad Chattopadhyaya, Professor of Philosophy, Jadavpur University, Calcutta, India, and Chairman, Indian Council for Philosophical Research.

Tad S. Clements, Professor of Philosophy, State University of New York, Brockport, New York.

William Horosz, Professor of Philosophy, University of Oklahoma, Norman, Oklahoma.

Francis J. Kovach, Professor of Philosophy, University of Oklahoma, Norman, Oklahoma.

Jitendra Nath Mohanty, George Lynn Cross Research Professor of Philosophy, University of Oklahoma, Norman, Oklahoma.

Kai Nielsen, Professor of Philosophy, The University of Calgary, Canada.

Walter S. Wurtzburger, Rabbi of Congregation Shaaray Tefila, Far Rockaway, New York, and Visiting Associate Professor of Philosophy, Yeshiva University, New York City.

PART I

FROM THE PHILOSOPHICAL PERSPECTIVE

CHAPTER 1

LINGUISTIC PHILOSOPHY AND 'THE MEANING OF LIFE'

KAI NIELSEN

I

Anglo-Saxon philosophy has in various degrees 'gone linguistic'. From the faithful attention to the niceties of plain English practiced by John Austin, to the use of descriptive linguistics initiated by Paul Ziff in his *Semantic Analysis*, to the deliberately more impressionistic concern with language typical of Isaiah Berlin and Stuart Hampshire, there is a pervasive emphasis by English-speaking philosophers on what can and cannot be said, on what is intelligible, and on what is nonsensical. When linguistic philosphy was first developing, many things were said to be nonsense which were not nonsense. However, this is something of the past, for linguistic philosophy has for a long time been less truculent and more diffident about what it makes sense to say, but only to become – some would say – unbelievably bland, dull and without a rationale that is of any general interest.[1]

Critics from many quarters have raised their voices to assault linguistic philosophy as useless pedantry remote from the perennial concerns of philosophy or the problems of belief and life that all men encounter when, in Hesse's terms, they feel to the full 'the whole riddle of human destiny'. Traditionally the philosophical enterprise sought, among other things, to give us some enlightenment about our human condition, but as philosophy 'goes linguistic', it has traitorously and irresponsibly become simply talk about the uses of talk. The philosopher has left his 'high calling' to traffic in linguistic trivialities.

Criticism of linguistic philosophy has not always been this crude, but there has typically been at least the implied criticism that linguistic philosophy could not really do justice to the profound problems of men with which Plato, Spinoza or Nietzsche struggled.

It is my conviction that such a charge is unfounded. In linguistic philosophy

---

1. John Passmore remarks in his brief but thoroughly reliable and judicious *Philosophy in the Last Decade* (Sydney University Press: 1969) 'Philosophy is once again cultivating areas it had declared wasteland, or had transferred without compunction to other owners', p. 5.

there is a partially new technique but no 'abdication of philosophy'. Surely most linguistic philosophy is dull, as is most philosophy, as is most anything else. Excellence and insight in any field are rare. But at its best linguistic philosophy is not dull and it is not without point; furthermore, though it often is, it need not be remote from the concerns of men. It is this last claim – the claim that linguistic philosophy can have nothing of importance to say about the perplexities of belief and life that from time to time bedevil us – that I wish to challenge.

With reference to the concepts of human purpose, religion and the problematical notion 'the meaning of Life', I want to show how in certain crucial respects linguistic philosophy can be relevant to the perplexities about life and conduct that reflective people actually face. 'What is the meaning of Life?' has been a standby of both the pulpiteer and the mystagogue. It has not come in for extended analysis by linguistic philosophers, though Ayer, Wisdom, Baier, Edwards, Flew, Hepburn and Dilman have had some important things to say about this obscure notion which when we are in certain moods perplexes us all and indeed, as it did Tolstoy and Dostoevsky, may even be something that forces itself upon us in thoroughly human terms.[2] I want to show how the use of the analytical techniques of linguistic philosophy can help us in coming to grips with the problems of human purpose and the meaning of Life.

Part of the trouble centers around puzzles about the use of the word 'meaning' in 'What is the meaning of Life?' Since the turn of the century there has been a lot of talk in philosophical circles about 'meaning' or 'a meaning criterion' and a good measure of attention has been paid to considerations about the meanings of words and sentences. But the mark (token) 'meaning' in 'What is the meaning of Life?' has a very different use than it has in 'What is the meaning of 'obscurantist'?' 'What is the meaning of 'table'?' 'What is the meaning of 'good'?' 'What is the meaning of 'science'?' and 'What is the meaning of 'meaning'?' In these other cases we are asking about the meaning or use of the word or words, and we are requesting either a definition of the word or an elucidation or description of the word's use. But in asking: 'What is the meaning of Life?' we are not asking – or at least this is not our central perplexity – about 'What is the meaning of the word 'Life'?' What then are we asking?

Indirection is the better course here. Consider some of the uses of the general formula: 'What is the meaning of that?' How, in what contexts, and

---

2. A. J. Ayer, 'The Claims of Philosophy', in M. Natanson (ed.), *Philosophy of the Social Sciences*, Random House, 1963.

for what purposes does it get used? Sometimes we may simply not know the meaning of a word, as when we come across a word we do not understand and look it up in a dictionary or ask the person using it in conversation what it means. It is not that he is using the word in an odd sense and we want to know what *he means* by it, but that we want to know what is meant by that word as it is employed in the public domain.

There is the quite different situation in which it is not about words that we are puzzled but about someone's non-linguistic behavior. A friend gives us a dark look in the middle of the conversation in which several people are taking part and afterwards we ask him 'What was the meaning of those dark looks?' We were aware when we noticed his dark look that he was disapproving of something we were doing but we did not and still do not know what. Our 'What was the meaning of that?' serves to try to bring out what is the matter. Note that in a way here we are not even puzzled about the meaning of words. The recipient of the dark look may very well know he is being disapproved of; but he wants to know what for. Here 'What is the meaning of that?' is a request for the point or the purpose of the action. In this way, as we shall see, it is closer to the question 'What is the meaning of Life?' than questions about the meaning of a word or a sentence.

We also ask 'What is the meaning of that?' when we want to know how a particular person on a particular occasion intends something. We want to know what *he means* by that. Thus if I say of some author that he writes 'chocolate rabbit stories' you may well ask me what I mean by that. Here you are puzzled both about the meaning of the phrase 'chocolate rabbit stories', for as with 'the pine cone weeps' or 'the rock cogitates' it is a deviant collection of words of indeterminate meanings, and about the point or purpose of making such a remark. After all, the point of making such an utterance may not be evident. Suppose I had said it to a stupid and pompous writer blown up with a false sense of his own importance. I could explain my meaning by saying that I was obliquely giving him to understand that his stories, like chocolate rabbits, were all out of the same mold: change the names and setting and you have the same old thing all over again. And the point of my utterance would also become evidence, i.e., to deflate the pompous windbag. The phrase 'chocolate rabbit stories' has no fixed use in human discourse, but language is sufficiently elastic for me to be able to give it a use without generating any linguistic or conceptual shock. To explain my meaning I must make clear the use I am giving it and make evident why I choose to use such an odd phrase.

'What is the meaning of Life?' is in some very significant respects like this last question though it is of course also very different. It is different in being non-deviant and in being a profoundly important question in the way the other question clearly is not. But note the likeness. In the first place when we or other people ask this question we are often not at all sure what we are asking. In this practical context we may in a way even be puzzled about the word 'life', though, as I have said, the question does not primarily function as a request for the explanation of the use of a word. There is a sense in which life does and there is a sense in which life does not begin and end in mystery. And when we ask about life here we are not asking Schrodinger's question or J. B. S. Haldane's. We are not in search of some property or et of properties that is common to and distinctive of all those things we call 'living things'. We are typically concerned with something very different and much vaguer. We are asking: 'Is life just one damn thing after another until finally one day we die and start to rot? Or can I sum it up and find or at least give it some point after all? Or is this just a silly illusion born of fear and trembling?' These are desperately vague, amorphous questions, but – as Wisdom would surely and rightly say – not meaningless for all that. And for some of us, and perhaps for all of us, *sometimes*, they are haunting, edging questions, questions we agonize over, then evade, then again try to come to grips with.

First, I want to say that, like 'What is the meaning of calling them chocolate rabbit stories?', 'What is the meaning of Life?' does *not* have a clear use; but that it does not have a clear use does not, I repeat, entail or in any way establish that it does not have a use or even that it does not have a supremely important use.[3] Secondly, 'What is the meaning of life?' most typically – though not always – functions as a request for the goals *worth* seeking in life though sometimes it may serve to ask if there are *any* goals worth seeking in life.[4] We are asking what (if anything) is the point to our lives? What (if anything) could give our lives purpose or point? In anguish we struggle to find the purpose, point or rationale of our grubby lives. But if this is the nature of the question, what would an answer look like? For this to be a fruitful question, all of us must ask ourselves individually: what would we take as an answer? When we ask this we are apt to come up with a blank; and if we are readers of philosophical literature we may remember that, along with others, a philosopher as persuasive and influential as A. J. Ayer has said that all such questions are unanswerable. But if they are really unanswerable – or so it

---

3. John Wisdom has driven home this point with force. In particular see his 'The Modes of Thought and the Logic of 'God'' in his *Paradox and Discovery* (California, 1965).
4. Ronald Hepburn has correctly stressed that this for some people may not be what is uppermost in their minds when they ask that question. See Hepburn's essay in this volume. See also Ilham Dilman's remarks about Hepburn's analysis in 'Life and Meaning', *Philosophy*, 40, October 1965.

would seem – then they are hardly genuine questions.

I will concede that *in a sense* such questions are unanswerable, but in a much more important sense they *are* answerable. We can be intelligent about and reason about such questions. Any analysis which does not bring this out and elucidate it is confused and inadequate. In destroying pontifical pseudo-answers the baby has frequently gone down with the bath. In showing what kind of answers could not be answers to this question, the temptation is to stress that there are no answers at all and that indeed no answers are needed. I want to try to show this is wrong and what an answer would look like.

II

How then is it possible for our life to have a meaning or purpose? For a while, oddly enough, Ayer in his 'The Claims of Philosophy' is a perfectly sound guide.[5] We do know what it is for a man to have a purpose. 'It is a matter, Ayer remarks, 'of his intending, on the basis of a given situation, to bring about some further situation which for some reason or other he conceives to be desirable.'

But, Ayer asks, how is it possible for life *in general* to have a meaning or a purpose?

Well, there is one very simple answer. Life in general has a purpose if all living beings are tending toward a certain specifiable end. To understand the meaning of life or the purpose of existence it is only necessary to discover this end.

As Ayer makes perfectly clear, there are overwhelming difficulties with such an answer. In the first place there is no good reason to believe living beings are tending toward some specifiable end. But even if it were true that they are all tending toward this end such a discovery would not at all answer the question 'What is the meaning or purpose of life?' This is so because when we human beings ask this exceedingly vague question we are not just asking for *an explanation of* the facts of existence; we are asking for a *justification* of these facts. In asking this question we are seeking a way of life, trying as suffering, perplexed, and searching creatures to find what the existentialists like to call an 'authentic existence'. And as Ayer goes on to explain,

---

5. See Ayer, *op. cit.* The rest of the references to Ayer in the text are from this essay. His brief remarks in his 'What I Believe' in *What I Believe* (London: 1966) pp. 15–16 and in his introduction to *The Humanist Outlook*, A. J. Ayer (ed.), (London: 1968) pp. 6–7 are also relevant as further brief statements of his central claims about the meaning of life.

a theory which informs them merely that the course of events is so arranged as to lead inevitably to a certain end does nothing to meet their need. For the end in question will not be one that they themselves have chosen. As far as they are concerned it will be entirely arbitrary; and it will be a no less arbitrary fact that their existence is such as necessarily to lead to its fulfillment. In short, from the point of view of justifying one's existence, there is no essential difference between a teleological explanation of events and a mechanical explanation. In either case, it is a matter of brute fact that events succeed one another in the ways they do and are explicable in the ways they are.

In the last analysis, an attempt to answer a question of why events are as they are must always resolve itself into saying only *how* they are. Every explanation of why people do such and such and why the world is so and so finally depends on a very general description. And even if it is the case, as Charles Taylor powerfully argues, that teleological explanations of human behavior are irreducible, Ayer's point here is not all weakened, for in explaining, teleologically or otherwise, we are still showing how things are; we are not justifying anything.[6]

When we ask: 'What is the meaning of life?' we want an answer that is more than *just* an explanation or description of *how* people behave or *how* events are arranged or *how* the world is constituted. We are asking for a *justification* for our existence. We are asking for a justification for why life is as it is, and not even the most complete explanation and/or description of *how* things are ordered can answer this quite different question. The person who demands that some general description of man and his place in nature should entail a statement that man ought to live and die in a certain way is asking for something that can no more be the case than it can be the case that ice can gossip. To ask about the meaning of our lives involves asking how we should live, or whether any decision to live in one way is more *worthy* of acceptance than any other. Both of these questions are clearly questions of value; yet no statement of *fact* about how we in fact do live can by itself be sufficient to answer such questions. No statement of what ought to be the case can be deduced from a statement of what is the case. If we are demanding such an answer, then Ayer is perfectly right in claiming the question is unanswerable.

Let me illustrate. Suppose, perhaps as a result of some personal crisis, I want to take stock of myself. As Kierkegaard would say, I want to appropriate, take to heart, the knowledge I have or can get about myself and my condition in order to arrive at some decision as to what sort of life would be most meaningful for me, would be the sort of life I would truly want to live if I could act rationally and were fully apprised of my true condition. I might say to myself, though certainly not to others, unless I was a bit of an

---

6. Charles Taylor, *The Explanation of Behavior*, Routledge and Kegan Paul, 1964.

exhibitionist, 'Look Nielsen, you're a little bit on the vain side and you're arrogant to boot. And why do you gossip so and spend so much of your time reading science fiction? And why do you always say what you expect other people want you to say? You don't approve of that in others, do you? And why don't you listen more? And weren't you too quick with Jones and too indulgent with Smith?' In such a context I would put these questions and a host of questions like them to myself. And I might come up with some general explanations, good or bad, like 'I act this way because I have some fairly pervasive insecurities'. And to my further question, 'Well, why do you have these insecurities?' I might dig up something out of my past such as 'My parents died when I was two and I never had any real home.' To explain why this made me insecure I might finally evoke a whole psychological theory, and these explanations about the nature of the human animal would themselves finally rest, in part at least, on various descriptions of how man does behave. In addition, I might, if I could afford it and were sufficiently bedevilled by these questions, find my way to a psychiatrist's couch and there, after the transference had taken place, I would eventually get more quite personalized explanations of my behavior and attitudes. But none of these things, in themselves, could tell me the meaning of life or even the meaning of my life, though they indeed might help me in this search. I might discover that I was insecure because I could never get over the wound of the loss of my father. I might discover that unconsciously I blamed myself. As a child I wished him dead and then he died so somehow I did it, really. And I would, of couse, discover how unreasonable this is. I would come to understand that people generally react this way in those situations. In Tolstoy's phrase, we are all part of the 'same old river'. And, after rehearsing it, turning it over, taking it to heart, I might well gain control over it and eventually gain control over some of my insecurities. I could see and even live through again what *caused* me to be vain, arrogant and lazy. But suppose, that even after all these discoveries I really didn't want to change. After stocktaking, I found that I was willing to settle for the *status quo*. Now I gratefully acknowledge that this is very unlikely, but here we are concerned with the *logical* possibilities. 'Yes, there are other ways of doing things', I say to myself, 'but after all is said and done I have lived this way a long time and I would rather go on this way than change. This sort of life, is after all, the most meaningful one. This is how I really want to act and this is how I, and others like me, ought to act'. What possible facts could anyone appeal to which would prove, in the sense of logically entail, that I was wrong and that the purpose of life or the meaning of life was very different than I thought it was? It is Ayer's contention, and I think he is right, that there are none.

'But you have left out God', someone might say. 'You have neglected the possibility that there is a God and that God made man to His image and likeness and that God has a plan for man. Even Sartre, Heidegger and Camus agree that to ask 'What is the Meaning of Life?' or 'What is the purpose of human existence?' is, in effect, to raise the question of God. If there is a God your conclusion would not follow, and, as Father Copleston has said, if there is *no* God human existence can have no end or purpose other than that given by man himself'.[7]

I would want to say, that the whole question of God or no God, Jesus or no Jesus, is entirely beside the point. Even if there were a God human existence can, in the relevant sense of 'end', 'purpose' or 'meaning', have no other end, purpose or meaning than what we as human beings give it by our own deliberate choices and decisions.

Let us see how this is so. Let us suppose that everything happens as it does because God intends that it should. Let us even assume, as we in reality cannot, that we can know the purpose or intentions of God. Now, as Ayer points out, either God's 'purpose is sovereign or it is not. If it is sovereign, that is, if everything that happens is necessarily in accordance with it, then it is true also of our behavior. Consequently, there is no point in our deciding to conform to it, for the simple reason that we cannot do otherwise'. No matter what, we do God's purpose. There is no sense in saying it is *our* purpose, that it is something we have made our own by our own deliberate choice. I have not *discovered* a meaning for my life and other people have not *discovered* a meaning for their lives. If it were possible for us *not* to fulfill it, the purpose would not be God's *sovereign* purpose and if it is His sovereign purpose, it cannot, in the requisite sense, be *our* purpose, for it will not be something that necessarily happens to us because of God's intentions. If we are compelled to do it, it is not *our* purpose. It is only our purpose if we want to do it and if we could have done otherwise.

On the other hand, if God's purpose is not sovereign and we are not inexorably compelled to do what God wills, we have no reason to conform to God's purpose unless we independently judge it to be *good* or by our own independent decision make it our purpose. We cannot derive the statement 'x is good' from 'that Being whom people call 'God' says 'x is good'' or from 'that Being whom people call 'God' wills x' unless we *independently* judge that whatever this Being *says* is good *is good* or whatever that Being wills *ought* to be done. Again, as Ayer remarks, this 'means that the significance of our behavior depends finally upon our own judgments of value; and the

---

7. See his discussion of existentialism in his *Contemporary Philosophy*.

concurrence of a diety then becomes superfluous'.[8]

The basic difficulty, as Ayer makes clear, is that in trying to answer the questions as we have above, we have really misunderstood the question. 'What-is-the-meaning-of-that?' and 'What-is-the-purpose-of-that?' questions can be very different. We have already noted some of the differences among 'What-is-the-meaning-of-that?' questions, and we have seen that 'What is the meaning of Life?' in many contexts at least can well be treated as a 'What-is-the-purpose-of-that?' question. But 'What is the purpose of life?' is only very superficially like 'What is the purpose of a blotter?' 'What is the purpose of brain surgery?' or 'What is the purpose of the liver?' The first is a question about a human artifact and in terms of certain assumed ends we can say quite explicitly, independently of whether or not we want blotters, what the purpose of blotters is. Similarly brain surgery is a well-known human activity and has a well-known rationale. Even if we are Christian Scientists and disapprove of surgery altogether, we can understand and agree on what the purpose of brain surgery is, just as we all can say Fearless Fosdick is a good safecracker, even though we disapprove of safecrackers. And again, in terms of the total functioning of the human animal we can say what livers are for, even though the liver is not an artifact like a blotter. If there is a God and God made man, we *might* say the question 'What is the purpose of human life?' is very like 'What is the purpose of umbrellas?' The human animal then becomes a Divine artifact. But, even if all this were so, we would not – as we have already seen – have an answer to the *justificatory* question we started with when we asked, 'What is the meaning of life?' If we knew God's purpose for man, we would know what man was made for. But we would not have an answer to our question about the meaning of life, for we would not know if there was purpose *in* our lives or if we could find a point in acting one way rather than another. We would only know that there was something – which may or may not be of value – that we were constructed, 'cut out', to be.

Similarly, if an Aristotelian philosophy is correct, 'What is the purpose of life?' would become very like 'What is the purpose of the liver?' But here again a discovery of what end man is as a matter of fact tending toward would not answer the perplexity we started from, that is to say, it would not answer the question, 'What is the meaning of life, how should men live and die?' We would only learn that 'What is the purpose of life?' could admit of two very different uses. As far as I can see, there are no good reasons to believe either

---

8. While I completely agree with the central thrust of Ayer's argument here, he has, I believe, overstated his case. Even if our behaviour finally depends on our own standards of value, it does not follow that the concurrence of the deity, if there is one, is superfluous, for we could still find crucial moral guidance from our grasp of something of God's wisdom.

that there is a God or that the human animal has been ordered for some general end; but even if this were so it would not give us an answer to the question: 'What is the meaning of life?'

This is so because the question has been radically misconstrued. When we ask: 'What is the meaning of life?' or 'What is the purpose of human existence?' we are normally asking, as I have already said, questions of the following types: 'What should we seek?' 'What ends – if any – are worthy of attainment?' Questions of this sort require a very different answer than any answer to: 'What is the meaning of 'obscurantism'?' 'What is the purpose of the ink-blotter?' and 'What is the purpose of the liver?' Ayer is right when he says: 'what is required by those who seek to know the purpose of their existence is not a factual description of the way that people actually do conduct themselves, but rather a decision as to how they *should* conduct themselves'. Again he is correct in remarking: 'There is – a sense in which it can be said that life does have a meaning. It has for each of us whatever meaning we severally *choose* to give it. The purpose of a man's existence is constituted by the ends to which he, consciously or unconsciously, devotes himself'.

Ayer links this with another crucial logical point, a point which the existentialists have dramatized as some kind of worrisome 'moral discovery'. Ayer points out that 'in the last resort ... each individual has the responsibility of making the choice of how he ought to live and die' and that it is logically impossible that someone else, in some authoritative position, can make that choice for him. If someone gives me moral advice in the nature of the case I must decide whether or not to follow his advice, so again the choice is finally my own. This is true because moral questions are primarily questions about what to do. In asking how I ought to live, I am trying to make up my mind how to act. And to say I deliberately acted in a certain way implies that I decided to do it. There is no avoiding personal choice in considering such questions.

But Ayer, still writing in the tradition of logical empiricism, often writes as if it followed from the truth of what we have said so far, that there could be no reasoning about 'How ought man to live?' or 'What is the meaning of life?' Thus Ayer says at one point in 'The Claims of Philosophy': 'He [the moral agent] cannot prove his judgments of value are correct, for the simple reason that no judgment of value is capable of proof'. He goes on to argue that people have no way of demonstrating that one judgment of value is superior to another. A decision between people in moral disagreement is a 'subject for persuasion and finally a matter of individual choice'.

As we have just seen there is a sound point to Ayer's stress on choice vis-à-vis morality, but taken as a whole his remarks are at best misleading. There is reasoning about moral questions and there are arguments and proofs in morality. There are principles in accordance with which we appraise our actions, and there are more general principles, like the principle of utility or the principles of distributive justice in accordance with which we test our lower-level moral rules. And there is a sense of 'being reasonable' which, as Hume and Westermarck were well aware, has distinctive application to moral judgments. Thus, if I say, 'I ought to be relieved of my duties, I'm just too ill to go on' I not only must believe I am in fact ill, I must also be prepared to say, of any of my colleagues or anyone else similarly placed, that in like circumstances they too ought to be relieved of their duties if they fall ill. There is a certain *generality* about moral discourse and a man is not reasoning morally or 'being reasonable' if he will not allow those inferences. Similarly, if I say 'I want x' or 'I prefer x' I need not, though I may, be prepared to give reason why I want it or prefer it, but if I say 'x is the right thing to do' or 'x is good' or 'I ought to do x' or 'x is worthy of attainment', I must – perhaps with the exception of judgments of intrinsic goodness – be prepared to give *reasons* for sayng 'x is the right thing to do', 'x is good', 'I ought to do x' and the like. (Note, this remark has the status of what Wittgenstein would call a grammatical remark.)

It is indeed true in morals and in reasoning about human conduct generally that justification must come to an end; but this is also true in logic, science and in common sense empirical reasoning about matters of fact; but it is also true that the end point in reasoning over good and evil is different than in science and the like, for in reasoning about how to act, our judgment finally terminates in a choice – a decision of principle. And here is the truth in Ayer's remark that moral judgments are *'finally* a matter of individual choice'. But, unless we are to mislead, we must put the emphasis on 'finally', for a dispassioned, neutral analysis of the uses of the language of human conduct will show, as I have indicated, that there is reasoning, and in a relevant sense, 'objective reasoning', about moral questions. It is not at all a matter of pure persuasion or goading someone into sharing your attitudes.

I cannot, of course, even begin to display the full range of the reasoning which has sought to establish this point. But I hope I have said enough to block the misleading implications of Ayer's otherwise very fine analysis. Early linguistic philosophy was primarily interested in (1) the descriptive and explanatory discourse of the sciences, and (2) in logico-mathematico discourse; the rest was rather carelessly labeled, 'expressive or emotive discourse'. But the thrust of the work of linguistic philosophers since the Second World War has corrected that mistaken emphasis, as recent analytical writing in ethics makes evident. Here I commend to you R. M. Hare's *The Language of Morals*, and his *Freedom and Reason*, Stephen Toulmin's *An Examination of the Place of Reason in Ethics*, Kurt Baier's *The Moral Point of View*, Marcus Singer's *Generalization in Ethics*, P. H. Nowell-Smith's *Ethics*, Bernard Mayo's *Ethics and the Moral Life*, or George von Wright's *The Varieties of Goodness*. They would also reinforce the point I tried briefly to make against Ayer, as would an examination of the essays of Philippa Foot or John Rawls.[9]

III

There are, however, other considerations that may be in our minds when we ask 'What is the meaning of life?' or 'Does life have a meaning?' In asking such questions, we may *not* be asking 'What should we seek?' or 'What goals are worth seeking really?' Instead we may be asking 'Is *anything* worth seeking?' 'Does it matter finally what we do?' Here, some may feel, we finally meet the real tormenting 'riddle of human existence'.

Such a question is not simply a moral question: it is a question concerning human conduct, a question about how to live one's life or about whether to continue to live one's life. Yet when we consider what an answer would look like here we draw a blank. If someone says 'Is anything worthwhile?' we gape. We want to reply: 'Why, sitting in the sunshine in the mornings, seeing the full moon rise, meeting a close friend one hasn't seen in a long time, sleeping comfortable after a tiring day, all these things and a million more are most assuredly worthwhile. Any life devoid of experiences of this sort would most certainly be impoverished'.

Yet this reply is so obvious we feel that something different must be intended by the questioner. The questioner knows that we, and most probably he, ordinarily regard such things as worthwhile, but he is asking if these things or *anything* is worthwhile *really*? These things *seem* worthwhile but are they in reality? And here we indeed do not know what to say. If someone queries whether it is really worthwhile leaving New York and going to the beach in August we have some idea of what to say; there are some criteria which will enable us to make at least a controversial answer to this question. But when it is asked, in a philosophical manner, *if anything, ever* is really worthwhile,

---

9. I have discussed these issues in my 'Problems of Ethics' and 'History of Contemporary Ethics', both in Vol. 3 of *The Encyclopedia of Philosophy*, Paul Edwards (ed.), Macmillan, 1967.

it is not clear that we have a genuine question before us. The question borrows its form from more garden-variety questions but when we ask it in this general way do we actually know what we mean? If someone draws a line on the blackboard, a question over the line's straightness can arise only if some criterion for a line's being straight is accepted. Similarly only if some criterion of worthiness is accepted can we intelligibly ask if a specific thing or anything is wortly of attainment.

But if a sensitive and reflective person asks, 'Is anything worthwhile, really?' could he not be asking this because, (1) he has a certain vision of human excellence, and (2) his austere criteria for what is worthwhile have developed in terms of that vision? Armed with such criteria, he might find nothing that man can in fact attain under his present and foreseeable circumstances *worthy* of attainment. Considerations of this sort seem to be the sort of considerations that led Tolstoy and Schopenhauer to come to such pessimistic views about life. Such a person would be one of those few people, who as one of Hesse's characters remarks, 'demand the utmost of life and yet cannot come to terms with its stupidity and crudeness'. In terms of his ideal of human excellence nothing is worthy of attainment.

To this, it is natural to respond, 'If this is our major problem about the meaning of life, then this is indeed no intellectual or philosophical riddle about human destiny. We need not like Steppenwolf return to our lodging lonely and disconsolate because life's 'glassy essence' remains forever hidden, for we can well envisage, in making such a judgment, what would be worthwhile. We can say what a meaningful life would look like even though we can't attain it. If such is the question, there is no 'riddle of human existence', though there is a pathos to human life and there is the social-political pattern problem of how to bring the requisite human order into existence. Yet only if we have a conception of what human life should be can we feel such pathos'.

If it is said in response to this that what would really be worthwhile could not possibly be attained, an absurdity has been uttered. to say something is worthy of attainment implies that, everything else being equal, it ought to be attained. But to say that something ought to be attained implies that it *can* be attained. Thus we *cannot* intelligibly say that something is worthy of attainment but that it cannot possibly be attained. So in asking 'Is anything worthy of attainment?' we must acknowledge that there are evaluative criteria operative which guarantee that what is sincerely said to be worthy of attainment is at least in principle attainable. And as we have seen in speaking of morality, 'x is worthy of attainment' does not mean 'x is preferred', though again, in asserting that something is worthy of attainment, or worthwhile, we imply that we would choose it, everything else being equal, in preference to something else. But we cannot intelligibly speak of a choice if there is no possibility of doing one thing rather than another.

Life is often hard and, practically speaking, the ideals we set our hearts on, those to which we most deeply commit ourselves, may in actual fact be impossible to achieve. A sensitive person may have an ideal of conduct, an ideal of life, that he assents to without reservation. But the facts of human living being what they are, he knows full well that this ideal cannot be realized. His ideals are intelligible enough, logically their achievement is quite possible, but as a matter of *brute fact* his ideals are beyond his attainment. If this is so, is it worthwhile for him and others like him to go on living or to strive for anything at all? Can life, under such circumstances, be anything more than an ugly habit? For such a man, 'What is the meaning of life?' has the force of 'What *point* can a life such as mine have under these circumstances?' And in asking whether such a life has a point he is asking the very question we put above, viz. can life be worth living under such conditions.

Again such a question is perfectly intelligible and is in no way unanswerable any more than any other question about how to act, though here too we must realize that the facts of human living *cannot* be sufficient for a man simply to read off an answer without it in any way affecting his life. Here, too, *any* answer will require a decision or some kind of effective involvement on the part of the person involved. A philosopher can be of help here in showing what kind of answers we cannot give, but it is far less obvious that he can provide us with a set of principles that together with empirical facts about his condition and prospects, will enable the perplexed man to know what he ought to do. The philosopher or any thoughtful person who sees just what is involved in the question can give some helpful advice. Still the person involved must work out an answer in anguish and soreness of heart.

However, I should remind him that no matter how bad his own life was, there would always remain something he could do to help alleviate the sum total of human suffering. This certainly has value and if he so oriented his life, he could not say that his life was without point. I would also argue that in normal circumstances he could not be sure that his ideals of life would permanently be frustrated, and if he held ideals that would be badly frustrated under almost any circumstances, I would get him to look again at his ideals. Could such ideals really be adequate? Surely man's reach must exceed his grasp, but how far should we go? Should not any ideal worth its salt come into some closer involvement with the realities of human living? And if one deliberately and with selfunderstanding plays the role of a Don Quixote can one justifiably complain that one's ideals are not realized? Finally, it does not seem to me reasonable to expect that *all* circumstances can have sufficient meaning to make them worthwhile. Under certain circumstances life is not worth living. As a philosopher, I would point out this possibility and block those philosophical-religious claims that would try to show that this could not possibly be.

Many men who feel the barbs of constant frustration, come to feel that their ideals have turned out to be impossible, and ask in anguish' – as a consequence – 'Does life really have any meaning?' To a man in such anguish I would say all I have said above and much more, though I am painfully aware that such an approach may seem cold and unfeeling. I know that these matters deeply affect us; indeed they can even come to obsess us, and when we are so involved it is hard to be patient with talk about what can and cannot be said. But we need to understand these matters as well; and, after all, what more can be done along this line than to make quite plain what is involved in his question and try to exhibit a range of rational attitudes that could be taken toward it, perhaps stressing the point that though Dr. Rieux lost his wife and his best friend, his life, as he fought the plague, was certainly not without point either for him or for others. But I would also try to make clear that finally an answer to such a question must involve a decision or the having or adopting of a certain attitude on the part of the person involved. This certainly should be stressed and it should be stressed that the question 'Is such a life meaningful?' is a sensible question, which admits of a non-obscurantist, non-metaphysical treatment.

IV

There are many choices we must make in our lives and some choices are more worthwhile than others, though the criteria for what is worthwhile are in large measure at least context-dependent. 'It's worthwhile going to Leningrad to see the Hermitage' is perfectly intelligible to someone who knows and cares about art. Whether such a trip to Leningrad is worthwhile for such people can be determined by these people by a visit to the Museum. 'It's worthwhile fishing the upper Mainistee' is in exactly the same category, though the criteria for worthwhileness are not the same. Such statements are most assuredly perfectly intelligible; and no adequate grounds have been given to give us reason to think that we should philosophically tinker with the ordinary criteria of 'good art museum' or 'good trout fishing'. And why should we deny that these and other things are really worthwhile? To say 'Nothing is worthwhile since all pales and worse still, all is vain because man must die' is to mistakenly assume that because an eternity of even the best trout fishing would be not just a bore but a real chore, that trout fishing is therefore not worthwhile. Death and the fact (if it is a fact) that there is nothing new under the sun need not make all vanity. That something must come to an end can make it all the more precious: to know that love is an old tale does not take the bloom from your beloved's cheek.

Yet some crave a more general answer to 'Is anything worthwhile?' This some would say, is what they are after when they ask about the meaning of life.

As I indicated, the criteria for what is worthwhile are surely in large measure context-dependent, but let us see what more we can say about this need for a more general answer.

In asking 'Why is anything worthwhile?' if the 'why' is a request for *causes*, a more general answer can be given. The answer is that people have preferences, enjoy, admire and approve of certain things and they can and sometimes do reflect. Because of this they find some things worthwhile. This, of course, is not what 'being worthwhile' *means*, but if people did not have these capacities they would not find anything worthwhile. But *reasons* why certain things are worthwhile are dependent on the thing in question.

If people find x worthwhile they generally prefer x, approve of x, enjoy x, or admire x on reflection. If people did not prefer, approve of, enjoy or admire things then nothing would be found to be worthwhile. If they did not have these feelings the notion of 'being worthwhile' would have no role to play in human life; but it does have a role to play and, as in morality, justification of what is worthwhile must finally come to an end with the reflective choices we make.

Moral principles, indeed, have a special onerousness about them. If something is a moral obligation, it is something we ought to do through and through. It for most people at least and from a moral point of view for everyone overrides (but does not exhaust) all non-moral considerations about what is worthwhile. If we are moral agents and we are faced with the necessity of choosing either A or B, where A, though very worthwhile, is a non-moral one, we must choose B. The force of the 'must' here is logical. From a moral point of view there is no alternative but to choose B. Yet we do not escape the necessity of decision for we still must *agree* to *adopt* a moral point of view, to *try* to act as moral agents. Here, too, we must finally make a decision of principle.[10] There are good Hobbesian reasons for adopting the moral point

---

10. I have discussed the central issues involved here at length in my 'Why Should I Be Moral?' *Methods*, 15, 1963.

of view but if one finally would really prefer 'a state of nature' in which all were turned against all, rather than a life in which there was a freedom from this and at least a minimum of cooperation between human beings, then these reasons for adopting the moral point of view would not be compelling to such a person. There is, in the last analysis, no escape from making a choice.

In asking 'What is the meaning of Life?' we have seen how this question is in reality a question concerning human conduct. It asks either 'What should we seek?' or 'What ends (if any) are really worthwhile?' I have tried to show in what general ways such questions are answerable. We can give reasons for our moral judgments and moral principles and the whole activity of morality can be seen to have a point, but not all quesitons concerning what is worthwhile are moral questions. Where moral questions do not enter we must make a decision about what, on reflection, we are going to seek. We must ascertain what – all things considered – really answers to our interests or, where there is no question of anything answering to our interests or failing to answer to our interests, we should decide what on reflection we prefer. What do we really want, wish to approve of, or admire? To ask 'Is anything worthwhile?' involves our asking 'Is there nothing that we, on reflection, upon knowledge of ourselves and others, want, approve of, or admire?' When we say 'So-and-so is worthwhile' we are making a normative judgment that cannot be derived from determining what we desire, admire or approve of. That is to say, these statements do not entail statements to the effect that so and so is worthwhile. But in determining what is worthwhile this is finally all we have to go on. In saying something is worthwhile, we (1) *express* our preference, admiration or approval; (2) in some sense imply that we are prepared to defend our choice with *reasons*; and (3) in effect, indicate our belief that others like us in the relevant respects and similarly placed, will find it worthwhile too. And the answer to our question is that, of course, there are things we humans desire, prefer, approve of, or admire. This being so, our question is not unanswerable. Again we need not fly to a metaphysical enchanter.

As I said, 'Is anything really worthwhile, really worth seeking?' makes us gape. And 'atomistic analyses', like the one I have just given, often leave us with a vague but persistent feeling of dissatisfaction, even when we cannot clearly articulate the grounds of our dissatisfaction. 'The real question', we want to say, 'has slipped away from us amidst the host of distinctions and analogies. We've not touched the deep heart of the matter at all'.

Surely, I have not exhausted the question for, literally speaking, it is not one question but a cluster of loosely related questions all concerning 'the human condition' – how man is to act and how he is to live his life even in the face of the bitterest trials and disappointments. Questions here are diverse, and a philosopher, or anyone else, becomes merely pretentious and silly when he tries to come up with some formula that will solve, resolve or dissolve the perplexities of human living. But I have indicated in skeletal fashion how we can approach general questions about 'What (if anything) is worth seeking?' And I have tried to show how such questions are neither meaningless nor questions calling for esoteric answers.

V

We are not out of the woods yet. Suppose someone were to say: 'Okay, you've convinced me. Some things are worthwhile and there is a more or less distinct mode of reasoning called moral reasoning and there are canons of validity distinctive of this *sui generis* type reasoning. People do reason in the ways that you have described, but it still remains the case that here one's attitudes and final choices are relevant in a way that it isn't necessarily the case in science or an argument over plain matters of fact. But when I ask: 'How ought men act?' 'What is the meaning of life?' and 'What is the meaning of *my* life?, how should I live and die?' I want an answer that is logically independent of any human choice or any proattitude toward any course of action or any state of affairs. Only if I can have that kind of warrant for my moral judgments and ways-of-life will I be satisfied'.

If a man demands this and continues to demand this after dialectical examination we must finally leave him unsatisfied. As linguistic philosophers there is nothing further we can say to him. In dialectical examination we can again point out to him that he is asking for the logically impossible, but if he recognizes this and persists in asking for that which is impossible there are no further rational arguments that we can use to establish our point. But, prior to this last-ditch stand, there are still some things that we can say. We can, in detail and with care, point out to him, describe fully for him, the rationale of the moral distinctions we do make and the functions of moral discourse. A full description here will usually break this kind of obsessive perplexity. Furthermore, we can make the move Stephen Toulmin makes in the last part of his *The Place of Reason in Ethics*. We can describe for him another use of 'Why' that Toulmin has well described as a 'limiting question'.[11]

Let me briefly explain what this is and how it could be relevant. When we

---

11. Stephen Toulmin, *An Examination of the Place of Reason in Ethics* (Cambridge University Press, 1950).

ask a 'limiting question' we are not really asking a question at all. We are in a kind of 'land of shadows' where there are no clear-cut uses of discourse. If we just look at their grammatical form, 'limiting questions' do not appear to be extra-rational in form, but in their depth grammar – their actual function – they clearly are. 'What holds the universe up?' looks very much like 'What holds the Christmas tree up?' but the former, in common sense contexts at least, is a limiting question while the latter usually admits of a perfectly obvious answer. As Toulmin himself puts it, limiting questions are 'questions expressed in a form borrowed from a familiar mode of reasoning, but not doing the job which they normally do within that mode of reasoning'.[12] A direct answer to a limiting question never satisfies the questioners. Attempted 'answers' only regenerate the question, though often a small change in the questions themselves or their context will make them straightforward questions. Furthermore, there is no standard interpretation for limiting questions sanctioned in our language. And limiting questions do not present us with any genuine alternatives from which to choose.

Now 'limiting questions' get used in two main contexts. Sometimes, they merely express what Ryle, rather misleadingly, called a 'category mistake'. Thus someone who was learning English might ask: 'How hot is blue?' or 'Where is anywhere?' And, even a native speaker of English might ask as a *moral* agent, 'Why ought I to do what is right?' We 'answer' such questions by pointing out that blue cannot be hot, anywhere is not a particular place, and that if something is indeed right, this entails that it ought to be done. Our remarks here are grammatical remarks, though our speaking in the material mode may hide this. And if the questioner's 'limiting question' merely signifies that a category mistake has been made, when this is pointed out to the questioner, there is an end to the matter. But more typically and more interestingly, limiting questions do not *just* or at all indicate category mistakes but express, as well or independently, a *personal predicament*. Limiting questions may express anxiety, fear, hysterical apprehensiveness about the future, hope, despair, and any number of attitudes. Toulmin beautifully illustrates from the writings of Dostoevsky an actual, on-the-spot use, of limiting questions:

He was driving somewhere in the steppes ... Not far off was a village, he could see the black huts, and half the huts were burnt down, there were only the charred beams sticking out. As they drove in, there were peasant women drawn up along the road ...
 'Why are they crying? Why are they crying?' Mitya [Dmitri] asked, as they dashed gaily by.
 'It's the babe', answered the driver, 'the babe is weeping'.

12. *Ibid.*, p. 205.

And Mitya was struck by his saying, in his peasant way, 'the babe', and he liked the peasant's calling it a 'babe'. There seemed more pity in it.

'But why is it weeping?' Mitya persisted stupidly. 'Why are its little arms bare? Why don't they wrap it up?'

'The babe's cold, its little clothes are frozen and don't warm it'.

'But why is it? Why?' foolish Mitya still persisted.

'Why, they're poor people, burnt out. They've no bread. They're begging because they've been burnt out'.

'No, no', Mitya, as it were still did not understand. 'Tell me why it is those poor mothers stand there? Why are people poor? Why is the babe poor? Why is the steppe barren? Why don't they hug each other and kiss? Why don't they sing songs of joy? Why are they so dark from black misery? Why don't they feed the babe?'

And he felt that, though his questions were unreasonable, and senseless, yet he wanted to ask just that, and he had to ask it just in that way. And he felt that a passion of pity, such as he had never known before, was rising in his heart, that he wanted to cry, that he wanted to do something for them all, so that the babe should weep no more, so that the dark-faced, dried-up mother should not weep, that no one should shed tears again from that moment ...

'I've had a good dream, gentlemen', he said in a strange voice, with a new light, as of joy, in his face.[13]

It is clear that we need not, may not, from the point of view of analysis, condemn these uses of language as illicit. We can point out that it is a muddle to confuse such questions with literal questions, and that such questions have no fixed *literal* meaning, and that as a result there are and can be no fixed literal ways of answering them, but they are indeed, genuine uses of language, and not the harum-scarum dreams of undisciplined metaphysics. When existentialist philosophers and theologians state them as profound questions about an alleged ontological realm there is room for complaint, but as we see them operating in the passage I quoted from *The Brothers Karamazov*, they seem to be not only linguistically proper but also an extremely important form of discourse. It is a shame and a fraud when philosophers 'sing songs' as a substitute for the hard work of philosophizing, but only a damn fool would exclude song-singing, literal or metaphorical, from the life of reason, or look down on it as a somehow inferior activity. Non-literal 'answers' to these non-literal, figurative questions, when they actually express personal predicaments or indeed more general human predicaments may, in a motivational sense, *goad* people to do one thing or another that they *know* they ought to do or they may comfort them or give them hope in time of turmoil and anxiety. I am not saying this is their only use or that they have no other respectable rationale. I do not at all think that; but I am saying that here is a rationale that even the most hard nosed positivist should acknowledge.

13. *Ibid.*, p. 210.

The man who demands 'a more objective answer' to his question, 'How ought men to live?' or 'What is the meaning of Life?' may not be just muddled. If he is *just* making a 'category mistake' and this is pointed out to him, he will desist, but if he persists, his limiting question probably expresses some anxiety. In demanding an answer to an evaluative question that can be answered independently of any attitudes he might have or choices he might make, he may be unconsciously expressing his fear of making decisions, his insecurity and confusion about what he really wants, and his desperate desire to have a Father who would make all these decisions for him. And it is well in such a context to bring Weston LaBarre's astute psychological observation to mind. 'Values', LaBarre said, 'must from emotional necessity be viewed as absolute by those who use values as compulsive defenses against reality, rather than properly as tools for the exploration of reality'.[14] This remark, coming from a Freudian anthropologist, has unfortunately a rather metaphysical ring, but it can be easily enough de-mythologized. The point is, that someone who persists in these questions, persists in a demand for a totally different and 'deeper' justification or answer to the question 'What is the meaning of Life?' than the answer that such a question admits of, may be just expressing his own insecurity. The heart of rationalism is often irrational. At such a point the only reasoning that will be effective with him, if indeed any reasoning will be effective with him, may be psychoanalytic reasoning. And by then, of course you have left the philosopher and indeed all questions of justification far behind. But again the philosopher can describe the kinds of questions we can ask and the point of these questions. Without advocating anything at all he can make clearer to us the structure of 'the life of reason' and the goals we human beings do prize.

VI

There is another move that might be made in asking about this haunting question: 'What is the meaning of Life?' Suppose someone were to say: 'Yes I see about these 'limiting questions' and I see that moral reasoning and reasoning about human conduct generally are limited modes of reasoning with distinctive criteria of their own. If I am willing to be guided by reason and I can be reasonable there are some answers I can find to the question: 'What is the meaning of Life?' I'm aware that they are not cut and dried and that they are not simple and that they are not even by any means altogether the

---

14. Weston LaBarre, *The Human Animal*, University of Chicago, 1954.

same for all men, but there are some reasonable answers and touchstones all the same. You and I are in perfect accord on that. But there is one thing I don't see at all, 'Why ought I to be guided by reason anyway?' and if you cannot answer this for me I don't see why I should think that your answer – or rather your schema for an answer – about the meaning of Life is, after all, really any good. It all depends on how you *feel*, finally. There are really no answers here'.

But again we have a muddle; let me very briefly indicate why. If someone asks: 'Why ought I to be guided by reason anyway?' or 'Is it really good to be reasonable?' one is tempted to take such a question as a paradigm case of a 'limiting question', and a very silly one at that. But as some people like to remind us – without any very clear sense of what they are reminding us of – reason has been challenged. It is something we should return to, be wary of, realize the limits of, or avoid, as the case may be. It will hardly do to take such a short way with the question and rack it up as a category mistake.

In some particular contexts, with some particular people, it is (to be paradoxical, for a moment) reasonable to question whether we ought to follow reason. Thus, if I am a stubborn, penny-pinching old compulsive and I finally take my wife to the 'big-city' for a holiday, it might be well to say to me: 'Go on, forget how much the damn tickets cost, buy them anyway. Go on, take a cab even if you can't afford it'. But to give or heed such advice clearly is not, in any fundamental sense, to fly in the face of reason, for on a deeper level – the facts of human living being what they are – we are being guided by reason.

It also makes sense to ask, as people like D. H. Lawrence press us to ask, if it really pays to be rasonable. Is the reasonable, clear-thinking clear-visioned, intellectual animal really the happiest, in the long run? And can his life be as rich, as intense, as creative as the life of Lawrence's sort of man? From Socrates to Freud it has been assumed, for the most part, that self-knowledge, knowledge of our world, and rationality will bring happiness, if anything will. But is this really so? The whole Socratic tradition may be wrong at this point. Nor is it obviously true that the reasonable man, the man who sees life clearly and without evasion, will be able to live the richest, the most intense or the most creative life. I hope these things are compatible but they may not be. A too clear understanding may dull emotional involvement. Clear-sightedness may work against the kind of creative intensity that we find in a Lawrence, a Wolfe or a Dylan Thomas.

But to ask such questions is not in a large sense to refuse to be guided by reason. Theoretically, further knowledge could give us at least some vague answers to such unsettling questions; and, depending on what we learned and what decisions we would be willing to make, we would then know what to do. But clearly, we are not yet flying in the face of reason, refusing to be guided by reason at all. We are still playing the game according to the ground rules of reasons.

What is this question, 'Why should I be guided by reason?' or 'Why be reasonable?' if it isn't any of these quesitons we have just discussed? If we ask this question and take it in a very general way, the question is a limiting one and it does involve a category mistake. What could be *meant* by asking: 'Why ought we *ever* use reason at all?' That to ask this question is to commit a logical blunder, is well brought out by Paul Taylor when he says:

... it is a question which would never be asked by anyone who thought about what he was saying, since the question, to speak loosely, answers itself. It is admitted that no amount of arguing in the world can make a person who does not want to be reasonable want to be. For to argue would be to give reasons, and to give reasons already assumes that the person to whom you give them is *seeking* reasons. That is it assumes he is reasonable. A person who did not want to be reasonable in any sense would never ask the question, 'Why be reasonable?' For in asking the question, Why? he is seeking reasons, that is, he is being reasonable in asking the question. The question calls for the use of reason to justify *any* use of reason, including the use of reason to answer the question.[15]

In other words, to ask the question, as well as answer it, commits one to the use of reason. To ask: 'Why be guided by reason at all?' is to ask 'Why be reasonable, ever?' As Taylor puts it, 'The questioner is thus seeking good reasons for seeking good reasons', and this surely is an absurdity. Anything that would be a satisfactory answer would be a 'tautology to the effect that it is reasonable to be reasonable. A negative answer to the question, Is it reasonable to be reasonable? would express a self-contradiction'.

If all this is pointed out to someone and he still persists in asking the question in this logically senseless way there is nothing a philosopher *qua* philosopher can do for him, though a recognition of the use of limiting questions in discourse may make this behavior less surprising to the philosopher himself. He might give him all five volumes of *The Life of Reason* or *Vanity Fair* and say, 'Here, read this, maybe you will come to see things differently'. The philosopher himself might even sing a little song in praise of reason, but there would be nothing further that he could say to him, philosophically: but by now we have come a very long way.

---

15. Paul Taylor, 'Four Types of Relativism', *Philosophical Review*, 1956.

VII

Ronald Hepburn is perceptive in speaking of the conceptual 'darkness around the meaning-of-life questions'.[6] We have already seen some of the reasons for this; most generally, we should remark here that people are not always asking the same question and are not always satisfied by answers of the same scope when they wrestle with meaning-of-life questions. And often, of course, the questioner has no tolerably clear idea of what he is trying to ask. He may have a strong gut reaction about the quality and character of his own life and the life around him without the understanding or ability to conceptualize why he feels the way he does. Faced with this situation, I have tried to chart some of the contexts in which 'What is the meaning of Life?' is a coherent question and some of the contexts in which it is not. But there are some further contexts in which 'meaning-of-life questions get asked which I have not examined.

There are philosophers who will agree with me that in a world of people with needs and wants already formed, it can be shown that life in a certain 'subjective sense' has meaning, but they will retort that this is not realy the central consideration. What is of crucial importance is whether we can show that the universe is better with human life than without it. If this cannot be established then we cannot have good reason to believe that life really has meaning, though in the subjective senses we have discussed, we can still continue to say it has meaning.[17]

If we try to answer this question, we are indeed brought up short, for we are utterly at a loss about what it would be like to ascertain whether it is better for the universe to have human life than no life at all. We may have certain attitudes here but no idea of what it would be like to know or have any reason at all to believe that 'It is better that there is life' is either true or false or reasonably asserted or denied. It is quite unlike 'It is better to be dead than to live with a tumor'. Concerning this last example, people may disagree about its correctness, but they have some idea of what considerations are relevant to settling the dispute. But with 'It is better that there be life' we are at a loss.

We will naturally be led into believing that 'What is the meaning of Life?' is an unanswerable question reflecting 'the mystery of existence', if we believe that to answer that question satisfactorily we will have to be able to establish that it is better that there is life on earth than no life at all. What needs to

16. Ronald W. Hepburn, 'Questions About the Meaning of Life'.
17. See in this context Hans Reiner, *Der Sinn unseres Daseins*, Tübingen: 1960. This view has been effectively criticized by Paul Edwards, 'Meaning and Value of Life', *The Encyclopedia of Philosophy*, Paul Edwards (ed.), Macmillan, 1967, Vol. 4, pp. 474–476.

be resisted is the very acceptance of that way of posing the problem. We do not need to establish that it is better that the universe contains human life than not in order to establish that there is a meaning to life. A life without purpose, a life devoid of satisfaction and an alienated life in which people are not being true to themselves is a meaningless life. The opposite sort of life is a meaningful or significant life. We have some idea of the conditions which must obtain for this to be so, i.e. for a man's life to have significance. We are not lost in an imponderable mystery here and we do not have to answer the question of whether it is better that there be human life at all to answer that question. Moreover, this standard non-metaphysical reading of 'What is the meaning of Life?' is no less objective than the metaphysical reading we have been considering. There are no good grounds at all for claiming that this metaphysical 'question' is the real and objective consideration in 'What is the meaning of Life?' and that the more terrestrial interpretations I have been considering are more subjective. This transcendental metaphysical way of stating the problem utilizes unwittingly and without justification arbitrary *persuasive* definitions of 'subjective' and 'objective'. And no other grounds have been given for *not* sticking with the terrestrial readings.

A deeper criticism of the account I have given of purpose and the meaning of life is given by Ronald Hepburn.[18] It is indeed true that life cannot be meaningful without being purposeful in the quite terrestrial sense I have set out, but, as Hepburn shows, it can be purposeful and still be meaningless.

One may fill one's days with honest, useful and charitable deeds, not doubting them to be of value, but without feeling that these give one's life meaning or purpose. It may be profoundly boring. To seek meaning is not just a matter of seeking justification for one's policies, but of trying to discover how to organise one's vital resources and energies around these policies. To find meaning is not a matter of judging these to be worthy, but of seeing their pursuit as in some sense a fulfillment, as involving self-realisation as opposed to self-violation, and as no less opposed to the performance of a dreary task.[19]

A person's life can have significance even when he does not realize it and even when it is an almost intolerable drudge to him, though for human life generally to have significance this could not almost invariably be true for the human animal. But one's own life could not have significance *for oneself* if it were such a burden to one. To be meaningful to one, one's life must be purposive *and* it must be a life that the liver of that life finds satisfactory in the living of it. These conditions sometimes obtain and when it is also true that

---

18. Hepburn's criticisms are directed toward an earlier version of this essay, 'Linguistic Philosophy and 'The Meaning of Life'', *Cross-Currents*, 14, Summer 1964.
19. *Ibid.*

some reasonable measure of an individual's purposive activity adds to the enhancement of human life, we can say that his life is not only meaningful to him but meaningful *sans phrase*.[20]

This is still not the end of the matter in the struggle to gain a sense of the meaning of life, for, as Hepburn also points out, some will not be satisfied with a purely terrestrial and non-metaphysical account of the type I have given of 'the meaning of Life'.[21] They will claim 'that life could be thought of as having meaning only so long as that meaning was believed to be a matter for discovery, not for creation and value-decision'.[22] They will go on to claim that 'to be meaningful, life would have to be *comprehensively* meaningful and its meaning invulnerable to assault. Worthwhile objectives must be ultimately realisable despite appearances'.[23]

However, even if they are not satisfied with my more piecemeal and terrestrial facing of questions concerning the meaning of life, it does not follow that life can only have meaning if it has meaning in the more comprehensive and less contingent way they seek. It may be true that life will only have meaning *for them* if these conditions are met, but this does not establish that life will thus lack meaning unless these conditions are met. That is to say, it may be found significant by the vast majority of people, including most non-evasive and reflective people, when such conditions are met and it may be the case that everyone *should* find life meaningful under such conditions.

It is not the case that there is some general formula in virtue of which we can say what the meaning of life is, but it still remains true that men can through their purposive activity give their lives meaning and indeed find meaning in life in the living of it. The man with a metaphysical or theological craving will seek 'higher standards' than the terrestrial standards I have utilized.

Is it rational to assent to that craving, to demand such 'higher standards', if life is really to be meaningful? I want to say both 'Yes' and 'No'.

On the one hand, the answer should be 'No', if the claim remains that for life to be meaningful at all it must be comprehensively meaningful. Even without such a comprehensive conception of things there can be joy in life, morally, aesthetically and technically worthwhile activity and a sense of

---

20. *Ibid.*
21. 'Questions About the Meaning of Life'. For arguments of this type see F. C. Copleston, 'Man and Metaphysics I', *The Heythrop Journal*, I, 2, January 1960, p. 16. See in addition his continuation of this article in successive issues of *The Heythrop Review* and his *Positivism and Metaphysics*, Lisbon: 1965.
22. 'Questions About the Meaning of Life'.
23. *Ibid.*

human purpose and community. This is sufficient to give meaning to life. And as Ayer perceptively argues and as I argued earlier in the essay, and as Hepburn argues himself, the man with a metaphysical craving of the transcendental sort will not be able to succeed in finding justification or rationale for claims concerning the significance of life that is any more *authoritative* and any more certain or invulnerable to assault than the non-metaphysical type rationale I have adumbrated. In actuality, as we have seen, such a comprehensive account, committed, as it must be, to problematic transcendental metaphysical and/or theological conceptions, is more vulnerable than my purely humanistic reading of this conception.

On the other hand, the answer should be 'Yes' if the claim is reduced to one asserting that to try to articulate a comprehensive picture of human life is a desirable thing. However, it should be noted that this is quite a reduction in claim. In attempting to make such an articulation, the most crucial thing is not to wrestle with theological considerations about the contingency of the world or eternal life, but to articulate a comprehensive normative social and political philosophy in accordance with which we could set forth at least some of the conditions of a non-alienated life not simply for a privileged few but for mankind generally. We need to show in some general manner what such a life would look like and we need to attempt again, and with a reference to contemporary conditions, what Marx so profoundly attempted, namely, to set out the conditions that could transform our inegalitarian, unjust, vulgar and – as in countries such as South Africa and the United States – brutal capitalist societies into truly human societies.[24] Linguistic philosophers and bourgeois philosophers generally have been of little help here, though the clarity they have inculcated into philosophical work and into political and moral argument will be a vital tool in this crucial and yet to be done task.[25] When this task is done, if it is done, then we will have the appropriate comprehensive picture we need, and it is something to be done without any involvement with theology, speculative cosmology or transcendental metaphysics at all.[26]

---

24. For a contemporary Marxist account see Adam Schaff, *A Philosophy of Man* London: 1963. But also note the criticism of Schaff's views by Christopher Hollis in 'What is the Purpose of Life?', *The Listener*, 70, 1961, pp. 133–136.
25. The strength and limitations here of linguistic anaylsis as it has been practiced are well exhibited in Ayer's little essay 'Philosophy and Politics'.
26. If what I have argued above is so, many of the esoteric issues raised by Milton Munitz in his *The Mystery of Existence* and in his contribution to *Language, Belief, and Metaphysics*, Kiefer and Munitz (eds.), New York: 1970, can be bypassed.

CHAPTER 2

PHENOMENOLOGY OF RELIGION AND HUMAN PURPOSE

J. N. MOHANTY

I

The title 'Phenomenology of Religion' has been used by many authors in recent times with no complete unanimity however regarding its subject matter, methodology and purpose. Holsten, writing on Phenomenology of Religion in *Religion in Geschichte und Gegenwart*,[1] distinguishes it from both History of Religion and Theology. It is not concerned with the historical development of religion. Unlike theology, it is concerned only with such phenomena as show themselves. The phenomenological *epoche* forbids us to look behind phenomena. More precisely, phenomenology of religion, according to Holsten, knows only of human acts in relation to God, not of God's acts. However, Holsten recognizes that since the religious phenomena is itself historical, phenomenology of religion cannot remain totally unconcerned with history.

Kristensen also distinguishes between phenomenology of religion and history of religion.[2] History of religion is neither systematic nor comparative. Phenomenology of Religion seeks to 'classify' and to 'group' religious phenomena of the same category (e.g., sacrifice, prayer, sacrament, etc.) appearing in different religions and at different times to get at their inner meaning and ideal connections. Just as this would be going beyond history, it would also be stopping short of philosophy, for Kristensen would not let phenomenology try to extract the essences of such phenomena. For him 'essence' is a philosophical concept, and so beyond the scope of phenomenology. But Kristensen also allows that phenomenology of religion is the systematic treatment of history of religion.[3]

However, the distinction between phenomenology of religion and history of religion is important and should not be obliterated. It is a misuse of the word

---

1. W. Holsten, article on 'Phänomenologie der Religion' in *Die Religion in Geschichte und Gegenwart*, Dritte Auflage, Band V, Tübingen: J.C. Mohr, 1961, pp. 322–324.
2. W.B. Kristensen, *The Meaning of Religion, Lectures in the Phenomenology of Religion*. E. Tr. by John B. Carman, The Hague: Martinus Nijhoff, 1960.
3. *Ibid.*, pp. 1–3.

'phenomenology' when it is used to designate the study of history of religions.[4] Eliade rightly sees that the historical conditions of an experience do not tell us what a religious experience ultimately is and what it means.[5] Religious phenomena may be historical, but they reveal a behaviour which, Eliade rightly remarks, goes far beyond the historical involvement of man.[6] In other words, phenomenology of religion cannot remain confined to a mere empirical study of religious phenomena, it has also to seek for their meaning, structure, significance or essence. What Kristensen regarded as a philosophical but not a phenomenological concern is precisely the concern of a phenomenological philosophy. It searches not for a metaphysical essence but for the morphological essence which shows itself in the phenomena.

But what sort of phenomena are the religious phenomena? In one sense, the religious phenomena are the whole spectrum of religious ideas, activities, institutions, customs, symbols, and myths; one cannot even exclude religious art and literature from the purview of such a study. But at the same time it is also true that phenomenology operates with a definite conception of 'phenomenon' which does not coincide with the ordinary conception of it.

The basic concept of phenomenology is the concept of intentionality. Introduced in modern times by Brentano with a view to distinguishing between mental and non-mental phenomena, this concept has demonstrated its effectiveness beyond that limited purpose. It in fact defines the whole subject matter of phenomenology, and also defines its methodology. Whatever is intentional comes under the scope of a possible phenomenological investigation precisely in so far as it exhibits intentionality; phenomenological description is not an empirical description of the Humean variety, but is intentional analysis making use of the key methodological notion of noetic-noematic correlation. Keeping this in mind, we may say that what a phenomenological study of religion has to do is not merely give an empirical description of the religious 'data' but to uncover the living intentions behind them, the acts and intentions through which the religious 'data' are constituted precisely in their character of religiosity.

As is well known, the concept of intentionality developed, in the writings of Husserl, through three distinct but interrelated stages: intentionality understood as the simple directedness of consciousness towards an object,

---

4. J. D. Bettis (ed.), *Phenomenology of Religion*, New York & Evanston: Harper Books, 1969, pp. 2–3.
5. M. Eliade, *The Quest, History and Meaning in Religion*, University of Chicago Press, 1969, pp. 52–53.
6. M. Eliade, *Images and Symbols*, E. Tr. by Philip Mairet, New York: Sheed & Ward, 1952, pp. 32–33.

intentionality as noetic-moematic correlation, and intentionality as constituting function. One may also need to recall the later Husserlian notions of intentionalities that are not acts, of unconscious intentionalities and finally the notion of operative intentionality. In post-Husserlian phenomenologists, this key notion took on the forms of the concepts of being-in-the-world (Heidegger), of transcendence (Heidegger and Sartre), nihilation (Sartre) and of bodily intentionality (Merleau-Ponty). These notions cannot be relevant for any discussions of phenomenology of religious experience.

Max Scheler, one of the pioneers in the field of phenomenology of religion, divides it into three parts: the first part is to be an essential ontology of the divine being ('die Wesensontik des Göttlichen'), the second part is to be a doctrine of the forms of revelation in which the divine reveals itself to man; and the final part is to be a doctrine of religious acts through which man prepares himself for the acceptance of the content of revelation.[7] However, it is highly doubtful if a theory of God's revelation to man can claim to be a phenomenology. Revelation is not a phenomenon, as Van der Leew rightly says. What is a phenomenon is rather man's reply to revelation.[8] The same may be said regarding Scheler's first topic for a phenomenology of religion. Phenomenology can concern itself with the divine only in so far as the divine is the noematic correlate of religious acts. In other words, phenomenology has to study the religious acts, both in their noetic and their noematic aspects. God or the Divine, after the phenomenological epoche, appears as the noematic correlate, as the intended object *qua* intended. It is with the religious intention that the phenomenologist is primarily concerned. The question, for example, whether God exists is of no concern to the phenomenologist. What concerns him is, what religious acts constitute, for the religious person, the divine being as an existent reality and as divine. He is concerned with the *meaning* of God's existence, and not with his actual existence which has been placed within the epoche.

II

A phenomenology of religious acts has been made possible by the modern discovery that feelings are not merely subjective states but are intentional in as much originary sense as cognitive acts. In other words, intentionality is not

---

7. M. Scheler, *Vom Ewigen im Menschen, Gesammelte Werke*, Bd. 5, Bern & Munchen: Francke Verlag, 1954, p. 157.
8. Van der Leew, *Religion in Essence and Manifestation*, E. Tr. by J. E. Turner. New York & Evanston: Harper & Row, 1963.

a characteristic of the cognitive states alone. Brentano of course, in a famous passage[9] speaks of love and hatred as being intentional. But while many would concede the seemingly uncontroversial fact that love implies an object loved, yet for most traditional philosophers love is not an originary intentionality inasmuch as it presupposes the intentionality of cognitive acts. An object that is loved is necessarily an object that is represented. As Brentano put it, every mental phenomenon is either itself a representation, or presupposes a representation. This Brentano doctrine, if taken seriously, leads to an intellectualism for which the primary intentionality is cognitive. Feelings may add a noematic quality. By being an object of love, the object may acquire a new noematic property of being loved, but its basic disclosure is to an act of representation. Now, one of the major philosophical insights we derive from the writings of Heidegger and Merleau-Ponty is that this intellectualist thesis is false. Feelings are originary modes of disclosure, they do not merely add colour to what has already been disclosed. This makes possible a further noetic and noematic study of religious acts which are basically non-cognitive in character. With the modern insight into the intentional structure of feelings, we need not any longer outright reject Schleiermacher's famous characterisation of religious experience. The 'feeling of absolute dependence' is meant to be an intentional experience, and not a mere subjective state.

The first and indispensable prerequisite for a satisfactory phenomenology of religious acts is that we bring into operation the phenomenological epoche, by which is meant that we neutralize our belief in the reality of the objects of religious acts (analogously with the neutralization of the belief in the reality of the world in a phenomenology of perception, and with the same meaning and methodological significance of 'neutralization'). We, instead of naively living in those acts, reflect upon them without disturbing their naivity, and yet we try to catch hold of their living intention directed towards their respective objects precisely as they are intended without taking it for granted that those objects are ontologically real or otherwise. For, as said before, the aim of a phenomenology of religion is not to arrive at a decision regarding the ontological status of the objects of religious acts, but to explicate their sense of those acts themselves.

The possibility and also relevance of such an epoche is brought out by the following logical features of intentional discourse. It has been brought out by Chisholm and others that intentional discourse is characterised by such

---

9. F. Brentano, 'The Distinction between Mental and Physical Phenomena', in R. M. Chisholm (ed.), *Realism and the Background of Phenomenology*, New York: The Free Press, 1960.

features as truth-value indifference, existence-independence and referential opacity.[10] In other words, if a sentence whose main verb is an intentional verb (e.g. 'S believes that p') with a propositional clause as its object ('p') then from the truth of this sentence nothing follows regarding the truth or falsity of the propositional clause. Further, if the main intentional verb has a name or a definite description for its accusative, then from the truth of the sentence nothing follows regarding the existence or non-existence of the entity referred to by the name or the description. Again, in intentional contexts substitution of extensionally equivalent expressions does not preserve truth-value. These logical features of intentional discourse reinforce the point of view that the mere fact that there is a certain intentional act directed towards an object does not entail either the existence or the non-existence of such an object. Intentionality is not a relation relating a mind to an object in a certain specific manner, for if it were a relation the subsistence of this relation would have implied – as with all relations – the reality of both the terms involved; whereas in the present case only the reality of the mental act is entailed; not the reality of the object of that act. This should warn us against making a too hasty transition from phenomenology to ontology, from a phenomenology of religious acts to an ontology of divine being or beings.

III

In the light of the above general remarks regarding intentionality, we may examine some of the claims made by Scheler about religious acts. First, Scheler regards relatedness to God as an essential feature of all religious acts. Acts directed towards any other sort of content – humanity, the nation, or ones own self – are not religious unless they all in the long run are directed towards God.[11] Now this seems to me to be a very narrow conception of religious experience, for there are obviously important religions which do not admit of God. Within the tradition of these religious communities – e.g. of Buddhism and some Hindu sects – religious experiences are recognized which however are directed towards God (as understood in the Christian-Judaic tradition) but towards the Self (Ātman) or the Nothingness (Sunyatā). To say that for these religions, the Self or the Nothingness itself serves as the God is to turn the thesis of Scheler into triviality, for in that case whatever a religious act may intend ultimately would become God for that act. We have

---

10. Cp. R. M. Chisholm, *article on 'Intentionality'*, in P. Edwards (ed.), *The Encyclopedia of Philosophy*, New York, 1967.
11. M. Scheler, loc. cit., p. 240.

then to look for a more generic characteristic or religious acts than the property of having God for their last intention.[12]

Religious acts, Scheler next tells us, belong essentially to human consciousness not because it is human (in the inductive-empirical sense) but because it is a finite consciousness.[13] The first secure truth of all religious phenomenology, according to Scheler[14], is that man, irrespective of the stage of his religious development, always and from the very beginning looks up at an ontological and axiological realm which is basically different from the empirical world. To look for the development of man into the religious point of view is absurd. Religion develops autogenetically and not heterogenetically. Now here again one should take care not to go astray from the path of phenomenology. It is one thing to plead for the uniqueness of religious acts, for their irreducibility to any other kinds of acts and to regard causal – psychological, sociological or otherwise – explanations as being irrelevant for a proper understanding of this uniqueness of religious acts *qua* religious. It is quite another thing to say that they follow necessarily from the finiteness of human subjectivity. How can one say that man in all ages and climes was and has been religious save through an empirical-inductive generalization? Surely the absence of the religious point of view in a human community is not inconceivable, and if we apply Husserl's method of free imaginative variation we may be entitled to refuse to give our assent to Scheler's proposition that the religious acts belong essentially to the human nature in so far as it is a finite consciousness. We may at best insightfully agree to the proposition that a finite consciousness must be characterized by transcendence and intentionality, but it does not seem evident that this transcendence should necessarily be a religious one. In fact, a phenomenology of religious acts need not take upon itself the larger task of ascertaining the essence of man; its humble task is to ascertain the essential features of religious acts themselves.

Religious acts cannot be mere desires or needs, just because they relate to objects of an altogether different type than the empirical objects towards which our desires and needs are ordinarily directed. They are thus not only altogether different from other sorts of acts of human consciousness, they are also not formed out of combinations of other intentional act types: ethical, aesthetic or logical. If by this attempt to separate the religious acts from the other types of intentional acts, Scheler intends to highlight their specific point of difference from the others he is surely justified. Religious experience is neither morality touched with emotion, nor the finite reason aware of its own

12. See also J. Hessen, *Religionsphilosophie*, Bd. I, Basel: Ernst Reinhardt Verlag, 1955, p. 268.
13. M. Scheler, loc. cit., pp. 242–243.
14. *Ibid.*, p. 170.

infinite potentialities. The moralist and the rationalist are both apt to miss the uniqueness of the religious act. However, it is not true that religious acts are given in isolation from the rest of man's conscious life. In fact, they are inextricable blended with, and they in fact lend colour and tone to, the entire conscious life of the religious man. Eliade recognizes that there are no purely religious phenomena and that it is by an epoche that we come to apprehend the purely religious moment.[15] In this sense, a phenomenology of religious acts should end up with the recognition that it can only be a phenomenology of the religious moment in the total life of a religious man. The religious acts do not exist side by side with the other acts, as do our intellectual acts, without touching them. They have the tendency to overpower them, suffuse them with their own aura and to transform the entire life. In this sense, every religious act has *global* intention, which Scheler owing to his emphasis on the other-worldliness of the religious object fails to recognize.

There are three other secure marks of religious acts, according to Scheler.[16] First, in their intentions they transcend the world, not merely the actual world which includes all things and persons even the religious person himself, but also any possible world.[17] The second feature follows from the first: the intentions of religious acts are fulfilled only through the divine understood as a world-transcending reality. Lastly, the religious acts, as distinguished from all other cognitive acts, even those of metaphysical thinking *demand* a reply, a reciprocal response from the object towards which the acts are directed. Revelation, in the broadest sense, is nothing but the mode of givenness of a divine being, such a mode being strictly correlative to the religious acts.[18] One therefore understands Scheler's contention that a doctrine of revelation and of its various forms ought to constitute a major part of a phenomenology of religion.

Again we note Scheler's over-emphasis on the other-wordliness of the religious attitude, which in fact renders his characterizations too narrow. For one thing, not all experiences which intend a transcendence of the world are *eo ipso* religious. Heidegger, as is well known, emphasizes certain ontological moods, like care and anxiety, where there is no specifiable object towards which they are directed but in which the world of entities becomes

---

15. M. Eliade, *Patterns in Comparative Religion*, E. Tr. by Rosemary Sheed, London & New York: Sheed & Ward, 1958.
16. *Ibid.*, p. 244 f.
17. Thus Scheler writes: 'Transzendenz im allgemeinen ist eine Eigentumlichkeit, die jeder Bewusstseinsintention zukommt ... Aber erst wo das also Transzendierte die Welt als Ganzes ist (mit Einschluss der eigenen Person), haben wir Recht, von einen religiosen Akt zu reden'. (loc. cit., p. 245).
18. M. Scheler, loc. cit., p. 249.

meaningless, insignificant, and in so far transcended. Such acts are not however for Heidegger religious. Further, not all religious acts transcend the world in their intention, they may discover a new significance in the world – and such a discovery would be precisely what fulfills their intention. Again, it is only in the context of theistic religions that one can speak of the demand for a revelation of the divine being in response to the religious acts of man. Outside that context, the notion of revelation becomes insignificant. The notion of discovery or disclosure becomes more important.

IV

Where Scheler's phenomenology fails, it is conditioned by his inability to take the multifarious forms of religious phenomena into consideration. It is precisely in this respect that the phenomenologies of Rudolf Otto, Van der Leew, and Mercia Eliade deserve our consideration, for both are aware of and take into consideration the vast domain of the religious phenomena that lies outside the Judaic-Christian tradition. Otto makes the notion of the holy his central notion, Eliade operates with the notion of the sacred, while Van der leew accords central pace to the notion of power.

Otto bases his phenomenology on Kantian-Friesian philosophy.[19] Accordingly, he searches for the *a priori* structure of religious experience. But Otto's *a priori* is not Kantian, but Friesian. The *a priori* for Fries is not a function of transcendental subjectivity as it is with Kant, but a psychological function, an inborn *Anlage*. Otto regards the complex category of holiness as an *a priori* element in this sense. He refers it back to the *Seelengrund*,[20] the bottom or ground of the soul. Otto gives a sort of proof that we have in the Holy an *a priori* category. He says that this proof can be had through introspection and 'a critical examination of reason such as Kant instituted'.[21] But the examination he undertakes is simply to show that the numinous experience involves beliefs and feelings which are qualitatively different from anything that natural sense-perception is capable of giving us. While this latter proposition may be conceded, this is far from entailing the truth of the thesis that the idea of the holy owes its origin to 'a hidden substantive source'. Phenomenology is under obligation to recognize the uniqueness of intentional acts where such uniqueness impresses upon us as a phenomenon, but this

---

19. R. Otto, *Kantische-Fries'sche Religionsphilosophie*, Tübingen, 1909.
20. R. Otto, *The Idea of the Holy*, E. Tr. by John W. Harvey, Fifth Impression, Oxford University Press, 1928, p. 116.
21. *Ibid.*, p. 117.

uniqueness need not lead us to find out a special faculty in the human soul as its source. Let us therefore pass over this part of Otto's doctrine, and turn to his analysis of the idea of the holy as the peculiar category of value that is experienced in religious acts. Religion in fact for Otto is *Werterleben*, experience of value; and the peculiar value that is experienced in it is the Holy. The idea of the Holy is indeed a complex idea consisting in both rational and non-rational components, and what interests Otto are the non-rational components of the *mysterium tremendum*, the *mysterium facsinosum* and the numinous value. The object of religious act is felt as absolutely overpowering (giving rise within us to the 'feeling of our creaturehood'), as awful and majestic, as the wholly other but also as uniquely fascinating. Otto claims that even the 'void' of the eastern mystics, the *sunyatā* of the Buddhist, the identity of the *Ātman* and the *Brahman* which the mystics of the Upanishads strived to realize – all these conform to his characterization of the Holy as the wholly other and the *mysterium tremendum*.

We may now make a few remarks regarding Otto's phenomenology of religious experience. In so far as Otto separates the idea of the Holy from that of God, he is on a more secure ground than Scheler.[22] But at the same time, in making this idea as an *a priori* category he also reduces it to a level of generality which raises itself above the diversity of religious acts and phenomena. In fact, what Otto gives us is a theory of the object of the religious act, and not a phenomenology of those acts themselves.[23] His is therefore not an act-phenomenology. But he at the same time seeks to provide religious experience with an ontological guarantee by making the acts themselves *a priori*, instead of showing, as does Scheler, that the acts being *sui generis*, demand a *real* object that is *sui generis*. Both attempts to provide an ontological guarantee for religious experience fall outside the scope of a phenomenology of religion, for such a phenomenology can only explicate the *sense* of the truth-claim of religious acts and *not substantiate* that claim.

Van der Leew operates with a more self-conscious phenomenological methodology. He is aware of the limitations, in fact, self-imposed limitations, under which a phenomenologist has to work. For example, he knows that phenomenology is not metaphysics and that existence is unattainable to the phenomenologist.[24] He also knows that 'Before revelation Phenomenology

---

22. Cp. J. E. Smith, 'The Experience of the Holy and the Idea of God', in (ed.) Edie, *Phenomenology in America*, Chicago: Quadrangle Books, 1967. Smith argues that there is no necessary logical connection between the experience of the Holy and the Judaic-Christian conception of God. The former belongs to the structure of life and the world and is not dependent on any definite religious belief.
23. Cp. J. Hessen, loc. cit., pp. 288–289.
24. Van der Leew, loc. cit. II, p. 675.

comes to a halt'.[25] Also: 'For Christian faith, the figure of the mediator is no 'phenomenon'; the phenomenologist cannot perceive where and how it enters history'.[26] However, though revelation is not a phenomenon, man's reply to revelation, his assertion about what has been revealed, is a phenomenon.[27] Again, 'Of heaven and hell however phenomenology knows nothing at all; it is at home on earth, although it is at the same time sustained by love of the beyond'.[28] Further, in recognizing that the phenomenon is neither pure subject nor pure object but the subject as related to the object and the object as related to the subject[29] he is aware that the phenomenon, for the phenomenologist, is defined by the notion of intentionality with its implied notion of noetic-noematic correlation. The range of the phenomena which he studies is also wide enough to help him avoid hasty generalizations.

Just as the central category for Otto is the idea of the Holy, for Van der Leew the central concept is that of Power. For the religious consciousness, things or persons have either power or not. Those that are powerful are sacred, those that are not are profane.[30] Phenomenology has to describe man's response to this Power. The sense of being in relation to a Power generates in human consciousness both fear and attraction. Man is also seized with dread and yet he loves it.[31] In directing itself to Power, human life is touched by Power and becomes sacred life.[32] Though much is *given* as sacred, life is yet regarded as something always to be filled with Power. Hence the importance of rites. Dread indicates the tension that exists between man and the Power. A man seized by dread may either live continuing to ignore the Power, or he may try to seize Power through *tapas*; or, he may rely on habit established through the rites and customs and feel secure; or he may fall back on faith in a possible reconciliation.[33] Thus religion is not mere acceptance of life as given. In one of its major strands, religion seeks power in life, seeks to elevate life, to enhance its value. It is 'the extension of life to its uttermost limit'.[34]

On the basis of this conception of religious life, Van der Leew works out in detail a phenomenology of the various forms of religious acts. Thus service

25. *Ibid.*, p. 565.
26. *Ibid.*, pp. 666–667.
27. *Ibid.*, p. 679.
28. *Ibid.*, p. 688.
29. *Ibid.*, p. 671.
30. *Ibid.*, p. 47.
31. *Ibid.*, p. 49.
32. *Ibid.*, p. 191.
33. *Ibid.*, pp. 468–469.
34. *Ibid.*, p. 679.

with its active, rhythmic swing of the body dramatizes the active participation of man in the Power and becomes a sort of 'sacred game'. The celebrations of festivals repeat what are regarded as the sacred moments of time – thereby implying the distinction between profane time and sacred time. While secular time and secular life are linear, sacred life and sacred time are cyclic. Every cult and rite is repetition. They do not symbolize events in linear time, they sybolize a cyclic order in which man seeks to participate. Like sacred time, sacred space has to be recognized as distinguished from profane space. Holy space is characterized by the existence of Power. Its effects are as it were visible there. Thus in all its dimensions, human life is touched, seized and transformed by Power. This, for Van der Leew, is the most essential feature of religion. This general feature makes room for various strategic moves that man may make in adjusting his relationship to Power. Man in fact takes up the challenge, but his responses are many and varied. Hence the diversity of religious phenomena.

Long complains that Van der Leew's phenomenology is too much under the influence of the objective and eidetic bias of the early Husserl.[35] This much is true that Van der Leew does not bring out the deep existential meaning of the religious phenomena. Reading his monumental volumes, one does not learn that religious acts arise out of existential needs of man and that they cannot properly be understood unless they are seen in that perspective. For these insights we have to turn to Eliade. It may also be said that Van der Leew overemphasizes the notion of Power. All religious experiences do not conform to this pattern, especially the Hindu search for the *Ātman* and the Buddhist striving after *nirvāna*. These latter religious hankerings have their origin in existential situations like pain and suffering and not in man's attempt to adjust himself to Power. There may be a sense of *tapas* according to which man seeks to acquire power to be equal to the gods. But this is not the primary, or even the main, motivation of the Hindu and Buddhistic religious life. Van der Leew interprets the Hindu ideal of seeking harmony with the universe as an attempt to unify human and cosmic powers.[36] But I have grave doubts if this interpretation can be sustained. What are sought to be harmonized are the individual consciousness and the spirit that is supposed to pervade the universe, the *Ātman* and the *Brahman*. And the notion of consciousness or spirit in the Hindu philosophies does not coincide with that of Power. However, to be fair, it must be said that one of the welcome

---

35. Cp. C. H. Long, 'Archaism and Hermeneutics', in J. M. Kitagawa (ed.), *The History of Religions; Essays on the Problem of Understanding*, Chicago: University of Chicago Press, 1967, p. 70 f.
36. Van der Leew, I, p. 36.

features of Van der Leew's phenomenology is that he has brought out the active, self-directing thrust of man in relating himself to the world and the Power. In fact, what a study of religious phenomena clearly brings to light is that man is not a passive instrument or medium for the working out of divine purpose, but that human intentionality, in its multifarious forms, constitutes and recreates the forms and patterns of life and behaviour which suit his existential needs.

The great merit of Eliade's studies on religious phenomena lies in their contribution towards relating the complex variety of religious phenomena to man's existential situation. Eliade is primarily concerned with the myths inasmuch as it is in the myths that the original intentions as of religious consciousness are preserved and can be read off. Myths are not primitive tales nor are they pre-scientific and pre-rational attempts to explain the origin of the universe. But what is intended in the myths? According to Eliade, the myths preserve the sacred history, the primordial history.[37] But sacred history is not history in our ordinary sense, it is not a linear succession of events. It is rather a cycle of significant archetypal patterns which the myths preserve and which the cults want us to repeat. Myth is the language of the sacred, and through myths man lives again in a timeless world. The distinction between the sacred and the profane is central to Eliade's thought. But the distinction does not mean a complete separation between the two worlds. For religious consciousness what is most important is 'the eruption of the sacred' in the profane world. The sacred space, for example, creates a centre through which not only communication with the transworldly is possible but also an orientation for the profane world first becomes possible. Similarly, sacred time, as relived in rites and services, gives a new significance and perspective to profane time which otherwise would be an endless series of moments. In general, the profane world receives organization, meaning and significance from the sacred, so that the world becomes apprehensible as a world first by being limited by and then by being diffused by the sacred. The myths show man's nostalgia for the sacred world. Eliade rightly insists that the existential situation is not as such a historical situation. There has been a modern emphasis on man's historicity which, for a true religious consciousness, errs by over-emphasis.[38] Religious consciousness rather tries to transcend historical existence, existence in profane history towards an existence in sacred

37. M. Eliade, *The Quest*, p. 72 f.
38. M. Eliade, 'It has been too lightly assumed that the authenticity of an existence depends solely upon the consciousness of its own historicity'. In fact, for Eliade, the more a consciousness is awakened, the more it transcends its own historicity (*Images and Symbols*, p. 33).

time. When therefore Eliade traces back the myths to man's existential situation he should not be understood as referring to man's historical existence. There is rather an essentialist strain in his thinking. The existential situations which the myths express are eternally there, and therefore their relevance for man is never superseded. The sacred is an element in the structure of consciousness, not a stage in the history of consciousness.[39]

Eliade's concept of the sacred has certain decided merits. It is wider in its application than Otto's notion of the Holy or Van der Leew's notion of the Power. Eliade's Sacred is not merely a structure of man's awakened, developed consciousness but also characterizes his subconscious. Symbolisms like the sky-symbolism, the symbolism of the 'unclean' and 'purification', the symbolism of origin belong to man's subconscious; myths are the language of the sacred. It is therefore an important philosophical task to relate the mythical element of the subconscious with the Freudean analysis of it. This task is undertaken by Paul Ricoeur.

The notions of sacred space and sacred time, as worked out by Eliade, are phenomenologically valid. But Eliade seems some times to be speaking the language of two worlds, so that for him religious consciousness would seem to be concerned with the sacred as distinguished from the profane. It is true, he also speaks of 'the eruption of the sacred' in the profane world, but the distinction and the consequent *via negativa*, seem to stand out prominently in his thought. This needs correction in two directions. First, it needs to be shown that the sacred world *qua* sacred is constituted by the peculiar intentionalities of religious consciousness – 'constituted' in that peculiar sense of 'constitution' in which Husserl used that word. It needs also to be pointed out that the goal of religious life is not the distinction itself but its annulment. For the truly religious soul, the profane is also the sacred. As the Buddhist philosopher Nagarjuna said, *samsara* and *nirvāna* are one and the same.

The creativity and constitutive function of religious consciousness is amply recognized by Eliade when he says, as final remarks to his *The Quest History and Meaning in Religion*, that spiritual creation is irreducible to a pre-existent system of values and that in mythological and religious universe every creation recreates its own structures.[40] To be noted is that he says 'recreates'. The phenomenologist cannot but be impressed by the recurrence of some fundamental patterns. But eidetic phenomenology must yield place to constitutive phenomenology. Patterns of religious expressions (myths, symbolism, rites, cults, etc.) must show the way to patterns of religious intentionalities in which they are constituted.

39. M. Eliade, *The Quest*, Preface.
40. *Ibid.*, p. 173.

V

Ricoeur[41] distinguishes between three dimensions of religious symbolism: the cosmic, the oneiric and the poetic. Man first reads the sacred on the world, on some elements or aspects of the world – the heavens, the sun, the moon, waters and vegetation. There is then a gradual movement away from the cosmic symbol towards the psychic which is best expressed in dreams. The cosmic and the psychic are two aspects of the same reality. 'I express myself in expressing the world; I explore my own sacrality in deciphering that of the world'.[42] As a philosopher, Ricoeur proceeds with the principle: 'Symbols give rise to thought'.[43] First there are the symbols as contingent cultural facts. Then, from amongst the world of symbols the philosopher chooses his own orientation: in Ricoeur's case it is the Judaic-Christian tradition which determines his point of view. It is good that he explicitly says this. Finally, he is led into the 'depths' of the intentionalities imbedded in the symbols. 'To understand (for phenomenology) is to display the multiple and inexhaustible intentions of each symbol, to discover intentional analogies between myths and rites, to run through the level of expression and representation that are unified by the symbol'.[44]

Every symbol, for Ricoeur, is finally a manifestation of the bond between man and the sacred. It is also an index of man's situation at the heart of being. The symbols like those of deviation, wandering, captivity and myths like those of chaos, blinding, mixture, fall – all these speak of the situation of man's existence in the being of the world.[45] Perhaps to this it should be added that man's situation in the heart of being is not as such religious unless a religious intention intervenes to relate man's existential situation to the sacred.

It was said before that one of the tasks with which a phenomenology of religious symbolism is confronted is that of reconciling its findings with the Freudean psycho-analysis. For, as Ricoeur has pointed out, every symbol has these two aspects in one: the cosmic and the psychic. The attitudes of phenomenology and psycho-analysis also differ.[46] Phenomenology does not seek to explain, but describes. Psycho-analysis tries to understand the

---

41. P. Ricoeur, *The Symbolism of Evil*, E. Tr. by Emerson Buchanan, New York, Evanston & London: Harper & Row, 1967.
42. *Ibid.*, p. 13.
43. *Ibid.*, p. 19.
44. *Ibid.*, p. 353.
45. *Ibid.*, p. 356.
46. I have derived the following material on Ricoeur's views on Freud from Stewart, J.D., 'Paul Ricoeur's Phenomenology of Evil', *International Philosophical Quarterly*, Vol. IX, No. 4, December 1969, 572–589.

religious symbolism by its function, not by its intention. Phenomenology entertains the question of the truth of symbols in so far as the intention calls for fulfillment. For psycho-analysis the symbolism is an illusion and nothing more than it. Phenomenology of religion looks upon the symbols as expressing man's relation to the Sacred, for Freud they express the 'return of the repressed'. Can these different systems be unified? Ricoeur considers each to be legitimate within its own order. In fact, he allows for two different ways of understanding consciousness: either by going back to the pre-conscious or the unconscious, or by going forward to its more comprehensive unfolding in the Absolute. The latter is the path of Hegelian phenomenology of spirit, the former is the path of Freudean psycho-analysis. It is a measure of Ricoeur's deep insight into the human situation that he rejects both these extremes. Both 'humiliate consciousness' and 'decenter the origin of meaning'.[47] Consciousness has this two-fold dependence: on the Sacred as much as on the Unconscious. Symbols are symbols of this dependence.

It is this ambivalence in the human situation which the religious symbols best express, this unstable union of passivity and spontaneity, of non-being and being, of evil and good. This is what Ricoeur calls man's 'affective fragility', the 'fault' of man's being, the *dukha* of the human existence (according to Buddhism). Religious symbolism both gives expression to it and points towards its transcendence through its annulment.

VI

The Indian philosphers started philosophizing with reflection on the fact that human existence is characterized by the basic fact of suffering (*dukha*). So did the Samkhya and also the Buddha. By 'suffering' or *dukha* they did not mean the mere fact that life is characterized by pain and frustration. They had in mind a more fundamental ontological fact that human existence is characterized by passivity and receptivity as also the fact that it is characterized by a perpetual self-transcendence. It is this experience of being subjected to a state of passive receptivity (of pleasure or pain) which generated in them the idea of freedom and complete spontaneity. Ever since the time of the Upanishads, this ideal of freedom and complete spontaneity has remained the goal of Indian spiritual life. What interests us in the present context is the fact that the religious acts have their origin in a certain human situation, they are always existential in their significance. The notion of 'religious intention'

---

47. Quoted by Stewart in his article cited in footnote 46.

has been used earlier in this paper. These intentions have their origin in peculiar existential situations, but they are not merely reflections on those situations. Reflection leaves the situation out of which it arises untouched. But the religious acts, arising out of pre-reflective human situation, tend to modify those situations by conferring on them a new noematic quality. Thus situations like death or frustration, trust and love, situations of the sort which Karl Jaspers called the *Grenzsituationen*, may generate religious intentions which *transform those situations from being merely human experiences into being experiences* of the holy, the sacred or the Power.

While thus a pre-reflective (and even pre-religious) existential situation may be transformed by an overwhelmingly religious intention into a religious *concern*, this concern at the same time posits its own object demanding a total surrender on the part of human subjectivity, an object which is such that, in the pertinent words of Paul Tillich, it 'makes us its object whenever we try to make it our object'.[48] We meet here with one of the most puzzling and yet compelling results of a phenomenology of human consciousness. Human intentionality is not only both receptive and constitutive, it confronts as given precisely that which it has constituted. To be an object for it is to be constituted by its meaning-giving function. The religious intention dominating an existential concern constitutes an Absolute, the correlate of an unconditional concern, which demands utter passivity and self-surrender on the part of the constituting intentionality. This is not to say that God or whatever else may be the object of Tillich's unconditional concern is an imaginary projection. To be constituted is not the same as to be projected by one's imagination. The religious object is the noematic correlate of the religious intention, and the sense of the reality or givenness of this object is the sense of such intention being fulfilled. Phenomenology cannot go beyond this point and recommend that there are or are not appropriate modes of fulfillment of the religious intention. What is pertinent in the above remarks is the contention that an existential situation, and an existential concern, is not *eo ipso* a religious situation, or a religious concern. Attempts to show that existentialism has to end up in an existential theology if it wants to be consistent are doomed to failure. Neither Heidegger nor Sartre have the least temptation towards a religious philosophy. This fact does not prove anything, but suggests that the transition from existential thought to religious thought is not straight and logically compelling, not even existentially compelling. But there is a way, the doors are not closed. The Buddha took this road. Many others did the same. The leap requires the coming into play of a religious

---

48. P. Tillich, *Systematic Theology*, Vol. I, University of Chicago Press, 1951, p. 12.

intention of some sort, which generally arises out of a therapeutic motive. Thus Tillich concedes that whereas modern existentialism does not provide any way of overcoming the ontological threat[49] and whereas psycho-therapy cannot remove the ontological anxiety,[50] religion provides the answer: 'Divine love is the final answer to the questions implied in human existence, including finitude, disruption and estrangement'.[51] This is alright so far as it goes (we may have to substitute 'divine love' by 'fulfillment of the religious intention'). But the answer presupposes the question, and the question presupposes a definite orientation towards the existential situation. It is at this last point that the transforming creativity and spontaneity of the religious intention comes into play taking the decisive step.

By way of conclusion it may be said, that a phenomenology of religion does *not* show that man is in his essence a religious being, it does not show that human consciousness, situated as it is, is bound to transcend towards the Absolute of religious consciousness – while it *does* show that the religious phenomena are constituted by a form of intentionality that is *sui generis* but which makes use of other constituted domains, especially of nature, art and the human situation, to constitute the peculiarly religious noematic quality which is grafted on to them. The combination of active spontaneity and receptivity which characterizes religious experience is nothing strange, for it characterizes the intentionality of human consciousness at all levels. But at all levels, intentionality is constitutive. The peculiarly novel component of the religious intention is the therapeutic motive, the motive of overcoming the human limitations, of getting beyond '*dukha*', of achieving freedom. The noematic correlate of this intention is precisely the supreme object of religious concern. In this sense, and it is only in this sense that human purposiveness underlies religious phenomena. But the basic category is not so much the concept of purpose as that of intentionality. We come face to face with a strange and novel form of human intentionality operating in all the diverse forms of religious phenomena, and this intentionality does not merely disclose, it is not merely *of* an object, it, like all intentionality, also constitutes that which it is of ...

49. *Ibid.*, p. 189.
50. *Ibid.*, p. 191 ff.
51. *Ibid.*, p. 286.

CHAPTER 3

THE CONCEPT OF PURPOSE IN A NATURALISTIC HUMANIST PERSPECTIVE

TAD S. CLEMENTS

Purposive behavior, irregardless of how it is conceived or defined, may be quite extensive in the animal kingdom. But, though it may not be confined to the human animal, it still characterizes human existence, or at least some of the manifestations of human existence, to an exceptional extent (indeed to such an extent that purpose as manifested in the human domain is generally conceived as constituting a difference in kind from its manifestations in the rest of the organic world). It is, therefore, not surprising that concepts of human purpose have come to occupy positions of fundamental importance in a large number of the conceptual-aspirational frameworks[1] men have developed. Indeed, these conceptual-aspirational frameworks themselves are often simply (or at least in large measure) manifestations of the human search for purpose. That is to say, many, perhaps all, of the conceptual-aspirational systems men have developed have been developed in order to create or elucidate structures which satisfy the human desire for a sense of purpose (in some sense of that term).

However, as the parenthetical qualification at the end of the previous sentence suggests, these varied conceptual systems have adopted and utilized different, often conflicting, views of the nature and status of purpose in the world. What purpose means, whether it is capable of being justified or not, and, if so, on what basis, are matters of dispute among those who accept different systems. Not only do religious, aesthetic, scientific and philosophic theories frequently disagree on the answers they give to these (and related) questions; even within any one of these provinces there is considerable disagreement. We see, therefore, that preliminary clarification is essential to our present project.

Let us begin, then, by noting what may be a rather obvious point, namely, that within our present context of inquiry the meaning(s) of purpose, the status of purpose(s) in the world and the question of whether or not

---

1. By a 'conceptual-aspirational framework', I mean any ostensibly explanatory system which also lays stress on certain goals or values to be striven for.

Horosz, W. and Clements, T. (eds.), Religion and Human Purpose
© 1986, Martinus Nijhoff Publishers, Dordrecht – Printed in the Netherlands

purpose(s) can be rationally justified can only be ascertained when we have agreed on an answer to the questions: What is meant by 'a naturalistic humanist perspective?' Are there different types of perspectives which are naturalistic and humanistic? If so, which type is involved here?

Now, I intend to take the expression, 'a naturalistic humanist perspective', to refer, generically, to any conceptual framework (albeit usually restricted to certain kinds of philosphic or religious systems) in which certain dimensions of human existence (in contradistinction, for example, to certain alleged theological facts) are taken as constituting values for human beings and in which these dimensions of human existence, in turn, are treated as resultants of natural processes exclusively. In other words, the expression is used to refer to any conceptual framework in which ultimate human values as well as instrumental values are understood in terms of human nature and the non-human environment within which human organisms, individually and as a species, have their being and possibilities.

Thus conceived, it becomes immediately obvious that there are many, diverse, indeed, fundamentally incompatible, varieties of naturalistic humanist perspectives. For instance, the expression would fit the ethical and metaphysical systems of such diverse thinkers as Epicurus, Spinoza, R. W. Sellars, Karl Marx and John Dewey. All of these men, along with a large assortment of others who are even more diverse in their fundamental philosophic perspectives, accept the view that 'nature' (in some sense which the individual thinker adopts) constitutes all of reality, together with the view that 'human nature' (in some sense which the individual thinker adopts), as this nature expresses itself within natural contexts, constitutes the ultimate basis for human value. It thus becomes important that we delineate the species of naturalistic humanist perspective with which we are here concerned. Such a delimitation will serve to identify one group of perspectives and exclude a great many other kinds.

The defining characteristic of this species of scientific humanism and its varieties is the importance placed upon science. These Naturalistic humanist perspectives insist on the supremacy of science, both methodologically and as a system of knowledge. While these perspectives recognize and admit that no empirical knowledge is absolute and that, therefore, the natural (or 'empircial') sciences cannot give us logical certainty, they do claim that the natural sciences give us the best knowledge claims available and, for this reason, the most reliable bases for value determinations and value attainments.

Nor is this claim arbitrary and without foundation: the justification for the claim is to be found in the logical and controlled experiential grounds of the methods employed by these sciences and the pragmatic consequences which arise from their employment.

This emphasis on science in our cognitive and valuational enterprises leads to the exclusion of men like Sartre and Heidegger who, despite their claim to accept some kind of naturalism and humanism, place supreme cognitive value on something other than the methods and fruits of the natural sciences, namely, on phenomenological descriptions of human subjectivity.

However, it seems possible and desirable to restrict our framework still further. Although many naturalistic humanist perspectives are not opposed to the desirability of the Unity of Science program or other physicalist and related reductionist models[2]; it is important to note that certain extreme reductionist views (those which are perhaps best designated as the 'nothing more than views', i.e., those which claim that mental events, human values, etc. are *unreal* because they are totally reducible, without remainder, to physical entities, relations and processes) are unacceptable as humanist perspectives. It may well be the case – and indeed increasing, cumulative, convergent evidence suggests strongly that it is the case – that mental and valuational terms, propositions and judgments are, at least in terms of future possibility (i.e., in principle), translatable into non-mentalistic and non-valuational terms and propositions whose referents occur within the domains of physics, chemistry, physiology, ecology, sociology, etc. But, whether this is the case or not, what needs to be noted is that (1) at least for now such a possibility is only a program, for the most part; we are not, in fact, able, to any considerable extent, to translate without residue mental and valuational activities or mentalistic and valuational linguistic formulations into physical, physiological, etc. realities or linguistic forms; (2) as *experienced*, thoughts and values are at least as real as the physical and biological constructs used to explain them, even though, as increasing evidence implies, they are or are produced by whatever these physical constructs represent.

These considerations, as well as others, point to the fact that, at least for the present (and perhaps in the future as well), an acceptable naturalistic humanist perspective must take sufficient cognizance of the data of direct experience. Indeed, this is simply a matter of giving fair recognition and weight to the content of experience out of which, in part, the conceptual structures of modern science develop and through which they are ultimately tested. It implies the exclusion, for our purposes, of simple mechanistic accounts which allow, as real, only one type of causal connection and only

2. Nothing dyslogistic is intended in referring to theoretical schemas and principles of procedure by means of the term 'reductionist': there are good reductive systems and procedures and poor ones.

one order of real entities.

Another group of theories of science and nature which are excluded are those which accept (indeed, rest upon) outmoded conceptions of cause, substance, law, etc. As modern science has developed during the last four hundred years, it has found it necessary to abandon or modify many of its fundamental conceptions. This has resulted, for example, in the replacement of Aristotelian, Thomistic, Cartesian and, to some extent, Newtonian conceptions by notions which permit the contemporary scientific enterprize to be carried out more effectively. In fact, this process of conceptual modification is continuous and clearly evident today. Nor is it limited to the physical and biological sciences. We have seen, in very recent times, early unsophisticated Freudian 'explanations' of behavior, in terms of 'Id' and 'Superego' (and other such constructs) branded as pseudo-explanations which either commit fallacies of hypostatization or amount to untestable utterances. Early behavioristic psychology which sought to ban mentalistic language and trace all behavior to a single level of explanatory principles has been modified, for example, by the introduction of principles of operant learning. Parallel modifications have occurred in nearly all of the natural sciences (crystallography is possibly an exception).

What these considerations imply is that no science can be taken as final, in terms of its criteria, methods, fundamental conceptions, or conclusions, but that some pictures of science and its fundamentals are more defective than others and some are completely unacceptable as theories of contemporary science.

Now, from what has been said, it is clear that I cannot hope to supply a definition of science which will be completely accurate and beyond reasonable criticism, for the word 'science' refers to diverse human activities which involve varying kinds and degrees of change. I will, therefore, insist only on the following points before proceeding: (1) science must not be understood in terms of conceptions which it has outgrown; (2) it must not be conceived so narrowly that it *seems* to 'explain away', as unreal, well attested phenomena which ordinary forms of human experience reveal, e.g., valuing, purposing, having meanings, etc.; (3) it must be seen as a group of *human activities*; not, as is all too common among philosophers today, as an isolated conceptual, symbolic system or frame of reference; the symbolic systems exist in intimate relationship to human activities such as observing, manipulating instruments, experimenting, tabulating, inferring, guessing, etc. and a scientific symbol system must never be completely dissociated from the factual (empirical) content of human experience; (4) science is necessarily confined to 'natural' conditions, conditions which, at least in principle, can be understood in terms of the categories and principles of explanation employed by the sciences; (5) wherever possible, accounts which are to be given scientific status must be testable. This is not to deny that some explanations employed by scientists are simply useful but not testable. Nor does it deny that testability is always a matter of degree, that confirmation is never conclusive.

From what has been said, it follows that (among other things) human purposes, whether considered in terms of specific goal-directed behaviors, i.e., specific means-end relationships, or in terms of overall senses of meaning and direction for individual or group existence, must be traceable, in this perspective, at least in principle, to the natural conditions of human life; for these conditions alone are able to find a place within the cognitive structures of science. It also follows that explanations of human purposing must be testable by reference to the same sorts of natural conditions of human life; for, unless such testing is possible, the accounts involved claim to be scientific.

Since the natural conditions of human life are of such fundamental importance in understanding human purpose within a naturalistic humanist perspective, we must ask: what is to be understood by 'the natural conditions of human life'? We should begin by noting that such conditions are not limited to external factors. Of course, environmental complexes are important, but at least equally important are the human organisms themselves. Indeed, the two expressions 'the human organism' and 'the external environment' refer, in actuality to functionally interdependent complexes. They are abstracted for convenience of conceptualization. It is the interactions among such bio-psycho-social beings and between them and various non-human environmental complexes which must be taken into account if we are to understand human purposive behavior in a way acceptable to both contemporary science and a scientifically oriented philosophy. Hence, plausible and testable (but, of course, not completely verifiable) models of human nature and of the environmental conditions in relation to which human purposes gain expression must be developed.

Of course, for this to be possible, there must be something, a common essence, whether conceived as static substance or as dynamic and variable process, correctly designated by the expression 'human nature'. that there is such an essence is vigorously denied by many thinkers, even by a fairly large number within the scientific community and within various 'humanistic' (e.g., literary, existential) orientations. In fact, there are some thinkers who are naturalistic (and scientific) humanists in the sense we are concerned with here, who deny that there is any sort of common ground 'plan' for human beings (cf., for example, G. Williams book, *Humanistic Ethics*). And certainly support seems to be added to the views of these varied scholars by the plethora of simplistic accounts and definitions of human nature which a wide assortment of thinkers, ancient as well as modern, have offered. It is completely understandable why men should be sceptical of all claims that human beings are exemplifications of a single 'blueprint', when it is observed how, throughout the ages, some of the greatest thinkers have come up with radically incompatible definitions and descriptions of human nature, definitions and descriptions which, it can now be seen, are gross oversimplifications. And besides, both ordinary experience and the investigations carried out by the various social sciences clearly reveal diversity of human interests and activities. Variability and relativity appear to be the manifest facts of human existence.

However, the fact that various oversimplified or false descriptions of human beings have been given in no way justifies the assumption or the inference that, therefore, human beings have no nature(s). For, if one were to proceed in that way, one would be guilty, it seems clear, of committing some form of the *Argumentum ad Ignorantium*, or at least of accepting some form of superficial analysis. Men are, I suppose it will be admitted, life forms and all life forms have natures. Regardless of how difficult it may or may not be to give adequate accounts of these natures, and regardless of the well-recognized fact that true but very diverse (because partial) descriptions can be given of any species or individual, the life forms have natures which, at least in principle, are susceptible of adequate descriptions. Organisms of considerably less complexity than man show extremely diverse forms of behavior in spite of very similar genetic constitutions (consider, for example, two German Shepards from the same litter, one used as a seeing eye dog and the other as a guard dog). In an analogous way, two identical human twins might, through quite varied experiences, possess quite different character traits and interests. With increased genetic and physiological complexity and, especially, through diverse cultural socialization processes, the diversity of behavioral patterns is proportionately increased. But this in no way negates the possibility that there is a human species nature which universally seeks expression and gratification of its fundamental requirements, albeit in varied ways. However, because of limitations of space, I will not attempt to develop and defend in detail a theoretic account of the components of human nature at this time. Instead, I refer the reader to my attempt to do this in Part II of my work, *Science and Man: the Philosphy of Scientific Humanism*. For our present purpose, I hope it will suffice simply to indicate, in little more than outline form, some of the main points of the treatment of human nature developed in that work.

My argument there is to the effect that organisms, of whatever sort, reveal their natures indirectly in what they do, i.e., in their patterns of behavior. This point should be qualified with the admission that what is thus revealed is not the complete nature of the organism and that the revelation is never direct, i.e., inference and interpretation are requisite. The point is, however, that certain basic requirements – expressing themselves as various kinds of demands, tendencies, felt needs, desires, interests, etc. – which can reasonably be thought of as essential (of nearly essential) aspects or components of the nature of an organism, can be plausibly inferred by scrutinizing the organisms' activities.

Now, I maintain that, in part, an analogous route can be and should be employed in an attempt to gain some understanding of the nature(s) of human organisms. In the case of human organisms, however, analysis consists largely in seeking correlations between two sets of data: the one set consisting largely of the sort of basic determinants which can reasonably be inferred in seeking to explain why men, transculturally and transhistorically, engage in various activities (e.g., art, religion, work, love, etc.); the other set of data consisting of introspective examination of one's own motivations together with the reports of others. These two sets of data, where they correlate, point to certain universal, or nearly universal, human characteristics. I further suggest, however, that the search for such nearly universal elements of a species nature for man should not blind us to the reality of individual differences, differences which are also discoverable by means of the same sorts of analyses. So much, then, for 'human nature' as one of the fundamental component complexes involved in the 'natural conditions of human life'. Undoubtedly a great deal more needs to be said on this subject, but this must suffice for now.

As to the 'external complexes' or 'external contexts', within which human nature operates, I will merely say that these expressions refer to all of the more or less clearly demarcated non-human domains studied by (or open to possible study by) the natural sciences. In other words, these expressions refer ideally to whatever would be susceptible to the methods of the natural sciences apart from human organisms. Since, however, it is impossible to isolate the non-human from the human domains, scientific (or even ordinary) study of the former always brings in references to the latter: 'external complexes' always must include, by implication, references to those dynamic complexes called 'human nature'. With these preliminary remarks in mind, let us now turn to human purpose.

In this work, I am concerned with purpose only in the sense of purpose in life, where 'purpose in life' is synonymous with such expressions as 'sense of meaning or significance in life', 'feeling that existence makes sense', 'sense of direction in life', etc., rather than with an analysis, within the perspective I have indicated, of specific means-ends relations. The matter to be explored can best be articulated by framing the following questions: What meaning does my own life have, i.e., why am I here? In other words, what purpose does my life serve? How do such senses of purpose come to be? Are they capable of being evaluated? These are the questions with which I shall be mainly concerned. An analysis of purposes, in the sense of specific cases of goal-seeking behavior, is not our primary concern here.

However, I think it is rather obvious that, both existentially and conceptually, there is a connection (perhaps a connection which holds universally) between the two kinds of purposes and between the two notions of purpose, i.e., between the specific and general senses of purpose. Generally, perhaps universally, a very enduring sense of well-being, a persistant feeling that one is functioning well, a general sense of overall direction within sequential life situations, is the result of three interacting complexes: (1) the personality structures which have previously been developed, (2) various life projects – past, present and anticipated – which one has adopted or will adopt, and (3) the conditions which permit these projects to be actualized in ways which are satisfying to the personality structures already formed or in process of formation or which will be formed at some later stage of development. If any one or more of these dynamically interacting complexes is defective, in any number of ways, there will not be an overall sense of purpose in life, or at least not to the same extent such would otherwise be possible.

Though all of these complex ingredients are important, the one I wish to focus on here is 3; for 3 is, in large measure, the reality factor in human life. I mean by this that it includes all those aspects of the world which must, to a sufficient degree, be recognized and adequately dealt with if the demands set by one's personality structure and one's projects are to be optimally satisfied. But certainly if the demands set by one's nature and life projects are to be 'adequately dealt with', this implies that certain effective means are employed to attain specific goals. In other words, 3 includes specific means-ends relations within an ongoing experiential continuum. The specific, limited cases of goal-seeking are among the objective conditions by means of which life-projects and personality structures are actualized. And successfully conducted life-projects, together with certain kinds of personality structures, are among the fundamental causes of the generalized sense of purpose in life. Let us turn to a hypothetical but not unrealistic case to illustrate this point.

Suppose we consider the case of a famous medical pioneer, Dr. X, who appears, in terms of the various tests open to medically and psychologically trained personnel, to be functioning well in his life situations; that is, as far as such evaluative procedures can assess his life processes, he seems healthy and adapted to the conditions of his existence. Furthermore, he generally has a sense of fulfillment and promise: for him, as experienced and reported, life has an overall direction which is, for the most part, satisfying and valuable. How could such a state of affairs come about? Well, obviously, the specification of all (or even most) of the factors involved in the case of Dr. X (or in any particular case) or of the probably innumerable combinations of conditions which might possibly bring about such states of affairs, would border on omniscience. Hence, a complete, or completely acceptable, account is out of the question. However, all of human experience, attests that it is reasonable to think that Dr. X's case would not manifest the existential traits which it does unless he had previously reached certain other points (for example, graduation from medical school) in his unique development, that he would not have reached such points in his development unless he had attained a number of lesser goals (for example, passing his biochemistry examinations), and that these lesser goals would not have been attained if certain means (for example, certain methods of studying for examinations) had not been employed effectively. So there is a frequent, but not invariable, connection within human experience between purposing in the sense of specific goal-seeking (and the means-ends relations these define) on the one hand, and purpose in the sense of an overall sense of significance and direction in life, on the other hand. There are, of course, reasons why such connections are not invariable, and I shall deal with some of these at greater length shortly. For now, I will simply indicate that it is all too possible for human beings to develop delusional worlds attended by spurious senses of well-being, i.e., senses of well-being having no objective correlates.

Throughout this presentation, I have made use of such expressions as 'the natural conditions of human life', 'environmental conditions', 'environmental contexts', 'environmental complexes', 'the conditions which permit life projects to be actualized', etc. As previously indicated, all of these varied expressions were meant to convey the view that human purpose, within a naturalistic humanist perspective which takes science as a fundamental conceptual framework, is derivative from natural processes, some of which are best conceived as external to human selves. However, such expressions also hinted at another point which must now be made explicit and (if possible) defended, namely, that human purposes are caused, that determinism holds for the domain of human purposing. I shall argue that 'external' states of affairs and self-states, both antecedent and concomitant, determine the forms and directions human potentialities can and will take and that these actualized potentialities in turn produce the feeling of well-being, the sense of significance and direction, which constitute human purpose in the sense which interests us here. Of course, the same sorts of considerations would lead to an understanding of the importance of determinism in understanding cases where a sense of futility and lack of significance and direction develop, but this is not our present concern.

Can a deterministic account of human purpose be justified on rational grounds? If the answer to this question is affirmative, what implications – moral, educational, etc. – does this have? Now, obviously, if these questions are to be answered in a philosophically adequate manner, some preliminary clarification is needed. To begin with, what is to be understood by 'determinism'?

By 'determinism', I mean the doctrine that all occurrences have causes, that there are no uncaused events. And by an 'event' or 'occurrence' I mean any phenomenon, i.e., anything which seems to form (either through direct perception or through inferences based upon such direct perceptions) a coherent part of experience and which can, therefore, at least in principle, be assigned determinate temporal and spatial loci in some natural order. What this ultimately amounts to is the theoretical possibility that the thing or pattern being dealt with can form a consistent part of some system of scientific explanation and can be manipulated through some of the methods of science applied in accordance with at least some of the cognitive criteria of the natural sciences.

If this is what is to be meant by 'determinism', understood in a generic sense, there are still a number of difficult clarificatory problems to be dealt with. Are there different and irreducible kinds of deterministic accounts? If the answer to this question is affirmative, which type(s), if any, can give a true account of human purpose? Along a different but related line, it should be noted that the question – Can a deterministic account of human purpose be justified on rational grounds? – presupposes satisfactory answers to the queries: What constitutes a 'justification on rational grounds'? Are there different sorts of rational justifications which are appropriate to different sorts of rational justifications which are appropriate to different kinds of problems? If the answer to this last question is affirmative, then we are naturally led to ask which sense of 'rational justification' is appropriate when one is seeking to establish the doctrine that human purposes are determined? Unfortunately, although all of these problems are relevant to our project, I cannot treat them in a thorough manner at this time because they are all extremely complex problems requiring lengthy and careful treatment.

There are, obviously, different kinds of causal accounts. The kinds of causes referred to in sociology, for instance, are usually not the same kind of causes referred to in physics or, for that matter, in biology or psychology. The phenomena dealt with in these areas of investigation are explained in terms of quite disparate categories. Physical facts are not the same as social facts, political facts, etc. As a consequence, these domains constitute different orders of human experience and cognition. However, even though the causal notions employed in such diverse universes of discourse are quite distinct, it is still legitimate and reasonable, to ask whether causes of one kind might be reducible to, i.e., translatable without residual meaning in terms of, causes of one or more other kinds. Or, since this is usually what is at issue, are all causal accounts ultimately reducible to (= expressible in terms of) elemental physico-chemical laws? For, in the final analysis, it appears clearly possible that all cognitive domains which deal with matters of fact may simply be selected aspects of a unified experience, in which case the diverse facts, causes, laws, categories, etc. of the various fields of empirical (factual) knowledge represent simply convenient abstractions useful for the conceptual manipulation of experience.

Be this as it may, an honest answer to the question of ultimate reducibility must be that although the possibility of such translations may serve as an ideal for the sciences, they are not for the most part, at least for the present, a practical possibility. This means that for now, at least, we must accept the existence of different irreducible deterministic accounts, even though it is worthwhile to chip away at this unfortunate fragmentation wherever possible. I say 'unfortunate', because although separate universes of discourse (different kinds of descriptions) are conceptually useful, it would also satisfy a deep-seated human craving (for the unification of all scientific knowledge) if translatability were more than an abstract ideal possibility.

Are any of these different kinds of deterministic accounts applicable to human purpose? If so, which kind? Can such application be rationally justified? Now, it seems manifest that the kind of deterministic laws which hold for the classical Newtonian physics are not properly applied to the phenomena usually designated 'human purpose', for these laws are applicable to relatively simply, abstracted properties and relations, whereas human purposes involve extremely complex patterns and processes. Of course, this is not to deny that there are certain kinds of processes which human bodies enter into which accompany purposive behavior and that these processes are expressible in terms of Newtonian mechanistic principles; but only that such principles cannot satisfactorily account for human purposing. And, obviously, twentieth century non-Newtonian, quantum-mechanical physics does not help us here either; for such physical accounts are not, in any strict sense, deterministic at all. But here again, it would be a mistake to think that, therefore, contemporary quantum physics is completely irrelevant to purposive structures. What this comes to is the fact that physical deterministic accounts (and indeterminacy accounts) do not contribute *appreciably* to an understanding of human purpose.

When, however, we turn to biological accounts and especially those which attempt to relate behavioral patterns to physiological (including biochemical and genetic), as well as ecological factors, we find principles and concepts which are, increasingly, able to account for human purpose in both the narrow means-end sense and in the sense of an overall sense of direction in life. However, such accounts, as these have been developed within the frameworks of the physiological and ecological biologists, are in need of supplementation from psychology and the social sciences. If one selects judiciously from the explanatory principles to be found among or logically consistent with the biological (including the biochemical and biophysical), the ecological, the psychological and the social sciences, one can account, to some extent, for patterns of human purpose. It must be candidly admitted, however, that such accounts, whether cautiously applied to the individual case or to classes of human beings, are never more than reasonable (in some sense of that word).

This last point brings us to the question: Can the application of such accounts to human purpose be rationally justified? Now, the answer to this question depends on what one means by 'rationally justified' or 'rational justification'. If one means by these expressions possessing deductive certainty, then, of course, the application of such accounts to human purpose is not rationally justified for it is always logically possible to make false causal assignments. But this is not warranted, because to require such a restrictive meaning for 'rational justification' would have as a logical consequence the judgment that no scientific accounts, except those within the domain of formal logic and mathematics, are rationally justified or justifiable.

If one means by 'rational justification' a procedure or set of procedures which objectively result in a high probability for the things being asserted, then here again the application of such accounts to human purpose is not rationally justified, because it is not possible, at least at present, to say with logical assurance that explanations of human purpose in terms of such scientific constructs are highly probable. Indeed, unfortunately, except in regard to a relatively few sorts of situations (e.g., certain sorts of psychological states which accompany certain neurological conditions), it is not even possible to establish that a given scientific account of human behavior is more likely than alternative accounts.

What I think may be reasonably meant by the expression 'rationally justified', in connection with human purpose, is (1) that the causal account does not contradict any well attested knowledge about human beings, (2) the account is suggested by an analysis, subjective and intersubjective, of human experience and (3) the account is useful. This does not place human purpose in a unique, unscientific position, for there are a large number of doctrines accepted within the sciences which are in the same sort of logical position. That is, there are many hypotheses and principles accepted and utilized by the various natural sciences, not because their status is logically certain or highly probable, but simply because in any explanatory system some things need to be assumed and they are consistent with empirical data which human beings want to explain and integrate. This means that the explanation of human purpose in terms of causal explanatory principles to be found among relevant sciences, or consistent with such principles, are on a par with many ontological and methodological postulates whose justification is ultimately pragmatic.

However, the justification is not solely pragmatic nor does the pragmatic appeal amount to an arbitrary subjective preference. What evidence there is – and this is already considerable, cumulative and convergent – supports our 'faith' in deterministic accounts of human behavior. We have no good reasons for not applying such accounts to human behavior and many, diverse reasons for applying them.

In *Science and Man*, I sugest that among the most powerful determinants of human behavior are certain basic motivations – biological and psychosocial – which transcend cultures and historical periods and which are, therefore, to be viewed as essential, fundamental components or aspects of human nature, i.e., species characteristics of man *qua* man. To these species traits are superadded various modifications resulting from unique individual hereditary, experiential and cultural factors. These two sets of factors – designated the *whatness* and *thisness* of a man's nature – constitute the conceptual model of an individual's human nature.

Given such a human nature and a complex set of environmental factors interacting at some moment in time, a number of alternative life plans are possible, *if* the individual apprehends them. If he does not, he is completely set into an existing pattern: his present course, then, is rigidly structured in terms of past determinants. In such a case, the individual is, for the moment at least, completely and blindly enslaved to the resultants of past complex interactions between his own past states and past environmental complexes. But let such an individual, through unplanned or planned experiences, become aware of other life modes and the possibility arises that he might break out of his present mold. However, whether such an individual does in fact develop a new pattern of response and aspiration will depend on the establishment of a new motivational set for him. And the establishment of a new motivational set will in turn depend upon certain insightful experiences which cannot antecedently be guaranteed. In other words, there is no guarantee that a person will in fact become sufficiently aware of the determinants and structures of his present existential pattern and sufficiently motivated to change some or all of these so that a new mode of life emerges for him, no matter what experience(s) he has. In practice, what this means is that, in the present state of knowledge, guidance, education, psychological devices, etc. cannot give assurance that an individual will be able to see more than one alternative course open to him, or, even if he does see this, will actually be able to pursue a course other than the one he is presently pursuing. We know from ordinary as well as scientific experience that all three possibilities can be found: (1) an individual may be almost completely unaware of possible alternative life modalities for him; (2) an individual may, through suitable experiences, be aware (as mere logical possibilities) that alternative life modalities are open to him, but with no ability, as he is presently constituted, to act on any of these; and (3) an individual may be able, through suitable experiences and previously formed personality structures, not only to see in general outline alternative life gestalts open to him but be in the (enviable?) position to choose one of these.

Now, in the cases suggested by (1) and (2), purposing becomes little more than a kind of blind habit. Individuals who are thus affected have aspirational lives which do not, in practice (for there are still, theoretically, possibilities for such individuals *if* certain things occur) differ markedly from some of the animal relatives of men. Such individuals are barely human, in terms of distinctively human possibilities for seeing alternatives as *real* alternatives open to them. To bring out these human possibilities requires intensive but cautiously applied educational techniques. Philosophic and scientific procedures which tend to create critical questioning are essential here.

But even in connection with (3) there are problems, for is it not possible to choose irrationally or rationally and to develop life patterns which are life promoting or life defeating? And if so, is it not possible to speak reasonably of human purposes which are wise or unwise in certain respects? Again, is it not possible to attain, and perhaps even to sustain, a sense of significance and direction in life through various abnormal physiological states (e.g., those induced by alcohol and various drugs), or through various functional psychological aberrations (e.g., psychoses, etc.). Answers to these questions are possible *and* acceptable only if we accept certain criteria for the evaluation of various life patterns and these criteria in turn must reflect certain ultimate values. Unless certain desiderata are accepted as ultimate for human beings *qua* human beings and for any particular individual with his ideosyncracies, we cannot rationally appraise alternative life modes. Are there such ultimate values? What do they depend upon?

As pointed out previously, it is possible to infer from the evidence available that men have a species nature which is modified by a somewhat unique heredity and set of experiences. I have also argued that human purposes are emergent products of deterministic interactions involving the human organism and its past, present and anticipated future environmental complexes. I wish now to maintain that it is these factors – the nature (whatness and thisness) of the individual and the conditions imposed by the environmental complexes within which that nature originates, develops and realizes some of its possibilities – which define and establish the nature of ultimate values for man, individually and as a species.

My argument runs as follows: What is ultimately good for any organism, individually or as a species, is what will promote that organism's well-being in the long run. By an 'organism's well-being' is meant a condition of healthful functioning as determined by the various tests open to the biological sciences. Such healthful functioning, it is well known, depends on two conditions being maintained within certain limits: the physiological states of the organism and its environment (especially those parts of the environment upon which it is most directly dependent, e.g., the organisms it feeds upon, etc., but not limited to these). Hence, if any organism or group of organisms is acting in any way which probably will destroy either the physiological basis or the ecological basis or both, and thus its well-being, this can reasonably be judged as bad for that kind of organism.

Man is no exception to this. Man, individually or as a species, has his well-being, i.e., his effective functioning, dependent on the maintenance of certain physiological states in dynamic (varying within limits) equilibria with the rest of the environment. But this cannot be accomplished in any way one might think it can. Alternative more or less successful courses are possible, but not all courses can be successful nor successful in the same way or to the same extent. Not all courses which might be open can satisfy the natures of men optimally over the longest period of time possible. The only courses that can do this are those which establish lasting dynamic balances between the species and the total relevant environment. All others, in one way or another, to one extent or another, result in ineffective and unhealthy physiological states and, sooner or later, recognizable misery, i.e., unhappiness. Hence, it appears clear, some overall senses of purpose are better and some worse, or, in more simplistic terms, some are good and some are bad, because, when translated into courses of action and life plans, for individuals or groups or the species as a whole, they are more or less life-fulfilling and life-promoting or life-frustrating and life-defeating, depending on whether they tend to produce ecological equilibria or disequilibria.

But are these the only ultimate values in terms of which evaluation of alternative life patterns is possible within the sort of naturalistic humanist perspective being considered? What about human happiness or satisfaction, especially if we are concerned not with transitory happiness or satisfaction for individuals or groups but with lasting happiness or satisfaction? And, while we are on this topic, let us at least consider a serious problem for the naturalistic humanist: What justification can there be for rejecting other, including 'non-natural', ultimate values as bases for evaluating alternative life styles and their underlying and concomitant purposes? These are all important problems, but in the space available to me I cannot hope to deal with them effectively. Again, for a more detailed treatment of these problems, I recommend that the reader turn to *Science and Man*.

I will merely say that the terms 'happiness' and 'satisfaction' are much less open to precise scientific definition and description than are 'physiological health' (or even 'psychological health'), 'life-promoting' or 'life-frustrating' activities. 'ecological equilibria' or 'ecological disequilibria' etc. In the case of 'happiness' and 'satisfaction', or their opposites, what is being designated is far less agreed upon. Nonetheless, it does seem to make sense to say that happiness or satisfaction, at least in some sense of these terms, are ultimate values. Would anyone be likely to agree, if such could be the case, that a world in which there were a well established ecological balance and everyone were functioning well (healthfully and effectively) within it, but in which everyone always or almost always felt miserable, would be a good world? I do not think so. Happiness or satisfaction, in some sense(s), must also, then be an ultimate value and should enable us to evaluate alternative life modes and purposes they reflect. However, an important point in the last statement is contained in the expression 'in some sense(s)'. The point is that the terms 'happiness' and 'satisfaction', as well as their opposites, are ambiguous terms and while some meaning(s) for them may be able to serve as bases for evaluative principles within a rational, scientifically oriented system, some other senses may not be able to do this. Or, to put the matter in a different perspective, the point is that some senses of 'happiness', etc. are compatible with the other ultimate values mentioned while others are not. In other words, some kinds of happiness or satisfaction can accompany states of affairs which are life-frustrating and/or ecologically disruptive, while other kinds of happiness or satisfaction are at least normal accompaniments of life-promoting states of affairs. We are therefore in a position to say that although healthful functioning and ecological balance are good, they need the third value – logically compatible happiness or satisfaction – to make them complete as ultimate values. And we are also warranted in asserting that other forms of happiness or satisfaction – those which are life-destroying or life-frustrating – are bad. This means that drug induced euphorias which lead to the deterioration of the person and/or which cause the person to deal with the real world and its problems ineffectually are bad. It would also justify the condemnation of religious myths which lead people to live warped semi-human lives and/or to deal with the natural world in unrealistic ways.

This is, I think, the appropriate place to make some comments about certain questions which are frequently found in discussions about purpose. Questions such as 'Why is there a world?', 'Why is the world the way it is?', 'Why am I here, i.e. what is the purpose of my existence?' are not reasonable questions. They point for their answers to a realm outside of the natural and/or human worlds open to scientific investigation. They presuppose a transcendent teleological realm for which there is no satisfactory evidence whatsoever. There are of course many things about the universe and about ourselves for which we have no satisfactory answers. We do not even know which of the rival scientific cosmologies is correct (although there is increasing evidence for one of these and so we know which one is to be preferred). But this lack of completely adequate answers in no way justifies wild speculations about a 'divine', 'supernatural' (or at least non-natural) telic realm.

For the most part, we do have reasonable scientific answers concerning the way in which our earth, its life forms (including the human species and its social forms) have developed. The sciences of astronomy, geology and biology, together with the social sciences, are, for the most part, able to translate such 'why' questions into 'how' questions with reasonable answers. And where this is impossible – as in the case of the question, 'What is the purpose of my existence?' – the trouble does not lie with the sciences, but rather with the question. Questions such as this beg the question of whether there is a cosmic designer operating behind the scenes of nature. As usually understood, they have no place in a rational, scientific philosophy. If one's existence seems to have a purpose, i.e., a meaning and direction, this is (at least in principle, since, in fact, the question is almost hopelessly difficult) answerable in terms of what factors (genetic and experiential) have produced this result. To seek more than this is to commit oneself to the quicksand of theological speculation and religious myth. This itself is a form of delusional world-building, i.e., a species of unrealistic and hence perverse purpose which should be condemned.

For similar reasons, the present practice of contemporary industrialized nations, such as the United States, which results in the want on destruction of ecological balance and wastage of natural resources are to be judged as evil ways of life reflecting perverse purposes, for they are destroying one of the fundamental bases of human value.

What of other values, both natural and non-natural? Are they logically compelling reasons why one or more of these should not occupy a position of fundamental importance in the assessment of alternative life styles along with their attendant purposes? Now, answering these questions is not a simple matter; because, along with other serious difficulties, the questions raise the most serious problem of all, namely, whether there are cognitively compelling reasons for preferring a naturalistic metaphysics wedded to a humanistic value system of a certain sort to all other metaphysical and value combinations. The defense of such a thesis is obviously beyond the scope of this work and, perhaps, is beyond the scope of any work. I do, however, think that there are compelling reasons for preferring an empirical, naturalistic metaphysics combined with a humanism of the sort being considered here, but limitations of space will not permit the full development of the requisite defense at this time. As a matter of fact, however, I have attempted, along somewhat different lines, such defenses in my work, *Science and Man*, to which I have previously alluded, and in the chapter 'Metaphysics as Metascience', in the *Marvin Farber Festschrift*. I recommend both of these works to the reader interested in a further defense of such a metaphysical and axiological standpoint.

Therefore, at this point I will merely make the following statements: It must be admitted that the conceptual structures of science are logically compatible with most refined metaphysical systems. This is so, because it is one of the marks of a well developed metaphysical hypothesis to be able to account for all of human experiences and its varied interpretations, including the scientific, in terms of the categories of the metaphysical hypothesis. Nonetheless, logical compatibility is not the only consideration. The natural sciences (which give us the most reliable knowledge claims we have) all presuppose certain fundamental doctrines and cognitive criteria and only certain kinds of empirical naturalisms take these doctrines and criteria as fundamental in developing and defending their own speculations. Such naturalisms become the metaphysical systems ideally suited to the sciences because they deliberately take the sciences as their own foundations. And, of course, the humanism I have been discussing is simply an attempt to develop and justify those human values which are found through a philosophic examination of the scientific study of men in relation to their natural environment. As such it is simply one dimension of an empirical naturalism, namely the human dimension with its characteristic emphasis on purpose(s).

CHAPTER 4

THE RECOVERY OF HUMAN PURPOSE IN THE RELIGIOUS LIFE

WILLIAM HOROSZ

Religion's great challenge is human purpose. The current debate between religion and secularism, if it is to be resolved, depends on how this challenge is met. In the past religionists have flirted with purpose, courted it, competed with it, deprecated it, made substitutions for it, and even used it to establish the normative priority of religious systems of totality. On the whole they have not come to grips with human purpose as the central topic in the debate between religion and secularism. While they have used purpose in its holistic meaning to establish final systems of religious coherence, they have simultaneously denied the effectualness of human purpose as an effective guide to the religious life, especially on issues of ultimate concern and salvation. Because of apologetic interests and for the alleged dualism between divine and human purpose, they have never explored critically the relevance of purpose to the religious quest. By the imposition of 'final purpose' on religious designs they have created undue tension and anxiety in the heart of man. Through such totalistic designs for living they made certain totalitarian claims on life that modern man is still trying to forget.

Is there an alternative to the holistic use of purpose in the religious quest? Is holism the final relevance of purpose to religion, or is it merely a post-purposive reading of the comprehensive designs and their normative claims on life? The timely debate between religion and secularism makes it imperative that we face up to some hard alternatives of the use of human purpose in the religious quest. Briefly stated, the alternative is: either we posit the primacy of a religious system of totality and give man a pie-slice share of the qualities in the system, or we posit the primacy of the human orderer as he participates in the religious quest and we conceive such totalistic designs for living as provisional aids in man's search for meaning. The choice we face is between a holistic use of purpose in religion and a self-directive use of purposiveness that gives the human orderer real credit in existence for the religious quest.

Horosz, W. and Clements, T. (eds.), Religion and Human Purpose
© 1986, Martinus Nijhoff Publishers, Dordrecht – Printed in the Netherlands

I. THE HOLISTIC USE OF PURPOSE IN RELIGION

The first alternative envisions man's life in terms of the primacy of comprehensive designs, holistically conceived, utilizing the definition of purpose in terms of wholes, unities, totalities, or final purpose. This is a rather prevalent use of purpose in traditional religions. Such religious systems of totality, as when God, for example, is defined as the 'ground of being' or 'being-itself', are given theological priority to the human orderer's quest for religion. They are often equated with ultimacy, divine purpose, and with normative claims in general. Man's ability to form such systems of totality is disclaimed and his purposive nature is barred from playing a creative role in these final designs for living out of piety for the source of one's being. These monolithic structures of religious meaning are, then, passed of as 'ultimacy in secular experience' or as the 'Other' confronting man in given experience.

Two examples should suffice to see the omnipotent role the holistic use of purpose has played in the field of religion. Paul Tillich and John E. Smith both endorse its primacy. Tillich especially gives it classic formulation when he states: 'Life universal moves towards an end and is elevated into eternal life, it's ultimate and even present end ... Creation is for the end: in the 'ground', the 'aim' is present'.[1] Speaking of the 'religious dimension of experience' Professor Smith states: 'This dimension marks man as the religious animal in the sense that he is the one being in whom the question of the purpose of existence as such becomes explicit both as a *question* and as a supreme *interest* ... He differs from all other finite beings, however, in his ability to envisage a whole of existence – in part through conception and in part through imagination – and to ask for a final purpose for that whole ... Understanding the religious dimension solely in terms of an interest that human beings display and a question about the purpose of existence is inadequate unless it is also shown how this question and interest are related to the religious question of God ... We must go on to show that the question and interest point to God as answer'.[2]

Viewed as confrontations in life both encounter-experiences, that of wholeness and of God, and their coupling, are believed to be free of human design and construction. They are a matter of direct participation in existence, and not mere products of the mind and imagination. Man is attributed a religious drive for wholeness and ultimacy in experience that is prior to human self-direction and purposiveness. The term 'interest' should be viewed in

1. Paul Tillich, *Systematic Theology*, Vol. III, Chicago: University of Chicago Press, 1963, p. 398.
2. John E. Smith, *Experience and God*, New York: Oxford University Press, 1968, pp. 55–56.

terms of an ontological need. This drive for wholeness is a unifying principle in human life only because man is first rooted in his participation, directionality, and responsibility, in the religious system of totality. Human purpose is a secondary and reactive phenomenon to this primal drive for a final purpose, answer, or God. The coupling of the concept of immediate wholeness to the notion of God is what we have been calling a monolithic structure of meaning or dominant purpose for life.

A more functional and pluralistic version of holism is well supported by R. W. Hepburn. By allowing for multiple purposes for life 'with trajectories of varying reach, scope and seriousness', the author is rejecting the monolithic perspective in order to expand the linguistic search for the meanings for life. He would reject the coupling of the purpose for the whole with ultimacy or God because of the meaning that is lost when the question: 'What is the purpose of life?' is translated to read: 'What are people for?' What is lost in the translation is man's dignity, for he becomes 'an instrument, a tool, or organ in a living body'. Hepburn thus rejects the monolithic structuring of life, of seeing life in terms of one dominant purpose, or of identifying the reality of God with the whole purpose for existence, and views it as the peril of subordination. The ends of life are more pluralistic in design.[3]

II. A SELF-DIRECTIVE USE OF PURPOSE IN RELIGION

The second alternative postulates a new dimension of purpose for the religious life. Before man is part of a system of religious totality he is self-directing in existence as a human orderer. In the light of this perspective religious holisms are provisional designs for living and integral with man's search for meaning. Whether we have a highly structured meaning for life, or many anologies of meaning, as in Hepburn's functional holism, life is still goal-directed in its quest and the purpose(s) of life are given an external design. The self-directive use of purpose in religious experience is a more serious venture as *a search* with provisional meanings on the way. Religious holisms are projects of human self-direction in existence. If they are seen as an integral part of the search, and viewed in the context of human *participation* in existence, rather than outside it, they have legitimate roles to play in the religious quest. They have little worth as final answers to human questions about the wholeness of existence. This view, then, regards human commitment to religious systems of holism a contribution of purposive being in existence, formed and designed

3. Ronald W. Hepburn, 'Questions About the Meaning of Life', *Religious Studies*, April, 1966, pp. 126–130, 140.

by man's purposive nature in search of meanings and goals in life. The coupling of the purpose of life with the reality and final coherence of God is primarily a search in self-direction before it is man's need to strive for wholeness.

Whatever else systems of religious holisms may mean, when we postulate their ontological primacy, they stand for systems of totality making totalitarian claims on human life. Langdon Gilkey has such a view in mind in defining God as ground of being: '(1) Ultimacy appears in our experience, first of all, as the *source*, ground, or origin of what we are, and therefore of the finite and its characteristics. It has, therefore, neither the form nor the feel of an entity amidst the finite. Rather in conditioning ourselves and other entities totally, it cannot be in turn conditioned by them – at least as another entity would be conditioned. More concretely, this experience of an unconditioned ground is manifested in the awareness that our being and its meanings are *given* to us; thus are we aware that they are not subject to the bidding, control, or direction of our intelligence or powers, but on the contrary, are the foundation or presupposition of our possession and use of those powers. (2) Ultimacy also manifests itself in relation to an awareness of our *limits*, when we experience a fundamental or essential – not provisional or temporary – threat and helplessness ... (3) In its positive role this principle of ultimacy is also the source and basis of our *values* ... (4) Because of these essential characteristic of source, limit, transcendence, and sacrality, and because of the strange dialectic of negation and affirmation involved in the experience of the ultimate, there is an element of *mystery* with regard to ultimacy'.[4]

Gilkey's perspective, imitative of Tillich, is a typical statement of the primacy of religious holism over the self-direction of the human orderer in existence. The fact that man's purposive nature is needed to raise the question of origins, the question of wholeness, and the coupling of the purpose for life with the eternal, is totally ignored by this view. The fact that self-transcendence, which makes all this work, is merely an *abstraction* from man's capacity for self-direction in existence, is similarly neglected. If man's purposive nature is needed to establish and mediate such schemes of religious totality, as the ground of being or being-itself, how can we establish the primacy of such systems of religious totality over the human orderer and his quest for religious meaning? Is this the demand of life itself or is it the requirement of piety and a post-purposive view of the religious life? In this chapter we shall attempt to show that the holistic use of purpose in the

---

4. Langdon Gilkey, *Naming the Whirlwind: The Renewal of God-Language*, New York: Bobbs-Merrill, 1969, pp. 313–14.

religious quest may not be as determinative of human life as Gilkey, Smith, Tillich, and others, hold.

We have developed the ontological relevance of purpose to existence elsewhere.[5] Here we need only to develop its religious implications. If we construe the deepest meaning of human purpose in terms of man's capacity for self-direction in existence, then, we can postulate systems of religious holisms, and human commitments to them, as projects of this ontological capacity in man. This ontological meaning of purpose in the religious quest has priority to systems of totality identified with religious designs. At the same time, we need not deny other layers of meaning in human purpose, such as the phenomenal, analytic, and artifactual levels of purposiveness. According to our theory, systems of totality in the form of religious holism arise on the second level of purposiveness, the phenomenal layer of meaning. After all holisms are nothing more than long-range goal-directions. Such holistic goal-directions in existence presuppose a capacity on the part of the human orderer to be self-directing in existence. Systems of totality are thus *operational aspects* of man's ontological potentiality to be self-directing in existence. The holistic use of purpose is prevalent in tradition; it utilizes the meaning of purpose defined as end, aim, telos, goal. When religionists utilize systems of religious totality for normative and apologetic reasons they give the phenomenal meaning of purpose as goal-direction theological fixation and ignore the mediative role that human purpose has played in establishing and forming such systems of totality. To define wholeness, God as ground, ultimacy, being-itself, outside the context of human participation in existence (and yet as something experiencable in existence) is really an attempt to discount the importance of the human orderer in fashioning such schemes of religious totalities. Before man is responsible to such systems of totality, he is responsible to himself in self-direction, as purposive being in existence. This perspective takes seriously the definition of religion as a search. God is not a necessity of a system of totality unless he is first and foremost a project of ontological self-direction, a project of his participation in existence. This would make human purpose co-extensive, co-conscious, or co-experiential, with the purpose(s) for life. If man has the capacity to order and reorder such patterns of totality when he entertains religious designs in existence, they should be looked on as provisional patterns of meaning, as being posterior to purposive being in existence. They are in fact stopping-places in the religious quest, places of stock-taking in human self-awareness, rather than a

---

5. William Horosz, *The Promise and Peril of Human Purpose*, St. Louis: Warren Green, Inc., 1970. This volume appears in a new series called 'Modern Concepts of Philosophy', edited by Marvin Farber of the State University of New York at Buffalo.

transcendent and totalitarian claim on human life. When holisms are viewed as an integral part of man's search for meaning they become less offensive and more hospitable meaning-structures for human purpose.

The alternative to this course of action is the attempt to make claims of ultimacy for one's system of totality, as over against another. There is no way out of the pluralism among systems of totality and its corollary of relativism. The only instrument available for legislating the claims among such absolute totalities is one man's claim to ultimacy over another's. The problem of how one goes from his own ultimate to real ultimacy is never adjuticated by this process. In fact, it is the breeding ground for intolerance. When one's believed-system of totality is supported by one's ultimate sanctions there is no alternative but that of making totalitarian claims on human life. When religious commitment to these systems of absolute totality is seen for what it is, as an operational goal abstracted from the human capacity for self-direction, God as source, limit, ground, mystery, transcendence, sacrality, and ultimacy, takes on new meaning and human purpose comes to have a new relevance to the religious quest.

The simplistic modern solution that man asks the questions and God or the system of religious totality gives the answers is really a way of subordinating man to the system of totality and of keeping him faithful and responsible to it in primary ties. It would make more sense if we were to view religion as the only discipline that begins with answers and ends up with questions, that it remains a search to the end, with provisional meanings on the way, rather than viewing it in terms of totalitarian claims and ultimate systems. If man is ontologically self-directing in existence, human purpose should have a new relevance to the religious quest, even on issues of ultimate concern and schemes of totality. This view enables us to see religious holisms within the context of human participation in existence and lessens the dangers of religious authoritarianism. Unless man's designs are relevant to the religious quest, and to religious systems of totality, he is not responsible to them.

We do not escape human designs on systems of totality by claiming encounter-experiences with them. For man designs also by participating in existence, even in encounters with wholeness. This is the forgotten aspect in given systems of religious totalities. If purpose has an ontological relevance to existence, to participation in it, he is, then, a model-maker by participation in existence, even of his positionality in the scheme of wholeness that is alleged to be his source. There is as much perspectivalism in lived experience as there is in our perspectives of meanings about immediate experience. Man is a model-maker in lived experience fashioning schemes of holism *by participation* in order to make sense out of life. This perspective will be made more explicit as we examine various meanings of the ground of being as a system of religious totality.

It is essential to grasp that unless we view such systems of totality in terms of various *models of existence*, the only other alternative we have is to identify our models of existence with existence *qua* existence. We shall see examples of this identification in Martin Heidegger and Paul Tillich on the level of lived experience where man encounters being-itself.

III. HEIDEGGER'S PRE-PURPOSIVE MODEL OF THE GROUND OF BEING

The basic meaning of Ground is that of goal or final goal. Although the Ground has other significant aspects, its meaning as goal-direction is the most significant as Ground relates to man. It is alleged that man in touching his own Ground touches the meaning of Ground of Being outside man. This can be envisioned only in terms of some fixed goal. In Heidegger, for example, man is goal-directed towards 'the Being of beings' in a pre-purposive manner through the *Dasein* in him. The author views Ground through the pre-purposive model of existence. The term pre-purposive should be understood in a technical sense, to the effect, that it is a goal-directed model of existence prior to human self-direction. In the case of Heidegger, Ground is the prior primordial totality of which man is a 'thrown project', and to which he returns in given possibilities. The goal of *Dasein* is the Nothingness in Being, which plays its exemplary part by defining the ultimate boundary of man's finitude. Ground and goal are thus interchangeable holistic concepts. In fact, it is man's otherness to which he belongs both as possibility and as a dependent being amidst numerous beings which the Ground also supports.

In the case of Paul Tillich, man is post-purposively goal-directed to the Ground of Being which takes man beyond the finite structures of existence and gives man contact with the eternal. Both meanings of Ground signify Otherness which is needed to establish man's place in the system of totality, either at the boundary of finitude in the hiddenness of Being or beyond it in the dimension of eternity. Both meanings thus have holistic implications which suggest either a final coherence in which God has overcome man's distortions and limitations within existence (by the power of Being over Nonbeing), or a final disillusionment in which the Nothingness is accepted as Otherness with total implications for human finitude. The fact that man touches his own Ground in Otherness, and not in himself (for man is not his own), may be the crucial test as to whether these encounter-experiences are model-free in their meaning or whether they are *models by participation*. Ground represents such a final encounter or destination which one meets in the depths of one's experience.

In *Being and Time*, Heidegger claims that Ground 'becomes accessible only as meaning, even if it is itself the abyss of meaninglessness', and this is represented by the term *Abgrund* which is at the core of the *Grundsein*.[6] How the Ground enters the understanding of *Dasein* as it touches its own being is thus a question of the meaning of the Ground. Heidegger claims that such meaning is model-free in its interior possibility. If man has any designs on such meanings they are peripheral. The meaning is essentially structured by Being's directives and intentions in Being-there. Man belongs to its meaning, or hears its call, but he does not make artifactual structurings of its basic meaning. The givenness of the meaning-encounter is given. *Dasein* experiences this as revelation, disclosure, or as a being-discovering. Such an experience of disclosure is pre-conceptual, pre-purposive, and pre-predicative. It depends on man's closeness to it in his affective life. The meaning of Ground is thus dictated by the aim-directed relationship between *Dasein* and Being rather than by man's designs upon it. *Dasein's* openness to Being's openness is merely metaphorical and pre-purposive discourse to acknowledge the fixed goal-direction and its control over the meaning of Ground. Consequently man must endure the meaning of the Ground in dread, in care (by standing it), and stand in awe of its concealed nature and truth. In short, man must relate to the meaning of Ground in active passivity: in care, or in conscience as the 'call of care', or in pre-purposive 'resoluteness', and in the later writings in 'will-less' thought, releasement, waiting and even in creative emptiness. That is to say, man may become involved in its meaning but he cannot have designs upon it. That, at any rate, is the essential point of the meaning of 'The Way Back Into the Ground of Metaphysics'.

Heidegger's main concern, then, appears to be what designs the meaning of the Ground have upon man, to which man is goal-directed. The model is pre-purposive because the question of origins, the question of meaning, and the problem of man's positionality in Being, does not originate in man's purposive nature where man is ontologically self-directing in quest of his origins. The meaning of Ground is solved prior to man's purposive intervention or construction of its meaning. Such ontological self-direction which is prior to holistic ventures is a prior consideration to any kind of fixed goal-direction, which appears to be the meaning of purpose on the phenomenal level of human experience. Human self-direction is thus prior to

6. Martin Heidegger, *Being and Time*, trans., J. Macquarrie & E. Robinson, New York: Harper and Row, 1962, p. 194.

ontologico-existential or ontologico-spiritual goal-direction. These may be projects of self-direction, but they cannot assume an ontological priority to man's purposive nature as self-directing in existence. Our complaint is that human purpose, understood as ontological self-direction, is excluded from encounter-meanings both on the level of ontological immediacy and on the level of spiritual immediacy; that man can only respond to these final meaning-discoveries in a secondary manner. We must accept the meaning of Ground as the 'upon-which' we build our projections on, for human self-projecting is projection 'upon something'. Once we exclude man's designs on the Ground of Being, we should expect to abide both by its meaning and by its boundaries or limitations, for it is not a part of beings or a finite part of systems. It is their support; it grounds all beings and finite parts. It is the source of such systems. Thus, even in its abysmal nature it is free of model-making, holy and mysterious.

The main point is that we must come to terms with the meaning of Ground as the truth of Being. In accepting Otherness, we do not overcome it. Its limitations upon human existence are exacting and final. Otherness is not within our power. We are conditioned by its power and meaning. Even when its meaning appears meaningless and inarticulate, its reign is unchallenged because it is the Ground the support of beings. The inarticulate character of Ground, as regards man's involvement in its meaning, is voiced in many volumes. A passage from *What Is Called Thinking?* is quite representative:

Our sole question is, what is it that calls on us to think. How else shall we ever hear That which calls, which speaks in thinking, and perhaps speaks in such a way that its own deepest core is left unspoken?[7]

The meaning of Ground, although it reveals itself in temporal existence, is, nonetheless, abysmal, inarticulate, non-conceptual, pre-purposive, and ineffable. The language of thinking is designed as pre-purposive discourse to safeguard the pre-purposive goal-direction of *Dasein* to its Ground. The language of closure and openness fortifies the pre-purposive disclosure of the meaning of Ground.

In spite of the inarticulate nature of the Ground's disclosures its directives are made known to man in encounter-experiences. Man's being is thus closer to the things themselves than it is to the appearances around it. It is closer to its own Ground in the meaning of Ground than it is to anything else in its environment. *Dasein* understands this closeness through antecedent comprehension of Being, through the 'peepholes' in its own being. Its

7. Trans., F. D. Wieck & J. G. Gray, New York: Harper & Row, 1968, p. 232.

experiences is that of pre-ontological understanding of its Ground which is prior to the artifactual structuring of its meaning.

A fine summary statement of its unavailability to man is given by Professor Macomber when he writes:

Dasein relates not only to beings (*Seiendes*) but to being itself (*Sein*). Beings are determinate, intelligible, and potentially available; being is not. In relation to human intellection – but not to human life in its totality – being is absolutely opaque and impenetrable. It is a 'beyond' which is always present, even in the mode of absence, and human intellection comes closest to it in recognizing its own limitations, in the Socratic knowledge that we do not know. Heidegger sees its clearest traces in history, where it manifests its progressive absence as man comes increasingly to ignore the necessary limitations of his konwledge. Most of all it is absolutely unavailable to human design, and this is what, in Heidegger's view, marks it off from the God of Christian theology, Whom he regards – rightly or wrongly – as a being.[8]

If the meaning of Ground is the 'beyond' which is always present in beings, and this is revealed 'to human life in its totality', this should be understood in its narrowest sense. Care represents this totality of life in man, but care simply guards *Dasein*'s relationship to Being and its Ground. Life's totality, then, is to be understood in the context of the pre-purposive model of existence which demands *Dasein* be goal-directed to the Ground of Being. The unavailability of the Ground is to be understood as a contextual unavailability, the terms of which are dictated by the model of existence in which the meaning of Ground is conceived. The beyond that is present is to be understood as transcendence which is an outward-going response. To the extent this represents the ontological Other the Ground symbolizes a system of totality also outside the context of human participation in existence.

Each model has things working for it. It utilizes the directives of immediacy and dialectical directionality to guard the meaning of the Ground. The requirements of each are determined by the model of one's choice. Yet the claim is made by each author that the meaning of Ground is model-free. We do not mind such differences in interpretation. What we do mind, however, is that these differences are derived allegedly from the meaning of the Ground given. While Tillich will have other justifications for leaving the meaning of the Ground untouched by human and artifactual structuring than Heidegger, the result is the same, namely, model-free meaning of the Ground. Even when such untouched meaning is implicit and vague, abysmal and inarticulate, this does not come from inadequate constructionism. It is the requirement of the Ground that it be so. Perhaps this is the path in one's search for ultimacy in the Ground: to justify one's choice of values in a wider system of values to

8. W. B. Macomber, *The Anatomy of Disillusion*, Evanston: Northwestern University Press, 1967, p. 76.

make that choice look better. But if everyone has such rights to ultimacy it means that no one has the ultimate, even when it is alleged that the Ground dictates its own meaning in terms of its own claims of ultimacy. This is the only alternative we have if we deny man's designs on the Ground of Being.

Heidegger would have it the other way, however, in the final chapters of his work on *Kant and the Problem of Metaphysics*:

> The comprehension of Being which dominates human existence, although man is not aware of its breadth, constancy, and indeterminateness, is thus manifest as the innermost Ground of human finitude. The comprehension of being does not have the harmless generality which it would have were it just another human property ... Its 'generality' is the basic originality of the innermost Ground of the finitude of *Dasein*. Only because the comprehension of Being is the most finite in the finite, can it make possible even the so-called 'creative' faculties of finite human beings. And only because it takes place in the very bosom of finitude is the comprehension of Being characterized by obscurity as well as by the breadth and constancy which have been noted.[9]

The finitude of *Dasein*, which is more primordial than man itself, needs the infinitized temporal power, Being, to make it a limited whole in the system of Being. This is no longer, Heidegger tells us, an anthropological question. What is needed is a general ontology with its perspective of the Ground of Being rather than the Kantian answer of the subjectivity of the subject. The remainder of the volume is concentrated on making clear how the meaning of Ground is model-free. The question we would raise: is this ontological faith or poor constructionism, or both, which requires that the Ground give us pre-purposive meaning in the form of revelations and disclosures? Heidegger is of the firm belief that human construction only 'lays bare the internal possibility of that which holds sway over *Dasein*'.[10] Such 'true remembrance' must always 'interiorize what is remembered', that is to say, let it 'come closer and closer in its most intrinsic possibility'.[11] This means that we can have close-ups of the given meanings of the Ground, but we cannot have designs upon it. It is not amenable to human meaning or available to man's conceptualization. The 'existential analytic' of the meaning of Ground is allegedly a way of avoiding constructionism. From our point of view, such experienced meanings may well be preconceptual, but they are not pre-purposive. Human purpose is more than a function of subjectivity, or a function of the mind; it is a real part of man's being. As such it reveals a capacity to be self-directing in existence, even in such meaning-encounters as we experience in the Ground. If the human orderer is taken as a serious factor

---

9. Martin Heidegger, *Kant and the Problem of Metaphysics*, trans., James S. Churchill, Bloomington: Indiana University Press, 1962, pp. 236-7.
10. *Ibid.*, p. 242.
11. *Ibid.*, p. 242.

in participation, then, his capacity for model-making in lived experience should be taken into consideration. The Ground of Being, taken as a system of totality, shares this perspectival nature of lived experience.

Otherness remains the 'intrinsic possibility' of Ground and it remains within the sphere of the temporal. For Heidegger, finitude contains both the possibilities and the dependence of *Dasein* on the Ground. In this capacity, man can be actively passive towards its meaning. The Other is thus the irrational contender in the arena of Being bringing man's rational and purposive endeavors to a halt. There is no attempt in Heidegger to forestall this collision course between man and his Ground, nor is man prepared in his affective life to bring this downward trek of life to a halt. Man must accept finitude and stand within its despair. He must accept it and live it for no reason at all, except perhaps to satisfy the meaning of the system of totality. There is no overcoming of finitude and of surpassing the sphere of the temporal, for the 'rational animals must become mortal'. P. C. Smith, in his comparison of Heidegger and Hegel through the medium of Kantian themes, sees this clearly, when he comments:

Being and nothingness belong together ... because Being is in itself finite and reveals itself only in the transcendence of *Dasein* which is extended into nothingness ... Heidegger ... seeks a relationship between I and the other which in no way implies a *Negation der Negation*, a negation of the *Nichts* or otherness which consciousness encounters, but which instead is based upon acknowledgement and acceptance of otherness and the finitude of consciousness entails ... The limit (Grenze) is to be affirmed, to be 'lived with', for it is the condition of the possibility of authentic existence.[12]

If the goal of man (with *Dasein* in him) is to reach the Nothingness in the system of Being, the meaning of Ground as Otherness provides the basic directives for human life. This means that man is primarily guided by the oppositional unity of Being and Nothing, a dialectical approach which serves the system of totality. From our point of view any dialectical steering of life is posterior to man's purposive nature as ontologically self-directing. Dialectics may be projects of human self-direction. However, when they are given ontological priority to the directives of man's purposive nature, this may simply be the demand of the model of existence which controls the meaning of the Ground. Such an approach has problems of its own in the context of ontological immediacy because any dialectical system is a mediational approach and the term 'immediate' – as its prefix implies – means some experience which is not mediated. If man's affective life is dialectially

---

12. P. C. Smith, 'Heidegger, Hegel, and the Problem of Das Nichts', *I P Q* (nternational Philosophical Quarterly), Sept., 1968, pp. 397, 403.

ordered and goal-directed to its Ground, it is hard to see how the meaning of Ground is model-free.

If we summarize our points on Heidegger's view of Ground, as goal, as temporal, and as Otherness, in the context of model-free meaning, it is clear that the author does not need the tension of the temporal and the eternal, as does Paul Tillich, to discuss the meaning of Ground. But Heidegger has tensions of his own, as in two of the attitudes of authentic and unauthentic modes of life within the structures of existence. However, this is not our concern. What is our concern is that Heidegger will accept the directives of other agencies for the meaning of the Ground, other than the self-directives of man's purposive nature, and at the same time claim that its meaning is model-free. In Heidegger's case, the interior possibility of the meaning of Ground is directed either by ontological immedicay, or by dialectics, or by both. This is inadequate constructionism, for it lacks human purpose and cognition in designing the meaning of Ground. If man does not take responsibility for the meaning of his Ground, or for the extension of it to the Ground of Being, some other power will. Politics is not the only place where such things happen. How can man be made more responsible for his elemental levels of response to existence, or to the Ground of Being? Heidegger is not troubled by this question. His growing concern is to place man in the care and clearing of Being, and not with man's responsible stand in life. The system of totality is placed at the beginning of life. Man through *Dasein* is responsible only for his return to the source of his origin. He does not fashion that source by his participation in existence. The given system of ontological totality is there to be encountered.

IV. TILLICH'S POST-PURPOSIVE MODEL OF THE GROUND OF BEING

Tillich's model of the Ground has Christian content and is controlled by the Biblical standard of systematic theology. The philosophical meaning of Ground is thus given a religious analysis which proceeds by identifying the post-purposive model of existence with the experience of Christian faith. The meaning of the Ground is a matter of faith or 'ultimate concern' which is given existential interpretation as an elementary mode of response on the part of man toward the 'ultimate'. How pervasive the notion of Being is in Tillich's perspective of the religious dimension of man is attested to by his own remark:

It appears in the present system in three places: in the doctrine of God, where God is called being as being; in the doctrine of man, where the distinction is carried through between man's essential and his existential being; and, finally, in the doctrine of the Christ, where he is called the manifestation of the New Being, the actualization of which is the work of the divine Spirit.[13]

With respect to God the doctrine of Being means the power of Being over Nonbeing in the sense of a *transcendentale* signifying Being beyond the universal and the particular as in Medieval theology. As such Being is the 'eternal *aporia* of thinking'. Ground is the source of this power to conquer Nonbeing in existence. Its meaning penetrates to the core of Being-itself which is identified with the Christian God. Thus God is more than any other particular existent, for He is not a part of the system, or one finite Being among others. To distinguish Him from other beings, Tillich makes Him the source of all beings as the Ground or source of all that exists. Thus God's uniqueness is to be found in his Reality or Being as the 'creative Ground of essence and existence', not found 'within the totality of beings'. God as Ground of Being is thus 'a question of necessity or impossibility, but not of contingent 'existence''. Or, as Tillich views the matter:

> The word 'being' points to the fact that this power is not a matter of someone's good will but that it is a gift which precedes or determines the character of every act of the will.[15]

One may also add that since human purpose has no ontological import, it also determines the character of purpose.

Once we postulate the meaning of Ground beyond universals and particulars, and give Him the reality of being-itself, it precludes man from having designs on the meaning of Ground. From that point on His meaning is the givenness of the given as gift. Man's positionality in the Ground is free of model-making and constructual gains. One can show ultimate concern in the Ground through immediate or direct participation, but this is faith or ultimate concern. To the extent that Tillich is an existentialist (he is also to some extent an essentialist) he believes these divine-human encounters are model-free. That is to say, they are pure encounter-experiences, such as *The Courage to Be*.

What is most instructive about the ontological courage of response to God is that it totally ignores man's designs on the Ground. It says nothing about the courage to be 'what?' or about the courage to be 'where?' Man's designs are precluded from such ultimate concerns and from having a say about his positionality in Being-itself. A few characterizations of the courage to be will

---

13. Paul Tillich, *Systematic Theology*, Vol. II, Chicago: The University of Chicago Press, 1957, p. 10.
14. John E. Smith, *Experience and God*, pp. 118–20.
15. Paul Tillich, *Systematic Theology*, Vol. II, p. 125.

make this clear. The courage to be is: 1) an existential courage of confrontation within the unlimitedness of Being, 2) an act of faith-awareness in which choices are made on the most elemental levels of response to the meaning of the Ground (prior to cognition and prior to human purpose ontologically conceived as self-directing), 3) the opposite of the 'courage to despair' exemplified by atheistic existentialism, 4) a participant's view, not an observer's perspective of the given meaning of the Ground, 5) a kind of affirmation in the midst of Nonbeing whose source of courage comes from beyond the self and world, 6) the path to the overcoming of life's ambiguities and distortions by returning to the meaning of the Ground, for without it the existential man can never find his essential nature. Courage as an ultimate mode of concern also instructs mankind:

> The courage to be in all its forms has, by itself, revelatory character. It shows the nature of being, it shows that the self-affirmation of being is an affirmation that overcomes negation ... We could not even think 'being' without a double negation: being must be thought as the negation of the negation of being. This is why we describe being best by the metaphor 'power of being'.[16]

Courage to be also relates to the notion of transcendence which is different for Tillich in its primary meaning from what it is for Heidegger. As an aspect of faith it is 'the state of being grasped by that toward which self-transcendence aspires, the ultimate in being and meaning'.[17] Such an ultimate concern is a different transcendent goal-direction than Heidegger's. It is also motivated by a different dialectics, as we shall see below. In affirming the power of Being over Nonbeing the ontological courage to be reveals another facet of meaning in the Ground than what Heidegger found. The emphasis in Tillich is on the *overcoming* of Otherness or Nonbeing within existence, not on our accepting it, as in Heidegger. The primary task in Tillich's system is to actualize this courage in existence through the power of the Ground in us as we realize its given, revealing meaning for us. The affirmation of courage overcomes the existential anxieties of fate and death, guilt and condemnation, and the meaninglessness and emptiness of existence. Heidegger's 'courage of despair' remains on the level of acceptance and disillusionment. Thus the authentication process takes place in a different orbit of meaning for these two thinkers. For faith, ultimate concern, ultimate commitment, and creativity have a different content and directionality in each writer; yet each writer is claiming certain ultimate disclosures of meaning from the given Ground of Being to the effect that each thinks it is model-free meaning.

16. Paul Tillich, *The Courage To Be*, New Haven: Yale University Press, 1952, pp. 178–9.
17. Paul Tillich, *Systematic Theology*, Vol. III, Chicago: The University of Chicago Press, Vx 1963, p. 130.

Existential anxiety is something we go through in order to overcome it with the given meaning of the Ground, in Tillich. One remains within the contours of finitude and disillusionment in the Heideggerian system where there is no overcoming or real affirmation of Being over Nonbeing.

How is the meaning of the Ground model-free in Tillich's system? 1) The fact that one approaches Being-itself through the courage to be, an existential faith that is conceived as an encounter-experience, means that its meaning is a matter of direct participation; 2) to the extent that the courage to be is a mystical experience of God as Being-itself or Ground of Being it is also a direct confrontation; 3) to the extent that its meaning is a person-to-person relationship conceived as the divine-human encounter it is direct participation in the Ground; 4) to the extent it is participation by 'Absolute Faith' (the taking of absolute doubt about God into oneself and transcending it by the courage to be) man directly participates in the meaning of Being-itself. Also the fact that ecstatic reason, with its capacity for an intuitive apprehension of the meaning of Ground, makes it possible for us to participate in the Ground directly. In all these respects the meaning of the Ground is given and self-revealing. Man can confront this given meaning and through such an encounter overcome the anxieties, ambiguities, and the distortions of existence, but he cannot have designs of his own meaning on this Ground of Being. God as the source of all existence is free of human construction. As Ground, Being-itself is nonsymbolic. Such items must be grasped as existential acceptances of revealed meaning. One is 'being grasped by the power of Being-itself' in these occasions of immediate participation. As Tillich himself views it:

He who is grasped by this power is able to affirm himself because he knows that he is affirmed by the power of being-itself once he has accepted acceptance or God's forgiveness. In this point mystical experience and personal encounter are identical. In both of them faith is the basis of the courage to be.[18]

The meaning of the Ground of Being is thus marked off by the 'transpersonal presence of the divine'. Through its meaning, man is a part of the whole understood as Being-itself. We shall have occasion later to see how ecstatic reason gives one an encounter experience free of model-making. Meanwhile it is essential to cast the problem of the post-purposive view of Ground in a larger perspective. After this we shall give a critique of 'direct' or 'immediate' participation, which does not violate the meaning of the given Ground because its function is to accept its revelation in existence.

What does direct participation in Being-itself reveal about the Ground if it

18. Paul Tillich, *The Courage To Be*, p. 173.

is conceived as being model-free? For Tillich, it reveals the Christian God in its first intention, or as the first statement about the eternal, which is needed to explain some of the more personal aspects of the Christian faith like grace and forgiveness. In short, direct participation reveals the impersonal presence of the divine in human life, as the foundation for the personal experience of God. Tillich believes that the projection of something is always 'projection upon something' (the 'upon-which' of Heidegger). Being-itself is not a construct; its meaning structure is a given to which man belongs and responds or fails to respond. The Ground is identified with God as Being-itself. It is given further theological treatment in relation to Christ and revelation, the trinity and worship, and other Christian verities. The meaning of Ground itself makes these demands upon man, not man's designs on the Ground of being. Yet the content of Ground is given a partially post-purposive reading. The post-purposive model of existence controls the meaning of the Ground towards which man is goal-directed. Being-itself is the goal of man as being, because he belongs to it, to begin with and because the Ground of Being requires it.

Paul Tillich accepted the pre-purposive model of Heidegger into his system as early as the Marburg days when Heidegger was his colleague at the university. His need for System-building and the Hegelian quality of absorbing various tendencies into the System prompted him to accept this starting point for a theology uncritically, without realizing that there was a conflict of models of existence in the understanding of Ground or Being-itself. Since the author is unconscious of the battle of the models for the understanding of a system of totality, he proceeds to account for its revealed meaning post-purposively. The 'depth of reason' raises the 'question of revelation' but Being-itself as Ground gives the answer or discloses its interior meaning. This is a claim to be a meaning-encounter as in Heidegger. But it is obvious that the inner answers are different, that somehow they reveal the imprint of man's designs on the Ground. The goal is different, too. The fact that reason itself is 'driven beyond itself' to its 'ground and abyss' is something not of our own contriving, it is alleged. For it is an elemental response to the Ground. This is the negative side of the mystery of the Ground of Being, which is included in the positive meaning of mystery as when Being-itself makes itself manifest in revelation. This is primal thinking as primal encounter which points to Being-itself. It is instructive to note, however, that similar depth experiences do not point Heidegger in the same direction; they merely enhance his interest in temporality which concerns Being in Time, not in Eternity.[19] This is a crucial point.

19. Paul Tillich, *Systematic Theology*, Vol. I, section on 'Reason and Revelation', Chicago: The University of Chicago Press, 1951, pp. 81, 110.

Being-itself is somewhat vague and opaque, as in Heidegger, and it can be known only by encounter and by the symbolic approach which 'participates' in it. It has a similar quality of revealedness and hiddenness as the pre-purposive model, which Heidegger initially borrowed from the Christian tradition and made pre-purposive in design. The main difference with Heidegger's model of Ground would appear to be the notion of finitude and its possibilities within and beyond existence. Human finitude, it would appear, has the same 'ontological shock' – the threat of Nonbeing in the midst of Being – as in Heidegger's system but the solution or answer to the shock is different as Tillich conceives it. The author advocates going through Nonbeing with the courage to be by overcoming it with the aid of the eternal. He does not ask the same questions, nor does he give the same answers as Heidegger. For example, he does not ask 'Why is there something? Why not nothing?' Such a question, Tillich believes, points to something that 'precedes being'. Divine presence in Being-itself accepts the ontological shock of existence that existentialists talk about, and overcomes or transforms it by pointing to the eternal that resolves the ambiguities and frustrations of existence. In this respect Being-itself is the 'ground of Revelation'. The directives come from above, not from below, as in the pre-purposive model; they come from the 'divine ground of revelation'.

Although Tillich is influenced greatly by Schelling's philosophy of being (that Being precedes knowledge), as by Kierkegaard, our concern in this article is a comparison with Heidegger's model of Ground. While Being-itself is intuited, as we said earlier by the 'depth of reason', this is to be taken as an elemental encounter to Being as Ground, because such an 'ecstatic reason' combines both reason and spirit, and is already a religious reading of man's rational capacity. This view allows for 'ultimate concern' toward Being which is a mode of elemental response. It is akin to Schleiermacher's 'feeling' as awareness of the Unconditional Ground of Reality (Being-itself). Tillich himself has equated this ultimate concern for Being-itself, as it is encountered by man's ultimate concern in ecstatic reason, is apprehended 'immediately and ecstatically'. God as Being-itself is thus an 'accepted intuition of theology'. The revelations which derive from this intuitive encounter with Being-itself provide the ground and unity for cognitive reason which is frustrated and divided in its existentialist and essentialist claims to knowledge.

While the procedure of encounter is different from Heidegger's advocacy of encounter with meaning, which is less spiritual and valuational than Tillich's, the result appears to be the same, namely, that the meaning of the Ground of Being is model-free and does not depend on man's designs. Yet Heidegger sees the essence of Ground as encompassed by finitude and Tillich projects it on the screen of infinite and absolute Being. The ultimacy of the given thus appears to be the 'ultimacy' only within the context of each model of existence. The pre-purposive model of existence dictates its own terms of meaning for the Ground, and the post-purposive design of Ground does the same.

What is the givenness of the Ground given in Tillich's post-purposive model? What does ultimate concern, and ecstatic reason, as encounter experiences, yield about the Ground's given meaning? 1) That man is goal-directed towards the eternal as Ground or Being-itself, 2) that man's Ground is within eternity, not within temporality, 3) that man overcomes the distortions of existence and his finitude by the redemptive course which Being-itself provides as the 'ground of Revelation'. This means that existentialism must be given a post-purposive reading for it to reveal the great concerns of the Christian life, faith, and revelation (that Tillich has designed for the Ground of Being). This new perspective (a post-purposive reading of reason as 'ecstatic reason') is provided by Tillich. Rathbun and Burwick see this religious reading of existentialism clearly when they comment:

> This is provided by the 'ecstatic reason', which intuits the Ground of Being and exalts man and nature in terms of vitalism and dynamisms. The philospoer-theologian is then able to penetrate the gauze curtain of existential being to get at the objective structures of being behind that curtain. He then 'correlates' these obejctive structures with his experience of revelation.[22]

What are some of the other characteristics of the post-purposive model of the Ground of Being? If we continue the list above, Tillich's view of Ground as Being-itself is: 4) dynamic, which means that man can renew his openness to God in such meaning-encounters and accept the process of redemption or transformation which it promises to the recipient, 5) eschatological, which in the final analysis breaks with the ontological structures of existence and promises life eternal, and, 6) that Being-itself is 'unhistoric'.

It is our contention that such great divergent meanings cannot issue from the being-discoverings or revelations of the Ground itself, that the correlation which Tillich attempts between the pre-purposive model of Ground and its post-purposive reading is utter confusion. If these prior unities of meaning are attributed to the Ground, why does the meaning so disclosed come out in such divergent models of life (as the pre- and post-purposive versions of human finitude)? The other alternative, which we are suggesting is that man has

20. *Ibid.*, p. 389.
21. J. W. Rathbun & F. Burwick, 'Paul Tillich and the Philosophy of Schelling', *I.P.Q.*, Sept. 1964, pp. 374–9.
22. *Ibid.*, p. 389.

designs on the Ground of Being and these cannot be ignored if we are to avert confusion. This also means that man is self-directing (the ontological relevance of purpose to existence) in his encounters with the Ground; that he sees the meaning or meanings of the Ground of Being through his preferred models of existence in which his purposive nature, as ontologically self-directing in existence, plays a prior role. The meaning of Ground in each model of existence, whether Heidegger's or Tillich's, results from *our models of participation* in the Ground. Participatory situations are not free of model-making. For man's purposive nature, as self-directing, is the gathering focus of all elemental modes of response to Being. Elemental modes of response to the Ground thus reveal man's designs on the Ground of Being. Neither the finite Being of Heidegger, nor the infinite Being of Tillich is responsible for our elemental responses to the Ground. This means that 'direct' participation is a myth. When immediate participation is equated with the given field of meaning we believe this can be maintained only on the grounds of identifying our model of participation with the given meaning-structure, which we disavow. The identification of our model of existence, or of our model of participation with the meaning of the Ground or with existence *qua* existence may simply be the demand of the goal-directed models of existence (the pre- and post-purposive models). This identification is not a requirement of the purposive model.

This does not mean that the Ground of Being is the function of human desire or purpose, just as it does not mean that it is the function of the very structures of the givenness of the Ground given. It means that the meaning of the Ground of Being is co-experiential or compresent with man's purposive nature. Antecedent structural meanings of Grounds, to which both Heidegger and Tillich make claims, wrongly identify their models of existence with existence *qua* existence, or their model of Ground with the meaning of Ground, that there are no prior given meanings or structures in the Ground, because man is self-directing in such encounters within existence through elemental responses to life. Heidegger's pre-purposive model of existence requires one kind of meaning of Ground; Tillich's post-purposive view requires another. The ontological self-direction is very much in evidence in each author's designs on the Ground of Being.

But we must return to Tillich's post-purposive model of Ground and point out some of its features in contrast with Heidegger's meaning of Being. The last mentioned feature of Ground was that Being-itself is 'unhistoric'. This is not only a sharp contrast with Heidegger's concept of Ground but also a point of divergence with some Christian thinkers. Carl Michalson, for example, prefers a 'self-revealing God' in the domain of history over Tillich's God as

Being-itself. He cautions Christian scholars to reject both Heidegger's Ground of Being as the 'silent mystery on the horizon' and Tillich's Being-itself because they do an injustice to the nature of human history and God's self-disclosures therein.[23] The objection appears to be that revelation is a manifestation of the 'ground of being' manifest in existence. For Tillich does maintain that revelation is not 'information about divine things' but is the 'ecstatic manifestation of the Ground of Being in events, persons, and things', and that such manifestations have 'shaking, transforming, and healng' powers in existence.[24]

Tillich is aware of the difficulties in relating Being-itself to God, Revelation, Christ, and man, but he is not aware of the basic conflict of models of existence in interpreting the Ground. In communicating with other Christians he blames the uneasiness of this identification on the supremacy of the male-determined symbolism in Christianity, which he would correct in his own symbolic approach.

> In so far as it (Ground of Being) is symbolical, it points to the mother-quality of giving birth, carrying, and embracing, and, at the same time, of calling back, resisting independence of the created, and swallowing it. The uneasy feeling of many Protestants about the first (not the last!) statement about God, that he is being-itself or the ground of being, is partly rooted in the fact that their religious consciousness, even more, their moral conscience are shaped by the demanding father-image of the God who is conceived as a person among others. The attempt to show that nothing can be said about God theologically before the statement is made that he is the power of being in all being is, at the same time, a way of reducing the predominance of the male element in the symbolization of the divine.[25]

I wish the problem were that simple. In Tillich's system itself there are two models of the Ground. These systems of totality are not readily reconcilable. Both totalities are defined, in part at least, outside the context of human participation. The notion of the 'given' is similarly defined outside the context of human participation. If there are two notions of totality, whose given is such given meaning of the Ground? The problem of pluralism persists if we take Heidegger's totality and Tillich's as two systems of totality. How do we legislate such total schemes of existence (and Tillich's even goes beyond the totality of existence)?

When Ground is equated with a system of totality, and it must be at least that, we can direct the following criticisms against it.

1. The problem in Ground as a system of totality involves the issue of

---

23. J. M. Robinson & J. B. Cobb, Jr., *The Later Heidegger and Theology*, New York: Harper & Row, 1963, pp. 147, 155.
24. Paul Tillich, *Systematic Theology*, Vol. I, p. 156, Vol. II, pp. 166–7.
25. Paul Tillich, *Systematic Theology*, Vol. III, p. 294.

existentialism and essentialism. The problem is how to give the abstraction a lived quality. Tillich decides to shore up the system of totality with existential constructions, by emphasizing existential themes like ultimate concern, etc. He is thus using man's existence to an abstraction like Being-itself a form of life. As an impersonal system of totality, beyond the particular-universal distinction, it is a totality beyond totalities. Yet it is the same Being-itself that offers 'living presence' in existence to fragmentend man, when he is 'being grasped' by it. How Being-itself is more than a system of totality Tillich can only show by identifying his model of God with God-himself, and this off limits even for the Christian layman, let alone a theologian. Is this just another way of making claims to ultimacy within a certain system of totality? But if this is allowed for one system of totality, why not for another?

2. If we had the space to show how existential constructs are also designs by human participation existence, that they are not free of constructionism and model-making, Tillich would have a harder time breathing life into his system of totality. Encounter-experiences with the Ground of Being, like ultimate concern, can only be read as private responses to the eternal, and not as universal demands on man.

3. The dilemma which faces man in his religious quest is not the one which forces him to choose between competing systems of totality that offer him directionality prior to purposive being in existence, but one where he faces up to his responsibility for such systems of totality (for systems of responsibility). If religion is a search for the meaning of life, Being-itself as a finalized answer will not help the question along. Religion is the only discipline that starts with answers and ends with questions. The given Ground of Being, we have seen, was such an alleged final answer. Man not only molds his questions in life; he also molds the answers by participating in existence. We need not deny such totalistic notions. We need only to relate them more meaningfully to purposive being in existence to make some sense out of them. We cannot translate the meaning of life into the question: 'What are people for?' When the Ground is defined, in part, outside the context of human participation existence, there is such a translation of the purpose of life. To the extent that Tillich has given an existential quality to his system of totality (Being-itself), to that extent he has identified his model of God with God-himself.

V. TOWARDS A PURPOSIVE MODEL OF THE GROUND OF BEING

To the extent that a system of totality defines the nature and meaning of human participation, directionality, responsibility, it is designed as a destinarian notion. Such systems of totality are projects of purposive being in existence; they are filtered through our models of existence and schemes of participation. When man is 'being grasped' in 'direct participation' in the Ground, either from below or from above, this is already a model of immediate experience, and of encounter-experiences with the given Ground. Tillich portrays such a destiny for man in the system of Being when he defines man's freedom as consisting 'only in polar independence with destiny'. Ground symbolizes the larger structures to which the individual structure belongs. Totality has its way with man's freedom, directionality, and responsibility; it defines the patterns of given participations in the Ground.

It is unfortunate that human participation, defined as an immediate kind of encounter-experience, is first related to the system of totality, before it is seen in relation to man's being-agency. Apparently, there is no need to relate it to human directionality first because the system of totality has imprinted its fixed patern of goal-direction upon immediate experience. The paradox of participation can be summarized thusly: with all the emphasis on direct participation in the Ground, man has only a pie-slice of such immediate encounter-experiences, and only those designed for him by the system of totality or the Ground of Being. All aspects of man, but the human orderer himself, apparently participate in the Ground; he is there receiving the directionality and the assignments of responsibility from the Being-itself. He takes orders from the Ground for which he had no responsibility for shaping and forming in a creative way. The 'interdependence' between human freedom and destiny is thus a one-way street. The directives of Being-itself have the upper hand in molding human responsibility to the system of responsibility. Because man is not his own, he owes primary responsibility to the system of totality which functions as his Ground. The purpose of life is read off as: 'What are people for?'

What needs to be examined, then, in man's relation to the Ground, is the notion of 'direct participation' in the Ground. If direct experience is defined by the system of totality, it is not model-free, as both Heidegger and Tillich presuppose it is. Immediate experience denies only human mediation of it; it does not preclude its being mediated by the system of totality and its methodological servant, the system of dialectics. The issue is plain enough: the question is not whether immediate experience is mediated or not, but by whom or by what. In the case of pre- and post-purposive models of immediate participation in the Ground it is the system of totality that gives mediation to human participation, directionality, and responsibility (which is beyond man's hopes to mediate). This is a crucial problem in modern philosophy of religion, and the greatest myth of twentieth century thought, to believe that such lived and immediate experience can be justified without relating it to human directionality. What has happened in this neglected field of experience is that substitute directive agencies were called in to justify immediate experience, and to give it movement, mediation (like self-transcendence and dialectical patterns).

Once the notion of immediacy is related to human directionality, and participation is related to purposive being in existence, any notion of the 'given' can only be read in terms of participation in existence. The attempt to define the given Ground outside the context of human participation must, consequently be read as a form of abstractionism. Man is a model-maker in lived experience; he is not a catalyst, but a claimant in experience. It is in this context of participation that he designs and fashions the systems of totality that apply to man's search for meaning in life. When systems of totality are not read as the provisional aids in that search, and as an integral part of the quest, they are useless appendages of archaic religious systems.

Unless the human orderer is given the capacity to be a model-maker in lived experience, of correlating his models of participation with the process of lived experience, in the context of participation, then, the only other alternative we face is to identify our models of existence with existence *qua* existence. What we have in Heidegger and Tillich is such an identification of the model of the Ground with the Ground of Being-itself. The given Ground becomes a finalized answer, rather than a provisional scheme aiding man in his search for the meaning of life. If there is a distinction between the model of the Ground and the Ground of Being-itself, such a system of totality can still be a part of the religious search for meaning. What has prevented religionists from seeing this issue as a problematic was the external meaning of purpose as finalized goal-direction. Man participates in the Ground, but the Ground as a system of totality is beyond his participation. Religious holism exploits this external meaning of goal-direction in terms of the final purpose of the whole. What is needed in its place is a deeper conception of human purpose so that man can adequately participate in existence, rather than in some system of totality.

Some directive agency is in charge of direct participation. The real question is: who or what provides this gathering focus for human modes of participation in existence? In Heiddeger, 'the Being of beings' provides such guidance. For Tillich, the eternal as Ground of Being becomes the gathering focus. In both cases unmediated experience is exploited by the mediative roles of systems of totality. Immediate experience is pre-packaged by the given Ground.

Thus it makes a great deal of difference whether we view direct experience, such as the experience of the given meaning of the Ground, pre-purposively, post-purposively, or purposively. For Heidegger and Tillich the meaning of Ground needs no human justification. The proper stance of man is to receive the revelations of the Ground. We are claiming that this is only the requirement of the pre- and post-purposive models of existence, and not the demand of the Ground itself, or the demand of human nature. The purposive model disclaims such pure given meanings which are established prior to the intentions of man's purposive nature. Each model of existence has its own interpretation of the given meaning of the Ground.

What is apparent is that the meaning of the Ground is not an empirical given. For neither Being nor God are objects of human perception. They are thus philosophical givens. The notion of the 'given' is a problematic for philosophy and has been for some time, whether it was termed datum, qualia, revelation, interior possibility, or what not. Philosophical givens cannot be disassociated from man's purposive nature as self-directing. For man's quest for a foundation of his experience is the quest of a purposive being. Philosophy cannot get behind this prior claim and establish given unities of meaning in the Ground by disavowing human directionality in this quest. The very disavowel of man's designs on the meaning of the ground is an affirmation of man's directive claims therein. Heidegger gives it whatever content he wishes; and so does Tillich. The given is controlled by the models of existence.

Laurence Foss, in his penetrating study of the 'Myth of the Given', states the problem rather well:

What is taken to be given is in truth only partly given and partly conventional ... Heretofore, 'grass' was a color-property-word and 'building' a figure-property-word. Now they are color-activity and figure-activity words, respectively. It is against the backdrop of these revolutionary settings that we can demythologize the 'given' and realize that it has only pragmatic significance.[26]

If the given is merely a myth with pragmatic significance, and 'there is more to seeing than meets the eyeball' in the epistemological consideration of phenomology and linguistic philosophy, the orbit of meaning for Foss' demythologization of the 'given', how much more mythological is the concept of the meaning of ground which is not an object of seeing? It would appear there is more model-making present in the meaning of the Ground than in the meaning of objects of perception. From our point of view we not only see what our conceptual framework enables us to see, but our conceptual framework only sees what our models of existence allow it to see in the

26. Laurence Foss, 'The Myth of the Given', *The Review of Metaphysics*, Sept. 1968, pp. 56–7.

meaning of the Ground. Human reason is rooted in man's purposive nature. The mind's goals are the operational aspects of human self-direction. The meaning of such mental goals are inexplicable on their own terms. They need to be rooted in man's capacity for self-direction. For such conceptual frameworks are motivated by the deeper concerns of man's purposive nature. Thus even the pragmatic criterion of the given, with partly given and partly conventional meanings of the given, is controlled by Foss' model of existence.

The fact is that the distinction between invention and discovery (the given) is posterior to man's purposive nature as self-directing. It is meaningless, from our standpoint, to resolve the notion of given meanings or meaning-giving without a consideration of human purposiveness in such a problematic. In the purposive model of the meaning of the Ground the given meaning is the requirement of our model of existence which is an approximation of Reality. The more mythological the given is (and the given meaning of the Ground must be viewed as the most extreme case of the mythological for reasons stated above) the more our models of existence control its meaning and shape the activity of 'direct participation' in it. Tillich's view of Being-itself as the nonsymbolic is an attempt to evade the charge that the meaning of the Ground is mythological and a construct of our models of existence by participation. The meaning of the Given thus rests on many analogies of meaning. Man shows his ontological self-direction in inventing such analogies of meaning about the Ground.

If we utilize the perspective of a twentieth century humanistic psychiatrist, James Bugental, who relies both on Heidegger and Tillich for some of his insights, the mythological nature of the meaning of the given becomes even more pronounced. What man encounters in the given meaning of the Ground is the mystical 'All-ness of existence', on the level of primitive encounter and 'intercourse of awareness with existence'. Such awareness, which is most basic, which is prior to human purpose and cognition, as the product of this encounter, is model-free. The mystic notion of the All provides the map for the given meaning of the Ground. As if to cover up the problematic the author upholds the view that pre-purposive awareness is the 'medium' through which the given meaning of the Ground is best disclosed to us. Such awareness is part of our instant being, and is prior to human purpose as self-directing. In man's needs, anxieties, fears, and hopes, we 'invent-discover' such encountered given meanings, as the meaning of the Ground. The distinction between invention and discovery is thus prior to human cognition and human purpose. It is something our affective life makes in its encounter with existence *qua* existence. Man encounters the meaning of Ground through modes of existence and is thus open to the meaning of Ground in profound receptivity as he touches the Ground. Just as in Tillich the Church is receptive to the New Being of the Christ as the manifestation of Being-itself in existence or history. As Bugental proceeds to explicate his view of man's confrontation with existence and draws closer to his discipline of psychiatry he needs Tillich's view of *overcoming* to make therapy operative in human life. In fact, finally he surpasses Tillich's system in mystic sensitivity in postulating the mystic All as the Ground of Being. The path to mythology is now complete. In this context the author feels free to confuse the pre- and post-purposive designs for living as he opportunistically utilizes both designs to put across the new claims of psychiatry. The myth of the given meaning of the Ground leads one 'beyond the human frontier'.[27]

The upshot of the discussion thus far appears to be that 'direct participation in the given meaning of the Ground is not as 'direct' as it is claimed to be by each respective author. There is prior manipulation, or prior purposiveness, manifest in these encounters, which is not accounted for by the encounter-experiences themselves. Through direct participation Heidegger discovers the supremacy of the Nothingness in Being; Tillich discovers the Christian personal God based on 'the impersonal presence of the divine' as Being-itself; Bugental discovers the mystical All behind the human frontier. It is quite obvious that the givenness of the meaning-given Ground is a myth. There is no such thing as the uninterpreted model-free meaning of the ground. For it is either the product of the constructive effort of the mind or the constructive effort of models of participation or a mixture of both. The alternative approaches merely administer the claims of ultimacy to an otherwise insoluble problem. Both the pre- and post-purposive models of existence do not require the need to justify the pure given meaning of the ground. The authors who claim these positions write volumes to justify the fact they need no justification of the Ground. This in itself is a mystery. Or, is it perhaps the demand of the model of existence which they apply to the meaning of the Ground?

If the latter is the case of what is, the referential claims by direct participation (which point to the given meanings in the Ground of Being) are mediated references. Such directives are either usurped by immediate experience (in which case they are hidden within the directives of immediacy itself), or they are dialectically ordered (in which case such orderings are prior to human purpose), or they are ordered by the human orderer seeking fulfillment of human nature in existence (in which case the meaning of the

27. J. F. T. Bugental, *The Search for Authenticity*, New York, Holt, Rinehart, and Winston, 1965, pp. 282-3, 395-415. The New Virtues for the emergent man, based on the mystical meaning of the Ground, are: fantasy, suchness, freedom of awareness, creative emptiness.

Ground is intertwined with man's purposive nature as self-directing). The purposive model of the Ground of Being claims the third approach as being the more enlightened one. The search for the meaning of the Ground is in part man's designs on the Ground of Being and its meaning.

In Tillich's view man finds the experience of Ground by direct participation in the depths of experience, prior to cognition and purpose, as in the passage below:

> All these forms of insecurity and uncertainty belong to man's essential finitude, to the goodness of the creative in so far as it is created. In the state of mere potentiality, insecurity and uncertainty are present, but they are accepted in the power of the dimension of the eternal. In this dimension there is an ultimate security or certainty which does not cancel out the preliminary insecurities and uncertainties of finitude (including the anxiety of their awareness). Rather it takes them into itself with the courage to accept one's finitude ... If in the state of estrangement the dimension of the ultimate is shut off, the situation changes. Insecurity becomes absolute and drives toward a despair about the possibility of being at all.[28]

When the given meaning of Ground is discovered in the depths of experience Tillich finds the dimension of the eternal; Heidegger finds the Nothingness (which is not negated) in the system of Being; and Bugental finds the mystical All that is beyond the human frontier. Each author allegedly finds the meaning of the given Ground through direct participation in the depths of experience where man's being touches the Ground as its source. For Tillich, it means affirming meaning within the domain of meaninglessness; for Heidegger, it means asserting meaninglessness in the *Abgrund*; for Bugental, it means getting lost in the infinite see of All where individual identity is lost in the I-process and the latter is lost in the All. Quite obviously, the meaning of the Ground cannot be all these things. They are not the requirements of the given Reality, but the demands of man's designs upon Reality; and these demands are mediated by man's purposive nature as self-directing in the depths of existence.

Tillich's post-purposive reading of the meaning of Ground is only too clear when he advocates the 'third way' between naturalism and supernaturalism and conceives of God as the final dimension of existence:

> In this respect God is neither alongside things nor even 'above' them; he is nearer to them than they are to themselves. He is their creative ground, here and now, always and everywhere ... God as the ground of being infinitely transcends that of which he is the ground. He stands *against* the world, in so far as the world stands against him, and he stands *for* the world, thereby causing him to stand for him. This mutual freedom from each other and for each other is the only meaningful sense in which the 'supra' in 'supernaturalism' can be used.[29]

28. Paul Tillich, *Systematic Theology*, Vol. II, p. 73.
29. *Ibid.*, p. 7.

Of course, Tillich prefers the term supra-natural for signifying God. But even as the final dimension of existence, as its creative Ground, the meaning of the Ground is unclear if its meaning is conceived prior to ontological self-direction. Direct participation is thus post-purposively oriented towards God. In this perspective man is already a religious participant in the Ground to get such meanings out of the depth experiences of life. This means that we cannot read off the meaning of the Ground from direct participation in it, for direct participation in the meaning of Ground is already a model of participation in the Ground. Man's designs on the Ground are, therefore, vital and deeply rooted, when that relationship is conceived in terms of ontological purposiveness. Ontological purpose is very much in evidence whenever Ground is conceived of as goal or Otherness. Direct participation is unable in itself to give us these two meanings of the Ground. In the light of our thesis man's purposive nature is responsible for our models of existence and these control the meaning of the Ground.

If we cast the problem in a broader perspective, it can be said that we do not resolve the conflict between faith and reason in contemporary theology without relating these two modes of understanding to man's purposive nature as ontologically conceived. Faith, as a direct mode of participation or elemental mode of response to the Ground, has its gathering focus in man's purposive nature. Otherwise God is responsible for it, and offers it as a gift to man. This is an irresponsible view of faith perpetuated through the ages by orthodoxy. The purposive model of existence requires that we make man responsible not only for his thoughts, and acts, but also, for all his elementary modes of response to existence. Reason is also rooted in man's purposive nature and its mental goals cannot be explained apart from conceiving man as a purposive being in existence.

We may thus conceive of man's purposive nature as self-directing as having two basic contacts with existence: 1) because it is the gathering focus for elemental responses to existence we can attribute to the function of immediatizing or existentializing; 2) because it is the potentiality for mental goals we can attribute to it the capacity for essentializing or mediatizing; and 3) through these two operations and its basic potentiality for self-direction it is capable of producing models of existence through which we mediate Reality and our own self-relatedness in experience. Fundamental to this view is the definition of man as a subject-object dialogue mediated by man's purposive nature. Purpose is a part of man's being, not merely a function of his mind or subjectivity. This perspective casts light on the problem of faith and reason in contemporary theology, as well as on the meaning of the Ground and its basic meaning of Otherness.

If we indulge ourselves in more comparisons, the most instructive of these is between Reinhold Niebuhr and Tillich in the way they conceive God in terms of direct participation. Direct participation, for Niebuhr, means Hebraic dramatic and historical encounter with God, not the ontological participation of Tillich. God as Ground is beyond any conceivable rational structure, just as he is beyond ontological and existential structures.

> I do not believe that ontological categories can do justice to the freedom either of the divine or of the human person, or to the unity of the person in his involvement in and transcendence over the temporal flux or that the sin of man and the forgiveness by God of man's sin or the dramatic variety of man's history can be comprehended in ontological categories. If it is 'supernaturalistic' to affirm that faith discerns the key to specific meaning above the categories of philosophy, ontological or epistemological, then I must plead guilty of being a supernaturalist.[30]

Thus Niebuhr gives us another post-purposive reading of the meaning of the divine Ground, one that rejects ontological immediacy for spiritual and dramatic immediacy and direct participation. This is a battle of two post-purposive models for an understanding of the meaning of Ground. Niebuhr simply believes that God's creative power as Ground is beyond the limits of a rational ontology. Tillich's 'third way' is supplanted by the 'old way' of Biblican meaning of the Ground. Yet each author claims direct participation in the meaning of Ground, as each is 'grasped by' its meaning that is model-free.

If we pursue these comparisons and include the naturalistic perspective of Henry Nelson Wieman on the meaning of Ground, the battle of the models in the understanding of the meaning of the Ground will be very much in evidence. Wieman is religiously impressed with God as process, as creativity, as the Creative Good or Creative Event, as the meaning of the Ground. It is in fact, as one of the titles of his works suggests, *The Source of Human Good*. The model of God is pre-purposive rather than post-purposive, because it is the creative transformation of man from below by the Creative Good. The Creative Event is supra-human and transcendent in the naturalistic sense of coming from below man through the events in existence and history.

> The creative event, not man himself, creates this greater imagination and this more profound and discriminating appreciation ... What we have said demonstrates that man cannot be creative in the sense in which this term applies to the creative event we have been describing. Man's creative ability is something produced in him as a consequence of the prior working of the creative event ... The creative event is supra-human, not in the sense that it works outside of human life, but in the sense that it creates the good of the world in a way that man cannot do. Man cannot even

---

30. C. W. Kegley & R. W. Bretall (eds.), *Reinhold Niebuhr*, New York: Macmillan Co., 1956, p. 433.

approximate the work of the creative good. He would not come any closer to it if his powers were magnified to infinity, because the infinite increase of his ability would have to be the consequence of the prior working of the creative event.[31]

That is to say that the Creative Good is functionally, not metaphysically, transcendent. It is transcendent within existence itself, but not beyond it.

To this view Niebuhr replies that such a process of Creativity is ambiguous, that the human and divine persons are both beyond the process, although they are also immersed in it. God may well be in the structures of nature or in the processes of existence but He also transcends them. Both man and God are free beyond existential or natural structures in existence. Spirit in both requires this quality-transcendence. There is a mystery of creation beyond the temporal process that reaches into eternity. Thus God, for Niebuhr, is beyond the categories of science and naturalism which Professor Wieman advocates.[32]

It is the pre-purposive model of existence which Wieman requires to define God within the final dimensions of nature and process. It is the post-purposive Biblical model that Niebuhr requires to define God beyond the structures of nature, process, ontology, and beyond every conceivable order, to account for man's and God's freedom beyond rational or natural or existential structures. The meaning of the Ground is primarily the battle of the models for the understanding of its meaning. The other alternative is claims of ultimacy based on partial perspectives and uninformed faith and zeal. The mythological given meaning of the Ground is mediated by man's purposive nature as self-directing. These models of existence control the very meaning and direction of the Ground as source of human good.

These comparative estimates of the meaning of Ground lead us to pose an alternative and to make a choice among them. The alternative is that the meaning of the Ground is either free of human designs upon it or it is not. The first alternative which rejects man's designs upon the Ground claims that such meaning is model-free and dictates its interior meaning as revelation. It assumes, therefore, that the meaning is the requirement of the Ground as man encounters it. Suppose that each author makes a similar claim, as we found it to be the case, and that this meaning is established prior to human cognition and human purpose ontologically conceived; then, it follows that this plurality and variety of meanings in the Ground is the very demand of the Ground of Being upon man. We find this difficult to believe.

The second alternative course is wiser to believe, because it gives a

---

31. Henry N. Wieman, *The Source of Human Good*, Chicago: The University of Chicago Press, 1946, p. 76.
32. C. W. Kegley & R. W. Bretall, *Reinhold Niebuhr*, pp. 446-51.

justifiable human explanation for such variety and plurality on the phenomenal level of experience (where plurality of goals and meanings is an accepted fact), and yet it leaves intact the vacuous potentiality for self-direction on the ontological level, for it is a prior groping for goal-direction, not yet having made the choice of goals. On the level of ontological self-direction man is free of the problem of the plurality of goals. This problem arises with the choice of holistic goal-direction. The respective claims to ultimacy are thereby diminished by this new perspective, and yet such projected meanings of the Ground are relevant as projects of human self-direction.

What is the consequence of this perspective for the notion of direct participation? Man is in control of the actions of immediate participation. If this is the case, immediate participatory experience will not be used indiscriminately by various writers for apologetic purposes. This chapter is an example of how direct participation has been used for ontological and religious exploitation. When man is not in charge of his direct experience in his purposive nature direct experience is open to such exploitation as we have described in this chapter. If it is understood that it comes in at least three models of existence, the claims to ultimacy will be effectively reduced and communication in religion will be increased.

The purposive model, moreover, offers a new interpretation of Otherness, one of the meanings of the Ground. This point of view is developed in Part Three of *The Promise and Peril of Human Purpose*. Here we wish only to allude to its possibilities. Since God is not an object of perception, nor an other in the comparative sense as we find in common experience on the meso-level of existence (and since Otherness is to an extent shrouded in mythology), it is meaningful to say that Otherness has its source of meaning in man's purposive nature, which is compresent with such experience. We call it purposive alienation, or positive alienation. Human purpose disavows its own directives to be guided by the Other, whatever or whoever it may be. The Other is thus pre-conceptual as an experience, but it is not pre-purposive. Since it is mediated by man's purposive nature, it is, to that extent at least, co-experiential with Otherness. Since we are beyond the meaning of objects and beyond the ordinary perception of persons on the meso-level, we believe that purposiveness mediates more on this mythical level of human concern.

Thus the nature of the divine orderer in existence will manifest itself in clearer perspective if the human orderer is given his proper due in immediate experience. The purpose of this chapter is not to discard the various meanings of the Ground, but to make ontological purposiveness relevant to each such claim. While this is a modest claim, it is not an easy achievement. For the history of thought has neglected the ontological meaning of human purpose. It was much easier to use human purpose in other ontological settings, than to define purpose itself ontologically. In attempting to correct this inadequacy in the history of thought we have to teach ourselves anew about the importance of models by participation, whether it involves various sundry meanings in existence in general or the meaning of the Ground itself. Purpose is thus more relevant to the religious quest than what it was acknowledged to be in the history of religion.

We said at the beginning of the chapter that religion's great challenge is human purpose, that this is the central issue in the debate between religion and secularism. Instead of meeting the challenge, religionists have denied the relevance and effectualness of human purpose both to existence and to the religious quest. By adhering to the doctrine of the primacy of totality they have perpetuated a dualism between divine and human purpose. Should religionists continue to follow this course of belief and action (a policy of reaction to secularism) it will never meet the challenge, which is essential to the vitality of religion in the modern world, of relating purpose either to existence or to the religious quest.

PART II

FROM THE RELIGIOUS PERSPECTIVE

CHAPTER 5

ORTHODOX JUDAISM AND HUMAN PURPOSE

WALTER S. WURTZBURGER

I

As a theocentric religion, Judaism regards the universe not as a self-sufficient cosmos, but as the creation of a transcendent God who is the source of all existence, value and meaning. Since the purpose of all creatures is grounded in the Creator, all questions concerning the purpose of any being must ultimately involve the Divine Plan for His creatures. But, as the Book of Job so dramatically shows, the purposes of a transcendent, infinite God are completely beyond the ken of our finite, limited intelligence.

To be sure, the Jewish liturgy asserts that 'God created everything for His glory'.[1] But, as Maimonides suggests, this statement does not really provide a teleological explanation. It does not really help us to determine why a particular being should possess the specific set of charcteristics with which it is endowed. We have no way of knowing why a different set of characteristics would not have equally well served to glorify God. Actually, following Maimonides' explanation, the statement is merely the equivalent of saying that we are incapable of fathoming the ultimate purpose of any creature and that we therefore cannot go beyond the assertion that a creature exists because God, for reasons totally unintelligible to us, willed its existence.[2]

Since there is no conceivable set of circumstances that would invalidate the proposition, 'Whatever exists, exists for the glory of God', the proposition cannot be invoked as an explanation for the occurrence of any particular event or process. Yet, though devoid of explanatory value, the notion of an inexplicable Divine Purpose governing the universe has far reaching implications. Once the notion of a transcendent Divine Purpose[3] is accepted, it follows that the meaning of any particular event or process can no longer

---

1. Bab. Talmud, *Ketuvot*, 8a. Cf. also Mishnah *Avot*, (*Kinyan Torah*, 6:11).
2. Maimonides, *Guide for the Perplexed III*, 13 and 25.
3. To be sure Judaism does not merely operate with the notion of a transcendent God. God is at the same time immanent in His creation. But since Judaism insists upon divine transcendence, God's purposes cannot ever be completely intelligible to those that are within the natural or historic order. See also below, Section *V* of this Chapter.

be completely expressible in terms of an immanent purpose manifesting itself in history or in nature.[4] Natural processes or historic events, at the very most, disclose fragmentary meanings. Their full meaning can be grasped only from a vantage point outside of both nature and history. Thus, in the final analysis, faith in Divine Purpose merely provides the believer with the assurance that the Author of nature and history has a purpose for His creation which is discernible only to the extent that He chooses to disclose it to His creatures.

The perspective of the believer is radically different from that of the atheistic existentialist who asserts the basic meaninglessness of all existence. To be sure, both despair of discovering within the universe itself a meaningful structure. But there remains this fundamental difference. Whereas the atheistic existentialist is confronted with a world of absurdity in which all meaning and purpose amounts to nothing but the fabrications and projections of the individual, the believer finds himself in a universe that reflects the inexplicable purpose and the providential plan of a benevolent God. Even the manifest absurdities of existence are attributed to the limitations of the human perspective. How could reality be conceived as absurd if it represents Divine Creation and is governed by His Providence? This optimism comes to the fore in the Biblical account of Creation. The verdict 'It was very good' was pronounced upon the completion of the entire process.[5]

The assertion of the goodness and meaningfulness of the world is not shaken by the existence of evil. Understandably, there was considerable reluctance on the part of the Rabbis to attribute to God directly the authorship of evil. Thus the Jewish liturgy finds it necessary to reformulate the passage from Isaiah which refers to God as the 'one who creates evil'.[6] Instead, there is subsituted for this term which might prove offensive to some religious sensibilities the more neutral description of God as the 'one who creates all things'.[7] But subsuming evil under the category of 'all things', while removing a shocking linguistic expression, does not really solve the problem. In view of Judaism's radical monotheism, one cannot dispose of the difficulty by ascribing evil to a force antithetical to or independent of God. Classic Jewish sources are most emphatic in their denunciation of any form of

4. Rationalistic Jewish theologians have, of course, within their system room for an immanent teleology. Though Maimonides maintains that there is no rational explanation why God has created a world, he nevertheless affirms that the universe possesses a purposeful structure. It should also be noted that some rationalistic theologians (e.g., Bahyah Ibn Pakuda and Saadyah Gaon) go as far as to claim that the purpose of all of reality is the salvation of man who is regarded as the highest creature.
5. Genesis, 1:31.
6. Isaiah, 45:7.
7. Daily Morning Prayer.

dualism which would eliminate the problem of evil by limiting the power of God.[8]

Some leading Jewish thinkers are inclined to explain *away* the problem of treating evil as a sheer illusion or privation of good. They dismiss evil as a mere appearance, because they would view the existence of evil as incompatible with the goodness of God's creation. But this essentially idealistic approach does by no means reflect the preponderant Jewish attitude.

Notwithstanding the fact that Rabbi Akiva declared that 'whatever God does is for the good',[9] the distinction between good and evil is not abolished. While one blesses God for the evil in the same manner as one does for the good, there is a radical difference between the type of blessing recited on the respective occasions.[10] Those, however, who feel that a religion such as Judaism which takes history and normative ideals so seriously cannot dismiss evil as a mere appearance, are left with a serious problem. Why should an omnipotent God choose to create evil in order to promote the goodness of the totality? Recourse to the Leibnitzian notion of the 'best of all possible worlds' seems rather unsatisfactory, since it would set limits to the omnipotence of God.[11] Ultimately, one would have to resort to the notion of the incomprehensibility of the divine plan to man, the solution which appears to be preferable to any of the alternatives presented so far.

An even more disturbing feature of the problem of evil arises from the fact that the divine Providential plan seems to include even moral evil. The prophet Isaiah, for example, does not hesitate to describe the wickedness of Assyria as the 'rod of Divine anger'.[12] There can be no doubt that sages of the Talmud are sensitive to the problem as to how it is possible for a benevolent God to will that human beings perform morally wrong actions to achieve His purposes in history. In their non-systematic fashion, they wrestle with the problem when they speak of God's silence in the face of the destruction of His sanctuary[13] and develop the paradoxical notion that by His apparent withdrawal from the historic scene, God chooses to manifest His power and greatness.[14]

8. See especially Bab. Talmud, *Berahot* 33b and *Megillah* 25a and *Berahot* 54a.
9. Cf. Maimonides' treatment of evil as a mere negation. *Guide III*, 10–12.
10. Bab. Talmud *Berahot* 60b.
11. Any attempt to treat evil as necessary to the attainment to the greatest possible good subjects God to the domain of necessity. The Leibnitzian view is of no avail to anyone who is unwilling to surrender the distinction between logical and factual truth.
12. Isaiah 10:5. Cf. also Jeremiah's attitude towards Nebukadnezzar's role as an instrument of divine purpose (Jer. 25:9; 27:6; and 43:10).
13. Bab. Talmud, *Gittin* 56 b.
14. Bab. Talmud, *Yoma* 69b; Jer. Talmud, *Berahot* 6:3.

While the Rabbis were fully aware of the nature of the underlying paradox,[15] they made no attempt to offer a solution to it.[16] Similarly, they fail to come to grips with the difficulties inherent in the notion that an omnipotent God's purpose for history requires man's freely given cooperation. There is no systematic effort made to reconcile God's omnipotence and omniscience (which entails His fore-knowledge) with the existence of human freedom.[17] The Rabbis simply state 'All is in the hands of Heaven, except the fear of Heaven'.[18] Apparently Jewish religious thought employs what Raphael Morris Cohen has called 'scissorial concepts'. The emphasis upon man's utter dependence upon an omnipotent God must be balanced by the insistence upon human responsibility. Notwithstanding all logical difficulties, Judaism must postulate both divine omnipotence and human freedom. Without either of these two components operating in dialectical tension, the entire Jewish concept of Jewish piety, which revolves upon man's responsibility to an omnipotent God, would be utterly impossible.

Committed as it is to a thorough-going monotheism, Judaism cannot brook any limitations upon Divine Power. But God, according to the Jewish view,

15. Most of the discussions of the problem of evil in the Talmudic and Midrashic literature relate not to the question of how a benevolent God can permit the existence of evil, but rather to an entirely different issue involving God's justice: How can a just God permit a situation where there is apparently no correlation between the moral worth of an individual and his happiness?
16. A most illuminating discussion of the entire problem as to how an omnipotent God can be involved in historic process as the Lord of history is contained in Emil L. Fackenheim's *God's Presence in History*. Although the bulk of this essay was completed before the appearance of the book, I wish to record my indebtedness to Prof. Fackenheim whose views exerted a considerable influence on my own thinking on the subject.
17. It is often taken for granted that the problem as to how one can reconcile the postulation of human freedom with the foreknowledge of God is already posed in the famous Mishnah in *Avot* 3:15 which is usually translated as 'Everything is foreseen, but permission is given to man'. This translation follows, however, the interpretation of Maimonides (Commentary to Mishnah ad loc). In his recent volume, *Hazal, Emunot Vedeot*, Prof. Ephraim E. Urbach has shown that Maimonides has actually read his own philosophical views into the ancient Mishnah. Prof. Urbach adduces linguistic proof that the intent of the Talmudic passage in question has nothing to do with the metaphysical issue raised by Maimonides. The Hebrew term *Tzaphui*, does not at all suggest divine foreknowledge. It merely denotes that all is seen (by God) while permission is given to man. It may also be of interest in this connection to point out that Potesquiere caustically comments on Maimonides' attempt (*Hilhot Rabad of Teshuvah* 5:5) to resolve the paradox, that in view of the implausibility of Maimonides' solution, it would have been preferable, if he had refrained from raising the question altogether. See also Julius Guttmannn, *op. cit.*, p. 38.
18. Bab. Talmud *Berahot* 38b.

has for mysterious reasons, chosen to need man's *freely* given services. Creatures which lack freedom automatically contribute to God's glory, and fulfill their purpose because they are bound to act in accordance with His Will. But man is given freedom of choice, whether to fulfill the role Divine purpose has assigned to him. He can either glorify or desecrate God. Were man merely a helpless puppet in the hands of an absolute Deity, he could not possibly be regarded as the bearer of the image of the Divine.[18a] It must also be borne in mind that in the Jewish scheme, man fulfills the divine purpose not by blind submission to the divine will. Human reason and conscience play an important role in determining the meaning of the divine imperatives addressed to man. To be sure, Orthodox Judaism maintains that man can carry out his purpose only by obedience to the divine commandments which were revealed to man. But this emphasis upon revelation does not – à la Tertullian – result in the condemnation of reason and the elevation of absurdity to the supreme religious value. Viewed from Jewish perspective, true commitment to God entails the utilization of one's rational resources and ethical convictions, which must operate in dialectical tension with the content of the Revelation, in order to ascertain the true meaning of God's demands upon man.[18b] This is why the Jewish concept of Torah stresses so much man's creativity. Man, as it were, is a partner with God in creating the Torah. The very conception of an Oral Torah involves not merely blind submission to an authoritative body of revealed teachings, but also creative effort on the part of man, who employs his intelligence, reason and moral insights towards the shaping of a 'Torah of life'. This more earth-bound Torah is now entrusted for its proper interpretation to duly qualified human beings. Its true meaning becomes the product of interaction between the infinite God and finite man.

Since Jewish thought is compelled to harmonize human responsibility with the absoluteness of Divine power it is not surprising that it is marked by a rather ambivalent attitude towards the efficacy of human action. On the one hand, emphasis on divine omnipotence tends to make man's fate exclusively dependent upon Divine Providence. In the words of the liturgy, 'Heal us and we shall be healed, save us and we shall be saved'.[19] Saving power belongs only to God; His designs cannot be thwarted. 'Except the Lord builds the

---

18a. That the two notions are closely related appears to follow from the sequence of Rabbi Akiva's statements as recorded in *Avot* 3. The first (*Avot* 3:14) develops the notion that man is beloved because he is created in the image of God. It is after this statement dealing with the unique position of man, that the next Mishnah stresses man's freedom and responsibility.
18b. Cf. 'Autonomy and Theonomy', A. Carlebach, *Tradition*, Fall, 1963, pp. 5–28.
19. Daily Liturgy.

house, all the toil of its labors will be in vain'.[20] But it is significant that the Psalmist still emphasizes the need for man's toil. Without it, God will not build the house.[21] And for that matter the Bible places upon man responsibility for healing individuals, for man is charged with the responsibility of being a partner with God in the process of Creation.[22] While ultimately the result of human efforts may fall short of our expectations, 'it is not incumbent on you to finish the work, nor do you have the right to desist from it'.[23]

It is of course impossible to delimit the extent to which any human action can achieve its intended result, since the fate of the individual is governed by God's providential plan. We encounter within the Jewish tradition a wide spectrum of attitudes towards the relative weight to be assigned to human actions. In a famous passage, the medieval Biblical exegete, Ibn Ezra[24] disparages all human efforts designed to improve one's material well-being, which according to him is completely determined by God's Providence. Only matters of spiritual welfare, according to this view, are influenced by man's performance. Since man's material conditions depend exclusively upon Divine Providence, there is no point in attempting to improve one's lot. This fatalistic and quietistic approach which is adopted by some thinkers clashes head-on with the position advocated by the proponents of a more activist approach, who categorically reject a policy of passive submission to one's fate.[25] Implicit in the notion of human dignity and responsibility,[26] one might plausibly argue in accordance with this view, is the belief that at least to some extent man may shape his destiny and that he bears some responsibility for the state of his material condition.

Rabbi Soloveitchik, a leading contemporary Jewish theologian, attributes the ambivalence of the Jewish position with respect to the efficacy of human action to a dialectical tension inherent in man's ontological status.[27] That man

20. Psalms 127:1.
21. Rabbi Joseph B. Soloveitchik's 'The Lonely Man of Faith', *Tradition*, Summer 1965, pp. 5–67, contains a most relevant discussion of this issue.
22. Exodus 21:19. See also Bab. Talmud, *Bava Kama* 85a. See also Joseph B. Soloveitchik, *op. cit.*, p. 53. Bab. Talmud *Shabbat* 119b. See also Rabbi Joseph B. Soloveitchik, 'Ish Ha-Halahah', *Talpiot*, 1944, pp. 710–18.
23. Mishnah *Avot*, 2:16.
24. See Ibn Ezra's Commentary to Exodus 20:14.
25. See especially Rabbi Menachem Meiri, *Bet Ha-Beḥirah* to *Moed Katan* 28a and *Shabbat* 156a. Cf. also Ephraim E. Urbach, *op. cit.*, p. 251.
26. Cf. Rabbi Joseph B. Soloveitchik, 'The Lonely Man of Faith', *loc. cit.*, especially pp. 14–16.
27. Although this theme is developed primarily in his 'The Lonely Man of Faith', his earlier

is torn between feelings of self-importance and utter insignificance reflects, not any malfunction of the human psyche, but a complex ontological status which condemns him to perpetual restlessness. On the one hand, man is conceived as an exalted creature who in partnership with God is called upon to help perfect the world and to utilize his intelligence and energy to harness the forces of nature. On the other hand, man, confronted as he is by his inability to wrest ultimate meaning from the triumphs wrought in the conquest of nature, realizes the utter insignificance of all his achievements as a finite creature. It is only through a covenantal relationship with God that, according to Rabbi Soloveitchik, man can overcome a sense of absurdity and futility. In this encounter with God, man does not only experience God's care and concern for him, but becomes aware that God in turn, for mysterious reasons, has chosen to desire man's commitment to Him. But, significantly, this covenantal relationship which provides human existence with transcendental meaning does not allow man to escape from his existential reponsibilities in the here and now. 'The Torah was not given to the ministering angels' but to human beings;[28] and the transcendental significance of man derives precisely from the fact that he is commanded by God to perform actions which can be carried out only by spatio-temporal creatures operating in an ever-changing transient world. Man must not lose himself in the higher regions of being; he must carry out his divine tasks in a concrete existential world which, not in spite of, but precisely, because of the intrinsic limitations arising from its finitude, constitutes the proper scene of man's operation. It is here where the finite and infinite meet and where man can perform the deeds which while taking place in time have significance in the realm of eternity.

That God has revealed His Will to man is a cardinal tenet of Judaism. No attempt is made to explain the mystery why an omnipotent God should have chosen to entrust a finite creature with tasks necessary for the fulfillment of a divine purpose. But it is regarded as the very hallmark of our humanity to be the addressees of Divine Commandments. Some commandments (i.e., the so-called seven Noahide laws) apply to all human beings.[29] Being human, according to Judaism, implies to be singled out for the service of God. It is precisely the fact that God demands the fulfillment of a certain task from finite man that provides the measure of our humanity and endows our existence with transcendent relevance.

essays 'Confrontation', *Tradition*, Spring/Summer, 1964, pp. 3–28, and especially his Ish Ha-Halahah *Talpiot*, 1944, pp. 651–735, should not be overlooked.
28. Bab. Talmud, *Berahot* 25 b.
29. Bab. Talmud *Sanhedrin* 29 b.

Since God has chosen to enter into a special covenant with the people of Israel, he has placed upon it additional obligations designed to make it 'a kingdom of Priests and a holy nation'.[30] The imposition of numerous commandments, which are contained in the Oral and the Written Torah, is looked upon as a sign of special love, 'Because the Holy One, blessed be He, wanted to bestow a special privilege upon Israel He gave them so many provisions of the Torah and so many Commandments'.[31] Human existence possesses value to the degree that it is related to a divine task which is commanded by God. It is also revealing that the Book of Ecclesiastes which grapples with the meaning of human existence, after struggling with a variety of contradictory formulations, finally gives up the attempt to find a rationally appealing solution and concludes on the note 'The end of the matter, fear God observe His Commandments, because this is the whole man'.[32] A well known Rabbinic comment notes that it is this verse which provides the ultimate rationale for all existence.[33]

The Jewish religious ideal with its emphasis upon obedience to God's revealed Will does not seek the dissolution of man's individuality through mystic union with God.[34] Were man to lose himself completely in God and cease to function as an individual, he would no longer be able to stand in a covenantal relationship with God. For this relationship can exist only if man *qua* man responds to God's love and commits himself to His service. In the benediction which is recited after the reading of the Torah, God is extolled as 'having given us a Torah of Truth and thereby implanting within us a life of eternity'. The very finiteness of human existence, with all its intrinsic

30. Exodus 19:6.
31. Bab. Talmud, *Makkot* 23 b.
32. Ecclesiastes 12:13.
33. Bab. Talmud, *Shabbat* 30 b.
34. To be sure Judaism has its share of thinkers who advocate the mystic ideal of union with God. But it must be borne in mind that essentially Judaism revolves around Halahah which presupposes man's standing in relationship to God, not merging with Him. See Rabbi Joseph B. Soloveitchik, *Ish Ha-Halahah*, and my essay on 'Pluralism and Halakhah', *Tradition*, Spring 1962, pp. 221–40.
34a. Bab. Talmud, *Bava Metzia*, 59 b.
34b. Because Jewish religious thought is marked by the perpetual dialectical tension between divine omnipotence and man's freedom, it is not surprising that we encounter in Jewish theological writings such radical disagreement with respect to the question whether the divine Commandments must be accepted as a Divine Decree totally unintelligble to man, or whether human beings have the right or even the duty to seek rationally appealing explanations for them. For an interesting historical survey of the various positions taken by representative Jewish theologians see Isaac Heinemann, *Taamei Ha-Mitzvot Be-Safrut, Yisrael*, Vol. *I* and *II*.

limitations, does not represent an unmitigated metaphysical evil, but rather the condition in which man alone can execute the unique religious task which God has assigned to him.

A telling illustration of the Jewish attitude towards the transcendental meaning of our finite life is provided by the Kaddish prayer which is recited by the mourner who confronts the mystery of human existence. Although the Kaddish is a doxology which contains no reference whatsoever to the phenomenon of death, it indirectly serves as an expression of the Jewish response to the finitude of human existence. Confrontation with death does not lead to a declaration of futility or absurdity, because fragmentary individual human life is seen within the context of the ultimate eschatological goal of Judaism – the sanctification of the Divine Name. And even though an individual's life falls short of the realization of all its goals, it nonetheless possesses meaning because even its partial accomplishments may contribute to the realization of the Divine plan.[35]

II

Against this background it is easy to account for the this-wordly and life-affirming attitude of Judaism. One hour devoted to Torah and good deeds in this world are held to be superior to all the life in the hereafter, even though, according to Rabbinic belief, the satisfactions enjoyed in the hereafter are infinitely greater than those available in this world.[36]

In a philosophy of life that stresses man's total commitment to a God who is not merely the Author of life, but the Lord of history, there is no area that can be excluded from the claims of the all-demanding Sovereign of the Universe. The prescriptions of the Torah regulate the entire gamut of personal, interpersonal, social, economic and political concerns. The ultimate eschatological goal of all religious activity is the establishment of the kingdom of God where the Sovereignty of God will be acknowledged in all human affairs.[37] While the complete fulfillment of this ideal must await God's redemption of man in the Messianic age, it is the religious duty of the individual to devote his total existence towards this objective.

Contrary to wide-spread misconceptions, Judaism does not equate commitment to the service of God with mere compliance with formal rules of

---

35. Jacob B. Agus, 'The Meaning of Prayer', in Abraham Ezra Milgram (ed.), *Great Jewish Ideas*, p. 23.
36. Mishnah *Avot* 4:17.
37. See S. Schechter, *Some Aspects of Rabbinic Theology*, pp. 80–96.

the law. Actually, observance of the law is regarded merely as a necessary, but not as a sufficient condition of piety. There is no basis for the charge of 'legalism' which so often is raised by poorly informed critics, since the classical Jewish sources abound with maxims stressing the necessity of extending the domain of piety far beyond the area covered by legal requirements.[38] Hillel, one of the foremost Jewish legal authorities, prescribes that 'all one's actions should be performed for the sake of God'.[39] In keeping with this precept he was able to treat even such trivial tasks as tending to the needs of one's own body as acts of religious devotion.[40] Similarly, another Talmudic sage, Bar Kappara cites the verse 'In all thy ways thou shalt acknowledge Him',[41] as the underlying religious principle of the entire Torah.[42] According to the medieval scholar Nachmanides,[43] one strives for holiness and piety through the practice of self-restraint even in activities which from a purely legalistic point of view are perfectly legitimate.

The social consciousness is imperative. Indifference to the plight of others is regarded as a grievous sin. Concern for the welfare of one's fellow human being must express itself in the attempt to improve both his spiritual and material condition.[44] While Judaism is fully cognizant of the fact that unsatisfied material wants may at times be helpful in inducing feelings of dependency upon God and thus may be instrumental in disposing individuals towards the demands of piety,[45] there is in no way any suggestion that suffering should be condoned because of its potential spiritual boons. On the contrary, Judaism looks upon suffering (including poverty) as an evil to be eradicated. Individuals who do not contribute to *Yishuv Ha-olam* (promotion of social well-being) are stigmatized as morally defective.[46] Conversely, considerable religious significance is attached to those activities which enhance human welfare. Talmudic legislation was replete with ordinances promulgated for the improvement of the world (*Tikkun Ha-olam*).[47]

38. See Samuel Belkin, *In His Image*, pp. 214–248 and Ephraim E. Urbach, *op. cit.*, pp. 279–347.
39. Mishnah *Avot* 2:12.
40. Leviticus Rabbah 34:3.
41. Proverbs 3:6.
42. Bab. Talmud, *Berahot* 63a.
43. Commentary to Leviticus 19:2.
44. Maimonides *Hilhot Deot*, 6:7 *Hilhot Avel* 1–6. See also Solomon Schechter, 'Notes on Lectures in Jewish Philanthropy', in *Studies in Judaism*, Vol. 3, pp. 239–276 and Isadore Twersky, 'Some Aspects of Jewish Attitude Toward the Welfare State', *Tradition*, Spring 1963, pp. 137–158.
45. Bab. Talmud, *Hagigah* 9b, *Vayikra Rabbah* 13:4.
46. Bab. Talmud *Sanhedrin*, 24b. See also Samuel Belkin, *op. cit.*, pp. 90–92.
47. *Mishnah Gittin* 5:3.
    Hilhot Yesodei Ha-Torah 4:13; *Hilhot Deot* 7:8.

Maimonides goes so far as to say that many of the laws of Torah are primarily designed to promote social well-being on earth.[48] To be sure, for Maimonides, the socio-political objectives of the Torah were merely subsidiary to the ultimate end – man's intellectual and spiritual perfection.[49] But what matters for our purposes here is the fact that even for Maimonides, notwithstanding his stress upon intellectual rather than practical virtues, 'the preservation of the population of the country and its stability'[50] is not merely a purely socio-utilitarian desideratum, but represents a fundamental religious imperative. In this connection it should be pointed out that according to Jewish belief, one is not only morally obligated to prevent the suffering of one's fellow man, but one must not remain indifferent even to one's own material plight. An individual is required to prevent his own pauperization.[51]

As a general rule, Judaism maintains that 'your own life takes precedence over that of your fellow man'.[52] Judaism would not subscribe to Berdayev's epigrammatic formulation that 'bread for oneself is a material matter; bread for one's neighbor is a spiritual matter'. From a Jewish perspective, to secure bread for oneself and to avoid unnecessary suffering also constitutes a spiritual imperative. The endorsement of activities leading to the promotion of human welfare must not, however, be confused with a 'success' or 'work' ethics. There is no equivalent in Jewish sources to the Calvinistic emphasis on material success as an index of spiritual worth, nor is there an echo of the Lutheran notion of a 'calling'. While material wealth and success are regarded as blessings, there is no trace whatsoever of the suggestion that man as the steward of God's possessions has a moral obligation to augment them according to the best of his abilities. Judaism knows of no obligation to succeed. On the contrary, excessive preoccupation with material success is regarded as a severe handicap because it prevents the individual from devoting sufficient time and energy to the study of Torah and other spiritual pursuits.[53] While *Yishuv Ha-olam* (improvement of material conditions) and *Derech Eretz*[54] (activities necessary for the civilization of the world) are regarded as

48. *Guide for the Perplexed III*, 27, 33 and 35.
49. *Guide for the Perplexed III*, 23, 27 and 35.
50. *Ibid.*, III, p. 27. For a thorough discussion of Maimonides' position with respect to the social utility of the commandments see, Isadore Twersky 'Some Non-Halakhic Aspects of the Mishnah Torah', in Alexander Altmann (ed.), *Jewish Medieval and Renaissance Studies*, pp. 103-105.
51. Bab. Talmud *Ketuvot* 50a and 67b; *Araḥin* 28a.
52. Bab. Talmud *Bava Metzia* 42 a.
53. *Mishnah Avot* 3:5; 4:10. Bab. Talmud *Eruvin* 55a. See also Maimonides, *Hilḥot Talmud Torah* Chapter III.
54. For a discussion of the centrality of this concept on Jewish thought see Max Kadushin, *Worship & Ethics*, pp. 39-62 and pp. 244-250.

desiderata, they do not occupy the highest rank within the hierarchy of values. To make possible the concentration upon the study of the Torah, the ideal religious personality, the *Talmid Chakham* (the Torah Scholar) is urged to forego, if necessary, the satisfaction of many legitimate needs.[55] After all, in case of conflict, lower values must be sacrificed for higher values. What ultimately matters from a religious perspective is not the degree to which human activity is productive of socially desirable consequences, but rather the extent to which an individual is faithful in fulfilling his covenantal obligations to God.

III

As opposed to religious systems which view human efforts aiming at the transformation of the environment with indifference if not hostility because they supposedly represent undue concern with matters that should be more properly left to the Deity, Jewish writings never suggested that man's mastery over nature implicates him in guilt. When man harnesses the forces of nature to promote human welfare, he does not usurp powers rightfully belonging to God, but carries out the provisions of Divine Mandate. When the Bible condemns the building of the Tower of Babel, it is not because the exercise of human creativity and the display of technological prowess represents an intrusion upon the domain of God. We vainly search the Jewish sources for parallels to the Promethean myth where human achievement is treated as a threat to Divine prerogatives. What provokes Divine wrath, according to Rabbinic interpretations of the Tower of Babel story, is not man's success in the conquest of nature, but rather his idolatry – his arrogant rebellion against God through the assertion of his own independence and self-reliance.[56] A similar motif appears in the Biblical Tree of Knowledge episode where man defies God because he is deluded into thinking that he too, could play God. ('And you shall be as God, knowing between good and evil'.)[57] But to denounce outright defiance of God's supremacy is a far cry from maintaining that intellectual or technological attainments as such involve man in the sin of *hybris* or, as some other-worldly religions suggest, reflect an undue interest in basically mundane concerns which divert man's attention from what ought to be the true focus of his goals.

Judaism's positive stance towards so-called secular concerns aiming at the

---

55. Bab. Talmud *Berahot* 43b. See also Maimonides, *Hilḥot Talmud Torah*. Chapter *III*.
56. See Bab. Talmud *Sanhedrin* 109a.
57. Genesis 3:5.

improvement of human welfare rests on two basic premises.

1. Man's faith in God entails not an abdication of responsibility for the world, but rather a responsibility to God to 'walk in His ways' and promote the welfare of His creatures.

2. The contingency, transcience and finitude which characterizes empirical reality does not deprive it of metaphysical worth. To exist in time rather than in eternity does not constitute a metaphysical evil. Conditions prevailing in a world of constant flux do not lose their significance simply because they lack the aspect of timelessness which is the hallmark of the transcendental realm. The here and now matters to God, who according to Rabbinic tradition, seeks the in-dwelling of His Presence primarily among the lower regions of being.[58]

Thus concern for the transcendent does not provide the believer with an escape from the harsh realities of our existential world. Suffering and want cannot be dismissed as inconsequential. On the contrary, the alleviation of misery assumes the dimension of a religiously meaningful act.

According to Jewish belief, a special role in the Divine Plan for the redemption of the world and the establishment of His Kingdom has been assigned to Israel. Torah, worship, and loving kindness provide the spiritual foundations of the world and constitute the *raison d'être* of the Universe.[59] In an unredeemed world it is Israel that must act as God's witness[60] attesting to His Sovereignty and serving as the light of the nations.[61] Because he belongs to the people of Israel, a Jew cannot satisfy his religious obligations simply as a human being who confronts his God purely as an individual. Unless he also abides by the terms of the special covenant governing the singular relationship between the people of Israel and God he is derelict in his responsibility. He is commanded by God to consider himself as a member of the Jewish people and share in the unique religious vocation for which the people of Israel has been summoned.

IV

Although the meaning of human existence is found not in self-realization or self-fulfillment, but in the total commitment to a divinely appointed task, Judaism nonetheless maintains that the *summum bonum* is attained as a

---

58. Bereshit Rabbah, 19:13. Cf. also Rabbi Joseph B. Soloveitchik's Study *'Ish Ha-halahah'*, *op. cit.* Compare also note 32 above.
59. Mishnah *Avot* 1:2.
60. Isaiah 43:10.
61. *Ibid.* 44:8.

consequence of a life dedicated to this ideal. Eternal beatitude is vouchsafed under those who align themselves with the divine purpose. To be sure, under ideal circumstances, the quest for personal salvation should not enter as a motive of piety. 'Do not act like servants who serve the master for the sake of reward'.[62] Those who truly love God do not have to be prodded towards religious behavior by the prospect of eternal bliss. As Maimonides put it, those who are influenced by expectations of reward serve God not out of love but out of fear.[63] But while ideally concern for personal salvation should not be a factor, Judaism possesses far too realistically a conception of human nature as to frown upon appeals to self-interest as an inducement to piety.[64] Following the Biblican precedent which links loyalty to the covenant with the enjoyment of divine blessings, Rabbinic Judaism harps upon the great rewards awaiting the faithful in the world to come. A well known Rabbinic dictum unabashedly recommends that one look upon this world as merely the ante-chamber to the next. 'One should prepare one's self in the ante-chamber in order that one may enter the palace itself'.[65]

This attitude also comes to the fore in the opening statement of one of the most popular pietistic treatises. In his *Mesilat Yesharim*, Rabbi Moses Chaim Luzzatto advises the believer to base all behavior upon the realization that 'Man was created only for the purpose of finding bliss in God and enjoying the radiance of His presence in the world to come'.[66]

It is of special interest that many of the rationalistic Jewish thinkers look upon the beatitude granted the faithful in the hereafter not as an extraneous reward conferred by God as a gratuitous compensation for good deeds, but rather as a spiritual achievement wrought by pious conduct and the cultivation of a religious personality.[67] For the rationalist, a regimen aiming at spiritual perfection is bound to yield spiritual rewards.

Though proceeding from entirely different premises, Kabbalistic thought, too, harps upon the centrality of human initiative and effort in the realm of the spirit. It is revealing that for a leading eighteenth century exponent of Rabbinic Judaism who operates largely with Kabbalistic categories, the achievement of immortality emerges as an aspect of man's creativity.

---

62. Mishnah *Avot* 1:3.
63. *Hilḥot Teshuvah* 10:1–2.
64. See especially Lipman Heller, *Tosaphot Yom Tov ad Avot* 1:3.
65. Mishnah *Avot* 4:16.
66. Moses Chaim Luzzatto, *Massilat Yesharim*, Chapter *I*.
67. According to Maimonides, immortality of the soul is not something given, but it is gained by the human soul through moral and intellectual efforts which actualize a potentiality for immortality.

According to Rabbi Chaim of Volozin[68] 'there is simply no ready made hereafter for which a man can qualify by dint of his piety. It is man himself who must create through his own spiritual efforts the realm of spirituality which constitutes his portion of the world to come'.[69] Viewed from this perspective, immortality is no longer postulated simply as an inducement to religious piety or as a solution to a theological dilemma posed by God's creation of a world where apparently there is no correlation between moral worthiness and the enjoyment of happiness; it rather represents a manifestation of the unique capacity for creativity which is possessed by man by virtue of his singular ontological status as a member of both the natural and the spiritual realm. It is because in man the finite encounters the infinite that he plays such a dominant role in the redemptive process. According to the Kabbalistic scheme, human initiative is needed to start a cosmic chain reaction whose repercussions are felt in the highest regions of being. The process of *Tikkun*, involving the redemption of Universe from evil and the ultimate reunification of God with His *Shehinah* (Divine Presence), must originate with man's creative efforts.[70]

V

The anthropocentric orientation of the Kabbalah represents by no means a radical break with the Rabbinic tradition. Numerous Talmudic statements could be adduced in support of the thesis that man as the 'crown of creation'[71] must provide the *raison d'être* for the entire Universe. This is one of the reasons why the destruction of human life is regarded as the equivalant of the destruction of the entire Universe.[72] Because of the sanctity and importance attached to each human life, every person should look upon himself as if the entire Universe was created for his sake.[73] Another Talmudic saying admonishes an individual to recognize that his actions may not only determine his own fate, but that of the entire world.[74]

To be sure, one encounters considerable dissent from the notion that man holds a preeminent position within the order of creation. Among medieval

68. Rabbi Hayyim of Volozin, *Nefesh ha-Hayyim I*, 12, *Ruah Ha-Hayyim I*, 1. See also my essay on rabbi Hayyim of Volozin in Leo Jung (ed.) *Guardians of our Heritage*, p. 205.
69. *Ibid.*
70. Cf. Gershom G. Scholem, *Major Trends in Jewish Mysticism*, pp. 265–84.
71. For a thorough discussion of this topic consult Ephraim Urbach, *op. cit.*, pp. 190–226.
72. Mishnah *Sanhedrin* 4:5.
73. *Ibid.*
74. Bab. Talmud *Kiddushim* 40 b.

philosophers it was especially Maimonides who emphasized that the Jewish tradition must not be read in an anthropocentric fashion.[75] Although in his legal works many of the maxims stressing man's personal responsibility for the world are incorporated, a metaphysics which reflects an excessive human parochialism is totally unacceptable to a Maimonides, who sees no need to accord man a preeminent metaphysical status in order to buttress his position as the bearer of the image of the Divine.

With man dethroned from his supremacy in the hierarchy of created beings, it is not surprising that Maimonides[76] accepts the opinion of those Talmudic Rabbis[77] who look upon the Messianic Redemption merely as the emergence of a new kind of social order, which, notwithstanding its great importance to man, is not really treated as an event of overriding cosmic significance. It is readily understandable that for rationalistic theologians it is difficult to ascribe more than merely human significance to the redemption of mankind through supernatural intervention. The situation, of course, is altogether different for those religious thinkers for whom history rather than natural philosophy provides the basic matrix of their thought. It has often been pointed out that Judaism is a historic religion which emphasizes God's concern and involvement with the historic process.[78] Significantly, as Rabbi Yehuda Halevi[79] and Nachmanides[80] have stressed, the Decalogue invokes not the God of Creation, but the God of history. The exodus of Egypt constitutes the dominant religious motif of Judaism and a host of religious practices, observances and institutions are directly related to this central event which at the same time is also regarded as the paradigm of the ultimate redemption.

It is not merely an accident that representative Jewish thinkers take such divergent positions in their evaluation of the importance of the role which the historic process plays in the Divine scheme. There can be little doubt that the disagreement manifests the dialectical tension between the Immanence and the Transcendence of God which is built into the very foundations of Judaism. The more one stresses the absolute transcendence of the Creator, the more one recoils from involving God in the historic process. Conversely the more emphasis is placed upon God's Immanence, the more one is prone to accept doctrines which reach their most radical formulation in the daring mystic notion that God whose *Shehinah* is in exile in some sense is redeemed together

75. See especially *Guide for the Perplexed III*, 15.
76. *Hilḥot Melachim* 12:1–2.
77. Bab. Talmud *Sanhedrin* 91b.
78. See Emil L. Fackenheim, *op. cit.*, especially Chapter *I*.
79. Kuzari, Chapter *I*.
80. See Commentary to Exodus 20:2.

with the redemption of the world.[80a] This dialectical tension which gives rise to a host of intellectually disturbing paradoxes provides much of the thrust and vitality of the Jewish religious experience. It prompts the Jew while recognizing that his righteousness is of no avail to God ('if he be righteous, what boon is this to Thee')[81] to consider himself responsible for the sanctification of the Divine Name and for discharging his religious obligations sustained by the faith that man's actions either strengthen or weaken the power of the Divine.[82]

It is to be expected that a religious system which views God both as a transcendent Creator as well as a God of history is bound to give rise to troublesome paradoxes which are beyond intellectual solution. But it should be borne in mind that the belief in a God of history in itself – apart from any problems posed by the concurrent postulation of a transcendent Creator – engenders its own polar tensions.

Man is charged with the responsibility for the state of the world and is bidden to bring his creative resources to bear towards the solution of the agonizing problems besetting mankind. Yet, according to Jewish doctrine, the purpose of the historic processes cannot be realized without Divine direct intervention in the redemptive process. This in a sense is the gist of the Messianic idea which according to Gershom Scholem represents an 'anti-existentialist idea'[83] inasmuch as it allegedly makes it impossible to attach any significance to actions which are performed by unredeemed individuals. If ultimately the meaning of history is completely in the hands of God who alone through supernatural intervention brings about the Redemption, then, so this distinguished authority on Jewish mysticism argues, concrete acts performed by individuals within the historic process are deprived of true value. They cannot really matter with respect to the attainment of the supernatural objective which alone confers meaning upon historic acts. But it appears that Professor Scholem's characterization of the Jewish attitude as anti-existentialist is rather one-sided. The very fact that ultimately God finds it necessary to intervene in the historic process in order to fulfill it does not only underscore the intrinsic limitations of all human endeavors, but also points to their radical importance in the cosmic scheme. Human efforts to establish justice and to promote benevolence are not senseless gestures without any hope of success. However limited their relative import may be, there is a

a. Bab. Talmud *Megillah* 29a, Jer. Talmud *Taanit* 1:1. Mekhilta de- Rabbi Ishmael, 1, 114.
81. Neilah Prayer of the Day of Atonement Liturgy.
82. Midrash Rabbah, Lamentations 1:35. See also Rabbi Hayyim of Volozin, *Nofesh Ha-Hayyim*, I, 3–4. Cf. Abraham J. Heschel, *The Prophets*, especially pp. 221–323.
83. Gershom Scholem, *Judaica*, p. 74.

divine guarantee that ultimately, with the establishment of the Kingdom of God, these ideals will prevail.

The all out resistance to the deification of man and the refusal to place upon his shoulders sole responsibility for the historic process does not within Judaism lead to the kind of quietism which so often in the history of religion has stifled all human initiative and reduced man to a puppet manipulated by the omnipotent deity. Judaism has never been characterized by 'the abandonment of self-responsibility' which for William James constituted the hallmark of the religious attitude.[84] Instead, veering forever between antithetical poles, Judaism summons man (individually as well as collectively) to uphold his dignity and worth without risking the plunge into the abyss of self-idolization which has plagued modern secular man.

---

84. William James, *The Varieties of Religious Experience*, p. 229.

CHAPTER 6

LIBERAL JUDAISM AND THE HUMAN PURPOSE

JACOB B. AGUS

I

It has long been acknowledged that religion draws its perennial vigor from two sources, existential anxiety and the moral-rational conscience.[1] While the proportion of these two components will vary in diverse faiths and at various times, we can always discern their presence in any living religion. We may take it for granted that the element of fear predominated in primitive religions; yet, as far back as historic research goes human societies were organized and structured, and in every such structure there was an effort, however feeble and naive, to coopt occult powers for the purpose of preserving the values as well as the life of society.[2] Whether this effort was carried out by means of rites which were believed to coerce the numinous powers or ceremonies which petitioned and persuaded them, it remained true that the component of social values was an inseparable part of even the most primitive faith. On the other hand, a living faith is always more than a society for the promotion of ideals or the celebration of sancta, be they ever so lofty. There is always the note of responding to an external Power. The numinous is an active force, dark and mysterious. Man is embraced and seized by it, commanded and coerced as well as loved and favored. So, religion is an act of personal surrender of self as well as of affirmation of value.

In confronting the mystery of Being, man becomes aware of his own 'creatureliness', and he then seeks solace in the negation of his assertiveness and in some form of 'rebirth'. In the awareness of his powers of judgment, ethical, esthetic and rational, man knows himself to be akin to the supreme governing power of the cosmos.[3] He then projects his values and those of his

---

1. The Greeks spoke of fear as 'the father of the gods'. Abraham asks, 'shall not the judge of all the earth do right?' (Genesis 19, 25). Immanuel Kant combined the existential stance with the voice of conscience in his famous observation that a person may not say, 'it is morally certain that there is a God', but only, '*I am* morally certain ...' (*Critique of Pure Reason*, 2nd ed., p. 856).
2. Bronislaw Malinowski, *Magic, Science and Religion*, Boston: Beacon Press, 1948, p. 68.
3. In the twenty third Psalm, the author begins on the note of dependence and trust, 'The Lord

society unto the numinous powers. He seeks to join the company of the Divine in the land of the living.[4] Without the elemental fears of danger and death there is no religion, but man lives on a sub-religious plane as long as he has not learned to attribute moral concerns to the cosmic forces that control his destiny.[5]

In the highly developed polytheistic faiths of the near Eastern world, there were already powerful thrusts toward the concept of ethical monotheism – the belief in the unity of supreme power and supreme value. In the Babylonian culture-sphere the belief in the universal sway of the laws of 'the assembly of the gods' was promoted by the contemplation and study of the stars. But this insight was marred by the astrological obsession with relentless fate. In Egypt the longing for immortality and the depth of the human soul were discovered and quickly overlaid with magical spells. In Canaan, the association of the gods with life was asserted, but this insight was diverted into sexual orgies and fertility rites. Throughout the Near Eastern world, the techniques of witchcraft and divination encumbered and smothered every attempt to rise to the high ground of a monotheistic faith.

The emergence of the Jewish faith constituted a great reform-movement in the Near-Eastern world, a movement which blended Babylonian reverence for cosmic law, Canaanite celebration of life and Egyptian awareness of the depth of the human soul into one philosophy of life that rejected determinism, sexual immorality and preoccupation with personal immortality. This achievement is not merely a fact of history, but a recurrent phenomenon in the spiritual life of the western world. Men are born pagan; they put their own needs first, seeking to manipulate the occult powers to their own advantage. They acknowledge ideals, at least within their own ethnic group, but each idea is discrete and fragile. Ethical monotheism sees all ideals as deriving from one overflowing fountain, which is also the ultimate source of power in human and cosmic affairs. Thus men are dependent for all their needs on one Power, and that Power is the validator and harmonizer of all ideals. The reading and reinterpretation of the Holy Scriptures dramatize for Jews and Christians the perennial struggle between paganism and monotheism, with the interests of a historic community being set over against its ideals, and with the diverse claims of varied ideals set against one another and against their inherent unity

is my Shepherd, I shall not want' and ends on the note of participation in a banquet, evoking the image of a prince in a King's palace.
4. Psalms 116, 9.
5. Rudolf Otto, *The Idea of the Holy*, 1923, stresses 'creature-feeling' and the sense of a 'mysterium tremendum'. In the Hebrew Bible, holiness and righteousness go together. See the nineteenth chapter of Leviticus. Also, Isaiah 5, 16.

in the experience of holiness. And within the monotheistic philosophy of life, every generation is likely to confront the tension between the manifest purposes of human life and the enveloping mystery of the Divine Being, in whose Will, human purposes are at once fulfilled and transcended.

The drive for self-transcendence is inherent in every creation of the human spirit, but it remains always short of total victory. Is not language the first distinguishing quality of mankind? Already, in man's use of language, we come to see our individual selves in the light of concepts and images that are meaningful to the society employing that language. By way of translation, meaning is conveyed from one language to another; yet, a residue of the untranslatable remains. It would seem that as the structure of one language is studied, a logical order of ideas is revealed which is universal. The logic of sentient beings cannot but lay claim to recognition as the universal Logos which determines the genesis and evolution of all existence. Still, all languages retain unique nuances, which resist all efforts at generalization. So, too, with our values of goodness, justice and harmony. We cannot affirm any human value without seeking to extend it into the universal scheme of things. But, in every historic community, a unique style of life is incorporated.

The impetus immanent in our experience of values is to transcend first the boundaries of selfhood, then of the community, then of humanity, but in the history of mankind this impetus was enchained and frustrated by the contrary tendency of celebrating the pieties and forms of the past. Each new generation had to be brought into the community by learning to revere the tradition of its elders. And it is easier by far to transmit the forms of a faith than to rekindle the living flame. Hence, while the inner impetus of the religious quest for value is dynamic and progressive, the momentum of religious forms and rites is static and even regressive. To many people, the external ritual acquires the aura of sanctity, far more than the inner intent of faith. How shall we convey to the young the need of living in a restless tension between reverence for the past and the imperative of transcending its limitations, between faith as celebration of values in society and faith as repudiation of invalid norms, between religion as a sacred heritage and holiness as an ongoing quest for an all-embracing perfection? Insofar as religion is the aspiration for the fullness of value, it is a restless, fluid phenomenon, tossed by the tides of history between ultra-conservatism and ultra-radicalism.

And this impassioned polarity is inevitably complicated by the other phase of faith, which taps the deepest springs of human nature. Man's 'ultimate concern' is after all existential as well as valuational. The worshipper asks, how do I fit into the nature of things? What is my destiny, fate or end? To become aware of these questions is to inject the personal absolute into social affairs. Total commitment is the *sine qua-non* of the existential component of faith. One cannot whithhold one's mind or conscience from the decision to put oneself completely in the service of God. All that is one's own, one's judgment, one's critical faculties, one's rational reservations, must be surrendered. The concerns of humanity and the compromises of common sense are marginal to the existential posture. In the leap of faith, there is no stopping in midpoint. 'All the nations are as naught before Him'. God is all and 'the superiority of man over the beasts is nothingness for all is vanity'. How idle and arrogant it is for the sophist to say, 'man is the measure of all things, of things that are that they are, of things that are not that they are not?' How can ephemeral man dare to pretend that he can dispose of being as he pleases? This anguished consciousness of man's frailty reduces the independent cognition of value to the vanishing point. True, the good, the true and the beautiful are rooted in the cosmic order of being, but our human limitations in perception and resolve are so momentous that we must submit without reservation to the guidance of tradition. Quite apart from the impact of the historic doctrine of 'original sin', the existential phase of religion compels the mood of one-sidedness, either the one-sidedness of activism or that of unbending conservatism. 'For my thoughts are not your thought; for high as are the heavens above the earth, so are My thoughts higher than yours'.[6]

Hence, ethical monotheism, which affirms the ultimate unity of value and being, fosters inevitably an inner tension between the tendency to project man's autonomous values unto the infinite cosmos and the feelings of limitation, even of anxiety and dread, deriving from the awareness of man's existential predicament. In Scripture, we find man asserting the dictates of his conscience as being absolute and inviolate, even against God. 'Righteous are Thou, O Lord, but judgment I shall speak with you – why is the way of the wicked prosperous?'[7] Characteristic is the posture of Abraham in his pleading for the corrupt city of Sodom. He is but 'dust and ahses'; yet, He asserts that God cannot but share his ethical imperatives – 'far be it from Thee to kill the righteous along with the wicked. Shall the Judge of the earth not do right?' The rabbinical tradition remained true to the biblical genius and continued to cherish the moral-rational polse as well as the existential one. 'If there is no wisdom, there is no fear [of God], if there is no fear [of God], there is no wisdom'.[8]

Throughout the entire course of Jewish history from Abraham to the

6. Isaiah 55, 8.
7. Jeremiah 12, 1.
8. Genesis 19, 25. Ethics of the Fathers, 3, 14.

present, this tension between being and value characterized the involutions of Jewish thought. The quest of value articulated the autonomous judgments of man, but the feelings of total dependence upon Divine power imposed severe limitations upon the human conscience and stressed the irrational and inexorable barriers to man's quest. The paradoxical feelings of holiness articulate man's awareness of his being close to God, but in the presence of God all human powers and faculties dissolve into the darkness of nothingness. Holiness is the awareness of this inner unity of the good and the beautiful and the true and the numinous; it affirms all that is peculiarly human as being also essentially divine, but somehow man's noblest ideals are absorbed, transcended and thereby also negated by the infinite majesty of the Divine Being. The Qabbalists pointed to the analogy of light coming from the sun, yet not existing as light in the sun itself.[9] Isaiah speaks of the Supreme Being as being 'sanctified through righteousness', but in his famous vision of the Lord enthroned in the Temple, he begins by asserting his own and his people's 'uncleanness' and ends by proclaiming a message that blinds and deafens man's senses, contradicting his cherished values and his faculties of judgment.[10]

II

The tension between the active assertion of ethical insights and submission to the all-pervasive Will of God is seen in the polarity between freedom and predetermination. All values belong to the domain of freedom – in the intellectual quest, freedom to search and reexamine in order to extend the horizons of knowledge; in the ethical field, freedom to choose the good, to overcome instincts and habits and to build up the vision of the good society; in the esthetic field, freedom is the mark of imaginative constructions in art and in public life which reflect the harmony, unity and peace of being.

So, the freedom of man is the basic postulate of the Hebrew Bible. God entered into a Covenant first with Adam, then with Noah, then with Abraham, then through Moses with the Israelites. A Covenant is meaningful and binding only among free parties. Indeed, the human party often failed in part at least to live up to its obligations. But since they were designed to be free, men can always 'return' and resume their part of the Covenant. In Judaism, the fall of Adam did not deprive men of choice, though without the

9. Mosheh Cordovero, *Pardes Rimonim*, 4, 4.
10. Isaiah 5, 16. Chapter 6.

blessing of Torah, it is very difficult to overcome the Evil Desire.[11]

In the Hebrew Bible, people are never 'saved' permanently; there is always the attached condition, 'if you will hearken ...'. The 'salvation-history' of the prophetic books presents a continous oscillation between the two alternatives, a good king with attendant good fortune for the people and a bad king with the inevitable, evil consequences. The Promise does not come signed, sealed and guaranteed. Even the patriarchs, we are told, were always fearful, lest they will not be found worthy in future trials.[12]

In general, Jewish theologians in ancient and medieval times stressed the doctrine of human freedom with virtual unanimity. Philo regarded freedom as the distinguishing quality of God and therefore of the Divine power in man.[13] In the Talmud, the doctrine of man being made in God's image is affirmed to be 'the great rule' of the Torah.[14] A bold talmudic master dared assert that only the first two of the Ten Commandments were spoken by God to all the Israelites – 'I am the Lord' and 'thou shalt have no other gods beside me'.[15] The first commandment identifies God as the Power that makes for freedom in history, hence also the source of freedom in the human personality; the second enjoins man from giving up the infinite quest and settling for less than this One God. Among the Jewish philosophers, Hisdai Crescas stands virtually alone in denying man's freedom, largely because he had to struggle desperately against the rationalists, who in his judgment, weakened Jewish resistance to the relentless pressure of the Christian mobs bent on the elimination of Judaism from the Spanish peninsula.[16] The Qabbalists who took the place of the philosophers in the sixteenth century considered the soul to be truly, 'a portion of God above'.[17] In modern times,

11. L. Ginzberg, *Legends of the Jews* volume V, p. 129, cites many passages maintaining that Adam was not responsible for the deaths of others. On the other hand, IV Ezra, the Apocalypse of Baruch and talmudic authorities speak of 'hereditary death', but not of 'hereditary sin'. Still, 'corruption' was injected into Eve by the serpent, according to Shabbat 146a, and only at Sinai was it removed. See B. T. Kiddushin 30b on the Torah as the 'spice' for the Evil Desire.
12. B. T. Berochot 4a.
13. Philo, *Quod Deus sit Immutabilis*, 10, 47 (Loeb Classics). 'For it is the mind alone which the Father who begat it judged worthy of freedom, and loosening the fetters of necessity, suffered it to range as it listed, and of that free-will which is His most peculiar possession and most worthy of His majesty gave it such portion as it was capable of receiving'. See H. Wolfson's *Philo* vol. I, chapter VIII.
14. Jerusalem Talmud, Nedarim. 9,4.
15. Babylonian Talmud, Makkot 24a.
16. Julius Guttmann, *Philosophies of Judaism*, transl. David W. Silverman, Holt, Rinehart and Winston, N.Y., 1964, p. 238. Jacob B. Agus, *The Evolution of Jewish Thought*, Abelard-Schuman, N.Y., 1959, p. 224.
17. Zohar on Genesis 2, 7. Moses Cordovero, *Ailima Rabbati*, 131. Sheneur Zalman, *Tanya*, 2.

the biblical concept of freedom was reinforced by the prevailing trends in the secular western world.

But the nuclear experience of religion implies an inescapable role for Divine Providence. In the Covenant itself, the two parties are not exactly equal; it is God Who commands and lays down the terms for Israel's obedience. And in the course of human evolution, it is God who works His Will. The prophets insisted that the Divine Plan was being carried out through the various vicissitudes of history. Some nations play the role of an 'axe' in the hand of God; others are onlookers, and still others are assigned the unenviable if exalted role of a Suffering Servant.[18] The apocalyptic authors left the element of free human choice almost completely out of their visions of the future. All events of the future had been foretold; the 'mystery' is known to the visionaries, the *eschaton* is already determined, and the 'elect' for salvation have been chosen from the foundation of the world.[19]

The rabbinic tradition eschewed the extremes of determinism. 'All is in the power of heaven, save the fear of heaven'.[20] The *eschaton* will come in its pre-destined time, if people generally and Israel in particular do not succeed in hastening the time of the Messiah's advent.[21] The Messiah will come in glory and with power, if the Jewish people prove deserving of this consummation; if not, He will come at the appointed time, but through incredible suffering and a series of horrendous disasters.[22]

Modern Judaism has reinterpreted the Messianic doctrine in secular terms. The Reform and Conservative movements of western Europe and America embraced the messianic hope with deep fervor as an act of faith in the continuous advance of mankind toward the goal of a redeemed universal society, when war and exploitation will cease, all the evils of life will be ocercome and all men will live together as brothers, under the Fatherhood of God. In this view, Jerusalem will be built, as Wm. Blake saw it, 'in every land'. And the biblical Promise to Israel is intended for all mankind. Israel was 'chosen', that is, called to serve as the 'first born son' in the human family; its destiny was to be a 'witness to the nations'; an example for others to follow, not a unique species, set over against the rest of humanity. The 'people of God' embraces in addition to the 'remnant of Israel' those of every faith and historic background who undertake to live as the heralds and

18. Isaiah 10, 15; 14; 12; 52, 13–53, 12.
19. IV Ezra 4, 33–44. Assumption of Moses I, 13,14.
20. Babylonian T. Berochot 33b.
21. Babylonian T. Sanhedrin 98a.
22. *Ibid.* The military successes and failures centered around the notion of a Messiah son of Joseph who will begin the task of redemption, but in spite of initial triumphs, he will die on the battlefield. Babylonian T. Sukkah 52a.

pioneers of this vision. So the Sages assert, 'Do not say thy 'sons', but thy 'builders''.[23]

The modern Zionist movement secularized the traditional messianic vision, setting as the immediate goal, the establishment of a social-cultural Jewish homeland, that would become in time a full-fledged Jewish state. Yet, the Zionist dream did not surrender the traditional hope for the universal 'kingdom of heaven'. On the contrary, its remarkable fervor was sustained by a mystical longing for the rebirth of the biblical genius for the life of faith. In the hearts of the people, realistic programs and political economic goals were fused in the fires of ancient dreams for the redemption from all evil. And the literary works of the great founders of the world-wide movement were attempts to restate in contemporary terms the visions of the biblical prophets. Moses Hess drew the outlines of the new 'Jerusalem', as a state built on the principles of Socialism; Ahad Ha'am dreamed of reviving in the land of Israel the ancient ethical genius of Moses; Theodore Herzl aspired to build a state along the lines of European liberalism, and Martin Buber evolved the vision of an ideal community, in which the 'I-Thou' relationship is attained all its perfection.[24]

With the emergence of the State of Israel, the character of the messianic hope was pushed into the forefront of discussion. Very slowly and gingerly at first, Jews began to fit the triumphant achievements of the Israeli into the pattern of the messianic vision as projected in Holy Writ and the Talmudic tradition. This trend was given additional impetus by the Six Day War of June 1967. It is now generally believed by modern Jews that the State of Israel must be considered as an integral portion of the messianic era.[25] The great universal society must embrace the redemption of peoples as well as of individuals. And of all the historic communities, the Jewish people were most in need of redemption; they were the most maligned, the most persecuted, the most envied and the most alienated. Homeless and insecure, their plight was aggravated by the fiendish myths concerning them that circulated chiefly in the Christian world, but also to some extent in the Moslem and Communist worlds. Hence, the existence of the State of Israel must be an integral part of the ideal society of the future.

23. The *midrashim* dealing with the visions of redemption were collected and edited by Yehudah Ibn Shemuel in *Midrashai Geulah*, Tel Aviv, 1954.
24. Kaufmann Kohler, *Jewish Theology*, first published in 1918. Reissued by Ktav Publishing House, 1968, pp. 389, 445.
25. Moses Hess, *Rome and Jerusalem*, translated by M. Waxman. Ahad Ha'am's essays were translated and edited by Leon Simon, Oxford, England, 1946. Theodor Herzl's works, edited by Ludwig Lewison, N.Y., 1955. Martin Buber, *Israel and Palestine*, N.Y., 1950.

However, nearly all Jewish theologians maintain that the messianic dream is not exhausted and fulfilled by the triumph of Israel. For the Orthodox, there are the goals of spiritual perfection, the rebuilding of the Temple, the Resurrection and the conversion of mankind. For the non-Orthodox theologians, the state is but an opportunity for a portion of the Jewish people to make their collective contribution to mankind. Ultimately the State cannot serve as a focus of loyalty for world Jewry without taking on the ideal lineaments of a holy society, prefiguring the universal kingdom of heaven. In the Diaspora, Jews work as individuals toward the same end; in Israel, the collective heritage of Jewish people may become the basis of the building of a 'schoolhouse' for many nations. Already, the fledgling state has provided training and technical assistance to many under-developed countries. Zionism, then, as modern religious Jews see it, is not a retreat of the Jew from the emerging great society, but an indispensable aid to the all-human perfection of the Messianic era.

Yet, it would be inaccurate to claim that a synthetic version of messianism has already been attained by modern Jews, a version that blends the vision of the Enlightenment with those of secular Zionism and the powerful myths of the orthodox tradition. For the moment, Jewish sentiment is still vacillating between the three alternative concepts. The splendid victory of the Israeli in the Six Day War, following the Arab threats of total annihilation revived the dormant dogmas of Armageddon and the medieval myths centering about the military Messiah, the son of Joseph, who is supposed to precede the spiritual Messiah, the son of David. Through the exhilarating impact of recent victories, the entire spectrum of Jewish thought was shifted toward the side of myth and mystery; Israel's uniqueness in the scheme of things, its special position in the design of Providence for 'the end of days', and the feeling that the predicted *eschaton*, in all its miraculous splendor is even now dawning.[26] So seductive is the appeal of ancient myths that even non-theists are tempted to magnify and sanctify the peculiar miracle of Israel's rebirth, with little or no reference to the universal values of humanity.

The basic issue is the character of God's revelation in history. Is it seen in the triumph of values, the potency of moral indignation, the hunger for freedom, the passion for righteousness, the longing for the good society? Or is it manifest in the salvation-history of the people of Israel, its unparalleled tragedies, its mysterious vicissitudes and its magnificient triumph? Various syntheses of these alternatives are possible, but for the present, one can only

---

26. The mood of the post-June war mentality is reflected in A. J. Heschel's *Israel, An Echo of Eternity*, where the events of the six-day *Blitzkrieg* are hailed as the miraculous fulfillment of biblical prophecy. It is published by Farrar, Straus and Giroux, N.Y., 1969.

speak of a blooming confusion of myths, a kind of psychedelic haze blurring the features of reality. Ancient visionary expectations are frequently mingled with down to earth practicalities and the residual appeal of the ideals of humanism. We must not forget that the Israeli ecstasy is not identical with the whole of Jewish experience; the vast majority of world Jewry continue to live in the Diaspora and to cherish the liberal ideals, which are in truth their breath of life.

Can we offer any prognosis as to the future of Jewish messianism? History has a way of giving an ironic twist to the realization of idealistic dreams. In modern times, the socialist version was fulfilled but also frustrated in the Soviet world, where the Communist vision of a proletarian paradise was turned into a living hell for the intellectuals and the non-conformists. The Liberal vision of the self-determination of nations, of man free and proud, living in open societies, was fulfilled in western Europe at the end of the first World War. For a brief moment it seemed as if the 'parliament of man' had become a reality in the League of Nations. That hope turned into a broken reed. The generation of Jews who had witnessed the horrors of the holocaust cannot put their trust wholeheartedly in liberalism. The Zionist vision of Jewish redemption has also been fulfilled in 1948, especially in 1967, but in circumstances which bid fair to launch another Hundred Years' War. Each of these visions retains a passionate following among Jewish people and a measure of plausibility. As to the future, we can only speculate and, in the good old-fashioned way, continue to hope.

III

The polarity between freedom and Providence in the history of Israel is also reflected in the concept of Torah, or the body of revelation for the sake of which the people of Israel were constituted.

In respect of Torah, we encounter the tension between man's free assertion of his values as a moral-rational being and the belief that the Israelites had obligated themselves to be the Lord's servants and therefore they were bound to obey His commands, no matter how arbitrary or irrational. The first was a reflection of the valuational phase of faith; the second, of its existential-mysterious character. In Kantian terminology, the first was autonomous, the second heteronomous.[27]

---

27. A ponderous and fundamentalist interpretation of the Six Day War in the light of messianic predictions of medieval and hassidic saints is presented in M. Kasher's Hebrew work, *Hatekufah Hagedolah*, Jerusalem, 1968.

Insofar as the Torah enjoins ethical principles, there is no conflict between freedom and obedience to the Law, for it is of the essence of man's free conscience to demand compliance with the moral-rational-esthetic laws of being.[28] But the Torah contains ritual and non-rational commandments. Why were these laws instituted?

Already in Scripture, we encounter the two antithetical sets of replies – the one humanist, the other supernaturalist. The Law is an expression of wisdom, or it is designed for human benefit, or it is in accord with the cosmic laws of being.[29]

On the other hand, the Law is the Will of the Master; good 'servants' know how to be properly obedient.[30]

In the Talmud, this tension is continued. We are told 'that the mizvot were given only for the purpose of 'purging' human beings through them' – that is, their ultimate purpose is the improvement of human nature. This phrase occurs in contexts where the absurdity of the Law, from a rational viewpoint, appears to be particularly manifest.[31] The import of that maxim is that even those laws that appear irrational to us are designed by Divine Wisdom for our good; in some mysterious fashion, they serve to purify and exalt the human personality.

But, we are also told that 'everything which the Holy One, blessed be He, has created, He made only for His own Glory'.[32] It is the role of the Israelites to be good servants, 'those who work for their Master without asking for any reward'.[33] Indeed, 'greater is he who serves in love than he who serves in fear', but he must serve trustingly, without asking questions. The more the requirements of the Law run counter to a person's desires, the greater is his reward. It is God's world, and humans are only workers in His vineyard. The

---

28. The contrast between these two categories of commands is already recognized in the Talmud – 'those which ought to have been written in the Torah, even if they were not written' and 'those which Satan and the nations of the world contradict' (Yoma 67b) (The phrase 'and the nations of the world' is missing in some versions). Saadia Gaon (882–942) classified the Commandments in two categories – the rational and the traditional. *The Book of Beliefs and Opinions*, translated by S. Rosenblatt, Yale University Press, 1948, p. 140.
29. That freedom contains a positive component, fidelity to the inner laws of being, was asserted in the Ethics of the Fathers, chapter 6 – 'for one is not free unless he is true to the Torah'.
30. Deuteronomy 4, 6. Isaiah 33, 6. Deuteronomy 4, 1. Amos 5, 14. Jeremiah 33, 25.
31. Isaiah 1, 3. Isaiah 42, 19. Ezekiel 20, 25.
32. Genesis Rabba, 44, 1. The context is the laws of Kosher-slaughtering – 'what difference does it make to the Holy One, blessed be He, whether the slaughtering is done from the neck or from the back? ...' Maimonides interprets this passage to mean that the Commandments are rational in their general intent, but that the details are often arbitrary. *Guide of the Perplexed* III, 26. Translated by S. Pines, University of Chicago Press, 1963.
33. Ethics of the Fathers, chapter 6.

Laws are His incomprehensible 'decrees'; it is man's duty to obey them, not to assess them in the scales of justice or compassion.[34]

The tension between these motivations is illustrated in a beautiful tale concerning the great Rabbi Yohanan ben Zakkai. When his son became sick, he asked his disciple, Hanina ben Dosa, to pray for his recovery. Hanina prayed and the young boy recovered. Yohanan's wife said to him, 'is Hanina greater than you?' – 'No', said Yohanan, 'but I am like a prince before the Lord, and he is like a servant'.[35] A prince shares in the purpose of the king; his loyalty is likely to be sophisticated and even tinged with skepticism. The servant's piety is untouched by doubts and unsullied by any hint of criticism; the servant's piety may be of a lower ontological order, but it is purer and more mystical.

Maimonides was the outstanding exponent of the moral-rational character of all the commandments. He laid it down as a general principle that no Divine commandment could possibly be either non-rational or non-moral, let alone irrational or immoral.

'The Law as a whole aims at two things: the welfare of the soul and the welfare of the body. As for the welfare of the soul, it consists in the multitude's acquiring correct opinions corresponding to their respective capacity. Therefore, some of them [namely, the opinions] are set forth explicitly ... and some of them are set forth in parables ...'.[36] Maimonides' view was opposed by traditionalists, who maintained that the Torah reflects God's Will, which is far beyond man's power to comprehend. The Qabbalists developed a complex theosophy, which related the performance of the Commandments to certain metaphysical processes that transpired in the numinous substance of the universe. Even man's prayer is not a function of his needs or an expression of his spiritual longing, but an act of participation in the work of redemption. Prayer is 'the food of the worlds'.[37]

Conservative and Reform Judaism are developments of the rationalist stream in Jewish theology. The non-rational laws are either abolished completely, as in Reform, or they are modified to suit contemporary ideals, as in Conservative Judaism. Thw laws are made for man, to enhance his life.

34. Ethics of the Fathers, I, 3.
35. Babylonian T. Sotah 31a. Babylonian T. Berochot 33b. 'Whoever mentions, 'Thy mercies extend to the nest of a bird' is silenced ... because He interprets the Divine laws as expressions of Mercy whereas they are only decrees'. Maimonides frankly repudiates this opinion. *Guide of the Perplexed* III, 48. The Jerusalem Talmud, Berochot 5, 3. interprets this passage in an ethical sens – God's Mercy is infinite, hence, any one instance of His concern is restrictive and therefore misleading.
36. Babylonian T. Berochot 34b.
37. *Guide of the Perplexed* III, 27.

Holiness is interpreted, not as a non-rational encounter with the Divine Being, but as the climactic unity of all the forms of man's outreaching – his quest for truth, goodness, harmony and being.[38]

What are the rewards of the Law? Are they other-worldly and transhuman? Or are they conceived in terms of man's life here on earth?

In Scripture, there are hardly any references to immortality and the resurrection. The nearness of God here on earth was felt so powerfully that the hope of immortality was shunted to the periphery of consciousness. Or it may be that the feeling of being in God's company here on earth was simply projected into the darkness of the hereafter as a virtual certainty. This is the way the medieval philosopher, Judah Halevi, interpreted the relative absence of references in the Hebrew Bible to the rewards of paradise and the penalties of hell.[39]

Halevi's conception of the good life was therefore thoroughly humanist in character, but in his view the ideal man was always aware of being in the presence of the Supreme Being and His angels. The man of piety was characterized by the confluence of three currents of feeling toward the Divine – fear and love and joy. And this complex of feelings *vis à vis* the numinous betokened at once man's fulfillment in joy, his awareness of finitude in fear and his clinging to the Divine in love.[40]

Maimonides' view of the consequences of the good life was also largely humanistic. The purpose of the ideal society was to produce saintly philosophers, who would be lovers of truth and habitudes of metaphysical contemplation. These elite sages would enjoy the nearness of God and the reality of His Providence here on earth. Their mind is likely to unite with Active Reason and thereby to attain immortality. Yet, these elite must not withdraw from the community. On the contrary, the distinctive mark of their piety is precisely an ardent concern for the community as a whole. If they are truly near to God, then they will engage in acts of kindness, righteousness and generosity, for their innermost desires will correspond to the Will of God for men here on earth.[41]

In his philosophical works, Maimonides does not even mention the horrors

38. 'The Physical performance of a *mizvah* creates a subtle spiritual effect, which ascends to the upper realms, till the foundation of the Throne ...' Moses Cordovero. *Shiur Komah*, 18.
    'The essence of prayer is to draw blessing and grace to the world ...' Moses Cordovero, *Pardes Rimonim*, 31,6. On the concept of prayer as a means of uniting the Sefirot, as food unites body and soul, see 'Nefesh Ha hayim' by Hayim Volozhim (ed.), N.Y. *Gate* II, ch. 6.
39. J. B. Agus, *Guideposts in Modern Judaism* Part One, chapters 3 & 4. Part Two, Section 3. N.Y.: Bloch Publ. Co, 1954.
40. Judah Halevi, *The Kuzari*, III, 20.
41. *Ibid.* III, 11.

of hell. His opponents championed the hopes and fears of popular piety, which derived from a simplistic reading of the literature of Talmud and Midrash. The anti-Maimonideans firmly believed in the trans-worldly rewards of paradise and the World to Come, which were virtually reserved for the Israelites and those who joined them. The purpose of life in this vale of tears was to earn these unearthly rewards and the danger of our brief span of existence was to fall into the clutches of sin and 'the other side'. The mark of true piety is contempt for the pleasures of this world and the awareness of the nothingness of all that life has to offer.[42]

Again, Conservative and Reform Judaism continue the trend of thought of classical philosophic piety. The dark shadows of the supernaturalist imagination are totally banished from contemporary thought. The doctrine of immortality is affirmed by the exponents of classical Jewish theology, such as this writer, but only in the Maimonidean sense. Some theologians have rejected this doctrine altogether. In their view, God is simply the name for the beneficient immanent forces in life or for the totality of potentialities in existence. A few would altogether eliminate all references to God from the liturgy.

The main body of the Orthodox adhere to the time-honored conceptions of popular Judaism, with some contingents of the modern Orthodox approaching hesitantly and cautiously the position of the Conservative and the Reform.

IV

The basic polarity between humanism and the trans-rational Divine fiat is perhaps best exemplified in the tensions within the concept of Israel. We have mentioned that Israel was conceived as 'the people of Torah'. Talmudic legend had it that the Torah was offered to every nation, but the Israelites were the only people that agreed to abide by its precepts.[43] The 'chosenness' of Israel was therefore predicated on its loyalty to the Torah. For this reason, the formula of the Synagogue service states, 'Who has chosen us from among all the nations and has given us the Torah'.

The concept of a 'people of Torah' is essentially humanistic, for it does not necessarily lay claim to the exclusive title, '*the* people of God'. On the contrary, it may well assume that God had inspired many other *Torot*, having

---

42. *Guide of the Perplexed*, III, 54.
43. On the anti-maimonidean trend and its consequences see Yitzhak Baer, *A History of the Jews in Christian Spain*, Philadelphia, 1961, pp. 234–306.

sent prophets to other nations even as he sent Moses and his successors to Israel.[44] The Talmud assumes a covenant with humanity, 'the children of Noah', that remained valid for all men, even after the Torah was accepted at Sinai.[45] This concept paralleled in rabbinic circles, the grand evolution of 'ius gentium' and 'natural law' by the contemporary Roman jurists. Furthermore, by means of the study and practice of this universal core of religion and ethics, a non-Jew could attain a state of holiness superior to that of the High-priest.[46] The term, 'people of God', in this view, transcends the boundaries of the Jewish community. 'The pious of all the nations share in the World to Come';[47] Gentiles need not convert to Judaism in order to serve the One God; they may employ their diverse historical faiths as so many vehicles of spiritual advancement, 'walking each in the name of its god'.[48] At the beginning of the fanatical fifteenth century, a Jewish philosopher maintained that several *Torot* could be ordained by the God of history for different peoples.[49] In the famous parable which sums up his entire philosophy, Maimonides maintains that philosopher-saints, regardless of their birth and ritual practice, come closer to God than those who are totally preoccupied with Talmudic lore.[50]

In opposition to this concept of Israel's 'chosenness', we encounter abundant expressions of what might be called 'sacred ethnicism' – that is, the belief that the people of Israel were endowed by birth with a unique and holy endowment.[51] In part, this conviction was due to the impassioned affirmation of man's powerlessness and God's implacable Will. So, Ezekiel chastises the elders of Israel who play with the notion of giving up their Israelite identity.

'What is in your mind shall never happen – the thought, 'Let us be like the nations, like the tribes of the countries, and worship wood and stone''. 'As I live, says the Lord God, surely with a mighty hand and an outstretched arem, and with wrath poured out, I will be King over you'.[52]

44. Babylonian T. Baba Kama 38a. Aboda Zara 2b. L. Ginzberg, *Legends of the Jews*, volume VI, p. 31, interprets this legend as implying that the nations were not *morally* ready for the Torah, since the general principles of religion and ethics are logically prior to the Torah-rites.
45. Numbers Rabbah 14, 34.
46. Babylonian T. Sanhedrin 56a.
47. Babylonian T. Yebamot 61a. See Tossafot ad loc.
48. Tosefta, Sanhedrin, 13.
49. Micah 4, 5.
50. Joseph Albo, *Sefer Haikkarim*, III, 13, translated by I. Husik, as the *Book of Principles* and published by The Jewish Publication Society, Phila.
51. *Guide of the Perplexed*, III, 51.
52. The Apocalyptic writers expressed this view emphatically. Note IV Ezra, 6, 55 – 'that for our sakes Thou hast created this world. But as for the other nations, which are descended from Adam, Thou hast said that they are nothing, and that they are like spittle ...' The

In part, however, the axiom of Israel's inescapable destiny was attributed to certain inborn qualities of the Jewish soul. The famed poet and philosopher Judah Halevi is particularly noted for his emphasis on the biological superiority of the Jewish people, insofar as things divine are concerned. Halevi regarded the Jewish people as a unique genus, standing between humanity and the angels. Yet, he did not claim for himself and his own generation so exalted a status, for Jews attain their full potential as a prophetic people only in the land of Israel and only when they are true to the life of Torah. Halevian romantic ethnicism was compounded in the Qabbalistic stream of thought, which was popularized by the Hassidic movement. In some forms of modern Zionism, the impetus of religious ethnicism continues to be felt. The national soul is still regarded as a quasi-biological quality, which is due to attain perfection in its own historic land, but that nature of this quality is now described in psychological or ethical terms. And the mystical feeling of uniqueness persists.[53]

Again, Conservative, Reform and some Neo-Orthodox Jews developed the concept of Israel along humanistic lines. Moses Mendelsohn was particularly effective in drawing the line of distinction between Israel as 'the people of Torah' and 'the people of God', which consists of all men of goodness and piety.[54] While some Reform rabbis followed Geiger in assuming a Jewish 'genius' for religion, the dominant trend of thought down to the first third of the Twentieth Century was definitely humanistic.[55]

The trauma of the holocaust caused some Jewish theologians to revert to Halevian ethnicism, because it is so congenial to the 'gut-thinking' of existentialism and the popular mood of militancy.

The question, 'what is a Jew?' which bobs up again and again in the turbulent society of Israel, is a reflection of this inner struggle between humanism and the ancient claim of Israel as a unique species of mankind – 'lo, a people dwelling alone, and not reckoning itself among the nations'.[56]

author speaks of Israel as 'only begotten', instead of 'the first born'.
53. Ezekiel 20; 32, 33.
54. Halevi's ethnicism was expanded and deepened in the Qabbalistic and Hassidic literature. See J. B. Agus, *The Evolution of Jewish Thought*, the chapters on Qabbalah and Hassidism. This ethnicistic interpretation of the difference between the Jews and the rest of humanity permeated the thought of East European Jewry, where the social and cultural isolation of the Jewish community was nearly total. Ahad Ha'am, the philosopher of 'cultural zionism' elaborated the import of a Jewish national soul that expressed itself in the quest of absolute justice. In his view, the Hebrew prophets expounded this ideal' however in the tragic years of exile, the ethical ideal was clothed in the harsh rituals of religion. In the new Zion, the old spirit will be revived.
55. Moses Mendelssoh, *Jerusalem*.
56. Kaufmann Kohler, *Jewish Theology*.

V

In sum, the tension between humanism and the Will of transcendent Deity has been embraced in biblical monotheism at its inception. This tension generated that remarkable pattern of piety and that all-embracing vision of the course of history that has made the Holy Bible the living focus and perennial text of western civilization. This tension has reached an unprecedented level of intensity in modern Judaism, ever since the Jews of the West were confronted with the stirring ideologies of the Nineteenth and Twentieth centuries. Should they resolve the tension by choosing to abandon ethnic insularity in an emerging, open liberal society? Should they identify their cause with that of the proletariat and join in building a socialist state, free from all 'capitalistic contradictions?' Should they proceed to build their own state, as a 'haven of refuge' for their persecuted brethren and as a beacon of light to all men? In the past generation, all three ideals were partly realized and partly transmuted. And the polar tensions are more severe than ever before. Each of the central concepts of Judaism – man's freedom and God's Will in history, Torah, the 'people of God' – manifest the dialectical consequences of this tension. The Nazi holocaust and the emergence of the state of Israel brought the tension within Judaism to the forefront of the international arena. If the lines of historical continuity offer any guidance for the extrapolation of future developments, we may assert that we shall not see a resolution of these tensions in the predictable future.

The tension between existentialism and humanism in the long history of Judaism is of universal significance. We note that in the creative periods of the Jewish faith – the prophetic period, the early rabbinic age, the Spanish efflorescence, the modern period – this tension was reasserted. The unity of Judaism was not shattered, but its inner turbulence gave rise to a dynamic diversity of beliefs and sentiments. In view of the central place of the Jewish faith in the grand evolution of western thought, may we not conclude that its impassioned affirmation of the unity of being and value, existentialism and humanism, corresponds to a basic quest that is inherent in the nature of the human personality? Man's dichotomy is real, but so is the aspiration for inner harmony and peace. To be human is to be aware of one's own deeper self and at the same time to be anxious over one's place in the realm of being and concerned with the claims upon him of his society. Man was designed to be tri-dimensional, relating himself to the depth of being, to the vertical dimension of values and to the horizontal dimension of his fellowmen.

In our contemporary world, the direction and focus of both forms of the human outreach have been put into question. God, the goal of man's ontic quest, is regarded by many analytical philosophers as a meaningless term. Already, Philo and a long line of medieval mystics have concurred in the proposition that 'God in Himself' was 'unknowable', hence that any proposition concerning Him was 'meaningless'. But, the theologians were concerned with the aspects of God's Being that enter into human exprience, or more simply with the image of God in man. Ultimately, the very concept of God is derived from two axioms – the unity of the cosmos and the unity of the self. But, neither the cosmos nor the self may now be treated safely as unities. In the present state of our knowledge, we cannot form a concept of the cosmos as a whole. At the very time, when we are engated in the so called 'conquest of space', we realize more and more keenly that 'there are more things in heaven and earth than are dreamt of in our philosophies'. Every day brings fresh discoveries which seem to burst through the boundaries established by earlier axioms. And the concept of personality has not yet recovered from the fragmentizing assaults of the Freudians, the behaviorists and the Marxists.

For many people, the unifying philosophy of ethical monotheism is now shattered. Some revert to primitivism, some to the nihilism of the Sophists. Babylonian fatalism reappears in the guise of scientism, Egyptian myth and magic in the quest of new and bizarre cults, and Canaanite worship of life and sex in the age old forms of 'sacred' prostitution.

Yet, the quest for self-transcendence cannot be permanently suspended. The existentialist movement of the past quarter-century was far more than a rebellion of philosophers against the abstractions of rationalists. Actually, it amounted to a reassertion of the individual's right and duty to build his view of the world on the promptings of his own deepest nature. If man cannot comprehend all of being in rational terms, he contains the mystery of being within himself. Hence, his right to evolve his own world, constructing a realm of meaning out of the inner rhythms of his sheer existence.

Existentialism has now become the living philosophy of our radical youth. Far stronger in their criticism of our so called 'sick society' than in their vision of what is to take its place, they reflect by their very naivete and irrationality the longing for cosmic meaning and human values. They sense the 'corruption' of all politicians, but they imagine that somehow they themselves could be incorruptible philosopher-kings. Their posture, for all its negativism and self-indulgence, is an articulation, however confused, of the religious quest of man, in one of its directions: that of depth. While in the past, the existentialist trend transcended the human values of their contemporaries in the Name of the Divine Will, the same impulse now leads to an unfocused, unscrutinized, utterly diffuse posture of love in general, freedom in general and faith in general. Without faith in God, this posture is devoid of self-criticism in the light of universal values and a rational grasp of reality.

Furthermore, the existential stance is balanced in a healthy faith by the outreach of the individual toward a structured society-hence, one governed by law, which is 'reason in action'. So, Judaism was long known as the religion of 'law and the prophets'. In Christianity, Roman law and stoic philosophy were preempted in order to provide a durable base for the ethic of love.

On the other hand, the quest for participation in an enduring society is sterile and reactionary if it is not balanced by the dimensions of depth and divinity. In that case the existing pattern of life tends to be sacralized and absolutized. In our day, we have become particularly aware of the inanities of 'natural law' and the theory of the 'just war'. Also, our youth today have been denied that fig-leaf of rationality that Marxist ideology provided for an earlier generation. Who can believe now in any utopian plan, any systematic ideology, any technocratic vision of static perfection?

But, while our social outreach in itself cannot afford security, it can complement and balance the romantic bias of our existential impetus, be it religious or atheistic. In all phases of life, as in art, the Nietzschean insight holds true – the Dyonisiac outburst of the primal energies of life and love must be molded, transmuted and guided by the Apollonian ideal of form and structure.

The humanist and existential impulses must be seen, as they indeed are, partial and fragmentary expressions of our being, in its quest of the unknown. And when we acclaim the Unknown as God, we acknowledge the inadequacy and sinfulness of all our efforts at self-transcendence. This acknowledgement is indispensable for the maintenance of an attitude of receptivity to change. Since no static synthesis is possible, we have to be alert to the voices of criticism and sensitive to fresh visions of the Good. The age-old Jewish affirmation of the unity of God reflects the indomitable quest of the human self for the unity of the several ways whereby it reaches out to reality. Like Socrates and the Hebrew prophets, we must assert that an unexamined life is not worth living, admit that we don't know the ultimates, while at the same time continuing our quest of the Hidden God, through reflection on the external universe and on our own inner self, and through building His Will ever more truly into the patterns of our life.

CHAPTER 7

HUMAN PURPOSIVENESS IN ST. THOMAS AQUINAS

FRANCIS J. KOVACH

I

There are various ways of treating the question of human purposiveness. St. Thomas Aquinas treats this question in terms of the ultimate end of man, and he does so both as a philosopher and as a theologian. This is to say that St. Thomas has a philosophical as well as a theological theory of man's ultimate end. Of these two, the philosophical theory is logically prior to the other since it serves as the speculative basis for the theological treatment, whereas the theological theory is much more elaborate and offers Aquinas' final answer to the question of human purposiveness.

For this reason it is understandable that Thomas' theological theory of man's ultimate end has been discussed much more frequently and extensively, and is much better known than his strictly philosophical theory of man's natural ultimate end. In this essay an attempt will be made to outline Aquinas' philosophical views on man's natural end as his relatively ultimate end in three steps. First the logical foundations of this philosophical theory within his philosophical system will be sketched; next, the theory itself will be considered; and finally it will be shown briefly how this philosophical theory is complemented by St. Thomas' theological theory of beatific vision as man's supernatural or absolutely ultimate end.

II

A. The philosophic foundations

1. The most fundamental doctrine on which Aquinas the philosopher builds his theory of man's natural end is the metaphysical doctrine of existence and essence in respect to God and the creature.

God, St. Thomas holds, is a being in which essence and existence are really identical, whereas in every other being the two are really distinct principles. This is to say that it is God's essence to exist or, that God exists essentially, in virtue of His essence, since His essence is existence; whereas every other being exists by participation, i.e., in virtue of God as its cause. More specifically, God is the exemplary, efficient, and the final cause of all other beings. God is the universal exemplary cause in the sense that He eternally conceives in His intellect the idea of every finite species as a mode of His own essence which is existence.[1] God is the universal efficient cause in so far as He gives existence to every being other than Himself. Since doing so precludes the use of any pre-existent material out of which the finite being could be made, God as the efficient cause of all finite beings is God the Creator, in Whom all creatures participate.[2] God is the universal final cause inasmuch as every creature naturally desires and tends toward God as its ultimate purpose or end. Since this doctrine is the generic theory of which Aquinas' theory of man's natural end is a logical continuation and an ethical specification, we must consider the reasons and some details of this doctrine.

2. As to the reasons for holding God's universal final causality, Aquinas argues first that the God-created world must have a purpose for three reasons. One is that every free agent necessarily acts for an end which serves as the principle of the agent's operative intellect. Another is that God, the most perfect agent, does everything in the most perfect manner, and that includes purposiveness. The third is that, since natural things have an end, so must, only even more so, the totality of the God-created world.[3] Next, Aquinas demonstrates with several arguments that this end of all creatures is God Himself. The principal argument is this. God, as already shown, acts for a purpose, and this purpose cannot be anything external to Him and to be attained by Him since only the imperfect agent acts for an external end to be attained. But the end of the agent is also the end of the work of that agent because of the dependence of the work upon its maker.[4] The formal aspect that makes God the universal final cause of creation, St. Thomas goes on reasoning, is His goodness mainly because it is the good that has the character of an end or purpose in which the appetite terminates; and also because what God, the perfect agent, wills for Himself is His own perfection to be communicated to the creatures, and His perfection is His goodness.[5] A

---

1. *Summa theologiae* (henceforth: *S.th.*) I, 3, 8, ad 1; 15, 1, ad 2, 3; *De veritate* 3, 2.
2. *S.th.* I, 44, 1; 45, 5; ;65, 1; *Summa contra gentiles* (henceforth: *S.c.g.*) II, 15; *Compendium theologiae* (henceforth: *Comp.*) cc. 68, 103.
3. *Comp.*, c. 100, R. A. Verardo (Ed.), (*Opuscula theologica*, Taurini: Marietti, 1954) nn. 191-193.
4. For this and other arguments see *S.th.* I, 44, 4; *Comp.* c. 109, n. 218; *S.c.g.* III, 17 (Pera (ed.), Taurini: Marietti, 1961) n. 1995; *S.th.* I, 103, 2.
5. *S.c.g.* III, 16, 1986; 17, 1995; *S.th.* I, 5, 4; 44, 4c; *Comp.* c. 101, n. 194. For additional

logically distinct second perfection for which God is the end of creation is His beauty, like goodness, is per se desirable and lovable.[6]

To the question of precisely how God, for His goodness and beauty, is the universal end of the entire creation, St. Thomas gives a detailed reply. Just as God wills His own perfection, so does every creature tend to achieve or preserve its own specific perfection. But the finite perfection of every kind of creature is a similitude of God's own infinite perfection. Therefore, by tending toward its own specific perfection, every creature tends to become similar to God and, thereby, tends toward God Himself, the eternal model or exemplar of all creation.[7] Now, this tendency of the creature toward its own perfection has two components: an existential-entitative, comprised of the existence and essence of the creature; and an operative-accidental, consisting of the accidental perfections achieved through the operations of the specific powers of the creature. The reason for this twofoldness is the fact that every creature from the first moment of its existence on is already in the possession of the fundamental perfection of existence, which is God's very essence, and also of its own essence, which is the particular mode of its own act of existing, whereas the operative perfection is something which can be attained only gradually. As to the existential and entitative perfection, the natural tendency of the creature is to retain these perfections; as to the operative perfection, the creature's natural tendency is to attain it. By the former, the creature tends to keep its initial metaphysical similarity to God; by the latter, it tends to increase in degree this similarity to God.[8]

3. Besides the metaphysical and cosmological foundations of Aquinas' philosophic theory of man's ultimate end, there are some psychological doctrines logically preparing and leading up to the theory in question. The most basic of these doctrines is the notion of man as a rational animal with two specific or unique powers, the rational intellect and the free will.[9] The proper object of the former is being as intelligible or, simply, truth; the proper object of the latter is goodness in general.[10] While these two specific human

arguments see *S.c.g.* III, 16, 1987; 17, 1990-1992, 1994; *S.th.* I, 103, 2; *Comp.* c. 101, n. 195.
6. (a) *S.th.* I, 5, 4, ad 1; I-II, 27, 1, ad 3; (b) *De divinis nominibus*, 4, 5 (C. Pera (Ed.) Taurini: Marietti, 1950) n. 353; 4, 8, 382, 390 f.; (c) *I. Sent.* 31, 2, 1, ad 4; *De div.nom.* 4, 10, 441; *De ver.* 22, 1, ad 12.
7. *Comp.* p. 2, c. 9, n. 574; *S.th.* I, 44, 4; *De ver.* 21, 5; *S.c.g.* III, 18, 2000-2002. For another argument see *S.c.g.* III, 19, 2004-2007.
8. *S.c.g.* III, 20, 201 5 f.; 21; *S.th.* I, 103, 4; *De ver.* 22, 1, ad 2, 3, 4; *Comp.* c. 103, n. 202; 109, n. 217; *I. Eth.* 10 (R. M. Spiazzi (Ed.), Taurini: Marietti, 1964) n. 119. Cf. *Comp.* c. 68, n. 116; 103, n. 202; and *S.th.* I, 65, 2.
9. *S.th.* I, 77, 4 and 7; *De anima*, a. 13, ad 10.

faculties differ in their proper objects, the two have this in common: each one, as any and every natural power, has a natural tendency toward its proper object. Thus, the intellect tends to know; the will desires the good. To understand properly this seemingly simple Thomitic doctrine, one must know what Aquinas means by natural tendency or appetite both in general and in regard to the human will, and also the relation of the above-mentioned natural desire of the intellect and the will.

Appetite can be taken in the broad, strict, and strictest sense. In the broad sense, it is the God-implanted, innate and necessary inclination of any natural being or any natural potency in any natural being, be it vegetative, sensory, or rational, to its own act or proper object which gives it fulfillment. In the stricter sense, it is a natural power or potency of the animal, the brute and human will, desiring the apprehended good. In the strictest sense, it is the human will tending toward the good rationally known.[11] In regard to the human will, natural appetite or desire means the necessary inclination as the initial and imperfect act of man's rational will to the good in general once it is rationally apprehended. As such, it stands halfway between the will as a mere potency and all the subsequent 'voluntary' acts or operations of the will, such as intention, choice, and joy, which flow either freely or necessarily from it as from their potency and principle.[12] While, then, man is not free in desiring good in general, he remains free in regard to every particular good because, by his reason, he can find some defect in every particular good;[13] hence the possibility of choice, the *par excellence* free act of the will. Thus, paradoxically enough, the principle of human freedom lies in necessity – the natural necessity of the will's desire for the good in general, so that we are not the masters of our acts of tending toward our end, although we are the masters of our acts choosing the means to that end.[14]

This realization does not only show that the principal or most noble act of the will is its natural desire, concerned with the end, instead of choice, concerned only with means,[15] but also the true relation between the intellect and the will. Since desire, the principal act of the will, is elicited only at the

10. (a) *S.th.* I, 5, 2; ;16, 2; 57, 1, ad 2; 58, 3; *III. De an.* 11 (A. M. Pirotta (Ed.), Taurini: Marietti, 1959) n. 762; *De ver.* 1, 9; (b) *De ver.* 22, 1c, ad 8; *S.th.* I, 20, 2; 79, 2; ;16, 1 and 3; etc.
11. (a) *S.th.* I, 78, 1, ad 3; 80, 1c, ad 3; *De ver.* 22, 3 ad 2; (b) *S.th.* I, 80, 2c, ad 1, 2; 80, 1, ad 2; *De ver.* 22, 4c, ad 1; 25, 1.
12. Cf. (a) *De ver.* 24, 1c; *S.th.* I-II, 10, 1, ad 2; 6, 4; *De potentia*, 4, 1, ad 2 *in contrarium; Comp.* p. 2, c. 1; and (b) *S.th.* I-II, 6, 1; 6, 2; 10, 1, ad 1.
13. *S.th.* I-I, 13, 6; *De ver.* 22, 6.
14. *De ver.* 22, 6; *S.th.* I, 82, 1, ad 3.
15. *De ver.* 23, 4.

moment when reason recognizes something as good, and since choice, *the* free act of the will, is impossible unless one knows by reason aspects of goodness and evilness in the particular good,[16] the human intellect is, at least operatively, superior to the will, being per se the proximate cause of its necessary and free acts. This is Aquinas' famous doctrine concerning the primacy of the intellect over the will, whereby he broke with the Augustinian tradition. St. Thomas' main reasons for this primacy rest, however, on the entitative superiority of the proper object of the intellect. For, the acts of the intellect are essentially rational; the operations of the will are rational only by participation. Besides, the proper object of the intellect is simpler or more absolute than that of the will, although he concedes that there are both entitative and operative respects in which the will is superior to the intellect.[17]

With all these metaphysical, cosmological, and psychological foundations in mind we can turn now directly to St. Thomas' philosophical theory of human purposiveness.

B. *The ethical theory of human purposiveness*

The first thing to know about Aquinas' position on human purposiveness, which means the theory of man's ultimate end, is that it is an integral part both of his philosophy and his theology. The reasons for this dualty are as follows. St. Thomas distinguished between imperfect happiness as man's 'proximate' or relatively ultimate end and perfect happiness as man's 'ultimate' or absolutely ultimate end.[18] Of these two, he considered the former to be attainable, at least imperfectly or in some manner in this life, and by natural means; the latter, to be attainable only in after-life, and only supernaturally.[19] This means that the absolutely ultimate end to be attained in after-life and *in the natural order* is, to St. Thomas' theologically oriented mind, at best a mere possibility or a conceivable alternative but not a genuine philosophic question since, as a matter of historical fact, God has elevated man through grace to the supernatural order and, consequently, there is

---

16. (a) *S.th.* I, 82, 4, ad 3; (b) *De ver.* 22, 15; *S.th.* I, 83, 3.
17. (a) *S.c.g.* III, 26, 2078; *S.th.* I, 82, 2; 4, ad 1; *I. Met.* 1, 2; (b) *S.th.* I, 82, 3; 4c, ad 1; I-II, 9, 1; *De ver.* 22, 1c, ad 5 and ad 1 *in contr.*; 12; 22, 13c, ad 2.
18. Imperfect vs. perfect happiness: *S.th.* I-II, 3, 3c and ad 2; 3, 7c; 4, 5c; 5, 3c and ad 2; 5, 5c and ad 3; 5, 6c; *I. Eth.* 10, 129. Proximate vs. ultimate end: *S.th.* I, 75, 7, ad 1; I-II, 4, 4c; 5, 6, ad 1; *III Eth.* 15, 549.
19. *S.th.* I, 62, 1; I-II, 5, 3; 5, 5; 5, 6 and ad 1; *I. Eth.* 10, 129; *S.c.g.* III, 26, 2282 f.; III, 52; *In Beoth. de Trinitate* 6, 4, ad 5; *De virtutibus in consummi*, a. 10.

merely the question of whether one will or will not attain in *after-life* the *supernatural* ultimate end of man.

The philosophical treatment St. Thomas gives the question of man's ultimate end logically begins with the notion and division of end; thus, so must this sketch of Thomas' ethical theory.

1. End, purpose, or final cause is that for the sake of which something is, or is done or made. Thus, it is the end either of the existence of a being or of the operation of an agent. Now, the end of any being or activity can be divided into proximate and remote;[20] and the remote into intermediate and ultimate end[21] so that proximate and ultimate end are two contrary opposites. Proximate end can also be taken in the broad sense so as to include both proximate and intermediate end, and to be opposed only to ultimate end.[22] Ultimate end, on the other hand, can be divided into relatively and absolutely ultimate end, where the former means the last end in a given area of human activities, like the art of medicine or military operations, and the latter signifies the last end with respect to all the activities of individuals in a given species.[23] Another meaning of absolutely and relatively ultimate end is this. Absolutely ultimate end is the good for the sake of which an agent of a species, like man, does everything it ever does; relatively ultimate end is the attainment or possession of the good constituting the absolutely ultimate end.[24] A third interpretation of relatively and absolutely ultimate end has reference only to man. The former means man's natural ultimate end; the latter, man's supernatural ultimate end.[25] All these divisions already indicate a certain hierarchy among the ends according to perfection. For a good may be sought only for the sake of something else; or both for itself and for the sake of something else; or else only for itself and never for the sake of anything else. The first kind of good, being a useful good, is a sheer means; the second kind, both a means and an end; the third kind, only an end. Applying this hierarchy to the original division of ends listed above, it is clear that what is a mere means is a proximate end; what is both a means and an end is some sort of remote end, viz., an intermediate end; whereas what is only an end and never a means, is the ultimate end.[26]

20. *S.th.* I-II, 1, 3, ad 3; cf. *S.th.* I, 65, 2, ad 2; 75, 7, ad 1.
21. *S.th.* I-II, 12, 2; *Comp.* c. 148, n. 296.
22. *III. Eth.*, 15, 549; *IV. Sent.* 3, 1, 2, ad 3; *S.th.* I-II, 21, 1, ad 2; 60, 1, 3a and ad 3; *De ver.* 23, 1, ad 3.
23. *S.th.* I-II, 16, 3. Cf. *S.th.* I-II, 11, 3; *I. Eth.* 9, 104f.
24. *S.th.* I-II, 3, 1, 16, 3; I, 26, 3.
25. E.g. *De virt. in communi*, a. 10, ad 1; cf. *ibid.*, corpus and *S.th.* I, 62, 1. Presently, we are concerned only with the former.
26. *I. Eth.* 9, 109 f.

This conclusion partly answers the question concerning the requirements of ultimate end in general. Since the proximate end is sought only as a means to some higher end, and since the intermediate ends, together with the proximate end, the ultimate end is obviously the highest good or the most perfect for the sake of which every other good is striven for, whereas it itself is never sought for anything else.[27] The first requirement or characteristic of ultimate end is thereby to be an absolute or highest perfection above or beyond which there is no further or greater good to be sought or found. The second requirement or characteristic of ultimate end directly flows from the first. The ultimate end, being the most perfect or highest good, is such that it is incapable of being increased through another good and, at the same time, has everything which the individual beings whose ultimate end it is can ever need or desire. This in turn implies that the ultimate end must be a good that can be attained by almost all or all individuals of a given species; like all or almost all men.[28] In brief, then, the ultimate end is that which is an absolute and self-sufficient good, attainable by all.

2. The next task is to identify man's ultimate end in terms of the good that is absolute and self-sufficient. St. Thomas readily gives us his answer on empirical grounds. Man's ultimate end, he declares, is happiness because, as commonly known from experience, it is happiness for which everybody strives in all his activities throughout his life, and strives so with necessity, being unable to will the opposite,[29] and without ever striving toward happiness as a means to something else, whereas whatever else man ever desires or wills he does so for the sake of his happiness. As such, happiness is the only end that fulfills the first requirements of the ultimate end.[30]

What, then, is happiness? Some may think that happiness as the ultimate end of man lies solely in delight, which is another way of saying that happiness means only the delightful repose of the will in the attained good but not the good itself which brings about this repose, or that happiness has no generic sense that includes both the supreme good as the object or cause of happiness and the enjoyment of the possession of that good. Others may even hold that happiness consists in corporeal pleasures. But, to Aquinas' mind, both of these views are wrong. As a matter of fact, St. Thomas never tires of heaping argument upon argument to prove both versions of the hedonistic position to be gravely erroneous. Should one insist, for instance, that suprasensory

---

27. *I. Eth.* 9, 111.
28. *I. Eth.* 9, 115; 14, 170; 9, 112.
29. *S.th.* I-II, q. 1, preamble; *De ver.* 23, 4; 24, 7, 6a and ad 6; *S.c.g.* III, 20, 2009-13; *Comp.* c. 109, n. 218.
30. *S.c.g.* III, 20, 2015-16; *I. Eth.* 9, 111-112, 116; *X. Eth.* 10, 2097.

delight must be the object of man's ultimate end because it is the ultimate perfection of operation, and because it is never desired for the sake of something else but always for its own sake, which is the characteristic of the ultimate end, Thomas gives the following reply. The first of these three reasons does not hold up. For delight is for the sake of operation (as beauty is for the sake of the youth), and not vice versa.[31] This can be seen from the additional facts that the goodness or desirableness of a delight depends on the goodness or desirableness of the operation to which delight is concomitant; and that in the order of natural things, too, delight serves and promotes the operation (e.g., sexual pleasure, the act of preserving the species).[32] But that which is a means is certainly not the ultimate end. The second listed reason, Thomas goes on arguing, that people seek delight for its own sake does not prove that delight is their ultimate end either. For one must distinguish between the supreme good whose attainment causes perfect delight, and the delight itself concomitant to the attainment of the good. Since the former of these two is naturally prior to the latter, whereas the latter depends on the former, the supreme good is willed first and essentially, whereas the delight taken in that good is desired in dependence upon the supreme good. Thus, although the objection rightly points out everybody's desire for happiness as being for delight, it fails to consider the unattainableness of this desire without attaining the supreme good which alone can cause happiness as delight in man.[33]

Having thus refuted, at least to his satisfaction, the suprasensory version of hedonism, St. Thomas considers the refutation of the inferior versions of hedonism a very easy task. Firstly, he argues, if the will's delight is only a means, so is, only even more so, corporeal pleasure. Secondly, man's ultimate end must be in something specifically human and supremely noble, whereas sensory pleasure is common to man and brute, and the suprasensory is more noble than the sensory. Moreover, sense pleasure is delightful only according to moderation, not per se, whereas the highest good is good per se. Also, if sensory pleasure were the supreme good, anything moderating it would be evil. But, being a moral virtue, temperance is good.[34]

This refutation of the two versions of hedonism is more than a negative doctrine. For, while arguing against the idea of beatitude consisting in delight, Aquinas indicated already that there must be some external good that is the proper object of man's desire for happineess, the attainment of which is

---

31. *S.c.g.* III, 26, 2089; in reply to n. 2073. Cf. *S.th.* I-II, 3, 4c.
32. *S.c.g.* III, 26, 2083–85; *S.th.* I-II, 2, 6; 4, 2.
33. *Quodlib.* VIII, 9, 2; *S.c.g.* III, 26, 2091 in reply to 2074. Cf. *S.th.* I, 26, 2 ad 2; I-II, 2, 6c.
34. *S.c.g.* III, 27, 2093–2101; *I. Eth.* 5, 60; 10, 125; *S.th.* I-II, 2, 6.

happiness essentially, and that, in turn, brings about the delightful repose of the human will as its natural consequence.[35] Thus, we must find out precisely what is the good which is the proper object of our desire for happiness and the attainment of which constitutes happiness and brings the will to a final and delightful repose. St. Thomas' answer is given both indirectly and directly. The indirect answer rejects all the human goods except one as demonstrably not being the proper object of man's happiness; the direct answer tells us that the solely adequate proper object of man's perfect happiness is God Himself, and why.

3. The overall frame of this indirect demonstration runs like this. The ultimate end of man is happiness. But happiness is attainable only through something that is a good of man, since only a good of man is man's specific perfection. Now the goods of man are partly extrinsic and partly intrinsic. The latter include the goods of the body and the goods of the soul. Now, the goods of the body comprise the goods of the body as a whole and the goods of the parts of the body; whereas the goods of the soul consist in the goods of the intellect and the goods of the will. But none of these goods, except one of the intellect, is the object of perfect happiness. Therefore the ultimate end of man consists only in one good of the intellect.

The last minor is proved in the following detailed manner.

First of all, St. Thomas argues, fame, glory, wealth, and power do not make man perfectly happy. Honor does not, because, unlike the ultimate end, honor is desirable only on account of some other good in man, and there is a higher good than honor, namely, being worthy of honor; and it is due to one predisposed to the end or one who has already attained this end.[36] Fame or glory does not make man perfectly happy either, because glory is sought for the sake of honor; meaning 'to be known', it is a lesser good than 'to know'; it is imperfect since its possession is uncertain and subject to error; and is one of the least permanent things.[37] Nor does wealth do so, because it is not sought for its own sake; it is subject to fortune; the highest good cannot be something that is beneficial if spent; and liberality and magnanimity are higher goods than wealth.[38] Finally, worldly power does not make one happy either, because its attainment depends on fortune; it is unstable; often comes to evil men; is relative to some other good as a principle, and can be abused.[39]

Moreover, Aquinas continues, happiness cannot lie in material or bodily

---

35. *S.th.* I-II, 1, 8; 2, 6; 2, 7; 3, 1; 4, 2; 5, 1; 5, 2; I, 26, 3; *I. Eth.* 14, 165.
36. *S.c.g.* III, 28, 2106 and 2108; *S.th.* I-II, 2, 2; *I. Eth.* 5, 65; *Comp.* c. 108.
37. *S.c.g.* III, 29, nn. 2111, 2113, 2115 f.; *S.th.* I-II, 2, 3.
38. *S.c.g.* III, 30, 2118-2123; *I. Eth.* 5, 72; 9, 110; *S.th.* I-II, 2, 1.
39. *S.c.g.* III, 31, 2124-28; *S.th.* I-II, 2, 4; *Comp.* c. 108.

goods in general because none of them is sought for its own sake; none of them can satisfy man's intellectual appetite; and, above all, the body and all its goods are for the sake of the soul, so that no amount of material goods can ever be a substitute for the immaterial goods.[40]

More specifically, the intrinsic goods of the body taken as a whole are not the proper object of felicity. For health, beauty, and strength can be possessed by both good and evil men; the goods of the soul are higher; the bodily goods are common to all plants and animals, and may be greater in some brutes than in man; they are due to vegetative activities, and these activities are not proper to man; and they are not sought for themselves, whereas that which is ordered to a higher end, as man is, cannot have its own conservation for its ultimate end.[41] Nor can man attain happiness through the goods of the senses, sc. food, sexual activity, sense perception or sensory pleasure, since they are common to man and brute; the intellect and its goods are higher than the sense and its goods; and the senses and sense knowledge are for the intellect.[42]

Furthermore, perfect happiness doesn't lie in the human soul or any of its goods. Not in the soul, because it is in potency to its acts and is, as such, ordered to those acts; and not in the potencies, habits, or acts of the soul, because they are all participated goods, whereas the human will desires the universal good.[43] More specifically, happiness is not reached through any of the goods of the will: either through the acts of the will (love, desire, delight), or through the habits of the will (moral virtues). Happiness cannot lie in any act of the will for three reasons. The first reason is that the ultimate end of any creature must be specifically suitable to the nature of that creature, and appetite suits both the cognitive and non-cognitive beings. The second reason is that the object of the will is prior to the act of the will, being the cause of that act; hence, what the will wants first cannot be its own act but rather some good. Thirdly, if any act of the will were the ultimate end of man, it would be either love or desire or delight, and neither of them can be that. Love cannot, since one can love a good not yet possessed; desire cannot, since its proper object is the absent good; and delight cannot, for reasons already given in the reasoning against hedonism.[44]

Furthermore, happiness cannot lie in virtue in general, since virtue is a habit, something between potency and act, and as such, inferior to the

---

40. *Comp.* p. 2, c. 9, n. 576. *S.th.* I-II, 2, 5.
41. *S.c.g.* III, 32; *S.th.* 2, 5; *I. Eth.* 10, 124; *Comp.* p. 2, c. 9, n. 576.
42. *S.c.g.* III, 33; *S.th.* I-II, 2, 6; 3, 3; *Comp.* c. 108; p. 2, c. 9, n. 576 f.; *I. Eth.* 10, 125.
43. *S.th.* I-II, 2, 7.
44. *S.c.g.* III, 26, nn. 2078-80; 2082; *S.th.* I-II, 3, 4; 4, 2; *Quodlib.* VIII, 9, 2c; *Comp.* c. 107. For the arguments against delight, see notes 31-33.

exercise of virtue, namely, the virtuous act.[45] More specifically, happiness does not consist in the moral virtues in general. For, among other things, all moral virtues control passions or exterior things for some higher end; and man cannot be most similar to God through these virtues since they can be predicated of God only metaphorically.[46] Nor does perfect felicity consist in the practical virtues of the intellect. It does not lie in the acts of prudence because these acts are concerned with and ordained to the acts of moral virtues which themselves are not the objects of happiness; and prudence itself is ordered to action as a means is to the end.[47] And perfect happiness does not consist in the acts of art, because art is a means ordered to making as an end; and the products of making are themselves means serving man as their end.[48]

With all these goods eliminated, one is left only with the contemplation of truth or, more specifically, with the speculative goods of the intellect, which are understanding, science, and wisdom. But understanding simply enables man to acquire knowledge about reality in general; science is demonstrable knowledge about the various parts or aspects of the material world; and wisdom is the only demonstrable knowledge of being in general in the light of God as its first cause.[49] Thus, understanding is imperfect or potential knowledge of being and a means to both science and wisdom; and the subject of science is inferior to and less noble than the subject of the 'divine science' of metaphysics, which is God.[50] From all this it follows then that, inasmuch as man's ultimate happiness in this life lies in some good of the intellect, it should be wisdom or metaphysics itself as it considers God Himself and, consequently, man's ultimate happiness lies in some intellectual consideration of God.[51]

4. Aquinas' direct line of reasoning, strongly influenced by Aristotle, consists of four main parts. The first part shows that happiness, our ultimate end, must have a per se rather than a per accident cause. The second part establishes that this per se cause of happiness must be an activity and, more specifically, an activity specifically proportionate to human nature. The third part demonstrates that such a human activity is necessarily that of the

45. *S.th.* I-II, 49, 3, ad 1; *I. Eth.* 12, 152.
46. *S.c.g.* III, 34.
47. *S.c.g.* III, 35, nn. 2–4.
48. *S.c.g.* III, 36.
49. (a) *S.c.g.* III, 37, 2152; *S.th.* I-II, 57, 2; (b) *I.Met.* 3 (M. R. Cathala (Ed.) Taurini: Marietti, 1964), n. 64; and *In Boeth. De Trin.* q. 5, a. 4c (B. Decker (Ed.), Leiden: E.J. Brill, 1959) n. 4, p. 195.
50. *S.c.g.* III, 37, 2159; *S.th.* I-II, 3, 6.
51. *S.c.g.* III, 37, 2152, 2160. Cf. *S.th.* I, 62, 1c; I-II, 2, 8; 3, 5; *Comp.* p. 1, c. 108.

speculative intellect. Finally, the fourth part explains why the only adequate object of the speculative intellect must be nothing less than God Himself. Let us now follow Aquinas through this four-fold positive argumentation step by step.

As Aristotle had already pointed out, happiness may flow from either a per se or determinate cause or a per accident or indeterminate cause. But there are at least three reasons why the cause of happiness cannot be a per accident or chance cause. First of all, what is caused per se is better, more perfect, more noble than what is caused per accident. Secondly, if happiness were caused per accident, happiness would be a matter of chance and, if this were so, man's pursuit of all goods would be seriously weakened, since every good is sought for the sake of the highest good. Thirdly, there is nothing in nature in vain. But if happiness were caused by mere chance, man might or might not attain it and, thereby, his basic natural desire for happiness would be in vain or radically frustrated.[52] From all this it follows then that happiness, our ultimate end, is caused per se by some good.

What, then, is this good? Goodness is perfection. The perfection of every being is twofold: first or original and second or final. The former in every being is the substantial form; the latter, its operation. Now, any finite being, including man, has its own proper mode of existing by virtue of its substantial form. On the other hand, since existence and every mode of existence, that is, every essence, is the finite analogate of God's essence which is existence, when man desires to stay in existence, what he desires is a similitude to God and, ultimately, although indirectly and implicitly, God Himself. This is what we may term the existential and entitative human desire for God as our ultimate end.[53] Moreover, the substantial form in every finite being is the ontological principle of all specific potencies whose operations impart the finite being its operative or final perfection proper to its species, as opposed to its first or basic perfection of existence and essence.[54] This is why, in addition to his existential and entitative desire for God, there is in every man, as in every finite being, also a second natural desire – a desire for his own second, operative, or final perfection that is specifically and uniquely human.

The next question is, the operation of which of the numerous powers rooted in the human soul will satisfy man's desire for ultimate or operative self-perfection. Clearly, no irrational operation will do so, since the desired self-

---

52. *I. Eth.* 14, 165, 171 f.; *S.th.* I-II, 1, 4c; *S.c.g.* II, 55, 1309; III, 48, 2257; III, 51, 2284; *II. De caelo* 16, 442; *Comp.* c. 104, n. 208.
53. *De ver.* 22, 2, ad 2; *S.th.* I-II, 10, 1; *S.c.g.* II, 55, 1298; *In Boeth. De Trin.* 1, 3, ad 4; *De ver.* 10, 12, ad 5.
54. See, e.g., *Quodlib.* VI, 2, 1 and *I. Eth.* 10, 119, 121.

perfection is by necessity proportionate to man's rational nature. Therefore, it must be either the operation of the will or of the intellect, because only these two are rational and, as such, proportionate to human nature. However, only the activities of the intellect are essentially rational and, as such, completely suitable to human nature.[55] Therefore, the supreme good suited to cause our felicity in this life is some activity of the intellect. Now, human reason is both speculative and practical, i.e., the principle both of man's speculative and practical life; and of these two, speculative life is per se superior to practical life and the only life that does not serve an ulterior end.[56] Therefore, of all the activities of the intellect, the speculative activities or the life of thought must constitute our ultimate felicity in this life. However, the speculative activities of the intellect include discursive, i.e., inductive and deductive, reasoning as well as contemplation in the strict sense.[57] Of these two, the investigation of truth cannot be said to be simply delightful because it is naturally arduous, laborious, often even fruitless, unsuccessful, if not the source of error, whereas the contemplation of truth is simply and per se delightful for both generic and specific reasons. The generic reason lies in the fact that every natural operation is, as such, delightful and, to man, it is natural to know, to possess the truth.[58] The specific reasons are as follows. Firstly, everything beautiful is per se delightful, and contemplation is essentially beautiful because proper proportion and clarity, the two principles of beauty that characterize contemplative operations, are rooted in and stem from the intellect. Secondly, in contrast to discursive thinking, the contemplation of truth consists in reflecting upon the fruits of intellectual investigations, that is, on the truth already recognized.[59] Since, then, happiness concomitantly or effectively consists in delight, the intellectual operation objectively and formally constituting happiness is not discursive reasoning but the contemplation of truth.[60] To these reasons comes the fact that happiness must consist in a continuous and lasting operation, and the most continuous and lasting human operation is the contemplation of truth, since we can persevere in reflecting upon truth longer than in any other activity.[61]

Having thus established contemplation of truth as the human activity in

---

55. *I. Met.* 1, 3; *S.th.* I-II, 3, 5.
56. (a) *S.th.* I, 79, 11; *De ver.* 3, 3c; (b) *S.th.* II-II, 182, 4 and 1; *De ver.* 11, 4, ad 2; (c) *S.c.g.* III, 25, 2063; 37, 2154, 2158.
57. (a) *I. Eth.* 10, 123, 126, 128; (b) *S.th.* II-II, 180, 4.
58. *S.c.g.* III, 37, 2152 f. and 2157; 50, 2277; *S.th.* I-II, 3, 5; II-II, 810, 7.
59. *S.th.* II-II, 180, 2 ad 3; *X. Eth.* 10, 2092.
60. *S.th.* II-II, 180, 3c, ad 1; 181, 1; 182, 1.
61. *X. Eth.* 10, 2089 f.; *S.th.* II-II, 180, 8c; 181, 1c.

which as in a per se delightful and lasting and, hence, perfect activity man's highest happiness lies in this life, there is only one final step to be taken. It is the realization that the most perfect activity requires the highest and noblest object to ensure its highest delightfulness.[62] Now, it is the objects of wisdom that are the highest and noblest, since wisdom concerns itself with the immaterial and lasting, with God, the most perfect, immaterial, and eternal being, in its center. Therefore, the contemplation of wisdom and, within this framework and above all, the contemplation of God, in so far as this is possible in this life, is the perfect operation in which man's ultimate happiness in this life lies.[63] It is for this reason that the contemplation of wisdom with its devine center is being sought always and only for its own sake, just as happiness itself is, whereas every other operation or perfection in man has the perfection of this contemplation as its natural, ultimate end.[64] Aquinas' indirect and direct arguments have converged, and reached the same conclusion, which is this. Man can find his ultimate happiness in this life in some sort of contemplation of God. And since this contemplation is uniquely and supremely delightful on account of the excellence and the consequent lovableness of its object, it is also true to say that our natural happiness lies in a kind of union with God attained through knowledge and love.[65]

5. Before taking up the final question of precisely what kind of knowledge it is of God that can make man most happy in life, let us attempt to sum up and unify the various cosmological, psychological and ethical doctrines of St. Thomas concerning man's natural ultimate end, so as to recognize the successive steps which can lead man to his natural end.

As every created being, man has both an existential-entitative and an operative tendency toward his own perfection implanted in him by the Creator. The former consists in his tendency or will to live, whereby he can preserve his existence and his specifically human essence. The latter or operative tendency aims at attaining his equally specific but accidental and ultimate perfection. Since man is a specifically rational being, this ultimate perfection is itself rational and, as such, attainable through the activities of his rational powers.[66] But man has two such powers: the intellect and the will. Thus, he has two operative natural tendencies. One is the innate tendency of his intellect to know the true in general and, ultimately, to know the first cause

---

62. *S.c.g.* III, 37, 2159; *S.th.* I-II, 3, 5; *Comp.* p. 2, c. 9, n. 579.
63. *X. Eth.* 10, 2083 f.; 12, 2123, 2125; *S.c.g.* III, 25, 2063; 37, 2155 f.; *S.th.* I, 62, 1; I-II, 3, 5; 3, 7; II-II, 181, 4, ad 2; 182, 1; *De ver.* 14, 2.
64. *X. Eth.* 10, 2097; *S.c.g.* III, 37, 2154, 2158; *S.th.* I, 62, 1; I-II, 3, 5; II-II, 182, 1.
65. *S.c.g.* III, 25, 2061; *S.th.* II-II, 180, 7c, ad 3. Cf. *Comp.* p. 2, c. 9, n. 591.
66. (a) *S.th.* I-II, 10, 1; (b) see note 8. Also, *S.th.* I, 62, 1c, ad 2.

as the ultimate explanation of everything. The other is the necessary desire of the will for the good in general and, ultimately, for happiness.[67] These two are two really distinct tendencies, just as the intellect and the will are, initially independent of each other. Yet, these two natural tendencies have something in common and are functionally interrelated. What they have in common is this. Both are, at least initially and in a way, abstract inclinations. For the intellect this means that what the first cause of everything actually is or that God is this first cause is at least originally or initially completely unknown to man. For the will this abstractness means that, while it necessarily tends toward the good in general or happiness in general, it does never desire in this life any particular good, not even God Himself, with necessity.[68] Thus, although God is, in fact both the first cause of everything and the supreme good or the object of happiness, one may or may not recognize God as being the terminus of his intellectual desire for knowledge, and he may desire God or something else as the sole object of his will's desire for happiness.[69]

The functional interrelatedness of the natural desire of the intellect and the will lies in the following. On the one hand, since the will naturally desires the good in general and, consequently, everything that is a good in any way, the will naturally desires not only happiness but the good or the proper object of every human power, including knowledge desired by the intellect. As a consequence of this, the final fulfillment of man's intellectual or cognitive desire is at the same time the attainment of happiness to the will.[70] On the other hand, long before this can happen, the will needs the intellect in such a basic manner that it cannot desire anything, not even the good in general, unless some good is first rationally apprehended.[71] Thus the following successive steps are needed for the fulfillment of the intellect's and the will's natural desire.

Initially, the intellect tends toward knowledge it does not have as yet, whereas the will is a mere potency without any natural desire. Then, at some time the intellect recognizes something as something definite and as being good. The being recognized as good, in turn, elicits in the will, that is up to this moment a mere potency, the natural desire for it, but only as it is good in general or a concrete instance of the good in general. Only from this moment on does the individual person necessarily desire happiness abstractly,

---

67. *I. Met.* 1, 2; *De an.* 13, ad 11; *S.th.* I-II, 10, 1, ad 2.
68. *S.th.* I, 2, 1c, ad 2; I-II, 5, 8c, ad 2; 10, 2; *De malo* 3, 3.
69. (a) *S.th.* I, 2, 1, ad 1; cf. *S.c.g.* I, 11, 67–70; *De ver.* 10, 12; (b) *S.th.* I, 82, 2c, ad 1; I-II, 5, 8; *De ver.* 22, 6c, ad 4; 27, 3; *II. Sent.* 38, 1, 2, ad 2; *IV. Sent.* 49, 1, 3, 1, ad 1.
70. (a) *S.th.* I-II, 10, 1; *De ver.* 22, 5; (b) *Comp.* p. 2, c. 1.
71. *S.th.* I, 82, 4, ad 3; II-II, 4, 7; *Quodlib.* VI, 2, 1; *S.c.g.* III, 26, 2078; *De ver.* 15, 3.

i.e., as being supreme goodness without anything particular being the object of this desire whose attainment fulfills this desire and in whose possession the will finds its repose and delight.[72] Once, however, the intellect comes to know something, it desires to know the cause of it; and every time it apprehends any other being, it wants to know the cause of that being too. This is to say that the true object of the human intellect's natural desire is not to know each and every individual being but only their natures and causes or explanations of all the things it has come to know as existent. This way the natural desire of the intellect has already, at least objectively, a natural terminus: the first of all causes, although no such cause is clearly recognized at this point.[73] Next, in the process of learning, man eventually discovers that there is order both within individual things and in the world as a whole; and thereby he acquires his initial and confused knowledge of God as the cause of all this order.[74] Later, upon discovering also change, contingency, and hierarchy of perfections, man can acquire a demonstrative knowledge of God.[75] Yet, even after this has been accomplished, Aquinas' emphasizes, the natural desire neither of his intellect nor of his will has found its true fulfillment: not his intellect, since all man knows is *that* God exists but not *what* He is; and not his will, since the will can desire an object only to the extent that the object is known to be good, and through demonstrative knowledge man knows that God is the supreme good only in a negative and abstract way.[76]

At any rate, the demonstrative knowledge of God's existence adds a new dimension to the human desire for knowledge, viz., to know what God is. But once we know one thing of His nature, we wish to know another, and even if we could ever learn everything knowable about God's nature, it would still be only an abstract knowledge of Him through universal concepts, and that kind of knowledge is per se potential and imperfect.[77] If we add to this the realization that, as long as the fruit of demonstrative knowledge is limited and imperfect, so is the delight taken in the contemplation of the results of such knowlege, we will suddenly realize that our natural happiness which we may attain, according to Aquinas, in this life through the life of contemplating God, is itself quite a limited and imperfect sort of happiness: a happiness which is proportionate to human nature that itself is limited and imperfect or

---

72. (a) *S.th.* I-II, 5, 8; *De pot.* 1, 5; *IV. Sent.* 49, 1, 3, sol. 3; sol. 1, ad 3; (b) *S.th.* II-II, 4, 7; *IV. Sent.* 33, 1, 1, ad 9.
73. *S.th.* I, 12, 8, ad 4; *S.c.g.* III, 25, 2065, 2067.
74. *In Symbolum Apostolorum* a. 1 (*Opuscula theologica*, II; *ed. cit.*) n. 869.
75. *S.c.g.* I, 13; *S.th.* I, 2, 3; *De pot.* 3, 5; *De ver.* 5, 2; *Comp.* c. 3; etc.
76. (a) *S.th.* I, 3, preamble; 13, 5; *S.c.g.* III, 49, 2270; (b) see n. 71.
77. *S.c.g.* III, 48, 2247; 50, 2276; *De an.* 18, ad 14.

happiness attained in the human way.[78]

6. Is then, this all we can expect in this life? St. Thomas has a twofold consolation for us in this matter, both, but especially the second, being almost completely overlooked by his interpreters.

One is a remark he makes in his commentary on Boethius' *De Trinitate*, quoting St. Hilary in support. Since, in His perfection, God is infinitely distant from the creature, the human mind can never find the terminus of its cognitive desire in God; yet it can endlessly move toward God by endlessly learning more and more about Him without ever exhausting His knowability or his own cognitive capacity.[79] With these words, Aquinas opens up a truly challenging horizon before us. For it means that man can never reach the point where he has no new thought on God to contemplate and meditate about, since as he keeps on discovering additional truths about God, he keeps on having a new fruit of intellectual achievement to contemplate and enjoy. Thus, human life appears to be an ever-exciting, endless voyage of the mind toward its Creator, with all the sweetness of the intellectual joy concomitant to it.

The other and completely overlooked optimistic component in St. Thomas' doctrine of human happiness is aesthetic in character. We know already the somewhat paradoxical nature of the happiness we can expect in this life. For this happiness is attainable only through the delightful contemplation of what we demonstratively learn of God – the contemplation of a knowledge that is, on the one hand, necessarily and essentially imperfect since it is discursive and abstract; and, on the other hand, potentially infinite in so far as there is no limit to its being incrased, widened, and deepened. Clearly, then, the perfection of this delightful contemplation needs improvement not in so far as we can endlessly enhance it and increase it, but inasmuch as it is discursive and abstract. But the knowledge which is per se superior and nobler and more delightful than the discursive and abstract is the intuitive and concrete. On the other hand, we cannot have an intuitive and concrete knowledge directly of God Himself in this life, since it would mean a *direct*, unmediated vision of God as He is in Himself, whereas in this life we can know only through mental abstraction.[80] Yet, an intuitive and concrete knowledge of God, that is *indirect* or mediated, is possible. What is it? The intuitive contemplation of the beauty of creation that mirrors (and thus gives us an idea of) the beauty of God Himself, the conceiver and maker of the beautiful created world. What is the basis of this teaching?

78. *S.c.g.* III, 48, 2246, 2254; *S.th.*, I, 62, 1.
79. *In Boet. De Trin.*, q. 2, a. 1, ad 7; quoting Hilary, *De Trin.* II, 10 (Migne, *Patrologia Latina*, vol. 10, col. 59a.).
80 *De ver.* 10, 11; *S.th.*I, 12, 11.

First, God Himself is essentially beautiful.[81] Thus, inasmuch as every creative idea in the divine intellect is a finite mode of the divine essence,[82] every creative idea is itself proportionately beautiful. Moreover, since the external realization of a creative idea essentially conforms to that idea unless the artist is incapable to realize his own creative idea, and since God is the infinitely perfect artist, every created being proportionately participates in its Maker's own beauty.[83] This is to say that every creature is individually beautiful, and so is the material universe in its totality, as a whole, reflecting and indicating the beauty of its divine Maker as a similitude or image of Him.[84] The application of this metaphysics of beauty to the question of human happiness is readily seen. If, in addition to contemplating the fruits of our demonstrative knowledge of God, we behold the amazingly complex order and glittering beauty of the universe as a whole, with the specifically and individually beautiful minerals, plants, brutes, and human beings as well as the heaven with the celestial bodies in it,[85] always bearing in mind that all this beauty is divine in its origin, then we get a glimpse, as if through a veil or a glass darkly, of the incomprehensible excellence and enigmatic beauty of God Himself. In this manner, our intellect comes to a genuinely intuitive and concrete, although still indirect and, as such, limited and analogous, contemplation of God.[86] And because everything beautiful is per se lovable and delectable, through this aesthetic contemplation of the universe precisely as God's handiwork and the mirror of His beauty, we can also experience the greatest possible delight as well as a profound admiration and irresistible love for the divine fountainhead of all the created excellence and beauty.[87]

81. *In Iob* 40, 1; 0iComp. p. 2, c. 9, n. 591; *De div. nom.0r 4, 11, 446, 448;* S.th. II-II, 34, 1, 1a; *In Psalmum* 26, 3.
82. *De I; I. Sent.* 36, 2, 1, ad 3; 2, 3, ad 2.
83. (a) Cf. *De ver.* 2, 7, ad 4; ;3, 3, sed c. 3a; *I. Sent.* 38, 1, 1, ad 3; *S.th.* I, 17, 1; (b) *De div. nom.* 4, 5, 349; *De ver.* 4, 4, sed c. 3a; *S.th.* I-II, 93, 1c; (c) *De div. nom.* 4, 5, 335, 337, 339, 345 f.; 4, 8, 390 f.; *In Iob* 40, 1; *In Psalm.* 26, 3; *I. Sent.* 46, 1, 4, ad 1; *De ver.* 3, 1, 6a.
84. (a) *De div. nom.* 4, 5, 355; 4, 11, 938; (b) *IV. Sent.* 47, 2, 2, II, sed c.; *S.c.g.* III, 72, 2482; *De ver.* 3, 1, 6a; *De div. nom.* 7, 4, 73; *De pot.* 5, 9, 4a, ad 4; *S.th.* I, 19, 9, 2a, ad 2; 48, 1, 5a; *Comp.* c. 170, n. 336; *In evangelium Ioanni*, 2, 1, lect. 2; (c) *In Symb. Apost.* a. 1, n. 878; (d) *De div. nom.* 4, 5, 337; 4, 18, 525; *IV. Sent.* 18, 1, 2, sol.; *In Psalm.* 44, 2; *S.c.g.* III, 64, 95, 97; *S.th. I, 15, 1.*
85. See, e.g., *De pot.* 5, 9, 4a, ad 4; *S.th.* I, 66, 1; 69, 2; 39, 2; II-II, 116, 2, ad 2; III, 18, 6; *De malo* 2, 4, ad 2; *IV. Sent.* 48, 2, 3, sol.; *In Hebraeos*, 1, 10, lect. 5; *S.th.* III, 36, 7; I, 47, 2; *In Symb. Ap.* 1, 873; *In Psalm.* 18, 1.
86. j(a) *In Symb. Ap.* a. 1, n. 878; *S.th.* II-II, 180, 4, the latter explicitly referring to St. Paul, I. Cor. 13, 12; (b) compare *S.c.g.* III, 80, 2551 with *S.th.* I-II, 31, 4, ad 3.
87. (a) *De div. nom.* 4, 9, 400, 408; 4, 10, 441; 4, 13, 463; *De ver.* 22, 1, ad 13; *S.th.* I-II, 27, 1, 3a, ad 3; I, 5, 4, ad 1; (b) cf. *Quodlib.* VIII, 9, 1 and *I. Eth.* 13, 161; (c) *Comp.* p. 2,

Summing up, in this concrete aesthetic contemplation, that is added to the more basic contemplation of the abstractly and demonstratively known God, and that is as interminably increasable as our metaphysical knowledge of God itself, we can experience perfect happiness '*inchoative*', getting a foretaste of a direct vision of God, so deep, so great, and so delightful as is possible at all for a being immersed in the finitude of matter and mind.

7. This picture, however grandiosely sketched by Aquinas of man's ultimate end attainable in this life, is not yet complete. For St. Thomas is well aware of the fact that contemplation of God through His handiwork at the metaphysical or even the aesthetic level is not possible for everybody. Moreover, Aquinas knows also that the rational intellect acts not only at the speculative but also at the practical level as the intrinsic principle of external activities,[88] and that man has also a second rational faculty besides the intellect; and, thus, it is only natural that the acts of the practical intellect and the will should also contribute to human happiness in a proportionate manner. The acts of the practical intellect which St. Thomas has in mind are the acts of teaching; and the acts of the rational will are the acts of the moral virtues. By the acts of teaching he means here the activities of intellectually helping and guiding one's friends or his fellow men in general in attaining their own happiness through an analogous recognition of God. Since this is a difficult task for which people do need help from others, intellectualy guiding one's friends toward their own happiness is quite naturally a source of great and deep satisfaction and joy in human life.[89] By the acts of the moral virtues, on the other hand, Aquinas means the acts of justice, temperance and fortitude, whereby man gains a proper rational control over his passions and external activities, and renders his life orderly and, as such, beautiful and delightful. This life of virtue is, in itself, an interminable and joyous journey of an ever-greater similitude to God and, hence, a gradually attained and increased happiness; whereas, in its relation to man's cognitive happiness, it properly predisposes man for the life of metaphysical and aesthetic contemplation.[90] Unlike contemplative life, virtuous life is possible for all men, and secures thereby some imperfect happiness for every man.

---

    c. 9, n. 591; *S.c.g.* II, 2, 860 f.; *De div. nom.* 4, 11, 448.
88. *S.th.* I, 79, 11; *De ver.* 3, 3.
89. *S.th.* I-II, 4, 8c. Cf. *Comp.* c. 103, n. 205.
90. (a) *I. Eth.* 13, 159 f.; (b) *S.th.* I, 3, 1, ad 2; 35, 2, ad 3; 93, 1, and 8; (c) *S.th.* II-II, 180, 2; 182, 1, ad 3; 182, 3. Cf. *X. Eth.* 12, 2120.

C. The theological doctrine of happiness

St. Thomas' theological doctrine of happiness as man's ultimate end is the logical and organic continuation of his heretofore discussed philosophical theory. Basically it consists of a negative and a positive part, both to be merely sketched here.

1. Everything that Aquinas the philosopher has got to say of man's ultimate end or happiness in this life, however noble, rich, lofty, and divinely oriented it may be, is quickly put in its proper finite perspective by Aquinas the theologian. He admits that this relatively ultimate end is truly great and most delightful since leading to God in a way. Yet, this end is great and delightful only in comparison to everything else in this life, whereas in itself it is quite limited and imperfect.[91] The reasoning supporting this sobering doctrine concentrates on the essential element of happiness in this life, viz., man's contemplative knowledge of God, and runs like this. The only types of knowledge man can ever have of God in this life is either common and confused, or demonstrative, or contemplative – intuitive, or one through the soul's self-knowledge, or one by faith.[92] But neither of these modes of knowing God secures truly perfect happiness. Not the first, the common and confused knowledge of God, which is the result of immediate reasoning based on the order of the universe as demanding some superior orderer, mainly because this knowledge is per se imperfect, hence, not a perfect operation.[93] Nor can perfect happiness lie in a demonstrative knowledge of God, mainly because it, too, is imperfect and indefinitely perfectible, while not universally attainable.[94] Even a contemplative or intuitive knowledge of God cannot make us perfectly happy, because not even the creatures are perfectly known to us; and because for metaphysical and epistemological reasons God cannot be perfectly represented by imperfect creatures.[95] Moreover, a knowledge of God through the soul's knowledge of its essence is only a conceivable alternative, because the soul simply does not have such a self-knowledge.[96]

91. *S.th.* II-II, 180, 7, ad 3.
92. A additional type listed and discussed by St. Thomas, knowledge of God through separate substances, who know God through knowing their essences (*S.c.g.* III, 41–46; *S.th.* I, 88, 1–2), can be neglected in this brief sketch.
93. See this and other arguments in *S.c.g.* III, 38, 2161–64, 2166; *Comp.* p. 2, c. 8, n. 569. Cf. *S.th.* I, 2, 1, ad 2; II-II, 2, 4.
94. *S.c.g.* III, 39, 2167–2172; *S.th.* I, 12, 12; *Comp.* p. 2, c. 8, n. 569; c. 9, n. 581.
95. (a)*Comp.* c. 105, n. 211; c. 12; *S.th.* I, 3, 5; 12, 2c; *S.c.g.* I, 24, 224; 16; 22, 25; 52, III, 49, 2266–2269; *De pot.* 7, 3; (b) *S.c.g.* III, 49, 2265; *S.th.* I, 56, 3; 12, 13, ad 1; (c) *Comp.* p. 2, c. 8, n. 596; c. 9, n. 590.
96. *S.c.g.* III, 46; *S.th.* I, 87, 1; *De ver.* 10, 8, 8, 6.

Finally, knowing God by faith is also insufficient for perfect happiness, mainly because in faith this imperfect knowledge may inflame our natural desire but not satisfy it.[97] The conclusion from all this is clear: there is no knowledge at all through which man could become perfectly happy in this life. But, as already demonstrated, only some kind of knowledge of God can make man perfectly happy. Consequently, man cannot attain perfect and ultimate happiness in this life.[98] St. Thomas uses also at least eight other arguments taken from the effective and concomitant sense of the term 'happiness' and from the empirical facts of life to show man's de facto failure to become perfectly happy in this life.[99]

2. In the light of all this, as a theologian, St. Thomas feels compelled to conclude that a truly beatifying knowledge of God as man's absolutely ultimate end or absolutely perfect happiness cannot be naturally, i.e., before death and in virtue of man's essential principles, attained at all.[100] On the other hand, he goes on arguing, and arguing this time in a positive or constructive manner, we must bear in mind that nature does nothing in vain. Since then we have a natural desire for perfect happiness, this end must be realized after death, and by virtue of grace, a supernatural principle absolutely freely given to man by God and enabling man to ahcieve a kind of knowledge that is adequate to make him absolutely happy.[101] This future knowledge of God is adequate because it is a direct knowledge of the essence of God, i.e., one similar to God's self-knowledge, hence a knowledge of vision, brought about by divine illumination.[102] As such, it elicits a proportionate effect in the will: perfect love for God in a never-ending life of perfect intellectual and appetitive fulfillment; that is, a cognitively and appetitively perfect happiness.[103]

III

The joyously optimistic theological portion of this brilliantly construed and awesomely intricate theory of human purposiveness, as it stresses man's chances to bring his desire for happiness to perfect fulfillment, is a powerful

---

97. S.c.g. III, 40, 2175–78; S.th. I, 12, 13, ad 3; Comp. p. 2, c. 1, n. 545.
98. S.c.g. III, 48, 2246; I. Eth. 16, 202.
99. S.c.g. 48, 2246–53; 2258 f.; S.th. I-II, 5, 3; Comp. c. 104.
100. S.c.g. III, 48, 2246; S.th. I, 12, 11; I-II, 5, 3.
101.
102.
103.

and timeless encouragement to everyone who shares Aquinas' own religious faith. The unquestionably somber philosophical theory, on the other hand, with its warning that no perfect happiness in this life is possible, advocates an almost stoical existentialism, i.e., that man ought to accept his earthly destiny that is connatural to the finitude of his essence. In so far, however, as this philosophical view is God-directed in respect to man's contemplative, moral, and practical life, it is not Aquinas' philosophical somberness that tempers the God-founded exuberance of his theological optimism, but the contageous joyousness of his theological views that permeates, by means of the ontological mystery of analogy, the measured soberness of his philosophic views on human destiny.

Is there any contemporary usefulness in St. Thomas' philosophic theory of human purposiveness? There is, and there is, interestingly enough, in such a way that to several major areas of human life promoting our earthly happiness, there corresponds some major trend in contemporary society. Thus, to the Thomistic doctrine of the axiological primacy of contemplative life over practical life there corresponds an enormous present-day intellectual upsurge of interest in every area of speculative knowledge, from the natural to the humanistic sciences to the liberal arts, promising an interminable intellectual progress and tending to promote the chances of mankind for contemplative happiness. Closely connected with this, we are witnessing today an impressive and ever-spreading interest in education, on the one hand, and an equally powerful widening and deepening of intellectual interest in beauty and art, both of these being, in Aquinas' opinion, important components in the attainment of relative felicity in this life. Regrettably, however, it is rather questionable that there is a universally growing concern with morality, the life of moral virtues, matching the powerful progress in speculation, education, and aesthetic appreciation. Even less encouraging is the present-day trend in the God-centeredness of aesthetic appreciation, due to the spread of skepticism and agnosticism in theology as well as philosophy. Nevertheless, very few people question that a more genuine concern with morality and virtuous life is, indeed, desirable for and contributive to the attainment of happiness in this life.

All in all, then, there is an amazingly wide area of agreement or conformity between what the highly sophisticated contemporary man does or values and what St. Thomas, the visionary wise man of a long-passed period in human history, had taught and advocated concerning human purposiveness.

CHAPTER 8

THE CONCEPT OF PURPOSE IN REFORMATION THOUGHT

ROBERT BRETALL

To imagine a language means to imagine a form of life.

Wittgenstein

Although the gospel came and comes every day through the Holy Spirit alone, nevertheless it came by means of languages, spread through them, and must also be maintained through them ... Languages are the sheaths in which the knife of the Spirit is contained. They are the case in which the jewel of the gospel is borne. They are the vessel in which the drink is held. They are the room in which the food is stored. And as the gospel itself tells us (Matt. 14:20), they are the baskets in which the bread and fish and fragments are gathered up.

Luther

In this essay 'Reformation thought' will mean the thinking of the sixteenth-century Reformers, especially Martin Luther; but it will mean also the thinking of those twentieth-century theologians – especially Karl Barth – whose orientation and attitude involve basically a return to Reformation principles, Reformation language, and thereby to Biblical principles and the language of the Bible. Whether or not they succeeded in their attempt, the Reformers wanted to think as the Bible writers thought: they wanted to re-create the Bible language after centuries of mere lip service amounting to neglect – centuries in which, as Luther and Calvin and the other Reformation leaders saw it, the Word of the Bible had been overlaid and obscured by layer upon layer of intellectualizing philosophical dust from Scholasticism. And a similar aim has led contemporaries like Barth and Brunner and Niebuhr and Nygren to a recovery of Biblical language and Reformation language long ignored – if not held in contempt – by a Protestant Liberalism which greatly preferred the language of philosophical Idealism or of Pragmatism.

So much by way of delimiting 'Reformation thought'. As for 'the concept of purpose', I wish to proceed on the later-Wittgensteinian assumption that *the* meaning of a term – even in a restricted context such as 'for the Reformers' or 'in Reformation thought' – is impossible to discover apart from the way or ways in which this term is actually *used* in relation to other terms in a 'language game' that we shall call 'the Biblical-Reformation

Horosz, W. and Clements, T. (eds.), Religion and Human Purpose
© 1986, Martinus Nijhoff Publishers, Dordrecht – Printed in the Netherlands

language' – meaning by this, the Biblical language as the Reformers and neo-Reformation theologians (especially Luther and Barth) have actually employed it. The first two sections of the essay will be devoted to what, I am afraid, will be a sketchy and inadequate account of this usage as it can be discerned in the two paradigm figures of Luther and Barth. Following this I want to come to grips with the philosophical problem raised by this language as described, *under a preliminary or tentative assumption of the verificationist theory of meaning* or some theory closely approximating thereto. Of course from the perspective of the *Philosophical Investigations* one might dismiss the problem by saying simply, 'This language game is played'. One might, but then again one might not; because the Biblical-Reformation language game isn't played so much any more – at least not by philosophers, the broader intelligentsia, or the younger generation. Perhaps out of a lingering fondness for this language game, I should like to pay it the tribute, at least, of taking it seriously enough to investigate its relevance under a tough-minded, empirical criterion of 'relevance'. The discussion of this will occupy the last two sections of the essay, section III stating the *problem* as sharply as possible and section IV suggesting a kind of answer, although an eclectic one.

I

A. The Reformation view of Purpose

'The central affirmation of Protestant Christianity concerns not man but God. It proclaims the sovereignty of God. God, the Creator and Redeemer, is not bound. He is not confined to limited forms of life, i.e., to historically relative, manmade institutions ... Protestant faith and life arise from the hearing of the speaking God who discloses himself when and how he chooses, and calls men into fellowship with himself ... In the name of the sovereign creative Lord of history who must be acknowledged ever anew as the source of all good, (Protestantism) protests against all absolutizations of the historically relative and against all tendencies toward the self-sufficiency of man. Whenever the natural and the historical are deified, the Protestant jealousy for the lordship of God is aroused. For the Protestant faith is: God is alive in history, but nothing historical can capture him'.[1]

Although this is not a *complete* characterization of the Reformation,[2] it will

1. Wilhelm Pauch, *The Heritage of the Reformation*, Boston: Beacon Press, 1950, pp. 149–150. Cf. Paul Tillich, *The Protestant Era*, p. 230 ff.
2. Pauck himself adds four other points to this first and central one: pp. 150–155.

serve to introduce the Reformers' view of purpose. Just as their basic affirmation concerned not man but God, so their thoughts about purpose are God-oriented. 'Purpose is a concept whose reference is above all to the divine purpose': i.e., the usage of the word is such that it refers to the divine purpose first of all and to human purposes secondarily. Such usage, the Reformers felt, was in accord with Scriptural usage – and one of the aims of the Reformation, so often noted, was to revive the language of the Bible.

The Greek word most frequently translated 'purpose' in the New Testament is *prothesis* from *protithemi* to place or set before; to lay out or display; to set up as a mark or prize; to propose to one's mind, or entertain.[3] And *Prothesis* is a distinctively Pauline word *in its usage as referring to God*. Non-Pauline occurrences of *prothesis* in the New Testament are only two in number (Acts 11:23 and 27:13), and in these it is *human* purpose that is being referred to. In only one place (2 Tim. 3:10) does Paul use the word in this way; over against this there are five passages in the Pauline and Deutero-Pauline corpus (Rom. 8:28 and 9:11; Ephes. 1:11 and 3:11; and 2 Tim. 1:9) which ascribe *prothesis* to God, and to God in a special sense. These passages speak of the divine 'purpose of the ages' (Ephes. 3:11), the divine pre-destining, and they are among the passages most often referred to and commented upon by the Reformers, Luther as well as Calvin.

In everything, as we know, (the spirit) co-operates for good with those who love God and are called according to his purpose. For God knew his own before even they were, and also ordained that they should be shaped to the likeness of his Son, that he might be the eldest among a large family of brothers; and it is these, so fore-ordained, whom he also called. And those whom he called he has justified, and to those whom he justified he has also given his splendour.[4]

... But that is not all, for Rebekah's children had one and the same father, our ancestor Isaac; and yet, in order that God's selective purpose might stand, based not upon men's deeds but upon the call of God, she was told, even before they were born, when they had as yet done nothing, good or ill, 'The elder shall be servant to the younger'; and that accords with the text of Scripture, 'Jacob I loved and Esau I hated'. What shall we say to that? Is God to be charged with injustice? By no means. For he says to Moses, 'Where I show mercy, I will show mercy, and where I pity, I will pity. Thus it does not depend on man's will or effort, but on God's mercy ...[5]

3. Liddell and Scott's *Greek-English Lexicon*, Abridged. Where *prothesis* is not used, the prepositional phrase 'eis touto' (---), 'to this (end)' appears in many passages expressing purpose. (Strong's *Exhaustive Concordance of the Bible*, New York & Nashville: Abingdon Press, 1955). In the Old Testament a number of different words are translated 'purpose'; the three used most often being *machashebeth* (from *chasab*, a 'primitive root'), *chephets*, and *etsah*.
4. Romans 8:28–30. New English Bible translation. For v. 28, J. B. Phillips has: 'Moreover we know that to those who love God, who are called according to his plan (prothesis), everything that happens fits into a pattern for good'.
5. Romans 9:10–16. New English Bible translation.

The 'cosmic', universalistic tone of the passages from Ephesians has often been noted:

... For God has allowed us to know the secret of his plan, and it is this: he purposes (protithemi) in his sovereign will that all human history shall be consummated in Christ, that everything that exists in heaven or earth shall find its perfection and fulfillment in him. And here is the staggering thing – that in all which will one day belong to him we have been promised a share (since we were long ago destined for this by the one who achieves his purposes with sovereign will), so that we, as the first to put our confidence in Christ, may bring praise to his glory![6]

To me, less than the least of all Christians, has God given this grace, to enable me to proclaim to the Gentiles the incalculable riches of Christ, and to make plain to all men the meaning of that secret which he who created everything in Christ has kept hidden from the creation until now. The purpose is that all the angelic powers should now see the complex wisdom of God's plan being worked out through the Church, in conformity to that timeless purpose (prothesis) which he centred in Jesus our Lord. It is in the same Jesus, because we have faith in him, that we dare, even with confidence, to approach God.[7]

For the spirit that God gave us is no craven spirit but one to inspire strength, love, and self-discipline. So never be ashamed of your testimony to our Lord, nor of me his prisoner, but take your share of suffering for the sake of the Gospel, in the strength that comes from God. It is he who brought us salvation and called us to a dedicated life, not for any merit of ours but of his own purpose (prothesis) and his own grace, which was granted to us in Christ Jesus from all eternity, but has now at length been brought fully into view by the appearance on earth of our Saviour Jesus Christ. For he has broken the power of death and brought life and immortality to light through the Gospel. [8]

These passages raise philosophical questions, some of which the Reformers may not have recognized or at any rate did not try to solve any more than St. Paul did. The Reformers – like St. Paul and unlike St. Thomas Aquinas – were first of all religious leaders and theologians, not philosophers – at least in the way 'philosophy' was understood by Scholasticism.[9] This does not

---

6. Ephesians 1:9-13. (*The New Testament in Modern English*, translated by J. B. Phillips, New York: The Macmillan Company, 1959). The New English Bible renders vs. 9–10: 'He has made known to us his hidden purpose – such was his will and pleasure determined beforehand in Christ – to be put into effect when the time was ripe: namely, that the universe, all in heaven and on earth, might be brought into a unity in Christ'.
7. Ephesians 3:8–12. Phillips translation.
8. 2 Timothy 1:7–10. New English Bible translation.
9. Luther's dislike of Scholastic philosophy and his strictures against it are well known. Cf. *The Table Talk of Martin Luther*, p. 42 in the Hazlitt translation, edited by Thomas S. Kepler (Cleveland: World Publishing Co., 1952), p. 30; and many passages to the same effect in *The Bondage of the Will*. It may be noted, however, that even in his most anti-philosophical mood Luther does not denounce the study of philosophy as such; on the contrary he 'approves thereof, so that it be within reason and moderation'. His contention is simply that 'philosophy understands naught of divin matters' and that 'to mix

mean, however, that no philosophical implications can be drawn from the five passages for a general view of purpose. That Luther drew some himself seems rather clear, and I shall try to state succinctly what these were.

1. *'Purpose' is a term which applies eminently to God*, in the Pauline usage which the Reformers wanted to follow. To put it only a little differently: according to the rules of the Pauline language game 'purpose' is predicated of God first of all, and only derivatively of human beings.

2. *In the Pauline language 'purpose' has its place in a pattern or constellation of terms such that no one term is definable apart from the others*: i.e., the terms in this Scriptural language game[10] are mutually supportive. This becomes clearer the better we become acquainted with the Biblical text in its original languages.

3. *God's purpose – because it is God's – is eternal and unchanging*, since with him 'there is neither variableness nor shadow of turning'. We might consider this 'trivially true', but Luther considers that it needs asserting because of passages that seem to speak of God's will as changing.[11] Perhaps such 'changes of will' or 'changes of mind' are to be seen *within* a larger encompassing purpose. On the other hand we may have here an instance of 'God and his masks'.[12]

4. Apart from the event and word of Jesus Christ, God's eternal purpose is *hidden from man*; it is a secret, a mystery impenetrable by human understanding or human imagination. The thrust of this, for Luther, is primarily against 'philosophy' which would attempt to reason from the creation to the Creator, from earthly and human phenomena to the divine Will or Purpose behind these phenomena. More of this in a moment.

5. *We must therefore draw a distinction* – indeed, the sharpest distinction

      philosophy up with divinity may not be endured'.

10. Luther, of course, would never have admitted that the 'Pauline language game' is idiosyncratically Paul's. It is the Scriptural language game with its terms used more rigorously than elsewhere in the Bible. While all of the canonical books are inspired, they are not all of equal weight or value. Thus Luther was able (i) to question whether some books belonged in the canon at all, e.g., 1 and 2 *Peter* and *Ecclesiastes;* (ii) to call James 'an epistle of straw'; and (iii) to claim Romans as 'the clearest gospel of all', a phrase which is significant in the present context. Paul's writings are central and crucial in that they use Biblical terms in a more rigorous way than they are used elsewhere. But Luther found a great many agreements with and anticipations of Pauline usage in, e.g., the *Psalms* and *Genesis*. See his extensive Commentaries on these books.

11. Cf. O. S. Rankin in *A Theological Word Book of the Bible*, edited by Alan Richardson, New York: The Macmillan Company, 1956, p. 183: 'The OT is not at all shy of the idea that God can change or modify his purpose'. Johan and Jeremiah 18:8 are cited over against Isaiah 14:24–27.

12. See §4 and §5, below.

possible – *between the God who is hidden, secret, transcendent and mysterious on the one hand, and the God who is revealed, clear, immanent and human on the other.* This distinction between 'God hidden' and 'God revealed', which Luther develops into the related distinction between 'God and his masks', is as the centre of Luther's theology, and it is the basis of almost everything he has to say which is of interest philosophically. I shall therefore want to deal with it at greater length.

6. *As much as we can know of God's purpose is in His Word, Jesus Christ; and this purpose is the free bestowing of love, mercy, forgiveness, salvation in His Son upon those who do not deserve it through any special moral or intellectual merit of their own.* They have absolutely no claim upon it, but It – God's purposed redemption – has claimed them from all eternity.

7. Finally: *Between God-as-known-in-Christ and what men generally have thought they knew about 'the hidden God' there is contradiction: there is a paradox.* The *form* of God's revealing himself is just this paradox: the sovereign God appears in a child born in a manger; he dies helplessly upon a cross. That God's purpose should contradict what reason tells us he is in himself is indeed 'foolishness' – foolishness to the reasoners, foolishness to the philosophers. Put in another way: God reveals himself without abandoning his mysteriousness.[13] His communication with man is 'indirect communication' from any rational point of view.

If these seven points may be taken as not unfairly summarizing Luther's views, I should like to select (somewhat but not quite arbitrarily) numbers 2, 4 and 5 for some degree of reinforcement, amplification and documentation.

Not long before his death, Luther wrote an account of 'his decisive conversion', the event which was also 'the fundamental theological perception of the Reformation'.[14] Whether or not it is biographically accurate – and there seems to be some doubt about this, as Ebeling points out – it is a passage of considerable interest for the light it sheds on Luther's *way* of thinking: i.e., on his theological method as well as on the 'turn' of thought that was to be decisive for him. It is therefore worth quoting at length.

A strange burning desire had seized me to understand Paul in the Epistle to the Romans; it was not coldness of heart that had stood in my way until then, but a single phrase in chapter 1: 'For in it the righteousness of God is revealed' (Rom. 1:17). For I hated this phrase, 'the righteousness of God', which I had been taught to understand philosophically, from its natural usage by all who teach doctrine, as referring to the so-called formal or active righteousness, by means of which God punishes sinners and the unrighteousness. But I who, however blamelessly I lived as

13. W. Pauck, *Op. cit.*, p. 19.
14. Gerhard Ebeling, *Luther: An Introduction to his Thought*, translated by R. A. Wilson, London: Collins, 1970, p. 39.

a monk, felt myself to be a sinner before God, with a deeply troubled conscience, and could not rely on being reconciled through the satisfaction I could carry out myself, did not love – no, hated – the just God who punishes sinners; and I silently rebelled against God, if not with blasphemy, at least with dreadful murmuring: Was it not enough that poor sinners, eternally lost as a result of original sin, should be cast down through the Law of the Decalogue, but that God should add one torment to another through the gospel, and even through the gospel should threaten us with righteousness and his anger? So I raved on with a wild and confused conscience; and yet I returned again and again to this very passage in Paul, burning with thirst to know what St. Paul meant. Finally, thanks to the mercy of God, and thinking ceaselessly of this matter one night, *I recalled the context in which the words occur*, namely: 'In it the righteousness of God is revealed ... as it is written. 'The righteous shall live by faith'.' *Then I began to understand the righteous lives, that is, by faith, and that this is the meaning of the passage*: through the gospel the righteousness of God is revealed, that is, passive righteousness, through which the merciful God makes us righteous through faith, as it is written, 'The righteous shall live by faith'. Then I had the feeling that straightway I was born again, and had entered through open doors into paradise itself. *The whole scripture revealed a different countenance to me. I then went through the whole scripture* in my memory and *compared analogies in other expressions*: for example, the work of God, that is, what God works in us; the power of God, through which he makes us powerful; the wisdom of God, through which he makes us wise; the strength of God, the salvation of God, the glory of God. As I had hated the phrase 'the righteousness of God' before, I now valued it with equal love, as the word which was dearest to me. Thus in truth this passage of Paul became the gate of paradise for me ...'[15]

What is remarkable here, I think, is not only the '*sola fide – sola gratia*' principle which became the cornerstone of the Reformation, but also – and more to our purpose – the way that principle was arrived at *through coming to see the usage of Scriptural words and phrases in a new light*. Luther's question was an existential one, arising out of deep trouble and concern. It was by no means a theoretical question about the exegesis of a text; and yet the question was answered, for him, by coming to a new understanding of Biblical language — a new perception of how various terms (like 'God', 'righteousness', 'faith') are inter-related *in their usage* throughout the Scriptures. 'The whole scripture revealed a different countenance to me' and 'I went through ... comparing analogies in other (Biblical) expressions'. As Professor John Wisdom might say, none of 'the facts' had changed: the words and phrases of the Scripture were the same as they had been before; no one had discovered that a certain passage was spurious, or that the Greek text of Rom. 1:17 should read differently. The difference was not in 'the facts'

15. Weimar edition of Luther's *Works* (Kritische Gesamtausgabe der Werke D. Martin Luthers, Weimar, 1883 ff.), Vol. 54, pp. 185-186 (yr. 1545). Translated by R. A. Wilson. Some current translators and commentators render the crucial quotation in Rom. 1:17 from Habbakuk 2:4 by connecting the phrase 'through faith' with 'the just' rather than with the verb 'shall live'. Thus: 'He who through faith is rigteous (or justified) shall live'. Anders Nygren, Commentary on Romans, Philadelphia: Muehlenburg Press, 1949, p. 65.

but in the wah 'the facts' fitted together and in the whole ensuing picture or pattern[16] which resulted. This new picture was *radically* new – showing that the question of linguistic usage involved (What is meant by 'the righteousness of God?' or: How is this phrase *used* in the Scriptures?) was a *central* one: the usage of other words and phrases depended upon it, because of the interrelationship of terms within a language. Furthermore and most importantly, the new picture or pattern that was formed spoke immediately to Luther's trouble and anxiety: it *answered* his worried questionings about divine 'righteousness' in relation to the guilty consciences of man.[17] His anxious questioning had received an answer in which his perplexity was dissolved.

The reason this could happen (on a philosophical, not theological level) was very clearly stated by Wittgenstein: 'To image a language menas to imagine a form of life'.[18] To imagine a *new* language – to *perceive* a new language, a language radically changed from what one had asusmed it to be – means nothing less than to envisage a *new* form of life, capable of making one a 'new being' through participating in it. And this is what happened to Luther. In the 'old' Scriptural grammar, 'the purpose of God' had a terrifying aspect: God's purpose, at least partly, was the exacting of justice: it was, at least partly, judgment and punishment. Now God's purpose was seen as mercy and love, because his 'righteousness' was viewed in a radically new way: not as an ethical justice which demands an equivalence or fitness in his treatment of men in typical Aristotelian fashion – 'giving every man his due' – but as a freely giving, forgiving, pardoning, and justifying righteousness whose aim was the salvation and transformation of men. Can a difference of language mean a change in one's 'form of life?' Martin Luther and the Reformation stand witnesses to this.

Luther's changed conception of the 'God's righteousness' and God's purpose in relation to man led directly to his sharp distinction between the hidden and revealed God. If God's purpose is to show love and mercy, the facts of nature and history seem to contradict this – *if we assume that nature*

---

16. Cf. Wisdom's *Philosophy and Psychoanalysis*, pp. 157–158.
17. '... The prevalence of the 'bad conscience' in reality, literature, and theory ... gives evidence for the assertion that the uneasy, accusing and judging conscience is the original phenomenon; that the good conscience is only the absence of the bad conscience; and that the demanding and warning conscience is only the anticipation of it'. (Tillich, *The Protestant Era*, pp. 137–138). Compare Albert Schweitzer's saying that 'a good conscience is an invention of the Devil'. But for Tillich it is possible, not to eliminate but to transcend one's guilty conscience – and this is exactly what Luther did. "Justification by grace', in Luther's sense, means the creation of a 'transmoral' conscience' (*Op.cit.*, p. 146).
18. *Philosophical Investigations*, paragraph 19.

and history can lead us to God. But Luther became more and more doubtful of this.

In nature we witness blossoming and withering, growth and decay; in history we see victor and vanquished, bane and blessing, rise and fall. But who hides behind all these masks? We sense the working of God in all life; we know that He is the cause and pulse beat of the world. But who is this God? ...

Who is the God encompassing us? Tree and rock are mute; nature utters no intelligible speech. Do flowers bloom merely to wither, or do they wither to produce new seed? Whose power is final, life's or death's? Is nature a realm of ineffable peace and tranquility which we seek when we flee to her from the bruised and battered world of man? Or is nature also subject to the never-ending conflict, subject to the never-ending conflict of dog-eat-dog? ...

History is no less mysterious and confusing. What is the meaning of the ceaseless alternation between ascent and descent, rise and decline? Does all this have a purpose and a goal? What about justice in a world in which the strong always conquer and disregard all laws? ... Is it not, after all, a game in which God alone participates by loading his musket at the nations and gloating as they topple? Is not this God a hardhearted, coldly planning, or perhaps planless Fate? ...

... Small wonder that Luther declared that this God, who dwells in everything that lives and whom he beheld there as clearly as every poet and philosopher[19] did, is a hidden God, a God to whom no path of our philosophical thinking can lead us ...[20]

'Therefore', said Luther, 'we are able to distinguish between God and His masks. The world is not able to do this'.[21] While God is veritably present in nature and history, he is not *unambiguously* present; and we cannot ascend from nature and history to a God whose character is clearly defined.

It makes a difference whether you say that God is present or whether you say that He is present for you. But he is there for you when he adds his word (to his presence) and binds himself, saying: Here you shall find me. When you have the word, you can grasp him and have him, and say: Now I have thee, as thou sayest. So it is with the right hand of God: it is everywhere, as no one can deny; but it is also nowehr – therefore you cannot apprehend it anywhere unless it binds and confines itself for your benefit to one place. This happens when it moves and dwells in the humanity of Christ. There you will most certainly find it. Otherwise you must run through all creation from end to end, groping and fumbling about, here and there, without finding it.

19. Both Luther and Calvin accepted a kind of teleological argument for the existence of God – or so it appears. They state it, however, in Biblical and 'everyday' language – not in Scholastic terminology. And the question is what significance they attach to it. See Calvin, *Institutes of the Christian Religion*, Book I, Chaps. 5 and 16; pp. 52–53 and p. 200 (The Library of Christian Classics, Vol. XX. Philadelphia: The Westminster Press, 1960). For references to a dozen or more passages in Luther affirming man's 'natural knowledge' of God, see N. Arne Bendtz, 'Faith and Knowledge in Luther's Theology' in *Reformation Studies: Essays in Honor of Roland H. Bainton*, edited by Franklin H. Littel, Richmond, Virginia: John Knox Press, 1962, pp. 21–23.
20. Heinrich Bornkamm, *Luther's World of Thought*, translated by Martin H. Bertram, St. Louis, Missouri: Concordia Publishing House, 1965, pp. 61–63.
21. Lectures on Galatians (1531), 40, I; 174, 3.

Although it is really there, it is not there for you.[22]

Nature and history show us not God but his masks. Natural theology and metaphysics have used the masks as evidence for the Being behind the masks – a precarious task (since for every mask its opposite may be found), but one which may have its meaning and value for cognition. Is our concern with God and his purpose a *cognitive* concern? Luther thought not, and made the sharpest possible distinction between cognition and faith.

> We must learn to put the question concerning God correctly. This is imperative ... Did we actually look for God when we sought Him in the aggregate of life? Or were we not groping rather for a concept of the ultimate unity of the world? To find the coherent elements of the world is the never-ending task of the philosopher, but this is not the core of the question concerning God. To trace the living world to its ultimate cause and deduce a philosophical system from this, and to believe in God, are two radically different matters. The former stems from our strong urge and thirst for knowledge and cognition. But the result of this philosophical investigation still has no bearing on my attitude and my conduct of life ... On the other hand, everything in life does depend on the question whether I truly believe in God. *A genuine faith in God must transform me into another man*. The real question concerning God is not only a question asked by us but also one addressed to us. The one is a question of cognition; the other, a question of life. The two can become one only if I know both ... Therefore we must learn to formulate the question concerning God correctly'.[23]

The voluntaristic-existential thrust of Luther's thinking about God comes out very clearly in the answer to a question in his Larger Catechism. Indeed it comes out in his formulation of the question itself: 'What does it mean to have a god, *or what is God?* – Answer: God is that to which I must look for all that is good and to whom I must flee in every need ...' Having God means 'to possess something on which the heart places all its reliance'. 'To whatever your heart cleaves and on whatever it relis, that is really your god'.[24]

To think of God and his purposes in this way is quite different from thinking of God in terms of cognition: What can we *know* about the source of life, the unity of the world, the *Ding-an-sich*, etc.? When the latter type of thinking runs up against the modern naturalisms, the refutations of the theistic arguments, and the bankruptcy of even the most sophisticated attempts[25] to revive and refurbish the God of metaphysics, it can only despair – or else view belief as 'a type of knowledge with less probability. A tragic confusion'.[26] Tragic in that we have been seeking God in a language unsuited

---

22. Weinar Edition of Luther's Works, 23: 151.
23. Bornkamm, *Op. cit.*, pp. 64–65. Italics mine.
24. Weinar Edition of Luther's Works, 30 I, 133–134.
25. See Paul Edwards, 'Professor Tillich's Confusions': *Mind*, 74, 1965.
26. Bornkamm, *Op. cit.*, p. 67.

to finding Him.

If we reject the metaphysical language for the language of Biblical faith, we must be very clear about the consequences: we shall *not have answers* to certain questions which may be raised. Certainly 'we must not ask for a concept of God equipped with all that appears to us necessary for and suited to God; we must not ask for proofs. There are none. We must not ask', either, 'for a categorical imperative'.[27] But there is another consequence, still, that we must face up to –another question we shall be unable to answer to the satisfaction of most philosophers:

> Where our blurred eyes behold nothing but darkness and tragedy in Jesus' life, there the eyes of faith see an immeasurable light bursting upon the world. God is concealed from the blind, but to the seeing He is revealed ... *But if some one should ask: 'Why must this be none other than Jesus*, this unphilosophical mind, this Jew from Palestine, that remote corner of the globe', *we have no reply to offer*. Whoever asks such questions has not yet comprehended the being of God. He still treats Him as a sort of president of the world with whose politics he is at variance and for whom he will not again cast his vote at the next election. This is not the way to deal with God. Whoever presumes to be able to prescribe to God how He should reveal Himself destroys the one thing in himself that he can do to meet God, namely, to behold where God's hand is to be seen and to hear where His Word is to be heard.[28]

Indeed – nothing the *petitio* involved in a statement such as the foregoing – we shall do well not even to say this much. One might do better to notice the curious similarity between this question ('Why this revelation rather than that one?'), so unanswerable by the fideist without begging the question, and another question which always seems to confront the metaphysician traveling the well worn Way of Analogy: 'Why choose *this* analogy, rather than some other one, to describe God?'[29] If the metaphysician is as embarrassed for an answer to this question (without *petitio*) as the fideist is for one to the question facing him, then the advantage might seem to be with the latter, insofar as he is *claiming* much less than the metaphysician. At this crucial point, as elsewhere, Luther's thinking lends itself to current empirical and analytical tendencies in the philosophy of religion[30] – tendencies in which talk about Jesus replace talk about God.[31]

27. *Ibid.*, p. 70.
28. *Ibid.*, p. 71.
29. See Paul Edwards' essay referred to above. Cf. Hume's *Dialogues on Natural Religion*, Section VII: 'We have no data to establish *any* system of cosmogony ... Our experience ... can afford us no probable conjecture concerning the whole of things. But if we must needs fix on some hypothesis, by what rule, pray, ought we to determine our choice? ... The Brahmins assert that the world arose from an infinite spider, who spun this whole complicated mass from his bowels, and annihilates afterwards the whole or any part of it by absorbing it again ... Here is a species of cosmogony which appears to us ridiculous ...

II

Just as we have taken Luther rather than Calvin for our paradigm of Reformation thought, so we shall take Barth – rather than Brunner or Niebuhr – as representing neo-Reformation theology in its clearest and purest form. Probably one could find more references to 'purpose' – and certainly to '*human* purpose' – in Calvin than in Luther; but what this means is that Luther's thinking is more purely, more distinctively Protestant in character; Calvin's is more mixed with Scholastic and classical elements. Something like this relationship holds also between Barth and Brunner: Brunner certainly has more to say about *human* purpose which is interesting philosophically; nevertheless Barth's is the most authentic voice of the Reformation in our time.[32]

A. The neo-Reformation view of purpose

Barth's theology is the theology of the Word of God. Herein is implied the same goal of *a renewed language* – the renewed language of Scripture – which motivated the sixteenth-century Reformers. The mark of Church 'proclamation' is above all *obedience*; it is obedient service rendered to the revealed Word found in Scripture even though it is not limited or bound by Scripture.

> Thus if human language claims to be proclamation, that can only mean that it claims to *serve* the Word of God, to point to its having previously been spoken through God Himself ..., Proclamation is human language in and through which God Himself speaks, like a king through the mouth of his herald, which moreover is meant to be heard and apprehended as language in and through which God Himself speaks, and so heard and apprehended in faith as the divine decision upon life and death, as the divine judgment and the divine acquittal, the eternal law and the eternal gospel both together.[33]

---

to take for a model of the whole universe. But still here is a new species of analogy ...'
30. Cf. R. B. Braithwaite's 'An Empricist's View of the Nature of Religious Belief'.
31. The 'Death of God' theology, having roots which are for the most part not empirical or analytical, nevertheless shares this characteristic with a view such as Braithwaite's. Bultmann and the later Bonhoeffer can also be seen as moving in this direction.
32. Although ecclesiastically Barth's affiliation was Reformed rather than Lutheran, quotations from Luther far outnumber those from Calvin. In the first volume of the *Kirkliche Dogmatik* the ratio is almost 2 to 1.
33. *The Doctrine of the Word of God* (Prolegomena to Church Dogmatics, being Vol. I, Part I), translated by G. T. Thomson, New York: Charles Scribner's Sons, 1936, p. 57.

The 'Otherness' for which Barth's theology is as well known is the underlying otherness of God's Word from all human words. This gives proclamation its dialectical character:

... All true prophecy has discerned that no man as such can possibly utter the word of God. If man's language about God claims to be proclamation, it claims to be not grace but the service of grace, the means of grace. Were the will here in question the will of man to reach out beyond himself, to put himself with his word about God in the place of God, it would be a blasphemous rebellion ...[34]

Man's purposing,[35] *qua* Christian, can only be 'concrete obedience' to the Word. This bears upon the distinction between general and special revelation and whether Barth accepts the former in any sense. Contrary to what many have supposed, the answer is unequivocally that he does:

The question, 'What can God do?' is different from the question, 'What is the *commisison* laid on us through the promise given to the Church?' ... God may speak to us through Russian communism or a flute concerto, a blossoming shrub or a dead dog. We shall do well to listen to Him if He really does so. But we shall not be able to say – that would mean that we considered ourselves the prophets and founders of a new Church – that we are commissioned to spread what we so hear as an independent proclamation. God may speak to us through a pagan or an atheist ... But that is not equivalent to saying ... that we should have ourselves to proclaim the pagan and atheist thing we have heard.[36]

Proclamation has two and only two forms: *preaching* and *sacrament*:[37]

Preaching is such proclamation: i.e., the attempt, essayed by one clled thereto in the Church, to express in his own words in the form of an exposition of a portion of the Biblical testimony to revelation, and to make comprehensible to men of his day, the promise of God's revelation, reconciliation and calling, as they are to be expected here and now.

A sacrament is such proclamation: i.e., the symbolic act consummated in the community of the Church according to the directions of the Biblical witness to revelation, which accompanies and confirms preaching, an act, the aim of which as such is to attest the event of God's revelation, reconciliation and calling, which not only fulfils but already proves the promise.

The Word of God is a language; it is communication. God's Word is God's language. 'Church proclamation is language. Holy Scripture is also language. But revelation itself and as such is language too'.[38]

34. *Ibid.*
35. In Professor William Horosz's terminology of pre-purposive, purposive, and post-purposive models of existence, Barth's would clearly be the post-purposive model, 'which construes immediacy in terms of supernatural and supra-rational directives. In this perspective we stand on different evidential grounds ...' ('Searching for a Sense of Immediacy', *South-western Journal of Philosophy*, Vol. 1, No. 3, Fall, 1970, p. 131).
36. *The Doctrine of the Word of God*, pp. 60–61.
37. *Ibid.*, pp. 61–62.

We have no reason for *not* taking the concept 'Word of God' in its primary and literal sense. 'Speaks' is not a symbol (as P. Tillich, *Rel. Verwirkl.*, 1930, p. 48) thinks, a designation and description, chosen by man on the score of his own judgment as to its greater or less symbolic force, of a totally different content ... foreign to the meaning of this proposition. But this proposition corresponds – certainly with human inadequacy, with the brokenness with which alone human propositions can correspond with the nature of the Word of God – with the possibility which God has chosen and realised at all events in His Church. We are not absolutizing the human possibilities of the intellect. We might very well be of the private opinion that it would be better and nicer if God had not spoken and did not speak with such deliberate 'intellectualism'[39] and that it would be more appropriate to God if 'God's Word' meant all sorts of different things, apart from 'God speaks'. But is this private opinion of ours so important, resting as it does upon some sort of philosophy? If perhaps it does not, let us simply stick to the fact, and not think beyond it, that in the form in which the Church knows God's Word – the one and only form which affects us at all necessarily because it affects us magisterially – in this form 'God's Word' means 'God speaks', and all further statements about it must be regarded as exegesis, not as limitations or negations of this proposition.[40]

Barth proceeds immediately to supply such exegesis: God's speech is also God's *act*, and God's act is also God's *mystery*.

But as only God's *act* is really *God's* mystery (and not any other sort of mystery), so only God's *speech* is really *God's* act (and not any other sort of act). The concepts 'act' and 'mystery' cannot therefore, because they are necessarily explanatory, point us away from the concept of speech or language, but because they are explanations can only point us back to it repeatedly as the original text.[41]

Surely the dispute between Barth and Tillich as to whether 'God speaks' is a symbolic statement can be settled easily enough. In Tillich's later use of 'symbol',[42] words would be signs rather than symbols – except for onomatapoetic words and words with strong associative overtones. However, what Barth means to assert is that the statement 'God speaks' is *not metaphorical*; whereas for Tillich it would have to be metaphorical, since *all* statements about God are metaphorical except for the single statement: 'God is Being-itself'.[43] It is hard to see how Barth can deny that some sort of metaphor or analogy is involved when we say, 'God speaks'. This is so clear that we may wonder whether Barth really means to deny this; and indeed he does not. What he is denying – as he makes quite clear – is not the metaphorical quality of 'God speaks' *in this usage* of the term 'metaphorical'; he is refusing to use the term in this 'philosophical' sense and using it, rather

38. *Op. cit.*, p. 150.
39. A polemical reference to one of Tillich's charges against Barth's theology.
40. *Ibid.*
41. *Op. cit.*, pp. 150–151.
42. Cf. *Dynamics of Faith*, New York: Harper, 1957, p. 41 ff.
43. *Systematic Theology*, London: James Nickel, 1953, p. 265.

in a theological sense. This sense has to do, as he says, with *the free choice of metaphors and analogies* which the poet, for example, exercises when his imagination leads him to coin an especially felicitous, vividly descriptive phrase. Barth is denying that in our language about God we may invent metaphors at will – or that the metaphors which occur to us can be assessed by any aesthetic or philosophical or religious criteria outside the Word of God. We may, of course, do this; but doing it is an ostensive definition (perhaps *the* ostensive definition) of 'sin'.[44]

'What does it signify for the concept of the Word of God, if Word of God means originally and irrevocably, God *speaks*?' Three things primarily: the '*spirituality* of the Word of God, spirituality as distinguished from naturalness, corporeality, from any physical event' – even though 'there is no Word of God without a physical event';[45] the *personal* character of the Word: 'it is not a thing to be described, nor is it a concept to be defined; ... it is not 'a truth', not even the very highest truth; ... God always utters a *concretissimum*, which ... can as such neither be anticipated nor repeated': finally and most appositely for us, 'the *purposiveness* of the Word of God', which 'might also be called its relatedness or pointedness, its character as an address'.[46]

We do not know the Word of God, either in its form of proclamation or of Holy Scripture or of revelation, as an essence that exists for itself or could exist only for itself. The sole way we know it is as the Word directed to us, coming home to us ... We cannot infer this fact from the general concept of language. It is so, but it might be different ... God had no need to speak to us; what God utters from eternity to eternity by Himself and to Himself might really be uttered as well and better without or being there, as an utterance which for us would be eternal silence. Only if we are clear on this point can we estimate what it means that God has created a world and ourselves – under no necessity on His side, but actually He has; that His love is valid for us – under no necesisty, but actually it is; that His Word is spoken to us, but actually it is. It is thus purposiveness, *free, actual, essentially unessential to God*, which meets us in proclamation, in the Bible, in revelation ...[47]

In discussing God's purposiveness, Barth notes these four points concerning it:

1. The Word of God as directed to us ... is such a word as we do not speak to ourselves, as under no circumstances we could ever speak to ourselves. Every human word ... even the word of the Bible, we perhaps could and can speak as such even by ourselves ... The Word of God always

44. Provided that God's Word has spoken to the individual doing it – and of this we are never able to be certain.
45. *Op. cit.*, p. 155.
46. *Op. cit.*, p. 158.
47. *Op. cit.*, p. 158.

tells us something new, which otherwise we could never have heard from anyone ... It is this otherness, then, which is yet related to us ... which stamps it as ... as *God's Word*, as *the Lord's* Word, compared with which all other words, however profound and fresh and arresting they may be, are not the words of the Lord.[48]

2. The Word of God is ... the Word which aims at and touches us in our existence. No word of man is competent to aim at us in our existence, no word of man has the power to touch us in our existence.[49]

3. The Word of God is ... the Word which has become and does become necessary for the renewal of the original relationship between us and him ... The Word of God under this third aspect of its purposiveness is the Word of reconciliation, i.e., of the *Reconciler*, of God who by a second creation sets up His covenant anew with us in judgment and grace.[50]

4. The Word of God is ... finally the Word by which God announces Himself to man, i.e. by which He promises Himself as the content of man's future, as He who meets him on his way through time as the End of all time, as the hidden Lord of all times. His presence as the Word is exactly His presence as He that cometh, cometh to fulfil and complete founded between us and Him and Creation, renewed and confirmed at the reconciliation. Once more this final Word cannot be a word of man. It is proper to God's Word, and only to God's Word, to be actually, as Word, the full, genuine presence of the Speaker, although of Him as Him that should come ... In that very way is the real righteous Lord the Lord of all lords. And whatever God may say to us, it will always be said too in this final, consummating eschatological relationship.[51]

We find that Barth's conception of 'purpose' agrees with Luther's in the following ways: (i) 'purpose – like 'person'[52] – is a concept that applies primarily and pre-eminently to God, and only secondarily and derivatively to human beings; (ii) 'purpose' is inseparable from language: we find out what a person's purpose is through his speech; his purpose is communicated through speaking; (iii) in God, who alone is truly Person, speaking and acting are not disjunct: God's language is therefore God's act in Jesus Christ;[53] (iv) philosopical discussions about 'human purpose' are irrelevant to theology, certainly to Christian theology;[54] (v) the theological concern with *human* purpose centers on man's response, both individually and collectively, to God's purposed act which is also his spoken Word to man, Jesus Christ; (vi)

48. *Op. cit.*, p. 160.
49. *Ibid.*
50. *Op. cit.*, p. 161.
51. *Op. cit.*, pp. 161–162.
52. Cf. *The Doctrine of the Word of God*, p. 157: 'The problem is not whether God is a person, the problem is whether we are. Or shall we find among us men one whom in the full and real sense of this concept we can call a person? But God is really a person, really a free subject'.
53. *Op. cit.*, pp. 162–164.
54. We *actually use* words like 'purpose' and 'intention' of human beings. Therefore to ask the question, 'Do human beings *really* entertain purposes' or 'Do they *really* have intentions, motives', etc. is as nonsensical as to ask the question, 'Do machines think?' – even though the answer might seem to be obviously 'Yes' in the one case, 'No' in the other.

this response is faith: not directly purposed itself (because it is a gift of God's grace), it changes and transforms human purposings and motivations which, apart from it, would be sinful in themselves;[53] (vii) the change and transformation wrought by the Word of God meeting and touching man in his existence are not so much changes in the *content* of his purposes[56] as they are a change and transformation of his ultimate purpose, the final goal for which everything is intended to be done. 'What is the *chief end* of man? To glorify God and enjoy Him forever'.[57] But God is the speaking of God of the Bible: he is Jesus Christ the reconciler, the redeemer.

III

Two problems of relevance arise to plague any such view as that of Luther and Barth. Broadly speaking, one problem belongs to christian social ethics, the other to epistemology.

God's purpose is transcendent; the Word of God differs qualitatively from the words of men. Likewise God's act in Christ differs qualitatively from the actions of men: hence 'God's act is also God's mystery'.[58] A man either responds or does not respond to God's Word; the response itself is a work of grace, for which no criteria can be laid down. It happens, or it does not happen; and its happening cannot be forced, insured, or guaranteed in any way. So much is clear; but are there *marks* by which the renewal of man's being may be recognized? It seems that there are not. As with Kierkegaard's 'Knight of Faith',[59] the Word of God is mysteriously hidden precisely in its 'worldliness':

When God speaks to man, this happening is never so marked off from the rest of what happens that it might not promptly also be interpreted as a part of this happening ... The Church in fact is also a sociological entity with definite historical and structural features ... The Bible is also in fact the document for the history of the religion of a tribe in Nearer Asia and of its Hellenistic offshoot. Jesus Christ in fact is alo the Rabbi of Nazareth, ..., one whose activity is ... a little

55. Compare Reinhold Niebuhr's remark that 'there is some sin contained in every act' of the natural man. Similarly, Article XIII of *The Thirty-Nine Articles* ('Of Works before Justification'): 'Work done before the grace of Christ, and the Inspiration of his Spirit, are not pleasant to God, inasmuch as they spring not of faith in Jesus Christ; ... yea rather, for that they are not done as God willed and commanded them to be done, we doubt not but that they have the nature of sin'.
56. To suppose this is the mistake of pietism generally.
57. *Westminster Shorter Catechism.*
58. *The Doctrine of the Word of God*, pp. 150, 184–212.
59. *Fear and Trembling*, Princeton: Princeton University Press, 1941, p. 49 ff.

commonplace alongside more than one other founder of a religion ... The veil is thick. We do not possess the Word of God otherwise than in the mystery of its worldliness.

In other words, we always have it in a form which as such is *not* the word of God ... Otherwise expressed, the self-presentation of God in His Word is not a direct one ...

The self-presentation of God in His Word is not comparable with any other self-presentation, inasmuch as all that elsewhere meets us as self-presentation is either direct communication, or if indirect, characterized by a certain correspondence and similarity between matter and form, ... This is the very thing that is excluded in the case of the Word of God. Its form is not a suitable but an unsuitable means for the self-presentation of God. It does not correspond to the matter but it contradicts it. It does not unveil it but it veils it ...

Moreover ... the place where God's Word is manifest is, objectively and subjectively, the place where sin rules. The form of the Word of God is therefore really that of the cosmos which stands in contradiction to God...[60]

Barth's dialectic of 'indirect communication', with its echoes not only of Kierkegaard[61] but of Luther's 'masks of God', poses the two following problems at least:

1. On this view, can any human purposes be recognized as relevant to God's purpose of self-communication in Christ? The 'wordliness' doctrine seems to make everything relevant; but where everything is relevant, isn't it a question whether anything is? To put the matter differently: man's *response* to the Word of God is all-important; but since this response is unpredictable, mysterious, etc. (not a work induced by human effort but a work of God's grace), have we any reason to see it as something determinate or to see *in* it implications for determinate social actions, determinate ways of changing (or of not changing) existing social conditions? The political conservatism of Luther in his later years is well known: could not this be seen as a natural outgrowth of the 'worldliness' doctrine plus the emphasis on transcendence and *sola gratia*? Where *all* temporal events are ambiguous – where divine meaning, divine purpose for human life – are not unambiguously present anywhere, what reason has the Christian to do this rather than that *as an expression of his faith*? For all that is said about 'worldliness', man's response to God's language seems to be so caught up in transcendence, that the world of human process is left just where it always has been – a part of the 'sinful cosmos'. Granted that this has the value Niebuhr and others have seen in it – of preventing us from absolutizing any human ahcievement or human perspective – does it not do this at the expense of leaving Christianity devoid of any social dynamic, any reason for altering the structures of society in which we are immersed? And if there are no reasons for *not* altering them either, then the Christian ethic, whatever else it is, would seem to be that of

---

60. *The Doctrine of the Word of God*, pp. 188–190.
61. Especially the *Concluding Unscientific Postscript* and *Training in Christianity*.

Thomas Mann's 'unpolitical man'[62] in the extreme. This – it may be argued – is the inevitable outcome and foregone conclusion of transcendence-without-immanence – of the God who is *totaliter aliter* – *however much one may talk simultaneously about the 'worldliness' of the Word and even about 'the humanity of God'.*[63]

2. The other problem is epistemological: it is the problem, so much debated lately, of *the meaningfulness of religious discourse*. This may seem to be especially acute for any theology accenting transcendence as Barth's does. And it is a *philosophical* problem, a part of man's attempt to think rationally, critically and comprehensively about religion. This entire enterprise may be questioned as to its *legitimacy* or its *effectiveness*.[64] The 'Reformation theology' has usually and sometimes drastically criticized it on the first ground, although it might do so on the second as well. It is noteworthy that the two representatives of what Professor Ferre calls 'the theological veto' against the enterprise are Luther and Barth. As philosophers we must set aside – not ignore – the theological veto. As Ferre points out, the philosopher's answer to it can be shown to be question-begging. 'This circle, however, is one which we may confidently enter'.[65] The philosopher, *qua* philosopher, must address himself to the question of the meaningfulness of religious utterances, the central question in the philosophy of religion today.

To see what the problem is for Reformation and neo-Reformation theology in particular we must take statements such as this theology would *characteristically* make, i.e., statements which are central or crucial to this theology, statements which are the *sine qua non* of *this* theology (rather than of other theologies) – statements like the following: 'God sent His Son into the world in order to redeem the world'; 'God has spoken to men finally and definitively in Jesus Christ'; 'the Word of God as directed to us always tells us something new, ... which otherwise we could not have heard from anyone';[66] 'through the gospel the righteousness of God is revealed, ... through which the merciful God makes us righteous through faith'.[67] For present-day Empiricism the problem is: how can such statements be understood in view of the widely accepted 'falsifiability' criterion of

---

62. Cf. *Betrachtungen eines Unpolitischer*, setting forth a view which Mann later repudiated in view of the Nazi atrocities and excesses.
63. See Barth's introduction to Feuerbach's *Das Wesen des Christentums*.
64. Frederick Ferre, *Basic Modern Philosophy of Religion*, p. 22.
65. *Op. cit.*, p. 25.
66. *Supra*, p.
67. *Supra*, p.

meaningfulness for empirical or informative statements?[68] It is not just that we could not dream of any way in which these statements could be publicly *verified* (this difficulty they share with metaphysical statements); but how could they ever be falsified: i.e., what evidence would a Reformation or neo-Reformation theologian accept as *counting against* them? That it is hard to be sure whether Jesus ever lived or not and much harder to know what kind of person he was? Obviously not: Barth himself states that 'on the evidence' one would not be especially impressed by Jesus.[69] That 'God' and 'Word of God' are transcendently beyond the power of man's mind to conjure up, verify, or imagine? Clearly this might make them extremely doubtful or questionable but it would not *falsify* them for Barth who insists precisely on this transcendence. That ther is a great deal of evidence in the world showing God, if He is also all-powerful and all-knowing, *not* to be 'the merciful God' – i.e., the age-old problem of natural evil? Many *apparent* believers have been shaken by this evidence (from Job to the present), but if Luther had really abandoned his assertion because of this evidence (with which he must have been even better acquainted than we are), he would not have been a beliver – or Martin Luther. It seems that there is no evidence the Reformation theologian is prepared to accept as falsifying his characteristic statements. This is partly because he refuses to accept any evidence as counting against what he says, and partly because the statements on their very surface seem to be immune from attack on the basis of empirical evidence.[70] What kind of meaning, then – if any – do such statements have?

IV

Only an intimation can be given of how these two problems might be dealt with in the framework of Reformation thought and (for the second especially) with the aid of modern linguistic analysis.

A. *The ethical-social problem of transcendence*

This is perhaps not so serious from within the Reformation framework. It is

---

68. See 'Theology and Falsification', *New Essays in Philosophical Theology*, edited by Antony Flew and Alasdair MacIntyre, London: SCM Press, 1955.
69. *Supra*, p.000. Cf. Kierkegaard's *Concluding Unscientific Postscript*, Princeton: Princeton University Press, 1968, pp. 25–35.
70. This, of course, would create difficulty under the older Positivistic criterion of verifiability and probably from any naturalistic, science-oriented point of view.

serious only if one insists on being able to deduce an ethic from a metaphysic of immanence– when there is no metaphysic of immanence! The history of the opposition to Nazism has shown men who were disciples of Barth, or strongly influenced by him, to have been among the most outspoken and most courageous enemies of totalitarianism: Martin Niemoller, Dietrich Bonhoeffer, Bishop Berggrav – not to mention Barth himself, whom the regime early recognized as one of its strongest critics. Protestant radicals like the strongly Barthian lay theologian William Stringfellow and the Rev. William Sloane Coffin Jr. carry on this tradition today. The theology of transcendence seems highly relevant to such men – precisely because of its transcendence. 'The kingdom of God is a totalitarian state' – and just for this reason, any human state which claims to be 'total' (explicitly or implicitly) has upon it the mark of the Beast and must be resisted.

So much for a pragmatic, individualistic answer – incomplete and unsatisfactory because it does not come to grips with the underlying problem. The real difficulty can be met – if at all – only by a renewal and revitalizing of something Protestants have neglected for over four hundred years: the doctrine of the Church, the crucified and risen Body of Christ. Fortunately something like this has been taking place in the ecumenical movement.

God's purpose for man is known 'by ostension', through pointing to Jesus. Man's purposive response to God's purpose is a response to Jesus, but not the exteriorized response of a separated, disrupted, alienated individual. It is possible only through participation in the life, death and resurrection of Jesus. This is accomplished (not merely told about referentially) through the Word of proclamation and the sacraments. The language of Word and sacraments is basically not constative but performative.[71] It is language in or through which something is *done*. What is done is that a fundamental purpose is laid at the base of one's life, from which there is no escaping.[72]

Historically, the doctrine of the secular 'orders' of society – structures such as the state, economic and legal systems, matrimony, occupational groups, etc. – has played an important role in Christian ethics.[73] These are 'the powers ... ordained of God', and the Christian's purpose in the world must first of all be mediated through them. Through them his responsiveness to the Word

---

71. See J. L. Austin, *How to Do Things with Words*, especially Lecture V.
72. 'The reason the Christian believes that story around which his whole life turns is, simply, that he cannot help it ... One neither seeks nor needs grounds for the acceptance of what he cannot help believing'. – Richard Taylor, 'Faith', in *Religious Experience and Truth*, Sidney Hook (ed.), New York: New York University Press, 1961.
73. For a contemporary Protestant expression of it see Emil Brunner's *The Divine Imperative*, Philadelphia: The Westminster Press, 1947.

becomes definite, structured, and specified; it becomes more than an indeterminate, unstructured, unpredictable responsiveness. A justified complaint of Protestant Liberals against Reformation theology is that so often these orders have been regarded as *fixed*, well nigh *unchangeable* structures expressing something of God's purpose for human life in this world. This has been a mistake.

> The new theology can learn from the Reformation doctrine of the orders that there are always given structural factors in human life which are what they are and which set the conditions under which the Christian life must be lived. But the new theology will also know that any *a priori* fixing of the possible transformation of the orders is unwarranted. The long testimony of history is against the notion that anything in human nature or society or perhaps even in physical nature is absolutely fixed. God is creator at every moment of time. In some degree, which is not given our minds to delimit, his world is always becoming new.[74]

The agency of this renewing of society is the Church – not indeed (or at least not primarily) the institutionally organized churches, but that body 'which no man can number or identify', of those who 'are not conformed to this world' of Vietnams and Cambodias and the power structure that has always produced them, but who work and pray – mostly in very 'secular' ways – for the renewal. In a society sick unto death, this may be the only ground of hope.

B. *The epistemological problem of transcendence*

Confronted with the falsifiability criterion, those who have wanted to find *some* meaning in religious utterances have taken two general directions, one to the left and the other to the right.[75] The latter group accept 'Flew's challenge'[76] head-on and try to *state* conditions under which 'talk about God' *would* be falsified. I. M. Crombie, Basil Mitchell, and John Hick are representative of this right-wing trend; and of these Hick's doctrine of 'eschatological verification' seems the most interesting move, as well as the one which best lends itself to statements about God's *purpose*. 'Eternal life' in the Biblical sense is a quality of life which can be experienced here and now; nevertheless certain of the New Testament promises could be verified or falsified (in one sense of those terms) by post-mortem experiences. This satisfies the verifiability criterion if all that is meant by this is that we can

---

74. Daniel Day Williams, 'The Liberal Theology in America', *The Journal of Religion*, Vol. XXV, no. 3, p. 177.
75. William T. Blackstone, *The Problem of Religious Knowledge*, Prentice-Hall: 1963, pp. 75–76.
76. As Blackstone notes, the principle of falsifiability was first stated by Karl Pepper in his Logic of Scientific Discovery.

imagine certain experiences that would confirm – although not falsify – *some* religious statements.

> There can be conclusive evidence for it (religion) if it be true, but there cannot be conclusive evidence against it if it be untrue. For if we survive bodily death we shall (presumably) know that we have survived it, but if we do not survive death we shall not know that we have not survived it.[77]

The cricitism of 'eschatological verification' by Kai Nielson[78] – viz., that Hick's reasoning is circular since we would have to know what 'God' or 'the Christ' means before a post-mortem experience of God or the Christ could be specified and thus counted as verifying it – is certainly valid if eschatological verifiability is being used to give meaning to statements in which *these* terms ('God' and 'the Christ') appear, or *a fortiori* to show that all religious statements are meaningful. As confined to a certain class of religious statements, however – viz., those referring to some kind of post-mortem existence in terms ostensively specifiable ('Jesus', 'streets paved with gold', 'large-eyed dancing girls' or whatnot) 'eschatological verification' would be a way of saying that for *these* statements there is no meaning problem – as long as we can make clear what we are talking about. But if we can do this, is it *religious* language we are using?[79]

If eschatological verification fails (as it certainly does) to show the cognitive claims of *all* religious language, this may suggest that 'religious language' is not all of a piece, and this I believe to be the case. Just as 'religion' can be defined only in terms of a list of 'religion-making characteristics',[80] so there exists among different samples of what would be generally recognized as 'religious language' a kind of 'family resemblance' in virtue of which they are so recognized. We shall not, then (as so many seem to have done) hope to find definitively that *all* religious language (or *all* Christian language or *all* Reformation language) is such that we can say of it definitively that it is cognitive or non-cognitive, informative or non-informative, falsifiable or non-falsifiable, emotive, conative, or heuristic, etc. We shall see that different kinds of religious language have different uses.

> Philosophy may in no way interfere with the actual use of language; it can in the end only describe it.

77. John Hick, *Faith and Knowledge*. Ithica, New York: Cornell University Press, *1957, p. 148.*
78. *Canadian Journal of Theology*, Vol. IX (1963), No. 4, pp. 271–281.
79. A test case might be 'I know that my Redeemer (Vindicator) liveth ...'
80. William Alston, *Religious Belief and Philosophical Thought*, New York: Harcourt-Brace, 1963, pp. 5–6.

> For it cannot give it any foundation either.
> It leaves everything as it is.[81]

'Leaving everything as it is' means – in the context of religion – paying attention to the way religious believers actually use the language they use, and not telling them how they *must* use it (if it is to be meaningful) in accordance with a pre-conceived canon of 'ordinary language'[82] or with dictates of a natural theology.[83] There are indeed confusions *within* a language that are the philosopher's business to clear up; but it is at least questionable whether this can be done *from outside* the language in question. That it can*not* be has been argued very cogently by Peter Winch:

> Criteria of logic are not a direct gift of God, but arise out of, and are only intelligible in the context of, ways of living or modes of social life. It follows that one cannot apply criteria of logic to modes of social life as such. For instance, science is one such mode and religion is another; and each has criteria of intelligibility peculiar to itself. So within science or religion actions can be logical or illogical: in science, for example, it would be illogical to refuse to be bound by the results of a properly carried out experiment; in religion it would be illogical to suppose that one could pit one's strength against God's ...[84]

And if we hold, with Wittgenstein, that a language expresses and articulates a form of life, the same thing Winch says about modes of social life, and actions within these modes, may be said of languages and of utterances within them:

> Reality is not what gives language sense. What is real and what is unreal shows itself *in* the sense that language has. Further, both the distinction between the real and the unreal and the concept of agreement with reality themselves belong to our language ...[85]

---

81. Wittgenstein, *Philosophical Investigations*, I: 123–124.
82. D. Z. Phillips has made this point very well in his philosophically important and religiously sensitive book. *The Concept of Prayer*, New York: Shocken, 1966.
83. Cf. Gareth Matthews, 'Theology and Natural Theology', *The Journal of Philosophy*, Vol. 61 (1964), pp. 99 ff. This is an able defense of what the author calls 'nonnaturalism' in the philosophy of religion, over against Flew. 'A given claim either is compatible with all conceivable states of affairs in the empirical world, or it is not. But suppose it is not. It would follow that the claim is subject to empirical confirmation or disconfirmation *only if we knew which conceivable states of affairs it is incompatible with*. Certainly one can understand that a given claim is incompatible with some conceivable states of affairs without knowing what the incompatible states are'. Although I have no interest in defending 'eschatological verification' beyond what was said above, this would pretty clearly be one way of doing it.
84. *The Idea of a Social Science*, London: Routledge, 1958, pp. 100–101.
85. Peter Winch, 'Understanding a Primitive Society', *The American Philosophical Quarterly*, Vol. I (1964), p. 309.

As Phillips puts it: 'To understand the distinction between the real and the unreal, one must take account of the context in which the distinction is made. One can say *within* any such context, whether it be science or religion, 'This is the rule which *must* be observed, this is the meaning which a word *must* have if it is to belong to this conceptual family'. But when philosophers say, 'This is the meaning which a word *must have*' without specifying any such context, they are guilty of arbitrary linguistic legislation. The 'must' is not a logical 'must', but simply the 'must' of their own preferences, or the 'must' of one context which they have elevated, consciously or unconsciously, to be a standard for all others'.[86]

We are now ready to note the different kinds of meaning – or some of the different kinds – that may inhere in different forms of religious statements made by persons in the Reformation tradition. While the term 'depth grammar' would be far too pretentious for what can be undertaken here, the classification will be in accordance with the actual *use* of the Reformation language from within the classically Protestant 'form of life'.

The language of Luther in the Larger Catechism, quoted earlier in this essay, shows us the most important divisions of this classification: 'What does it mean to have a god, or what is God? God is that to which I must look for all that is good and to whom I must flee in every need. To whatever your heart cleaves and on whatever it relies, that is really your god'.[87] In this brief statement all three of the major religious discourses are exhibited.

1. The statement is in the form of a definition. It is not informative, since the statement's whole structure is analytical. It answers the question, 'How are we to understand the term 'God'?' or 'How do we (in accordance with the Reformation form of life) use the word 'God'?' – not the question, 'What is there about God which *makes a difference* to the way things are in the empirically observable world?' Hence the statement is not empirically falsifiable – not because we 'refuse to let anything count' against it, but because it is not the kind of statement against which any empirical evidence *could* count, because any evidence brought in from outside the conceptual scheme would be irrelevant to that scheme. The scheme would stand 'regardless of anything', but this 'regardless of anything' does not mean a refusal to accept empirical evidence. The statement is thus meaningful although unfalsifiable.

It seems a far cry from Luther's simple statement to the Ontological argument and Barth's *Church Dogmatics*, but all three have a common structure. For the Ontological argument this has been shown in Norman

86. *The Concept of Prayer*, pp. 9–10.
87. *Supra*, p.

Malcolm's celebrated essay,[88] where '*necessary* existence' is shown to be a property of God in the theological language game, which has been set up (within the Christian-theological life form) in such a way that no empirical evidence against God's existence is relevant, since God, by definition, is not a contingent being who might or might not exist (and to whom, consequently, such evidence *would* be relevant).

> The idea of the necessary existence or eternity of God (is) an idea that is essential to the Jewish and Christian religions. In those complex systems of thought, those 'language games', God has the status of a necessary being. Who can doubt that? Here we must say with Wittgenstein, 'This language-game is played!'[89]

Thus Anselm showed clearly what he set out to show, viz., that one 'cannot meaningfully say or think' that there is no God, since 'God' – in the Judaeo-Christian language-game – *means* 'a necessarily existing being'.[90]

As Donald Evans has pointed out, Karl Barth's view of 'the biblical language-game' which he calls 'Church proclamation' or the Word of God is closely parallel to Malcolm's view of the Judaeo-Christian language-game as exhibited in Ansel's second Ontological argument. 'For Barth, dogmatic theology is similar to what Wittgenstein calls logical 'grammar'; *it exhibits the conceptual structure of biblical language. One does not attempt to justify or defend biblical language; one merely displays its inner logical connections*'.[91]

'In the Word of God', according to Barth, '*it is decided* that the knowledge of God *cannot let itself be called in question*, or call itself in question, *from any position outside itself* ...'

88. 'Anselm's Ontological Arguments', *Philosophical Review*, January 1960. Reprinted in *Knowledge and Certainty*, Englewood Cliffs, New Jersey: Prentice-Hall, 1963, pp. 141–162.
89. *Loc. cit.*, p. 156. Against J. N. Findlay, who (in the *New Essays*) had argued for the necessary *non*-existence of God on the ground that 'necessary existence' is contradictory, Malcolm points out: '... The view that logical necessity merely reflects the use of words cannot have the implication that every existential statement must be contingent. That view requires us to *look at* the use of words and not manufacture *a priori* theses about it' (*Ibid.*, p. 155). He then quotes from the Ninetieth psalm.
90. *Knowledge and Certainty*, p. 156. For a current treatment of religion along formally Wittgensteinian lines see Robert McDermott, 'The Religion Game: Some Family Resemblances' (*Journal of the American Academy of Religion*, Vol. XXXVIII, No. 4, pp. 390–400).
91. *The Logic of Self-Involvement*, p. 23. The italics are mine; and it should be noted that Evans himself does not accept 'the philosophical view of language as something to be divided up into language-games ... each self-justifying and autonomous'. (*Ibid.*) Cf. also John Lange, *The Cognitivity Paradox*, Princeton, New Jersey: Princeton University Press, 1970, p. 71 ff.

It is quite impossible to ask whether God is knowable, *because this question is already decided by the only ... meaningful questioning which arises in this connection. The only ... meaningful questions in this context are: how far is god known? and how far is God knowable?* These questions are ... meaningful because they are genuine questions of Church proclamation and therefore also genuine questions of dogmatics'.[92]

A three-word parenthesis in the *Philosophical Investigations* shows how congenial to Wittgenstein himself was this view of theological language: '*Essence* is expressed by grammar ... Grammar tells us what kind of object anyting is (*Theology as grammar*).'[93] With Wittgenstein's examples of 'grammatical utterances' ('One plays patience by oneself', 'Sensations are private', 'Every rod has a length', etc.[94]) Evans cites the following parallel from Barth: 'If the knowledge of a 'God' is or even can be attacked from without, ... then that 'God' is manifestly not God but a false god'.[95]

That the most momumental work of theology since Clavin's Institutes is something like 'a depth grammar of the Bible' thus seems clear. This does not mean that everything *in* the *Church Dogmatics* is theological grammar; and it does not mean that all *religious* language of classical protestantism is – since not by any means all religious language is theological.

2. While the form of Luther's *Catechism* statement is logical (or grammatical), its content suggests two other views of religious language: the *emotive* and the *performative*.

'God is that to which I must look for all that is good and to whom I must flee in every need'. The language here is that of an emotional reaction or an emotional attitude toward life situations and of 'God' as a term *used* in certain relationship to these situations.

The 'emotive theory' of ethical and religious language has been a familiar one since the days of Logical Positivism and in particular, A. J. Ayer's *Language, Truth and Logic*. As a general theory of religious discourse it has not recommended itself to very many outside the *Wiener Kreis* and its

---

92. *Church Dogmatics*, Vol. II, Part 1, Edingurgh: T & T. Clark, 1937, pp. 4–5. Italics are mine. Barth's theological method owes a good deal to Anselm, as Barth himself was aware. Cf. John McIntyre, *St. Anselm and his Critics*, London, 1954, p. 25. Moreover 'Barth's interpretation of Anselm is very similar to Norman Malcolm's'. (Donald D. Evans, *Op. cit.*, p. 23n.)
93. Philosophical Investigations, tr. G. E. M. Anscombe, Oxford, 1953, Part I, nos. 371 and 373.
94. *Pihlosophical Investigations*, nos. 248, 251.
95. *Church Dogmatics* II, 1, p. 7. Cf. one of the major principles of 'classical Lutheran orthodoxy': '*Theologia debet esse grammatica*'. This Principle one may find expounded at length in (e.g.) Gerhard's *Loci Theologici*; for a currently more accessible source see Mueller's *Christian Dogmatics*, p. 92.

immediate followers, and not even to all members of the Circle.[96] The important changes introduced into the emotive theory of *ethics* by Stevenson and others have not exactly been matched by corresponding changes in the theory as applied to religion; but rather clearly such changes would have to be made.

The emotive theory seemingly applies to a great deal of religious *literature* and probably to some of the best religious literature as such: religious poetry, psalms, hymns, liturgical materials, prayers, etc.[97] Of these we may say that whatever else they are, they *do* use language for expressive, emotive, or evocative purposes. And *as* using language in this way, their function is of course non-cognitive. Even when they contain what look like plain, categorical statements of fact, this is nothing but their 'surface grammar'. Their function is to express or communicate emotion – perhaps a distinctively *religious* emotion like Otto's *mysterium tremendum et fascinosum*, but still emotion.

All of this seems clear; and yet we may wonder whether even here – in what seems to be a purely emotive function of language – we really do get away entirely from a certain dependence on precisely what the emotive theory has been trying so hard to avoid – viz., *descriptive* meaning. Professor Ferre has argued cogently that we do not:

It is difficult to see how the emotive meanings of theistic language can function apart from the reintroduction of some kind of dependence on descriptive meaning. Sheer gibberish does not evoke penitence or express feelings of confidence and adoration. Clearly, theistic utterances are not utterly 'empty of content' in every respect ...
  The emotive powers of language are essentially parasitical upon provision of some kind of descriptive content. Theistic language *does* have emotive meaning. Therefore, it follows, theistic language cannot be entirely vacuous of descriptive definiteness ... We understand (the words in theistic utterances) because we know how to use them in nontheistic empirically falsifiable contexts. The words we employ about God ... borrow descriptive definiteness from ordinary usage. It is this descriptive definiteness that underlies whatever emotive power religious language possesses.
  ... Language about God has definiteness (such that even noncognitive uses logically presuppose) only because of its empirical content, (although) such language does not properly function to make empirical statements or give empirical information.[98]

A different answer to the problem of how expressive language is understood may be found in Donald Evans' *The Logic of Self-Involvement*. Evans introduced a new term, '*rapportive* language', to cover cases 'where an

96. Moritz Schlick, for example, took quite a different view in his *Fragen der Ethik*.
97. But see D. Z. Phillips' *The Concept of Prayer* for quite a different (i.e., performatory) view.
98. *Basic Modern Philosophy of Religion*, pp. 351–352.

utterance referring to an agent's action is *understood* only to the extent that one has an affinity and a rapport with the agent':[99] in such cases the utterance in question is called 'rapportive language'. 'Actions typically call for 'rapportive' utterances when they are *expressive* or when their *rationale is profound*'.[100] Both of these elements, according to Evans, 'are involved in the action of world-Creation'.

Whether or not we re-introduce descriptive meaning into emotive language as Ferre does, the conception of religious language as emotive in its function provides, *as far as this conception's applicability extends*, a satisfactory answer to the problem of falsification raised by Flew. Such language is not falsifiable because its function is not to describe or report or record any observable happenings or any observable states of affairs.

3. Luther's statement, finally, suggests and suggests strongly the performatory character of religious language. To say 'I believe in God' *means* that 'I look to him for everything that is good' and that 'I flee to him in every situation of need'.

Austin's account of 'performative language' in *How to Do Things with Words* was first applied to religious language by R. B. Braithwaite in his landmark essay, 'An Empiricist's View of the Nature of Religious Belief'. Braithwaite's 'conative function' view has become so well known as to be in no need of exposition here. A somewhat expanded and possibly preferable version of it appears in Ronald W. Hepburn's *Christianity and Paradox:*

We could describe as 'religious' any set of attitudes and beliefs that satisfies three conditions. First, the believer commits himself to a pattern of ethical behaviour. This way of life is simply decided for as an ultimate moral choice: empirical facts will be relevant to his choice, but he can *derive* his choice from no facts whatever, not even the commands of God, should he believe in a God. But (second) what will distinguish religious from moral language is that religious discourse provides a tightly cohering extended parable or myth that vividly expresses the way of life chosen and inspires the believer to implement it in practice. Third, the parable and its associated pattern of behaviour legislate not for any *fraction* of the believer's life but for every aspect of it. It commands his supreme loyalty and determines his total imaginative vision of nature and man ... Defined in this broad, formal way, a religious orientation of life would not necessarily include belief in a God nor in the possibility of speculative philosophy.[101]

The appropriateness of this view for all utterances of what H. H. Price has called the '*evaluative* belief-in' form (as distinguished from 'factual belief-in')[102] seems to me unarguable. We shall say, then, that the 'conative

99. *Op. cit.*, pp. 110–111.
100. *Ibid.*
101. *Op. cit.*, New York: Pegasus, 1966, p. 195.
102. 'Belief 'In' and Belief 'That'', *Religious Studies*, Vol. I (1965), pp. 21–13.

function' view is applicable to all *creedal and sacramental utterances* of a religion[103] – or to whatever can be reduced to such utterances. Language having this conative function is, in itself, 'no more subject to tests of truth or falsity than are finger-waggles or gavel-bangs. All are instances of doing, not asserting'.[104]

Ferre,[105] John Wisdom,[106] and R. H. Hare[107] have wanted to go beyond 'non-cognitivism' and see a 'quasi-cognitive' function for religious language. Ferre's attempt, quite carefully and elaborately worked out, takes the form of a Kantian theory of 'heuristic function'; Wisdom presses his well known law-court analogy, and Hare his equally familiar view involving 'Bliks'. Although these are all ingenious, I think that the price paid for achieving 'quasi-cognitivism' is too high – especially from the standpoint of the Reformation. Ferre and Wisdom want to re-introduce a kind of natural theology which would be rejected outright by Barth and whose congruence with Luther's doctrine of 'the masks' is at least questionable. Hare, it seems to me, does not want to do this, and his view may therefore be considered the most acceptable of the three on Reformation principles. It is, however, open to other objections.[108]

Is there a residue of religious statements that in all honesty will have to be considered plain, matter-of-fact statements capable of empirical falsification or (to a degree) of verification? Unquestionably there are factual, historical statements relating to the past which are supposed to be religious discourse by (e.g.) conservative Christians and Orthodox Jews. With Bultmann[109] I would

103. Typical verbs used in creedal utterances would be examples of Austin's 'Commissives'. 'The whole point of a commissive is to commit the speaker to a certain course of action' (*'How to Do Things with Words'*, p. 156). This is one of five groups of verbs which 'make explicit ... the illocutionary force of an utterance, or what illocutionary act it is that we are performing in issuing that utterance" (*Ibid.*, p. 149). The utterances involved in a sacrament are presumably *per*locutionary in their force: 'baptize' is an example used by Austin himself.
104. Ferre, *Basic Modern Philosophy of Religion*, p. 354.
105. *Op. cit.*, pp. 388–406.
106. 'Gods' in *Philosophy and Psychoanalysis*, reprinted in *Logic and Language*, first series, ed. Antony G. N. Flew, Oxford: Basil Blackwell, 1951; 'The Logic of God' in *Paradox and Discovery*, New York: Philosophical Library, 1965.
107. *New Essays in Philosophical Theology*, p. 100; 'Religion and Morals' in *Faith and Logic*, ed. Basil Mitchell, London: Allen and Unwin, 1957.
108. As Hare fully realizes, there are insane and quasi-insane 'Eliks' as well as 'normal' ones. But is 'normality' a criterion which can be rendered specific? If so, then this seems to undermine Hare's basic position; if not, then isn't it useless as a criterion? Cf. Ferre, *Op. cit.*, p. 369.
109. Cf. *Jesus Christ and Mythology*, London, 1960, p. 69. The affirmation of God as Creator,

like to deny that such statements are a part of *religious* discourse. Where they seem to be, a careful examination of language and context will show the statements to be not really neutral but 'self-involving'. Bultmann's example here is a good one and is borne out by the much more careful, more detailed analysis of Judaeo-Christian Creation-language by Donald Evans.

> Suppose, for instance, we knew people who foresaw the future; make forecasts for years and years ahead; and they described some sort of a Judgement Day. Queerly enough, even if there were such a thing, and even if it were more convincing than I have described, *belief in this happening wouldn't be at all a religious belief.*[110]

Another comment of Wittgenstein's summarizes what I have wanted to say, in this essay, about cognitivity, the Reformation language-game, and the Reformation form of life:

> ... Here we have people who ... base things on evidence which taken in one way would seem exceedingly flimsy. They base enormous things on this evidence. Am I to say they are unreasonable? ...
> I want to say: they don't treat this as a matter of reasonability.
> Anyone who reads the Epistles will find it said: not only that it is not reasonable, but that it is folly.
> Not only is it not reasonable, but it doesn't pretend to be ...
> Why shouldn't one form of life culminate in an utterance of belief in a Last Judgement? But I couldn't say 'Yes' or 'No' to the statement that there will be such a thing. Nor 'Perhaps' nor 'I'm not sure'.
> *It is a statement which may not allow of any such answer.*[111]

What I am suggesting is that Wittgensteinian agnosticism and 'Wittgensteinian fideism' are by no means inconsistent with the principles of 'Reformation thought'. Could the same be said of other theologies and other religious traditions? I doubt it, although attempts along this line might be interesting and worthwhile.

    according to Bultmann, *'cannot be made as a neutral statement*, but only as thanksgiving and surrender' (Italics mine).
110. L. Wittgenstein, *Lectures and Conversations on Aesthetics, Psychology, and Religious Belief*, Oxford: Basil Blackwell, 1966, p. 56. (Italics are mine).
111. *Ibid.*, p. 58. (Italics mine).

CHAPTER 9

THE LIBERAL COMMITMENT TO DIVINE IMMANENCE

WILLIAM HOROSZ

That Protestant liberalism made certain concessions to the modern world to establish the relevance of religion to experience is an acknowledged fact. For the standard of relevancy was a passion with liberals. This standard was accomplished by an appeal to experience and by certain commitments to divine immanence within experience. The very drive to understand the dynamics of faith and redemption in terms of the temporal process, in terms of the experience men live by, was enough to invite counter movements, familiar to us as crisis theology in Europe and neo-orthodoxy in America, that questioned this system of divine totality within existence. These charges were numerous, but the most open one was that liberalism neglected the given reality of Christianity, in terms of its own integrity, by its commitments to divine immanence, that it accepted certain secular standards over religious beliefs and sensibilities. What was uncertain in all this was the status of immediate experience as the judge of religious matters.

I. The liberal appeal to experience

My concern in this chapter is to reexamine this accommodating spirit of liberalism on the issue of divine and human purpose. It is a philosophical concern to see what commitments were made to God and to man in speculating on the relation of divine immanence to human purpose. How did Protestantism shape human experience by its appeal to experience, by its commitment to religious unity in experience? The thesis I propose is that no such concessions were made to human purpose in religious liberalism on its commitment to divine immanence. Man was still bound by a system of religious totality which both sustained and guided his life and its meaning. Man was still goal-directed to a system of totality that was immanent in the structures of existence in spite of the appeal to experience. Man still had a dominant purpose for life that was not his own because he was only a part of the whole. Man still needed religious holism to be whole again.

While there were many accommodations made to the secular world, such as the concessions (1) to the world-view of the physical sciences, (2) to historical relativism, (3) to the immanent goals of life and the striving for community (Kingdom of God), and (4) to persons of other faiths (love and tolerance),[1] these were all in a sense an appeal to the experience of modern man. But there was no accommodation to human purpose. The directives of immediate experience and the overall guidance of that experience by an immanent system of totality both had priority to human purpose. The directives of immediate experience and the overall guidance of that experience by an immanent system of totality both had priority to human purpose. What modern man was required to do was to make certain religious adjustments in life to fit into this system of totality. Responsibility, as the unifying principle of this system of religious unity, was obligatory on his part but it was not his own. It belonged to the system of religious immanence. Thus man was requested to make adjustments to scientific knowledge, to the evolutionary perspective, to social and historical reconstruction, to value reconstruction, in terms of the guidance that was offered him by the system of religious totality. The new standard of relevancy gave preference to the appeal to experience over tradition, scripture, confessional creeds, and to certain historical sensibilities perpetuated by orthodoxies. This appeal to experience gave birth to the accommodating spirit of liberalism, but it did not take with respect to human purpose. Man's capacity for self-direction was denied in preference for guidance by the idea of wholeness in the primal context of experience.

Experience was so broadly conceived as to include human actions and feelings in process. The key to the understanding of man was direct experience, his elemental modes of response to a system of immanent totality. Conformation to experience, meant for some, (1) that experience revealed wholeness and was our source of the knowledge of God, (2) for others, it was a sign of moral vitality and religious affirmations, (3) for still others, it was an opportunity for ushering in the Kingdom of God and community-building in general, (4) and for some, it was the testing ground for moral achievement, (5) for the critically minded it afforded many opportunities for attacks upon orthodoxy. In all these respects the appeal to experience aroused a new religious ferment among the American liberals and pointed to a new human quest in religion.[2]

If there was such a given structure of wholeness immediate experience could reveal it and men could observe and provide conditions for its growth. It was

1. Langdon Gilkey, *Naming the Whirlwind: The Renewal of God-Language*, New York: Bobbs-Merrill, 1969, pp. 76–7.
2. Daniel D. Williams, 'The Shaping of American Religion', *Religion in American Life*, J. W. Smith & A. L. Jamison (eds.), Princeton University Press, 1961, p. 448.

this optimism among the empirically oriented liberals in the twentieth century that enabled them to point to God as Fact, Object, Event, Process, Creativity, and Value. Charles Hartshorne put the matter as forcefully as any of them when he asserted that God 'exists as a datum in *every* experience'.[3] The intuition of the worshipful experience could give man more direction at this point than human purpose. Thus the liberals side-tracked the directives of man's purposive nature in existence for the directives of experience under the guidance of divine totality. This was their commitment to God and man. Man was given the role of responsiveness to divine totality. The instructions of man's elemental human nature (universally conceived) were that man was goal-directed to a system of wholeness in immediate experience. Man's intellect and purpose could only follow his feelingful life which was properly aligned with divine immanence.

With this perspective men could safely feel at home in the universe that had the assurance and guidance of divine wholeness. This, of course, led to a new sense of moral optimism (and here religious liberals shared the optimism with secularists). A whole cluster of religious affirmations supported this optimistic outlook: (1) belief in the continuity of God's creation in the temporal process, (2) belief in the continuousness of the Incarnation, (3) belief in the cumulative integration of life's values, (4) belief in the continuity of God's actions and man's responsiveness. Man was, after all, a co-worker with a cosmic worker in building the Kingdom of God on earth.

The liberal appeal to experience in defining divine immanence made religious holism more functional and operational in existence. The idea of wholeness was implied both in the dynamics of personal faith and in the process of redemption. Striving for salvation meant striving for healing and wholeness. To become whole one had to share and participate in wholeness. This participation was dictated by the Creator-creature doctrine (immanentized) and the whole-to-part logic of process philosophy which supported religious liberalism. The system of totality did for man what he could not do for himself. The fact that holism was made more operational in the temporal process did not lessen the religious claims on man. While God was brought closer to the secularization process, He remained the secular Other, as the Ultimate in secular experience. The cosmic worker could still do more and give better directionality than the individual worker. It is necessary to further pin-point the issue of the liberal challenge to human purpose.

---

3. Charles Hartshorne, 'Criteria for Ideas of God'. *Rice University Studies*, Vol. 51, No. 4, Fall, 1965, pp. 88-9.

II. The liberal challenge to human purpose

Thus the liberal commitment to divine immanence, in spite of its appeal to experience, remained a challenge to human purpose. Man's elemental human nature had more in common with the system of divine totality than with the human orderer. Human purpose was merely a reactive phenomenon to the self-disclosures of divine immanence in experience. It had no capacity to guide man. It could only follow the primal encounters of human nature with divinity. Human purpose had to face the Other in experience, rather than beyond experience, as in orthodoxy. The confrontation was closer, but it was still a confrontation. This is presupposed even in the doctrine continuity between divine action and human reaction. The two terms, however, are not equipollent in the relationship. The creator guides, the creature follows, even on the grounds of immanence and experience.

Human purpose is a matter of religious adjustment to divine immanence, to varying degrees of religious commitment. It is posterior to commitment, even in liberalism. Because purpose is posterior to religious commitment we shall call the liberal perspective of life a pre-purposive design for living. The issue of religious adjustment is made on the primal level of existence where elemental man confronts the elemental Other. Human purpose has neither the vision nor the energy to shape and form this encounter-experience or the system of immanence assumed. It is barred from the primal encounter-experience. In fact, we can view the history of liberalism as a procession in which caravans of secular Others confront the directives of human purpose rerouting them to a system of divine immanence. Ironically enough, an immanent deity requires a transcendent man to perform the work of redemption in the temporal process. Man must remain transcendent to aspire for wholeness in a system of totality. The deity may or may not be functionally transcendent to experience in its sense of wholeness. Pre-purposive human commitment is part of the parcel of religious adjustment that liberals required of man. Thus liberalism adjusted human purpose to varying degrees of religious commitment, to pre-purposive continuity with divine immanence in a system of religious totality.

The paradox of religious liberalism which suggests itself is this: that while it advised conformation to experience to secure religious affirmations, it neglected the human orderer and his purposive nature by which he could contribute directives to that experience. The reason for the paradox can be explained by the fact that liberalism already had a divine orderer in the primal context of experience. The reason for the paradox can be explained by the fact that liberalism already had a divine orderer in the primal context of experience. Man could assume a capacity for ordering human life only on a secondary level, following the leads of the divine orderer immanently structuring the value and meaning of experience. Thus liberalism guarded the secular Other against the encroachments of the secularization process (to which human purpose is rather central).

This issue may come into better perspective if we see it in terms of its background, in terms of its conflict with orthodoxy. The latter espoused a construct of religious unity that was transcendental, above the temporal and secularization process. Liberalism viewed this as a tissue of externals because it made the process of redemption somewhat superfluous in that it was not functional and operational in the temporal sphere. I shall call the orthodox model of religious unity post-purposive, as coming from above human processes and from beyond the temporal realm. Liberal thinkers substituted the pre-purposive model of religious unity for the transcendental model. However, liberalism was not an indiscriminate immanentism, for whatever was left of the transcendental model of unity was read functionally and operationally. If some liberals still adhered to elements of post-purposive unity, it was circumscribed by an immanent totality. It was not a metaphysical entity but only a certain kind of function within immanence. Thus liberalism did not defeat the transcendental unity of orthodoxy; it merely by-passed it as being irrelevant to the secular process. Implicit in the conflict was the belief that orthodox unity was a fabric of externals, a matter of irrelevancies, and a false construct of the religious experience. But the liberal view was real religious unity, the real dominant purpose for life, because it was true to man's immediate experience. The real destiny of man was thus misread by religious orthodoxy when it conceived of the Kingdom of God futuristically rather than in the present time dimensionality.

Obviously the stakes are high in such a religious conflict because the destiny of man is involved. But while the issue is hot and intensive it need not therefore be simplistic. The real problem is not the issue of which notion of religious unity is a construct and which the real one, but how each is a model of comprehensive religious unity defining the destiny of man and which approximates better our grasp of reality and human participation in it. Liberalism, with an air of self-confidence in its appeal to experience, conceived of its own construct of religious totality as being real. But in doing so it made certain identifications which need further justification.

First, it identified its construct of totality with divine immanence itself and this act presupposes omniscience. The process of human participation in cosmic reality is a prior process to the act of identifying that act of participation with cosmic process immanently conceived. Once it had the assurance of this false identification (thinking of it as primal experience on the same level as participation) it was led to a second and more pretentious identification by equating the first construct of divine immanence with a particular process in Nature, such as creativity, value. This move enabled liberalism to postulate man as co-worker with the cosmic worker explained earlier. In the following section we shall have ample opportunity to point to these two kinds of illicit identifications.

What liberalism had, then, was another model of divine unity than what orthodoxy preached, instead of cosmic reality itself. This pre-purposive model of religious totality was conceived as coming from below. A new pre-purposive language was devised to describe and explain it in such concepts as: growth, experiment, adjustment, continuity, responsibility, immediate experience. The appeal to experience which revealed these new nuances of meaning about wholeness in existence cleared the way for a new kind of pre-purposive language fitting to the pre-purposive model of religious unity. The idea of wholeness came from below, via process, and could be revealed in the present temporal and secularization process. Although liberalism introduced the pre-purposive outlook in talking about religious unity it did what orthodoxy did before, namely, it made claims of ultimacy for it. Man was advised to follow its directives and intentions. Since he was a creature of divine intent, goal-directed to a system of immanent totality he had not other recourse to become authentically whole. Both the pre- and post-purposive models of totality required of man to be goal-directed to their respective systems of totality. Both made claims of ultimacy on man's destiny. Both schools sought a premature religious solution to man's relations to the eternal without first consulting human purpose. The post-purposive model of unity required commitment to revelation to fulfill man's destiny. The pre-purposive model required commitment to direct experience devoid of purposiveness in primal encounter with God. In each model human purpose was denied a shaping and forming capacity in primal religious adjustment. Religious commitment was prior to human purpose. It had other leads and intimations to follow. Each school made a holistic use of human purpose in constructing the system of totality. Yet each denied the work of purpose by insisting on the given reality of its system of wholeness as having an integrity of its own, unmarred by human purpose. If such religious unities are not model-free, how can they be guides of human destiny both in pre- and post-purposive versions? On the issue of human purpose and its relationship to a system of totality, then, liberalism was not much different from orthodoxy. The religious claims on man were just as adamant in liberalism as they were earlier in orthodoxy.

In one respect, it was worse than orthodoxy when it identified the construct of totality with some process in nature-history and talked about the progressive realization of the possibilities of life in the same breath as redemption. This was open exploitation of immediate experience for religious advancement. But each respective school put an end to religion as a search beyond its own system of totality, theories of religious toleration notwithstanding. Calling the orthodox model of religious unity 'that old monistic hangover' (as Paul Van Buren does) merely restricts one's self-awareness towards the limitations of one's own system of totality (and Van Buren has one in the midst of his relativism, the Lordship of Jesus). It appears that the appeal to experience merely clouded the steps which a liberal took from his ultimate to 'the Ultimate'. The doctrine of continuity between divine and human purposiveness, as liberals conceived it in a system of immanence, was not so much a solution to human purpose (and its redeeming guide) as it was a new problem and source of frustration in time of despair. A new model of transcendental unity was soon to replace it in neo-orthodoxy which denied the coupling of immanent unity with some ongoing process in the world. The new emphasis was soon to establish a gap between divine and human purpose, both negating, contradicting, and simultaneously fulfilling it. But now it was the divine Other, not the secular Other, fulfilling human life.

Was this a romantic extravaganza on the part of liberals to claim an identity between the idea of religious wholeness and some ongoing process in life, with which human life was continuous in an elemental way? Was this a religious and empirical reading of direct experience? The belief that experience could reveal such wholeness in actual operation was an attempt to state the case for religious adjustment and interaction from below human purpose. This pre-purposive drive in liberalism made religious adjustment a different matter than what it was in orthodoxy (at least in its content), but in essence the form of model-making was the same. It was part and parcel of the same apologetic that would make God a necessity of human life rather than a project of human purpose which perchance mediates such claims of necessity, and finds the continual need to do so in the search for further meaning.

Perhaps the thoughts of Douglas C. Macintosch, Henry N. Wieman, Bernard E. Meland, and Daniel D. Williams, will add some content to this theme. In each thinker the pre-purposive model of immediacy and religious unity dominates the religious perspective and controls the limiting and restricting attitude towards human purpose that we mentioned above. Each will make a plea for the domination of human life in that system of religious totality he favors, which he has identified with the Ultimate itself (in spite of the fact this wholeness is dimly apprehended).

III. Some liberal commitments to wholeness

A. Douglas C. Macintosh

When we consider a sample of liberal thinkers in the twentieth century, the drive for wholeness is very much in evidence in their respective theologies. The one we shall consider first, Douglas Macintosh, made divine immanence into an objective reality. Wholeness was both revealed by immediate experience and certain aspects of it were even observable and available to scientific evaluation. He advised man to take many steps to achieve wholeness, by being goal-directed towards the given wholeness constituting divine immanence. Through aspiration and concentration, surrender and appropriation, and by response and persistence, man could fulfill his sense of wholeness by participating experientially in given totality. One may here legitimately speak of a third identification between wholeness as a given objective structure and the objectivating methods of science. The author not only identified his model of wholeness with divine immanence, and the resultant construct with the integrative process of value in experience, it was important for his scientific and experimental interests to characterize the given and its appropriation by objective standards.

Macintosh made his revisionist realism a plea to religious liberals as early as 1919, with the publication of *Theology As An Empirical Science*. Idealistic support for religious liberalism was by then bogged down with subjectivist claims. George B. Foster (along with Edward S. Ames of Chicago) viewed religion as 'the conviction of the achievability of universally valid satisfactions of the human personality'.[4] He had no directives to impart to religious liberals on how to relate the subject-object controversy in relation to cosmic reality. It was against the subjectivism of the Chicago School that Macintosh asserted the more pragmatic, experimentalist, and realistic position of liberal theology. Liberalism was bogged down with conflicting epistemological claims. While realism was not a solution to the problem of immediate experience it was, nonetheless, a viable alternative to the liberalism which sought support in idealism. The revisionist effort was thus an attempt to find, not a more direct route to cosmic wholeness, but a more objective one. Both philosopical schools made initial appeals to direct experience as the primal context for discovering God. Macintosh, by asserting a more objective content for the Christian faith and the objectivating conditions of divine wholeness, was

---

4. Georege B. Foster, 'The Function of Religion', *American Protestant Thought*, W. R. Hutchison (ed.), Harper Torchbook, 1968, pp. 145–6.

making religion more acceptable to a technological culture. Only a philosophy of experimentalism, with pragmatic overtones and more consonant with the mood of the day, could give support to the new goals of liberal theology, namely, to reach some standard of objectivity both for human appropriation of cosmic reality and for its given structure of wholeness. The challenge posed for modern man was to respond to a more objectivating system of divine totality, since God was viewed as Fact or Object.

This meant going one step beyond humanism and acknowledgement of the given structure of wholeness as somehow transcending experience functionally, but not metaphysically. Direct experience could reveal this cosmic reality beyond humanist claims even though the human mind could only dimly perceive the outlines of such wholeness in experience. Man knew its significance in the primal context of living. This is where all important religious adjustments to wholeness were made any way. They were not a matter of the head or of human purpose. Given wholeness was always more than man's striving for wholeness. Thus there was some barrier still between man and the divine in spite of the continuity asserted between divine acts and human responsiveness in the production of values in life.[5] It was taken for granted that God, as operationally immanent in experience, was somehow connected with man's 'ultimate well-being'.

Man's relation to the given cosmic reality was one of dependence and active religious adjustment. But this adjustment was only operational in the framework of dependence on a higher power since man's freedom was limited by his fallibility. Man's position in cosmic totality was thus controlled by the Creator-creature distinction (now made immanent), and the logic of organic relatedness discovered by process philosophy, a logic of whole-to-part.[6] With these limitations of man's response to wholeness, the dictates of divine immanence, active adjustment could mean at most only an active passivity. It is only when man's assertive freedom is controlled by receptive freedom (because human freedom is fallible) that religious holism can have dominance over human life. Even active experimentalism caters to this receptive immediate experience because that is where it, too, finds the confirmation of its truth. Consequently, when man's need for wholeness is sought in divine coherence God looks favorably upon such action and can be expected to continue doing so, to respond dependably to man's receptivity. For the author, this is an objectively observable phenomenon in the religious life.[7]

5. D C. Macintosh, 'Contemporary Humanism', *Humanism*, W. P. King (ed.), Nashville: Cokesbury Press, 1931, pp. 70–2.
6. Daniel D. Williams, *op. cit.* p. 462.
7. D. C. Macintosh (ed.), *Religious Realism*, New York: Macmillan, 1931, pp. 307–8, 326.

What is the source of man's dependence on divine immanence, man's drive for wholeness? Wholeness is a quasi-religious notion that is rooted in man's 'reality-feeling' since infancy, for Macintosh. It is the first response of an infant, and of primitive man, and it is attended by all sorts of specific religious reactions. Religion, then, has this in common with the world of mythology: in that it has a sense of solidarity, a sense of wholeness, a 'sympathy for the Whole'. Man's drive for wholeness, it is assumed, is the same elemental drive for cosmic reality. Only direct experience, man's elemental but universal human nature, senses this directionality and has the desire for completing it in something objectively real. The fact that this feeling for wholeness is part of infancy and is part of primitive man's consciousness is an indication perhaps that it is an essential and vital part of the life of man.[8] At any rate, the author thinks it important to root the drive for wholeness in man's elemental nature where elemental responses can send out feelers of expectancy in behalf of human fulfillment.

This means that cosmic wholeness is a given structure of totality and model-free. Human purpose has not shaped and formed either its features or intentions. The human orderer may be dynamically receptive in all this (active adjustment), but he is not assertive in the situation through his mind and purposes. Whatever commitments are made to divine immanent totality they are prior to the directives of man's purposive nature, for such commitments are made in the primal context of life form which purposiveness is barred. It follows that any appreciativeness of human values that it is rooted in such a given structure of wholeness will require of man to be responsible first to such a system of immanence. Responsibility to the whole of cosmic reality is the first consideration of the believer that would seek for wholeness of life. Reality-feeling is the form, and value-appreciation is the content in man's considerations of cosmic wholeness. But there must be an additional identification of cosmic reality immanently defined with values in the world. Seeking to define the 'distinctively religious interest' of man the author remarks (still making a plea for an original awareness of divine totality in experience):

Rooted in our awareness of reality and in our quest for values, the distinctively religious interest is an interest in the relation of reality to values. Not the relation of each and every reality to each and every value is that in which religion, as it develops comes to be and remains specifically interested. the relation, rather, of reality viewed as a more or less unitary whole, and especially of reality in its more mysterious and still somewhat transcendent aspects, to all genuine human values, individual and social – this it is that forms the focus of attention in all the more characteristic developments of the religious consciousness. May it not possibly be that social and

8. *Ibid.*, pp. 307–8.

moral values are somehow enforced by the mysterious and awe-inspiring power upon which we feel that we are ultimately dependent? Is there not an extrahuman factor or cosmic power at work for the promotion of genuine human values?[9]

That there is a divine purpose in the world integrating values, as from a functionally transcendent vantage point in a system of immanent totality, having as its aim cosmic unity, is something that immediate experience teaches us about existence. But we can only know directly the cosmic behavior of such a 'principle of concretion' and not the internal purposes of such a total divine mind and will in the universe. Its behavior one can study objectively, once the continuity between divine immanence and man is established, but certain features of cosmic motivation we can know only indirectly. But whatever we can apprehend of divine totality it does set limits to human freedom and purpose.

By way of summary, it should be noted, first, that by the time Macintosh was finishing his work at Yale, the reaction to empirical theology had already set in, even among his own students. The experimentalism in religious adjustment to an immanent totality was not working too well in America. But our concern is of different order, namely, that such active adjustment, in the framework of dependence and passivity, is in essence out of keeping with even a broad philosophy of experimentalism, without even a consideration of it as a strict scientific procedure. As a methodology it is opposed to simple empirical structuralism which accepts given structures as given. What religious experimentalism amounted to is simply a conformation of immediate experience in the domain of feeling that the immanent whole was at work in history. Man was not the source of value. He was not the director of value. Nor was he the integrator and conservor of values. In fact, man was not even responsible in the first instance for his state of well-being or that of humanity, for he was primarily responsible to the system of totality. It is only in a derivative sense, then, that man was even considering the state of well-being of mankind. In this situation of dependence and receptivity experimentalism as a methodology is merely an unfounded wish. Making religious adjustment to cosmic wholeness into an active process merely deepened the mood of receptivity in man. Experimentalism is an assertive methodology, not a receptive structuralism. What is more, the primal relation between elemental man and cosmic reality is one of fixed-goal-direction. No experimentalism could possibly change this theological orientation. The term 'experimental' is thus superfluous in the religious empiricism advocated. There already was an inner track of meaning of the cosmic wholeness to man, to which man was

---

9. *Ibid.*, p. 312.

already goal-directed, prior to the experimentation. The universe was already; pre-wired for immanent totality which the human orderer had to take into consideration to be authentic.

Second, if we further discount the epistemological problem which preoccupied religious liberals in the early decades of the twentieth century as a family quarrel, the problem of the liberal commitment to divine immanence may be pin-pointed and the alternatives faced. Meanwhile, suffice it to say that the issue of the subject-object split in relation to the immanent totality of God was somewhat premature. There was haste in relating to religious themes before it was adequately faced in relation to the human orderer in existence. There was no concern to face this issue, nor was there an attempt to justify the nature of immediate experience as used in process philosophy for its adaptation to religious use. The conflict between supporting philosophies of religious liberalism was between idealism and realism. Idealism was seen in terms of subjectivism. Realism was identified with objectivism. There were also mixtures of the two.

From the perspective of our theory, if it turns out to be that liberalism came up with a new model of religious unity, then, it had no right to make claims of ultimacy for it as being real and as permeating the secular world operationally. If what is at stake is only the model of religious unity, then, the subject-object issue can be regarded as setting up two kinds of pre-purposive models of divine immanence, as over against the post-purposive models of orthodoxy.

However, the contrary was the case. When liberals utilized idealism and subjectivism to state the case for totality, they assumed the reality of divine immanence. When the realistic liberals assumed a system of objective divine immanence, it similarly accepted this as real religious unity. During the ensuing conflict, the period of revision, each regarded the other's position as being a construct and his own as the real totality, as each identified his construct of totality with cosmic reality itself. Epistemologically speaking, then, it is possible to entertain the thought that ideas are model-oriented, following the pattern of the ontological models of existence. It is clear to me that both versions of idealism claimed the pre-purposive model of divine immanence, and this model controlled the meaning of religious unity and the methodological procedures which led up to it.

Thus we regard the subject-object controversy in liberalism as a peripheral issue. The real issue is whether the liberal view of cosmic reality is a model of divine immanence or the real thing. If it is a model of religious unity, its principle of concretion, or its operational vitality in the sphere of temporality is suspect. This is a more crucial issue for liberalism than subjectivism and realism. None of the writers that I will have covered, including Macintosh, are even remotely aware of the possibility that the notion of religious unity liberals espouse may only be a model of a system of totality which cannot be identified with cosmic reality itself. That the notion of the religiously given is a whole may be a construct of divine immanence mistakenly identified with real cosmic unity puts a new perspective on the liberal claims that man should have an attitude of wholeness to man's purposive nature on the part of liberals, which is itself a significant omission. For liberalism had already committed itself for the guidance of man to a system of religious totality.

By focusing on the real issue, then, the liberal postulate of a model-free divine immanence, and the claims for ultimacy on its behalf, we have a more central theme to discuss among liberal writers than the issue of subjectivism and realism in liberal religion. We turn now to the writings of Henry Wieman to see what restrictions a model-free religious totality places on man's purposive nature.

B. Henry Nelson Wieman

Since religious liberals rejected a metaphysical reference to the beyondness of experience they had to be content with functional transcendence, with the transcendent referenc in immediate experience pointing to the wholeness of experience. This was their system of divine immanence. The notion of wholeness was important to the entire liberal program. This appeal in direct experience to the whole of experience, on the primal level of immediacy, was something that claimed the concern of Wieman readily. Consequently, he thought of religion as a way of adapting 'the whole of life' to 'ultimate facts'. The concern for divine totality was thus the concern of the whole elemental man in total devotion to cosmic reality. The author contends that

Religion differs from other problem-solving in that it has to do with the ultimate character of events, rather than with the more superficial facts which engage the mind in other walks of life; and it requires the organization of all of one's experiences, the reconstruction of that totality of reactions, which make up the whole personality, rather than some department of the personality.[10]

As a process philosopher of religion, Wieman believed that human wholeness was achievable by seeking cosmic reality in and through immediate experience in feeling awareness. Empirical religion performed this unifying function for

10. H. N. Wieman, 'Religion and Illusion', *American Protestant Thought*, W. R. Hutchison (ed.), pp. 185, 188.

man, as it did for John Dewey also. One became a whole man not by an awareness of his capacities as a human orderer but by relating one's self to cosmic wholeness discoverable in direct experience. The appeal to wholeness was thus equivalent to an appeal to experience where points of contact with cosmic totality were available. Adapting to God as the supreme Fact was thus the beginning of any human reconstruction of the personality. Since this was the case, a radical empirical method was required to observe and test such growth in the direction of wholeness. It had to be an objectivating realistic program as that of Macintosh, with fewer 'surmises' and 'overbeliefs'. But man's pre-purposive goal-direction to a system of divine immanence was a prerequisite for the radical method. Man could only discover the operational conditions of the Creative Event. He could not create such events. Creativity came from below via the processes and events. Man could only give his purpose to the process of religious adjustment that was tuned in on the Creative Process. Once more, there is continuity between divine action and human reaction as the condition of authenticity.

His definitive work *The Source of Human Good*, identifies divine immanence with the Creative Event in the temporal process. Whatever residue is left from orthodox transcendental unity is regarded functionally, not metaphysically.[11] This enables Wieman to speak of divine immanence operationally and to regard cosmic wholeness as real. The traditional doctrine distinguishing Creator from creature is now conceived of as the difference between creative and created good. Creative good is the source of human value, the integrating factor in human events, having the ongoing unity of its own creativity spread out over concrete events. Cosmic wholeness is thus discoverable in experience. It is in sharp contrast to human effort and purpose (created good). Religious holism operationally conceived is available to observation, empirical testing, and to religious problem solving as man adjusts his life to ultimate facts and concerns.

Wieman's empirical theism thus establishes 'a new order of domination for man' which posits creative over created good in a system of religious totality.[12] It gives man a new 'sense of ruling purpose', 'a controlling purpose', which he cannot have on his own becauae what is needed in the first place is the 'creative transformation' of life. This new order of domination replaces the directives of man's purposive nature and puts religion in allience

11. *H. N. Wieman, The Source of Human Good,* Chicago: University Press, 1946, p. 264.
12. *Ibid.*p. 269. Cf., 'Reply To My Critics', *Religion in Life,* Vol. XXXII, No. 3, 1963, 'We are in dire need of a form of religion that can give a controlling purpose to human striving, not only for the individual and for special religious fellowships but also and preeminently for the conduct of the major institutions and for finding significance in human history'.

with education, government, science and technology, with a comprehensive reordering of life as its aim. A vital religious culture would dominate the life of the individual and give control to social striving. Underneath this human striving, individual and social, is the bedrock of 'creative exchange', the temporal manifestation of the Creative Process itself, giving man pre-purposive designs for living. Man is advised to give his ultimate devotion to 'creativity's winning supremacy', which is the operation of divine totality in and through 'creative exchange' in human experience.

Man's 'living responsiveness' to divine immanence is actually defined by the logic of organic relatedness in process philosophy which believes in the supremacy of the whole to the parts. Man is not the measure of his own values. If there is a structure of increasing value in history, it is sustained and measured by the scheme of religious totality. Divine immanence stands over against man as the creative source of human values. The immanent system of religious unity is the dispenser of human participation, responsibility, and purpose. Man is merely a responding part of the whole. His whole existence is defined by his positionality in the divine system of totality, which the author regards as 'supra-human'. 'Serving the creative event that renews itself', the author affirms, 'is the work of man – the supreme vocation of human history'.[13]

That which 'renews itself' is a deliberate choice of words by Wieman. It signifies that the Creative Process is itself model-free, undesigned by man in the primal context of immediate experience. This pre-purposive pattern for human directionality is self-renewing in its divine intentions for man and his world. It suggests a given structure of wholeness operating in the universe that has an integrity and directionality all of its own. The unifying power 'that renews itself' is an emergent force in life and produces structures and events prior to human initiative and purpose. All created good is dependent on this pre-purposive creative power and its transforming and redemptive work in history.[14]

Purpose, for Wieman, is that which 'refers to a direction of development wrought into the nature of human existence in such a way that if it is not allowed to occur, human life becomes self-destructive'.[15] Stated more

13. *Ibid.*, p. 74.
14. Cf. to my article, 'Is Creativity Free of Model-Making?' *The Journal of the Indian Academy of Philosophy*, Vol. VIII, No. 1, 1969, pp. 11–24. Wieman's section on 'Creative Good Is Supra-Human' (pp. 74–8) confuses two models of creativity. He borrows the language from the post-purposive model of creativity to use in explicating the pre-purposive view of it.
15. Henry N. Wieman, 'Purpose and Discipline in Education', *The Educational Forum*, 1963, p. 286.

specifically that power is 'creative exchange', the temporal manifestation of divine immanence, which sustains the human level of existence. Wieman is willing to call this emergent thrust in life 'revelation' and would convert all the venerable myths of the Christian tradition to his pre-purposive outlook. He is willing to identify divine immanence as a system of totality with Creativity and creative exchange in history, for the process of redemption can only be wrought 'amid the processes of human existence'. The 'what' and 'where' of divine purposiveness is thus of special concern to Wieman. The standard of relevancy, which we discussed at the beginning of the chapter, is the most vital problem of human life. Cosmic wholeness must, then, be operational, creative, and redemptive, in forms of creative exchange which creates community when individuals participate in shared values. This baseline of divine purposiveness creates all the needed value-structures to sustain human life in existence and give humanity the state of well-being that everyone longs for.

In view of Wieman's commitment to divine immanence, and the neglect of human purpose, we offer the following critical summary remarks. First, that the pre-purposive drive for cosmic wholeness, as something model-free, is a dominant theme with the author. Human purpose is self-destructive and sinful unless man finds some meaningful goal-direction on the primal level of existence with divine immanence. That this is the same process of redemption that the post-purposive model of orthodox Christianity believed in is assumed by him. Yet its directionality and immanent dominant purpose for life is altogether different from that espoused by the Christian tradition. Orthodoxy merely had a false construct of this Creativity for it did not ask 'where' this transforming activity took place. The content of redemption was empty. Wieman believes he has a model-free grasp of divine immanence whose redemptive work via creative exchange he can observe and test. But if the models of religious holism are different, how can he be so certain that it is the same process at work in existence?

What is Wieman's justification for the reality of functional divine immanence? What is the ultimate unity in process events? At first the author claims it is the abstract unity derived from processive events and calls it 'creativity'. Then, he goes on to say: 'The creative event is changeless, a unity, absolutely good and eternal in respect to creativity'.[16] When asked for concrete evidence of that unity in actual processes the author replies with an abstraction – 'in respect to creativity'. But creativity does not walk down the

---

16. Henry N. Wieman, *The Source of Human Good*, p. 299.

street, and neither does creative exchange. What concrete evidence is there for divine unity operating through these terms in the sphere of the temporal? The reply is that when such unity cannot be reproduced on the level of concrete, existential immediacy, postulate universal immediacy and view it concretely. The postulate of one single self-identical structure running throughout all the processes and events turns out to be an abstraction, a derivative notion from existential, concrete processes. But to speak of an 'identity of structure', where structure is derivative from concrete processes, does not solve the problem of immanent religious holism. It merely sets up new claims of ultimacy against the directives of human purpose.

The notion of immediate wholeness is not as direct as the author had presupposed. Yet universal creativity is something revealed in immediate experience. How this is the case is never demonstrated by the author. The positing of divine immanence amid the processes of human existence does not pin-point the redemptive whose meanings are construed in terms of universal immediateness. The only way such a realm of meaning can be reified, or made concrete is to illicitly identify the actuality of divine immanence whith the metaphysical assertion of the Creative Process. But even when we invest the latter with the 'principle of concretion' it can only take the form of universal immediacy. This we regard as a fiction.

Second, if universal immediacy is an abstraction, we can only know the wholeness that constitutes redemption, only indirectly. to identify the work of redemption with some process in human existence in some positive and direct way is not accessible to us. If the postulate of continuous Creativity is one of universal immediacy, then, the analogy of the part to the whole does not hold. There are many logics behind this analogy. The transcendental religious unity of orthodoxy was one model of it, the liberal version another one. The part-to-whole relationship is not one logic. We have various models of their relatedness. The notion of 'continuity' in the process of creation shares the model-making quality of the part-to-whole relationship. Although continuity comes to man as a paradigm of growth, we must construe it already as a model of direct experience. Immediate experience is neither continuous or discontinuous, immanent or transcendent. Whatever it is, the case is decided by human participation in experience, and not some wholeness that is beyond human participation in the final count. If this is true, there is as much model-making going on in immediate experience as in mediated forms of experience. It is only the pre-purposive model that holds immediate experience to be model-free, undesigned by the human orderer, and of one unitary piece. The given structures of immediacy are determined by human participation. Given experience is neither whole nor perspectival. These are already readings of immediate experience. If there is some credence to this position, direct access to the wholeness that constitutes the Creative Process is a fiction, one which can be supported only by special claims to universal immediacy which is already a reification of certain abstract meanings.

We turn next to Bernard Meland's writings, who has similar interests in the uncovering of the conditions which would unleash the healing balm of the Creative Process in our midst at a certain sacrifice to the directive of human purpose. The same problem remains, then, in Meland's perspective, namely how to harness human purpose to the directives of a higher power that can transform human life in a system of immanent totality.

C. Bernard E. Meland

We noted in the section above that the wholeness which constitutes the process of redemption consisted of universal immediacy. Meland accepts this as the primal context of the human situation. Although he moves from a narrow scientific concern in religion to more mystical and artistic preoccupations, man is viewed as a relational creature in the context of organic philosophy, with the exception of a few mystic overtones. The same logic of part-to-whole continues to concern him when he defines man as partially free and as partially following divine intent to achieve authenticity. But the language of immediate experience is made richer and more inviting for the modern man to throw his lot with divine immanence that is model-free. He makes more out of the universal immediacy of human nature than Wieman who had more neo-positivist interests. One may even view this as a shift in emphasis. Instead of concentrating on the universal immediacy of the wholeness that constitutes the process of redemption, there appears to be more emphasis laid on the universal immediacy of an elemental human nature that makes contact, appreciately, with divine immanence in history. The system of totality appears to be more seductive in its challenge to human purpose than the direct writing of Wieman.

In his later writings Meland prefers the phrase 'religious sensibility' to that of the 'appreciative consciousness'. For it conveys better the universal immediacy of human nature. It is more than a matter of style and taste. The religious sensibility is a capacity in all human being enabling them to partake of the influences of their culture and absorb some of its feeling-tone.

Sensibility as I use the term, however, implies something more than an extension of the appreciative dimension of common experiences. It presupposes a way of understanding man, the human mind. It partakes of the organismic view that sees the sensible and rational powers of man suffused and interrelated ... Sensibilities are thus the carriers of nascent and incipient acts of rational judgment or decision, and can be considered the persisting, durable source of structure of human perception and feeling from which over-acts erupt into conscious behavior.[17]

The passage seems to indicate that universal sensibilities are thus the carriers meaning and directionality of an enduring sort, and that the whole feelingful man is involved in such transactions, and not merely a part of him. The primal experience of these sensibilities dictates primordial meanings to the human mind and similarly informs human purpose. Human purpose is merely a reactive phenomenon to the purposes disclosed in and through such sensibilities, and like the human mind, it often over-acts. The sensibilities are steadier and surer guides to life than either cognition or purpose. They are geared to immediacy and its inner track of primal meanings and directives. Thus we see that much trust is placed in the universal immediacy of an elemental human nature and its sensibilities. They are the inner track of meaning which will contact the universal immediacy of wholeness constituting the process of redemption. They will lead man to a consideration of religious issues that go beyond the structures of human existence in the larger context of divine immanence.

A pre-purposive model of divine wholeness requires a pre-purposive theory of man for contact. A pre-purposive language in the form of process philosophy prepares the way for their proper communication. The next step is an easy one.

The context of human existence still presents to each of us a sense of something given, to which we are related in elemental ways. However far we develop and use our human powers we do not slough off this elemental condition of being creatures of a Creative Process that is not made by us, not really influenced or altered by us in anything that our sciences or philosophies undertake ... The realities of existence presented by this elemental fact of creaturehood persist in ineradicable circumstances of this living context. It is given as a primordial fact of our existence. We can obscure this sense of creatureliness, block it from view, proceed with the business at hand without thought of it, and, in our sophistication, we can disavow it. But this changes nothing except our attitudes and states of mind. The realities of existence presented by this elemental fact of creaturehood persist as ineradicable circumstances of this living.[18]

If one takes religious sensibility to imply responsiveness to what ultimately claims man, supports and judges his ways in the light of this primal context, one will be looking beyond religions as such, and beyond all human responses evidencing such behavior to the sovereign good that is the source of all religions and that stands in judgment of their human ways.[19]

17. Bernard E. Meland, *The Secularization of Modern Culture*, New York: Oxford University Press, 1966, p. 9.
18. *Ibid.*, pp. 117–18.
19. *Ibid.*, p. 118.

But the given creaturehood of man was viewed post-purposively, as coming from above and beyond creative processes, by orthodoxy. Which given system of totality is the right one, or is each merely a model about claimed cosmic reality? What is the evidence for such certitude, and the claim to ultimacy, except the identification of cosmic reality with the Creative Process, or simply the claim to omniscience? Just how is the wholeness which constitutes the process of redemption the same as the Creative Process? How is that Creativity a unification process in the multiplicity of events in history? How does the divine immanent wholeness of liberalism take its concrete steps in history, except through reified abstractions? How does the universal immediacy of human nature yield the ultimacy of cosmic reality? Is this a requirement of the pre-purposive model of man and cosmic reality, or of God himself? It is not the requirement of the transcendental model of religious unity promulgated by orthodoxy. Nor is it the requirement of the human orderer that has respect for the directives of man's purposive nature in existence. Why the confidence among liberals in their commitment to divine immanence? Is it the confidence of an intense religious reaction? Is it the call of the secularization process itself? There is the same primordial totality in Heidegger's 'Being of beings', but the dominant ontological purpose is different, and the basic issue of life hinges on the distinction between the authentic and unauthentic, rather than between the temporal and eternal dimensions of existence. Who is to decide and how. Why the call to premature commitment on the part of man, a call of ultimate devotion, as though one were not having commerce with a model of divine wholeness? Can there be such a living responsiveness on the part of man to what ultimately claims him, if the liberal commitment is to a model of immanence, to a perspective or symbol of immanence?

One can, of course, disclaim an actual identification between one's model and cosmic wholeness itself by admitting, at least in part, its projective nature, its perspectival character, or its symbolic nature. In all these and similar activities there is a beyondness to something else, to the wholeness that is ultimate, immanent, and given. But does such metaphorical language escape the problem of fixed goal-direction to an ultimate whole as the primal condition of man, to which human purpose can only react? Making wholeness more operational and functional in life does not lessen claims of ultimacy on man. Making wholeness into some kind of functional transcendence, where there is always the beyondness of particular experiences to the whole of experience, is just as deadly in its claims on man's purposive directives.

Besides the phrases 'appreciative consciousness' and 'religious sensibility' the author favors 'mythos', as distinghuished from mythologies, to put across man's elemental human nature. Myth is used in the sense of 'permanent' or 'presentational' in meaning; that is to say, they give direction to man's life.

> Myth, I would hold, is not to be identified wholly with mythologies. Rather it is the persisting sensibility and sense of wonder, abstractly referred to by Rudolf Otto as 'creature-feeling', functioning within any culture or community of people as a dimension of depth in their existence.[20]

'Reality-feeling' is thus correlated with 'creature-feeling' to produce 'salvation-feeling'. The given wholeness that constitutes redemption, as 'our relational ground' depends thus on the creaturely feeling, a response that has leads beyond human structures of existence.

Meland utilizes the neo-orthodox doctrine of self-transcendence, as a chastened neo-liberal, and makes an effort to relate it to the dominant theme of 'continuity' in process philosophy. Yet self-transcendence siginifies as its basic meaning the notion of 'discontinuity', as something that transcends immediate experience. In neo-orthodoxy it was a quality of the spirit. Here it is a quality of creaturely feeling. It is a rather uncritical use of a notion from another school, from the model of religious unity that is post-purposive rather than pre-purposive. Transcendence is not the 'tropism toward the More of existence' that William James has reference to and which Meland favors. It is a notion borrowed from another model of religious unity which comes from above processes and structures in existence. The neo-liberal interest in the notion of self-transcendence and its possible integration with process philosophy is of recent vintage and was not emphasized in liberalism prior to the counter movement of neo-orthodoxy. In the pre-purposive model of man the symbol of transcendence is a quality of the universal elemental man, not a quality of spirit. It is something prior to what mythologies and religions are about, and appears to be their substratum. Is self-transcendence a quality of universal immediateness that has intimations and yearnings in man beyond the structures of his existence? If it is, it is a dissonant note in process philosophy and suggests rather the mystic overtones in a processive interpretation of man, which Meland borrows from mysticism and neoorthodoxy. Is this an attempt to stretch process philosophy to enable religious sensibility and creature-feeling to rise above man in seeking the totality that constitutes the redemptive process? It would appear to be so. The plea that this commits us only to a 'marginal apprehension', an 'intimation' or 'yearning' of the More in existence (or beyond it), does not reduce the confusion in mixing two models of religious unity. He cannot have it both ways.

20. *Ibid.*, p. 125.

This transcendent outreach of the creaturely-feeling, beyond the human structure to divine immanence, becomes a new source of the empowerment of life and purpose, the author claims. It is a gift of grace, of divine immanence and, consequently, something beyond human purpose and command. This religious restraint on modern man and culture is to be welcome, the author contends. Man and culture are both under the judgment of the Ultimate Ground. To receive it, however, they must make the journey of receptivity by way of this creature-feeling. Receptive freedom defines man's more assertive moods. Religion gives one a foundation in being receptive to divine immanence and its directives through wholeness.

With man's drive for wholeness coupled with the transcendent outreach of his elemental nature, man's goal-direction to a system of immanent totality is set. Against this the theme of 'dissonance' which Meland emphasizes more and more in his later writings, cannot be taken too seriously. Man's dissonant quality is not a serious confrontation to divine immanence, because his freedom is both fallible and limited by divine intent. To the extent man is a creature of divine intent, 'he is obligated to pursue this freedom to fulfill that intent'.[21] The conflict in the encounter of man with divine immanence is apparent only. For man's destiny is sealed by immediate goal-direction to the Creative Process. The part can do only so much against the whole that constitutes redemption.

D. Daniel Day Williams

In reconstructing the liberal doctrine of divine immanence more in line with neo-liberal views Williams suggests the following revisions: (1) the Kingdom of God, while it is inclusive of human values, may also transcend them, which would extend the work of the Kingdom beyond the present experience; (2) it requires a processive theory of man capable of responding to divine immanence in terms of universal immediacy, for the relation between the divine and man is the processive logic between the whole and the part; (3) the continuous creativity of divine immanence in the process of secularization must be assumed in a world that has no *a priori* fixed limits, and this means the possibility of constant transformation of this life in the service of the Kingdom. Such is the perplexity and opportunity of a revitalized liberal perspective in America.[22]

21. *Ibid.*, p. 135.
22. Daniel D. Williams, 'The Perplexity and the Opportunity of the Liberal Theology in America', *The Journal of Religion*, Vol. XXV, No. 3, July, 1945, pp. 176–78.

Thus neo-liberalism is still bent on showing the relevance of the Ultimate in the secular process. Its appeal to experience for the standard of religious relevancy is still paramount, a standard freed from tradition and confessional creeds. Liberalism would still rather face the risks of religious participation in experience than to accept a transcendental religious unity for life that is empty. The appeal to experience is still significant for neo-liberals because it is felt that this theology has not yet accommodated itself properly to secular experience, not that it has accommodated itself too much. It is the same point G. B. Shaw makes to the effect that divine immanence has not yet been tried in experience. From the perspective of Williams 'Experience is transcended in the knowledge of God, but it is not eliminated from the knowledge'.[23] In spite of the bankruptcy of some of its doctrines and the tragic sense evoked in experience by the exigencies of the twentieth century liberalism remains undaunted in its program of showing man's goal-direction to divine wholeness as an immediate relation of man to God.

What is it, then, that immediate experience discloses about man's relation to divine immanence? The obvious answer by now is that although human truth about divine immanence is perspectival divine immanence and the whole which constitutes the process of redemption is not. There is a given structure of reality that is its own and whose work of self-disclosure is its own, having an integrity of its own that man does not fathom or fashion. Williams made this commitment to objective relativism as early as 1948. He defended the position on the grounds that (1) perspectivalism points beyond itself to something that is not a perspective, (2) and that such perspectives participate in the millieau of other perspectives in experience, that there is rewarding interaction 'in the clash and flux of the great democracy of experience itself' ('They are always in process').[24]

We have already alluded to the fact that projectionism, perspectivalism, and the symbolic approach (all three of which point to a reality beyond themselves), are still on the wave-length of goal-direction. Although it is a more subtle goal-direction we should still view it as a functional religious holism which makes claims of ultimacy on man. While the Ultimate is in the secular experience, He is there as the Other, notwithstanding. This perspective involves a notion of truth which should be examined.

Williams claims there are two kinds of truths. Truth I presupposes the truth of things in themselves, irrespective of what we think about it. It simply is what it is and that which is spoken about. Truth II, on the other hand, is our

---

23. J. W. Smith & A. L. Jamison, *Religion In American Life*, op. cit., p. 469.
24. Daniel D. Williams, 'Truth In The Theological Perspective', *The Journal of Religion*, Vol. XXVIII, No. 4, October, 1948, pp. 246–7.

relation to what is, or to what is spoken about. The author claims these two kinds of truth must be kept separate, that divine immanence is of the first kind and the human relationship to it, is of the second kind. Human purpose also belongs to the second kind of truth and has all the earmarks of perspectival truth. But divine intent is different. It is that given wholeness that characterizes the redemptive process in history.[25]

If man is to seek divine wholeness beyond his vision of its, he must listen to his elemental human nature and to presentational myths (both of which guide human purpose to its fulfilled destiny). Williams contends

> They guide us to realities, they envision the structure of life, and they motivate us in our reactions; but they do not yield truth. This can be derived only from the testing of discursive propositions ... It is part of the wisdom of both philosophy and theology to recognize their own myths, that is, those vivid, dramatic conceptions expressed in nondiscursive symbols in which the ultimate structure, unity, and worth of existence are simply grasped, and to recognize that these myths can never be wholly rationalized.[26]

This emphasis on the guidance-value of 'presentational myths' is in line with Meland's 'religious sensibilities'. They function as mediators in the field of universal immediacy between man and divine immanence. They are servants of that wholeness which constitutes the process of redemption. There is no attempt on the part of any liberal that I know of to relate the process of myth-making to man's purposive nature, and to view them as man's attempts to further grasp the meaning of life. It is assumed that if man is a 'member of totality', he should behave as such. As a part of the whole, he can make a worthwhile contribution 'to the life of the whole', which is his primary responsibility (because his well-being depends on totality). The highest kind of human participation in existence is the kind which is goal-directed toward the totality disclosed in divine immanence: 'for the problem of life is to find that unity and wholeness in the nature of things to which we can give ourselves with single-minded devotion'.[27]

Where does one discover one intelligible structure, or 'man's real good', if not amid the processes of human existence? In the midst of life we refer to it as an 'unrealized ideal' growing cumulatively in human history and beyond it. There in the human condition divine immanence turns out to be 'the problem of the value of life', which Williams defines as follows:

> God's unity is His goodness. God's goodness is his love. God's love is that the creative and

25. *Ibid.*, pp. 244–5.
26. *Ibid.*, p. 252.
27. Daniel D. Williams, *God's Grace and Man's Hope*, New York: Harper and Brothers, 1949, p. 63.

redemptive power which works unceasingly in all times and places to bring to fulfillment a university community of free and loving beings.[28]

That this system of religious unity is model-free and, therefore, prior to man's purposive nature, is evidenced by the language the author uses. The structure of love and goodness is actually the Christological structure of life. Man participates in an undesigning way in 'the life of the whole', 'in the total order of life'. By that participation in the real immediate wholeness of reality man achieves his destiny and wholeness. When the ultimate goal-direction of life is in proper focus the pattern of the whole becomes more visible and meaningful. This affirmation is made by the author in *God's Grace and Man's Hope* and in the recently published book *The Spirit and the Forms of Love* (1968). Williams contends that: 'While each gives itself to the whole each has its own claim upon the whole ... only a transformation of the human spirit into the willingness to give the self to the whole can suffice for the Kingdom'.[29] The phrase for it in the new book is 'the will to belong' to the 'whole creation and the Creator'.

'The will to belong' is a *sui generis* quality in man. In fact, it is the essence of man's humanity – 'this humanity which is between us and yet beyond us'. But it can be distorted by other systems of totality, with their patterns of belongingness. Consequently, there is need to talk about the relationship of sin to the will to belong (pp. 146–54), *The Spirit and the Forms of Love*). Thus it needs restoration and recreation in man. If it is constitutive of man's being, the task of recreating the spirit of belongingness along model-free lines is most urgent. Is this just another claim to ultimacy for one's system of religious totality?

While 'the will to belong' may be 'the formal possibility of our being in communion with the whole of creation and the Creator' it is that only through the mediation of man's purposive nature, and of the recognition that each system of totality makes and has its own 'will to belong', depending on the ultimate goal-direction it has postulates for its adherents. The will to belong 'to what', or the will to belong 'to which system of totality', and 'to which ultimate goal-direction and destiny', are rather significant questions in view of the possibility that our search for wholeness colors our systems of totality, even those for which we make claims of ultimacy.

---

28. *Ibid.*, p. 64.
29. *Ibid.*, pp. 79–80. Cf. also to *The Spirit and the Forms of Love*, New York: Harper and Row, 1968, pp. 146–54.

IV. The alternative – with some critical remarks

The criticisms which I shall offer in this section will all bear on the same issue, namely, that the wholeness which constitutes divine immanence is a project of man's purposive nature before it is the necessity of tradition, scripture, confessional creeds, or as in liberalism – the necessity of immediate experience, or the necessity of an elemental human nature. Man's purposive nature as ontologically conceived, necessitates that man be first self-directing in existence before he is a God-seeker or self-seeker. The alleged religious necessity imposed on immediate experience by religious liberals is a religious reading of immediacy, which has already had one other prior reading in terms of processive qualities, relations, and events. Man's purposive nature is already involved in such manipulation of immediacy. There is no awareness of religious liberals of this manipulation or exploitation of immediacy. Before man's relation to divine immanence can be stated in any one of these perspectives it must first be a project of human purpose. Religious commitment is posterior to it. I shall present these general criticisms in the following order: (1) the approach of immediate experience to the wholeness that constitutes divine immanence, (2) the given nature of divine immanence or wholeness, (3) the liberal claims to ultimacy for the wholeness of divine immanence.

First, let me consider the path of immediacy to the wholeness that characterizes divine immanence. Since I have dealt with this issue elsewhere[30] perhaps the issue can now be stated more briefly. The problem is: how do religious liberals go from the claims of existential particulars to their claims about universal immediacy (which is necessary in order to have an immediate grasp of wholeness that constitutes divine immanence)? Existentialists and process philosophies are both guilty of this shift of gears on the topic of immediacy. Is a processive reading of experience a model of experience, say, as in contrast to the existential construct of experience? Both schools deny the model-character of experience conceived either as process or as an existent. This would mean that human participation has lost its forming and designing power in existence. Man can participate in the bare given without affecting it or its character of wholeness (let it rest on its own integrity). Although it would be easier to claim this for existential or processive particulars (our theory disavows it even here), it is nearly impossible to uphold it on the level of universal immediacy. For this is immediacy by consensus. It involves the

---

30. William Horosz, *The Promise and Peril of Human Purpose*, St. Louis: Warren Green Inc., pp. 61–71.

identification of particular, existential processive participation in existence as having a universal outreach beyond itself and with humanity (in the claim of a common elemental human nature). This identification is not on the same level as the participation of a particular individual. Universal immediacy is thus part of man's search about models of human nature and cannot be separated and distilled from this process. The religious liberals have denied the model-quality of elemental human nature, just as they have denied the model-quality of the character of wholeness surrounding divine immanence. Thus we repeat what we stated earlier; unless it is part of man's search for models of human nature, it is a fiction. A model-free universal and elemental human nature is a fiction. The liberals are not exempt from constructing a model of man by an appeal to experience that would receive the idea of divine wholeness in terms of universal immediacy. There are exemplars of this search for a model of man, first in process philosophy, second, in religious mysticism, and in the combination of the two strains of thought.

Elemental modes of response do not make either correlations or identifications with cosmic wholeness. It is the human orderer in existence that does, using these elemental modes of response along with the existentializing capacity of his purposive nature. These experiences are not as mindless as existentialists say; they are, nor are they as purposeless as the religious liberals believe. The 'whole man" of liberalism is thus a model of man and as such assumes prior ontological purposiveness. The whole man is part of man's search for self-understanding and cannot be severed from that search. The liberal construct of man, the man in search of wholeness via ultimate wholeness in the context of universal immediacy, is not outside the context of self-understanding through such model-making. Before man is a searcher after wholeness, in his own fulfillment, or in his own fulfillment in the divine whole, we must assume that he is self-directing in such a quest. Before man is either a self-seeker or a God-seeker, we must first see him as self-directing in existence. Without the directives of man's purposive nature we cannot make much sense out of any of the above notions.

Without the directives of man's purposive nature contributing to his experience and being a part of human participation in existence, there is no other alternative but to settle for other mediators of man's lot, like 'creative exchange', 'the appreciative consciousness', 'religious sensibilities', or 'presentational myths'. While the liberals were confident that these approaches would significantly relate man to divine immanence, I am not so confident. They are substitute forms of human pre-wired with pre-purposive goal-direction to a system of divine totality.

Let me, then, summarize this section. Unless immediate experience is 'my experience', it is nothing. To postulate a universal pool of immediate experience, as the liberals have done, to go from 'one's ultimate' to 'the Ultimate', is to miss the point about the nature of immediacy. How does one universal direct experience to make the secular Other the requirement of immediacy? The reply is obvious. By prior purposive manipulation, which is disavowed by the liberals. Such immediacy may be more childish than childlike. 'My original awareness of my ultimate' is one thing. But the belief that universal original awareness reaches 'the Ultimate' on the level of immediate experience, is another. Such necessity is mediated by man's purposive nature ant its self-directives in existence. Unless man is first prepurposively goal-directed to divine immanence, there is nothing in immeidate experience itself to commend such fixed goal-direction. The liberals have given the twentieth century a tutored universal elemental human nature that knows his dues when appealing to experience. It is a religious posture in experience, towards man himself and towards the whole which constitutes divine immanence.

Second, the given nature of divine immanence and its constitutive wholeness in temporality is a special problem withl iberalism. The orthodox model of religious unity does not postulate this last theme. The given is both real and whole. In its given rality of wholeness it has an integrity of its own. Yet its wholeness is constitutive of unity in the temporal sphere, which the liberals identified with the Creative Process. Since the liberals also expressed belief in functional transcendence we may assume that the whole extends beyond the scope of particular experiences of man. Thus it is beyong human participation. Also in respect to truth, the given is beyond human participation. Thus it is constitutive of wholeness or unity in the temporal sphere without human participation. Man as 'co-worker' is a secondary construct in this context, because man does not constitute wholeness in experience. This is the prerogative of God, most liberals claim.

In contrast to the special status attributed divine immanence at the outer rim of experience and within it, let us view the participatory role of the human orderer in existence. He makes no contribution to the whole of experience *qua* wholeness, although he may contribute to some of the immanent goals of life as co-worker with God. He is a part participating in the whole. His primal dealings with the whole are prior to his intellect and purpose. He is advised to make a religious commitment prior to the exercise of these powers (his elemental nature makes the decision). He also takes many risks in this roles of religious participation. These points would suggest that the role of man's participation in existence is limited both by process philosophy and by mystic attachments to divine immanence. Man does not share equipollent power with the whole at none of these points of comparison. The nature and scope of participation is defined by the fixed goal-direction that defines the dominant purpose of his life. Again, his elemental nature made the decision pre-conceptually and pre-purposively to commit himself to such fixed goal-direction. The model of human participation in existence, in spite of the liberal appeal to experience, appears somewhat shabby. In contrast to the given whole, he comes out poorly, except for the promise of wholeness in the ultimate whole. Thus, even within experience, the immananent Other, is in control of human participation.

Liberalism worked itself into the embarrassing position of claiming an empirically given whole in the doctrine of divine immanence that was beyond human participation. Although God was a cosmic companion and worker divine wholeness transcended human participation in both his nature and work. One way to stave off criticism was to assume a functional, rather than a metaphysical transcendence for Him. But the problem given remains.

How can man state the claims for the given as given beyond the claims of human participation in it? How can one assume wholeness for the given when human participation is perspectival, particular, and fragmentary? Just because human projection, perspective, and symbolization point beyond themselves to a reality other than themselves does not establish the holistic nature of the given, especially since all these processes are themselves, as participatory functions of the human orderer, perspectival and fragmentary experiences. If this is the case, the given as given beyond human participation, must be an abstraction or myth. Moreover, the whole itself is an abstraction.

What would the given whole be like viewed in terms of human participation? Such systems of religious unity are temporary and provisional aids in man's search for religious meaning. That is all they have been historically. Alexander Allen mentions the historical conflict between the Greek immanent view of religious unity and the Latin transcendental version.[31] The transcendental Other of crisis theology and of neo-orthodoxy, reacting to the liberal commitment to divine immanence, was the 'wholly Other', an alienating experience to man (negating and contradicting the directives of human purpose, and somehow mysteriously fulfilling them, too). The history of Christian thought reveals the pendulum swinging from transcendence to immanence and vice versa with a regularity that ceases to

---

31. W. R. Hutchison (ed.), *American Protestant Thought*, pp. 57–68. Allen is interested in establishing the continuity between the Greek conception of religious unity and theliberal notion of divine immanence. The fact that he can point to various historical models of religious unity, however, points out the fact of historical constructs of religious unity. They appear to be cultural aids as well, in the search for religious meaning.

amaze man. They are models of religious unity that serve an epoch until another time period comes which demands another model of religious unity. Some, however, may claim the change in models is superficial, that under the models is the real given whole which sustains all models of religious unity, the one real God. But this is a claim beyond historical participation in the given whole, hard to sustain, even more difficult to demonstrate.

The more participatory theory of the given whole, then, assumes that such schemes of totality are temporary aids, individual and cultural, in man's search for further meaning, just as the notion of the 'whole man' is a temporary aid in man's further search in self-understanding. That man is self-directing in the quest for meaning, we must assume. They are projects of human self-direction, whether man extends the search towards the divine whole or towards some other scheme of totality.

These totalities are goal-directions for living stated in terms of some dominant purpose for life. They derive from man's phenomenal experience. Theology merely gives such phenomenal goals theological fixation and thus gives them ontologico-religious status. Once this process is achieved, piety demands that such religious wholes be given a reality and an integrity of their own. The process is only too familiar. Underlying even fixed goal-direction is man's ontological capacity for goal-direction. This means that it is man's participation in existence that creates such alleged given systems of totality. For the given has meaning only in terms of human participation. Without human participation in existence it remains the bare Otherness of human experience, nothing to speak of. The attitude of receptivity to given wholes beyond human participation is a concession to piety, not to human wonder and sensitivity and purpose. Human purpose mediates even that which inheres in the human structure as it mediates the claims of man to 'A-More-Than-Human-Reality'. Man's purposive nature mediates the Creator-creature doctrine, as well as the part-to-whole relationship which liberals continue to espouse.

This perspective presupposes a view of immediate experience, as a participatory phenomenon, which designs concepts of the given and of the whole. Man is a kind of designer in and through human participation in existence. If there is credence to this position, then, it follows that the identification of the wohle with the given, is a secondary function, derivative of human participation in existence. This perspective also presupposes various models of immediate experience. The equating of process with the given is another such model of direct experience. The mystic identification of the secular Other of liberalism with direct experience, while maintaining the functional transcendence of divine immanence above experience, is another such model of direct experience. If direct experience is available to us only in models of experience, as the human orderer participates in existence, then, universal immediacy, the liberal foundation for man's relation to God, is a fiction. We can neither identify our models of a living relationship, nor our model-making as a living relationship, because human participation, as perspectival participation in existence, presupposes a human order that has such designs in the midst of such participation. Had we examined the historical development of liberal notions of the secular Other the appeal to religious experience would have revealed many models of the other each varying with the changing experience of individuals and of cultures. To hold out for the constancy in the midst of such change is simply to deny the claims of human participation, and its potency for design therein. The phenomenon of history speaks out against this denial. The affinity between God and man in liberalism is thus a modeled relationship, serving its time as a model modern history. It depends on a model of man, on a model of divine immanence, and on the model of a living relationship between them. If human participation has this potency amid experience, its voice should not be denied in either of these three terms. To state the case for this triadic relationship apart from human motivation, where developed to its highest capacities, is simply a case of mistaken identifications, an awkward way of talking about all three terms.

How does man go from his given, from his Whole, to Ultimacy itself? By a set of mistaken identifications? Or, does he do it by human participation? Such is the alternative. If by the latter, then, human designs upon the given and upon the whole cannot be cavalierly discounted, as liberals have done. The pre-purposive model of religious unity is just as inadequate as the orhtodox view was and is, because both schools chose the path of mistaken identifications, rather than participation. If human participation in the given whole is real, its designing qualities cannot be denied. The issue of receptive and assertive freedom is a funcitonal aspect in such participation. They do not define human participation in the given whole or in existence.

Third, the liberal claims for the ultimacy of their model of religious totality has been documented. They assumed the reality of immanence over the empty version of religious unity presented by orthodoxy. The claims to ultimacy rested on certain mistaken identifications, as we noted. (1) They identified their model of religious unity with divine immanence. While this construct informed man of his fixed goal-direction to the eternal, it denied a shaping and forming power of human purpose of the given structure of the whole. It stood over against man as the Other. (2) It identified the above construct with some empowering force in nature-history. This took the form of creativity, value-integration, and assumed the ingression of unity in the multiplicity of processes and events in the world. (3) The realists among the liberals identified the first construct with more objective experiences and methods that would relate religion to a scientific culture. (4) All these identifications were made by an elemental human nature informed of the reality-feeling by its creature-feeling.

If these identifications are mistaken or illicit, then, the liberals have no grounds for their claims to ultimacy for divine immanence. Why do we regard them as mistaken identifications? They are illicit because: (1) they presuppose omniscience on the part of man, (2) they show a concern for the given beyond the notion of human participation in the given, (3) they identify the cosmic hwole with some process of empowerment in the universe, (4) they make these identifications with an inadequate and hasty theory of human nature in terms of universal immediacy, (5) they presuppose a model-free use of immediate experience which is suggestive of apologetic practice.

Let me put the matter more bluntly, human participation in existence is prior to such identification schemes. It is better to correlate our models of existence with reality via the process of participation, before practicing the identification process, a derived product from human participation. Human participation is always particular, existential, and fragmentary. If this is the case, then, the given can only be an object of human participation, the end term in the process of participation, actual or possible. It needs no prior identification with direct experience as the given structure of immediateness. It would be much easier to make a case for the perspectival nature of the given in experience than to construe it holistically, without identifying the given in experience than to construe it holistically, without identifying the given with immediateness, by simply saying it is the object of human participation. Since the given is only that (rather than a whole, or a brute fact, or the bare Other), the process of identification can be introduced as the second step in the procedure. If human participation in existence is prior to the process of identification, then, universal immediate experience should be viewed as a derived abstraction from direct experience, a secondary process. The liberals reverse this procedure for apologetic reasons and, consequently, exploited immediate experience, for religious reasons.

In the light of our theory, then, it is more likely that perspectivalism constitutes the given whole, rather than wholeness, if the given is merely an object of human participation. Man's view of participation in existence has thus been misconstrued, as coming in contact with the whole of existence or with the whole of reality, in terms of reality-feeling or creature-feeling. However, we need not commit ourselves to the process of identification so hastily, prior to human participation in reality. For it is human participation in experience which informs man how to procede with the identifications on hand. Man's perspectival comprehension of reality may simply mean a perspectival reality, if the given is viewed as an object of human participation or its possibility in existence. What good is the whole that constitutes reality, if it is beyond human participation? Is this the *a priori* requirement of the human mind or the demand of reality itself? The claims to a dim apprehension of the given whole, while assuming its pure given structure, are too numerous to mention. Why so many apologies? The reply is obvious? Because they have postulated a given beyond human participation and there is an uneasy feeling it is merely the *a priori* demand of the human mind and not the real whole after all.

Another likely alternative presents itself. Perhaps both the holistic and the perspectival views of given reality are already model-constructs of cosmic reality, that we should desist from making either assumption on the level of human participation, and admit it only after the process of participation has taken place. Perhaps we can have only model-constructs of reality and not reality itself. If we can only participate in reality in a designing and forming way, as we admit, amid the processes of existence, perhaps all we can have on the level of such participation is close-ups of reality, and never the reality itself, as it is in its given reality and its own integrity. Let us conclude then, that on the level of human participation we admit model-making in existence, that the given, even as Other, can never be seen apart from human motivation and purposive being. On the next, more abstract level, it is permissible to practice identifications. This should lessen the claims to ultimacy for any model of religious totality, including the liberal view.

In terms of our perspective, it is clear the liberal model of totality was as much a construct as the orthodox view, in spite of their identification of divine immanent wholeness with some process of empowerment in nature. This was only the foil for covering the mistaken identification as being the equivalent of human participation. The identification of religious totality with the creative process was thus unwarranted, if not damaging to mankind in its consequences. Human purpose was shoved to a corner, and regarded as a reacting phenomenon to these mistaken identifications. Only the claims to ultimacy held the religious totality together. When modern man was no longer subservient to these claims, the liberal mosaic for life was shattered, and crisis theology in Europe and neo-orthodoxy in America, tried to put it together once more (along the same lines of mistaken identifications), but without success, as the death of God theology was soon to question the new transcendental religious unity.

If my conclusion is to be brief, let me hasten to say that the inclusion of human purpose in the context of primal encounters with God (or in the encounter-experiences with any other given) should by now be regarded as the only necessity required of man. For it is purposive being that mediates the claims of necessity for God in liberalism and in other schools of thought. On the basis of this mediation in the context of a richer primal experience, from which the human orderer has not been excised or made passive, should flow more continuous relations between man and his world, or between man and God. If God is alleged to be a necessity of life, as the liberals claimed, this is so through the claims of human participation in existence, from which purpose cannot be excised. For man's purposive nature is there as model-maker in the very process of participation. This fact relieves man of the burden of identificaitons on the level of human participation in existence. It makes man responsible only for his role of participation in existence, not for identifications. If immediate experience is that level of human good where all goodies are to be found, then, we must conceive of immediateness in richer forms by including human purpose as part of primal experience.

At this stage of civilization it may be asking modern man too much to go back to the reality-feeling of infancy or to the creature-feeling of primitive man. This is an unwelcome note at a time when modern man aspires toward higher standards for religious knowledge. If it is the case that human participation in existence is perspectival, just as his thinking is, then, it follows that man cannot avoid model-making in existence, to make up for this deficiency and incompleteness. Although man is self-directing in human participation in existence, he is not self-sufficient. Because he is incomplete he needs to practice model-making in his participatory search in existence. There is nothing wrong with models of reality so long as we desist from making claims of ultimacy for them and resist identifying our constructs of wholeness, which are part of our search for wholeness, with cosmic wholeness itself. If they are viewed as temporary patterns of meaning which function as provisional guides for life, so much the better for them. But the recognition of this fact requires that we view purpose ontologically as an aspect of primal experience where its model-making powers count in shaping encounter-experiences.

One may, of course, continue to object to all this by saying that if the eternal is not prior to human purpose, then, man's purposive being is God. There is no attempt here to make the term 'God' superfluous in human experience. What is being attempted is to relate purpose more effectively to such encounters with God. The obvious reply is that what is inveighed against is that human constructs of wholeness are not prior to purposive being. The charge itself assumes the mistaken identification we disavowed throughout the chapter between construct of wholeness and cosmic wholeness itself. The objection assumes a separation between man's search for wholeness and cosmic wholeness itself. The basic point remains, namely, that whatever we may or may not affirm about God's wholeness we do so through human channels or models of human participation in existence. The remainder is mythology.

PART III

FROM THE PERSPECTIVE OF INDIAN RELIGION

CHAPTER 10

PURPOSE OF MAN IN THE TRADITION OF INDIAN ORTHODOXY

S. P. BANERJEE

I

The attempt at explaining the main spring of philosophical systems has been an interesting endeavour in philosophy. Until recently, it has been almost a commonplace in the subject to hold that philosophy starts either with the problem of nature, taken to imply objectivity, or of man, signifying subjectivity. That man himself is a combination of both or that nature includes man also has not been totally unknown, but in the question of laying emphasis, it has been laid either on the one or the other.

The early western thinking seems to have started with the problem of nature or the world. The Greek thinkers started wondering on the ultimate stuff of the universe and so, they are legitimately claimed to have also been the first scientists. It cannot, however, be an exclusive affair restricted only to nature. Some have naturally mused on the nature of mind (nous) and the master minds on the nature of human knowledge and values.

In the case of Indian philosophy it seems to have started the other way round. The seer of the *Ṛg Veda* has wondered at the natural objects, but the centre which has prompted him to explain or utilize them, has been man himself. To unfold the mystery of human nature, to clinch the essence of man has been the primary motivation of the traditional systems. *Ātmanam viddhi* (knowh thyself) is the 'go'-word of Indian philosophy. And this knowledge, as developed through the *Vedas, Upaniṣads*, and other systems based on them, is not a mere epistemic affair. Knowing is for being, they interpenetrate. The dichotomy between thought and action, between the knower and the agent, is transcended in the concrete being of man. It is the full man in his perfection (*Mokṣa*) that is the object of quest for the Indian systems. It is for the realization of man's true self, it is for his liberation that thought, feeling and action converge. This philosophical motif makes no rigid distinction between philosophy and religion. Philosophy is that of human existence or being; so, it is religion in practice and action. *Dharma* (a synonym for religion) is that which sustains a man, it is the philosophy of life. Philosophy and religion supplement each other, they tend to fuse together to depict the true nature of the concrete man, who does not only think but acts and feels too. With all its diversities and dimensions, life is one. Science of *Dharma* is the master science of life.

This has been a source of confusion to some who fail to seee anything in Hinduism more than a mass of codes for conduct. The real life seems to flow underneath these codes with the admission of immense diversity in life. Traditional Indian orthodoxy usually means the Vedic tradition which includes the *Vedas*, the *Upanisads*, the *Bhagavad Gitā*, and the philosophical systems,[1] which are based on the teachings of the *Vedas* and *Upanisads*. Though Buddhism and Jainism are claimed to be independent of the Vedic philosophy, they are in perfect concord with the spiritual outlook expressed by the tradition. Only the Cārvāka system, though sharing the same concern for man, presents an altogether different brand of thinking, rather materialistic in character.

It is too much to claim that the Vedas formulate an articulate philosophy of man. The *Ṛg Vedic* seer has wondered at the natural objects, at the manifestation of power but somehow he has started thinking from the standpoint of man. He has raised the problem of purpose and has given a historical meaning to the flow of events. This concern for the purpose of man prompts him to offer prayers to the gods and to seek the exact relationship between man, nature and god.

Philosophy has gradually crystallized through the *Upanisads* reaching full maturity in the systems. The key-problem seems to have been man's relation with nature and the spiritual reality, to find out the purpose and meaning of life. So considered, Indian tradition has to be reckoned as anthropocentric. One could try to answer the question by extolling man or the individual and trivializing the absolute. Or, one might trivialize the individual and capitalize between the two. By and large Indian traditional endeavour has been to achieve this harmony and derive all meaning from this harmony. No Indian system would maintain that human life is devoid of purpose. The denial of purpose goes against the anthropocentricity of Indian tradition. What this purpose is is the most important question.

We may try to understand the solution of this problem by trying to answer a few questions that may be formulated in this connection. They are:

1. The Indian tradition recognizes six systems as based on the *Vedas* and the *Upaniṣads*. They are known as *Sutra* philosophies of the Hindu *Sad Darsana*. They are as follows: *(Sāmkhya, Yoga, Nyāya, Vaiśeṣika, Purva Mimamsā* (or simply *Mimamsā*) and *Uttara Mimamsā* (generally known as *Vedānta*). These systems as called *āstika* systems as distinguished from the *nāstika* systems (like Buddhism, Jainism and *Cārvāka* philosophy) which are either independent of, or opposed to, the Vedic tradition.

1. What is the concept of man in the traditional systems? Is there a unity in this regard?
1.1. Does the individual have a choice of purpose? Or, is destiny controlling him, i.e., is there a freely chosen purpose or is it pre-ordained?
2. Is there a teleology in nature?
2.1. Is, then, human teleology a part of the wider teleology in nature, or,
2.2. Is human teleology the determining factor of the natural teleology?
3. What is the place of God in Hindu thought?

All these problems could be compressed into the following three and this paper will try to deal with them in an attempt to understand the nature of the individual and his purpose.

A. The relation of the individual to nature;
B. the relation of the individual to society, and
C. the relation of the individual to God/Absolute.

II

In a way, the answer to C would solve the basic problems involved in A and B. If Indian tradition in general advocates a purely theistic or absolutistic philosophy, there will be little scope for nature existing independently of such an all-comprehensive reality. Nature and man will be integral parts of reality and as such their relation will be one of that between parts of the same whole.

This may broadly be the line of thinking in Indian philosophy. But a close examination is called for. The logical alternatives one can think of in settling the relation between individual and nature may be of following types:
i) Nature is hostile to human existence with its values and purposes;
ii) nature is indifferent to human existence;
iii) nature is conducive to the pursuit of human purpose.

i) One does not generally come across such a view in Indian philosophy where it is maintained that human existence is not within the scheme of nature. The boundlessness of space and time has been a common background but there is nothing to show that nature is hostile to human existence. The so-called natural evil has to be explained from the moral point of view.

A principal reason for the absence of such a view could be that on its admission, 'physical living' itself becomes the primary value as it is for this that man would have to struggle. Other values, should they be accepted, slide downwards in a value-structure based on such an ontology. The *Cārvka* system, though without a developed scientific view on which such a theory has been offered, philosophically works on such a background. It takes nature to be indifferent, if not hostile, to human living. The value-structure that is developed is consequently primarily materialistic. The body, treated as a thing, becomes the sole value. Indian orthodoxy, generally known to be pessimistic, is not a tradition of despair. It does not look upon human existence as transitory always facing up to the challenge of death. Nature at least does not intend it. Physical death, again, does not mean much for the Indian system. A brief discussion on the role of human body will be made towards the end of this section.

ii) Absence of hostility is not necessarily to be construed as being congenial to human purpose. Nature could be regarded to be totally indifferent to human existence. Such a view would imply that there is no teleology in nature – explicit or implicit. This theory also does not seem to have been held by the Indian thinkers as they speak of purposiveness in nature. But some amount of naturalism has been accepted.

iii) Purposiveness in nature could be explained in two ways: (a) there is cosmic purpose and human purpose is only a part of it; (b) nature as such does not have a purpose of its own; but it serves human or divine purpose. Both these views have their difficulties. If (a) is adopted, human values might become insignificant as part of nature's own scheme. If (b) is advocated, the explanation of nature becomes completely anthropocentric and might go against an independent development of natural sciences.

It is not the case that the traditional thinking has been clear on the alternatives from the very beginning. The possibility of nature being indifferent to human endeavours for the realization of values has not been ruled out by the early Vedic thinkers, though there has always been an undercurrent for reading teleology all around in nature. The cosmogony of the *Ṛg Veda* presents an interesting picture. One finds here a dual suggestion of ordinary naturalism and divine purposiveness presented in the garb of mythology. The universe is regarded as the result of mechanical production on the one hand and the *Brahman*[2] (Supreme Being in the later development of Vedic thinking) is looked upon as the material cause of everything in nature, on the other.[3] In the Man-hymn[4] the Supreme Man is regarded as the lord of everything in the universe, and of immortality. The animate and inanimate things are nothing but his diffusion. The Supreme Man is supposed

---

2. Reference may please be made to *Satapatha Brāhmana* where the conception of *Brahman* acquires great significance as the supreme principle. Also compare *Svetāsvataropanisad*, Canto III, Sloka 13–15, 17.
3. *Ṛg. Veda*, X, 81.4 and also Macdonall, Vedic Mythology, p. 11.
4. *Ṛg Veda* X, 90 (*Puruśa-Sukta*).

to pervade the whole of the world with only a fourth part of Himself, while the remaining parts extend to the region beyond. He is beyond time – as He is at once past, present and future.

There has been an interplay of naturalistic and teleological tendencies in the course of later development of philosophy. In the vast Vedic literature with diverse philosophical thinking, it cannot be expected that there has been complete unity on the point. But there has been general unanimity in attributing some sort of broad purposiveness to nature without completely denying nature flow of events. In the *Upaniṣads*, nature is viewed more or less as fulfilling the divine purpose and this is further developed in some of the theistic systems; but the limited independence of nature is not completely taken away. The agreement in the attitudes may be brought out in the context of two philosophical systems, one believing in God and the other without such a belief. *Nyāya* system accepts God and Sāṁkhya rejects it; but both of them believe in the purposiveness in nature, though in varying degrees. What I intend to point out is that the teleology in nature may sometimes be independent of a belief in an Omnipresent God.

Nature is generally taken to be the background for the moral or religious struggle of man in his march towards self-realization. Nature not only does not repel human endeavour in the moral life but it sustains such an endeavour. Nature does this either in its own way or to fulfill divine purpose. Sṁkhya[5] philosophy presents independent teleology in nature. In this system two fundamental realities are accepted – *Puruṣa* and *Prakṛti*. *Puruṣa* stands for pure consciousness (*cit*)[6] or soul. *Prakṛti* is the unconscious principle (*acit*), the dynamic causal matrix of everything but *Puruṣa*. *Puruṣa* is unchanging, non-active and eternal. In its own nature, it is pure and free. But consciousness appears in conjunction with a body in the subjects of experience, i.e., the ordinary individuals. *Puruṣa* does not have any control over *Prakṛti*. *Prakṛti*, composed of three essential components (*guṇas*) like *Sattva*, *Rajas* and *Tamas*, is always envolving. This evolution is of two types – homogeneous (*svarupāvasthā*) and heterogeneous (*virupāvasthā*). In the homogeneous evolution the *guṇas* change into themselves and *Prakṛti* is non-creative at this stage. But in the heterogeneous evolution these elements get

5. *Samkhya-Kārika* with the commentary of *Vācaspati Miśra*.
6. *Samkhya* theory of pure consciousness seems very close to the *Advaita Vedanta* concept. But there are differences at least on two important points. Firstly, *Sāmkhya* does not consider the soul to be of the nature of pure intelligence and bliss as maintained in *Advaita Vedanta*. Secondly, while according to the *Advaita Vedanta* the individual souls (*jiva*) are illusory manifestations of pure consciousness which is non-dual (*advaita*) *Brahman*, according to the *Sāmkhya* system they are many and real.

mixed up one with another and this results in the emergence of things of nature. Human body itself is a product of *Prakṛti* and the ordinary ego or individual is an amalgam of consciousness and the body – a product of unconscious nature. The activiiy that belongs to the individual is due to the contribution of *Prakṛti* which contains the principle of activity and change. *Puruṡa* is present as a catalyst to move *Prakṛti* to creative (heterogeneous) evolution.

The entire scheme of this evolution appears to be intentional in a peculiar way. It is for the enjoyment of the *Puruṡa* that *Prakṛti* evolves. *Prakṛti* evolves for the pleasure and suffering of the different *Puruṡas* in accordance with their potency of activities.[7] *Prakṛti* thus engages *Puruṡa* in an intimate way and the *Puruṡa* falsely identifies itself with its body or the products of *Prakṛti*. But *Prakṛti* not only binds down the *Puruṡa* but also helps it to realize its nature by understanding its distinction from the *Prakṛti*. Thus *Prakṛti* always moves in a purposive way; there seems to be teleology all around. *Prakṛti* or nature presents *Puruṡa* with the results of its activities and finally helps it in liberating itself through proper knowledge of the category-mistake it commits by identifying itself with the unconscious principle. *Sāmkhya* does not accept the existence of God as the guiding force for the evolution of the *Prakṛti* (*Yoga* accepts God in that fashion). *Prakṛti* is independently purposive and the purpose is to involve and liberate *Puruṡa*.

This novel theory of the *Sāmkhya* system, which is one of the oldest of the systems of philosophy, tries to avoid the difficulties of cosmic purposiveness which might logically be independent of human purpose. The purpose of nature, completely independent both of the individual and of God, is to serve human purpose in assisting it by offering the suitable background for the realization of its moral values. There might be difficulties in accepting unconscious teleology, but the entire character of the ontological scheme is anthropocentric. Though ontologically distinct there does not seem to be a purposive duality between man and nature.

The basic concept does not appear to be different in a theistic view of nature. One may take up the *Vaisnava*[8] point of view for consideration as it is believed to be represent Indian theism at its best. It regards the whole of the universe as the *Lilākshetra* (play ground or sport) of *Visnu* – the Lord, God. Nature is regarded as the manifestation of God who offers it as the back ground for the devotees to work out their union with God. The devotees are His parts and parcels and nature presents the necessary field for the

7. Law of Karma is being referred to. Of this more later.
8. Of the three principal religious trends in Hinduism, *Vaisnavism* is one. A fuller discussion on them is given in this paper.

individuals to make their religious march. Nature, in this thinking, is taken to form a part of the cosmic divine purpose. Nature is like a body to God. While the details of this type of thesis will be taken later, we may briefly consider here the role of body in the tradition of India.

Except in the anti-orthodox *Cārvāka* system body has not been identified with human soul nor has it been regarded to be spiritual to be closely related to human soul. Consciousness is ordinarily taken to be embodied. Body is not just a 'thing' – it is a value, though an extrinsic one. It is created by moral values to some extent and is instrumental to a person's liberation. It acquires a level of subjectivity. It is compared to the temple where consciousness lives in. It is, again, compared to a chariot[9] with sense and motor organs as the horses. This chariot is driven by consciousness and the individual is the master of this chariot. Bodily value is not generally[10] neglected in the value-structure of the tradition, though it is not regarded as an end in itself. Properly trained and controlled, body may be of great assistance to the attainment of the ideal which is perfection.

This attitude to body may be taken to represent the Indian way of evaluating nature. Nature, dependent or independent, on the moral governor (God is accepted only as the efficient cause and the moral governor in the *Nyāya* system or an all-creating God, appears to be the background of the moral life of man. It exhibits purposiveness – primary or secondary. The separate existence of nature does not offer any special problem to Indian philosophy. In the teleological scheme, the passage from the nature to the individual is not difficult. Being is for knowing and knowing leads to greater realization of being. Nature's purposiveness does not necessarily imply that it is ontologically secondary or derivative. Its independence and telos may well go together. But the key-concept is that nature is either a means or the background of man's march to perfection. The march towards perfection might extend through many lives. The body might change, but the soul having different bodies in accordance with the law of *karma* has a continuous march. Thus body or nature is a necessary though secondary means for the successful pursuit of values.

The Indian idea of the world, of nature and of existence is not physical, but psychological and spiritual. Spirit, soul, consciousness are not only greater than inert matter and inconscient force, but they precede and originate these lesser things. All force is power, or means of a secret spirit;

9. Cp. *Kathopaniṣat*, Canto I, Chap. III & IV and Canto II, Chap. II, I and also *Svetāsvataropiniṣad* – Canto III, Sloka – 18.
10. *Kāma* is regarded as a value. Fuller discussion later. For a somewhat different view Buddha's early thought regarding body may be considered.

the force that sustains the world is a conscious Will, and Nature is its machinery of executive power.[11]

The Indian tradition, as has been pointed out here, does not look upon human existence as a chance entrance into an unfriendly environment. The environment or nature is to some extent the background of moral life as also it is to some extent determined by voluntary human activities. The Indian mind aspires to break through the vegetative existence as conditioned by the material and vital situation and reach the higher level of spiritual conscious existence through which alone human existence becomes meaningful. And in this spiritual significance of life consists the main spring of Indian tradition.

One may recount here with profit the broad scheme of the spiritual evolution as envisaged by the ṛsis (seers) of the *Upaniṣads*.[12] Material nature seems to be the first level of existence but it is surcharged with a deeper purpose. Matter seems to be in constant movement towards the higher and higher values. There is a 'nisus' in matter (*annamoy sattā*) towards vital existence (pranomoy sattā) which leads to the next higher level of psychical existence (*manomoy sattā*). There are different strata of knowledge corresponding to these differing levels of evolution. Psychical state finds its culmination in the state of wisdom (*vijñānamoy sattī*. Knowing, however, is not the final state of being. the fruition of this spiritual evolution is achieved in the state of perfection which is blissful (*ānandamoy sattā*). In this gradual progress of the spirit no barriers are recognized between matter and life, life and mind, and, mind and blissful soul. The unconscious nature with progressive stages of evolution reaches its climax in the blissful state of the human soul. But, for each man it may not reach the same level of development. One might be thing-like and live only in the material level while the other could attain liberation. Thus for one without proper wisdom all the different stages might be hard realities with rigid edges while for the other, the truth of spiritual unity might be the only acceptable position. Each has, however, to attain this state through the progressive march to perfection and the entire set up of the universe is the background for the march. The value-structure for each individual is the same, though different persons might be placed on different positions in the value-march.

---

11. Sri Aurobindo, The Foundations of Indian Culture, New York, 1953, p. 110.
12. *Svetāsvataropaniṣad*, Canto IV, Sloka 1-4, 10, & VI, II, 12. *Taittiriyopanisad*, Canto II, Saying 1-5 and III, 10. 5. *Bṛhadāranyaka Upaniśad*, 1.3.28.

III

In the previous section references have been made to spiritual evolution and to the law of action (known as *karma-vāda* in Indian philosophy). A fuller discussion, though not an exhaustive one, may be considered to be in order.

Karma-vāda and the theory of rebirth associated with it have always been regarded by the Hindus as a very necessary part of their tradition. It is largely so to the common Hindu even to-day. Even in Buddhism and Jainism there is general acceptance of this theory. Associated with it, there are certain fundamental problems and wide misconceptions about them. So, a presentation of the theory in its ordinarily accepted form and an examination of it on the philosophical plane is what is presented in this section.

Karmavāda or the law of *karma* implies among other things the belief that there is no loss of the potencies of the actions done with desire (*vāsanā*). There are intricate problems regarding the nature of the *karma* which is the object of consideration. But that need not detain us here. *Karma* or action would generally mean voluntary action of man motivated by a desire (*sakāma karma*). Every such action has certain potencies, good or bad, in accordance with the nature of the action. And these potencies must come back as results to the agent. So, broadly, the law of *karma* is a law suggesting conservation of moral values. The results might not all be actualized in the agent's lifetime; so, a continuity and a rebirth in some form also are logically implied by the law.

The *Ṛg Veda* speaks first about an inexorable moral law governing the universe in the *Ṛta-sukta*. Even the gods are not above the jurisdiction of the law. They are rather the keeper of the law (*Ṛtasya gopa*). Since the *Ṛg Veda*, this belief in a moral order appears, either explicitly or implicitly, throughout the vedic tradition. This law appears as *Apurva* in the *Mimāṃsā* system and as the law of *Adṛsta* in the *Nyāya*. The *Yoga* system gives a classification of the different types of *karmas*, with the approval, if not under the influence, of the Jainas. Whether it has a special name or not, the principle is accepted by all the traditional schools and by some others independent of the vedic origin, as already mentioned.

There is some amount of misunderstanding in some quarters regarding the nature and scope of *karma vāda*. It is pointed out that the law implies complete determinism which wrecks the possibility of moral life. The denial of freedom of choice or of action which the law is supposed to imply makes moral life unreal by negating moral responsibility and moral obligation. Should it be so, human pursuit of values which implies freedom becomes non-existent in the Hindu tradition.

On closer examination, however, the law would appear to do just the opposite; it makes moral life and progress a reality in the true sense of the term. Moral life without moral progress or evolution seems pointless. If moral progress is to be a fact, progressiveness in moral attainment does not necessarily imply a conservation of the values generated by the free activity of man. Not all results are obtained at the completion of an action. Nor can we take the action to be totally lost if we do not believe in a different metaphysical order and an altogether different value-structure. To believe in moral progress is to accept the theory that the potencies of the actions performed through freedom of choice must be somehow conserved to come back to the agent at the appropriate time. *Karma vāda* is simply this acceptance. It advocates conservation of moral values and their retribution to the agent in a regulated way.

Actions could be broadly of two types from the point of view of the presence or absence of potencies. Actions which have yielded results are morally exhausted (*prārabdha karma*); those which are yet to bear fruit (*anārabdha*) could be again of two kinds, e.g., those which have been performed and have not yielded results (*sancita*) and those which are in the process or the current actions (*sanciyamāna*) whose results are being accumulated. From the standpoint of merits actions could be classified into either bad *kṛṣṇa*), or good (*śukla*), or a mixed type (*śukla-kṛṣṇa*) neither good nor bad (*a-śukla-kṛṣṇa*). One does not have a control over the past actions or the potencies left by them. But one may carefully choose the present actions and try to reach the state of perfection through them. Should the actions be good, the agent must reap the good result and conversely in the case of bad actions. But if one chooses to perform the value-neutral activities (*Niṣkāma karma* as spoken of in the *Bhagavad Gitā*)[13] he may stop the process of accumulation of results and when the accumulated potencies are exhausted through their results, there remains nothing to be enjoyed or suffered by the individual. The ordinary process of birth, death and rebirth stops and the soul shines in its pristine glory.

This is the popular version of *Karma-vāda*. It may also be considered on a different level. But we may take up the implications of the popular view first. It seems clear that *karma vāda* is an attempt to put forward a reasonable explanation for the apportionment of good and evil in the world without bringing in the notion of God or any other agency. But the theory may well be maintained even in the context of theism, where God is regarded as the moral governor, the keeper of the law. The potencies of the actions done of

---

13. *Bhagavadgitā* – Chapter I–VI.

free choice comes back to the agent in the form of reward or punishment in the present life or life hereafter. It is popularly maintained that the nature of the next birth is determined by the potencies of the activities so that the enjoyment or punishment could come in the proper form and proportion. If the suffering earned by an individual by his actions in a birth(s) can be meted out only if he is born as any other animal other than man, he has to be born as such.

Such a suggestion opens up new fields of discourse. It becomes evident on the one hand that the moral world does not end only with the human world but it includes within its scope the whole of the kingdom of living animals, the whole of nature. This might imply the extention of the concept of moral responsibility to the non-human world. On the other hand, a belief in the conservation of values seems necessarily to imply the continuity of the soul with or without a body and this ushers in the question of immortality and transmigration of soul.

Indian tradition believes, as pointed out, in the beginningless, though not endless process of birth, death and rebirth in the process of the sojourn of the soul. Soul achieves its perfection only gradually. The realization of perfection is a gradual process extending through continuous life interpersed with physical deaths. But the soul does not die as in that case the question of appropriation of moral potencies is rendered pointless. It appears that a belief in the continuity of soul is quite reasonable for the pursuit of moral values. Immortality of soul is thus accepted as a postulate of moral life; but the justification sought to be given is not merely of practical necessity. Theoretical reasons, as ordinarily adduced, have been mentioned. There is nothing to assume that the clearage between pure and practical reason has been at all thought out. No barrier is suggested between thought and action, or in other words, between pure and practical reason.

There is an apprehension that the stock of potencies of activities might determine a good deal of the present life and in that case the freedom of choice becomes seriously narrowed down, if not completely denied. It may be that in a significant way, the individual is controlled by fate and the range of his activities is determined. Talk of perfection under such circumstances becomes an idle talk and the ideal might remain well beyond the individual's capacity to attain. An answer to this, though not always very clear, definitely points out the fact that all the activities of life are not pre-determined. The stock goes to determine the nature of the birth and some peculiar actions pertaining to that type of birth. Within that framework, there is enough scope for freedom and by a judicious choice of actions the individual might march to perfection. Absolute freedom, unless in the state of liberation, seems, however, to have been denied.

An explanation of evil on the assumption of the law of *karma* becomes rather easy. Individuals suffer or prosper in accordance with the potencies of the actions performed, either in that life or in the lives before. The question of the first birth seems illegitimate since any answer to it is nothing better than arbitrary. Those who believe in God make Him the moral governor, the keeper of the law. Those who do not, make the law self-operative; they would believe in moral naturalism. In any case, God may not be held responsible for the retribution one has for his actions. The law thus can be held independently of any belief in God or conjointly with a belief in such a being.

As to the question formulated earlier regarding freedom of choice and action, we have already indicated the answer. Both destiny and freedom of choice might have been accommodated in the law. There is no absolute freedom if that means complete indeterminism. The past is determined and the present and future are conditioned. Absolute freedom is the goal to be achieved. And in the way to its achievement man is controlled by destiny (*adṛṣṭa*) to some extent. But this should not be construed as leading to fatalism. Destiny is not inscrutable fate operating as an external agency. It is the accumulation of the potencies of actions done by free choice by the individual. But the point which confuses the modern mind is perhaps the notion of the individual itself. The individual seems to have a series of lives – *heretobefore* and *hereafter*. The 'I' in Indian tradition appears extended quite far – both ways – beyond the present 'I'. It recurs in changing bodies and carries on the march towards perfection. The individual thus is generally (in case is different in staunch theism like *Vaiṣṇavism*) the determining agent of his future. There seems to be a double-order concept of the individual. In one of these senses, the ordinary notion of the individual as the present 'I' with the common code of conduct and regulations seems to have been accepted. In the other sense, however, the present 'I' is only a member in the beginningless 'I'-series continuing endlessly either embodied or without it as in the final state of liberation. That 'I' then would either trivialize the ordinary notion of an individual vis-a-vis the absolute/God or it would trivialize the absolute/God and instal altogether a different concept of the individual. In either case, common morality and religion would become pointless. A synthesis in the theistic way has been attempted in the *Bhagatvadgitā*. All these problems will engage us in the last section.

From an analytic point of view, a few questions could be raised regarding the problem of rebirth and transmigration of soul, the complexity of the different types of free activities (e.g. some being concerned with beauty or general health, a pursuit of love or fortune or happiness or a pursuit of individual or collective objects). A blanket law like the law of *karma* might have to be readjusted, at least reinterpreted to do proper justice to the multi-dimensional character of human experience and action. A question regarding the types of world could also be formulated.

It appears that rebirth cannot just be taken mechanically. The soul is not to be taken as being impelled completely by the mechanism of the law of *karma* in an altogether determined way. There may be a gap between births and rebirth may not be understood as an automatic continuation of the previous personality with all its features. There has to be a rearrangement of the different components of the personality so as to prosecute the spiritual movement in a better way. This march is from the physical to the spiritual level through the vital and mental stages and all these phases are contained within the spirit itself. Different types of activities are the manifestations of the same spirit in different strata of development. The present individual is the end-product of his own previous actions and emotions, his inner and outer, vital and spiritual energies. But it is the end-product only in relation to what has been, and not what has yet to be. The reason why the law of *karma* is spoken of in terms of action may be that as no rigid distinction has been, or can be, admitted between thought, emotion and action – action has been spoken of indifferently. A more plausible reason could be that as action is the greater part of human life and is the norm for man's values for being, the law of *karma* is primarily expressed in terms of actions rather than in those of thought and passion. From a linguistic point of view too, one may note with interest that verbs express all ranges of human existence and activities.

The law of *karma*, though evidently suggestive of moral naturalism, is not a mechanical law of nature. Its significance is not in determining the spirit but in conditioning its functioning. The law in its simple application has a determining say with regard to the body and life, but in relation to the spirit it tends to become more complex and less rigid. Spiritual freedom manifests itself through the law and transcends the deterministic bounds of the law. Human progress is progressive realization of greater and greater freedom and in this process of spiritual evolution the law helps rather than hinders the process. This law, even if considered as a part of nature, does not stand out as completely indifferent or antagonistic to human purpose. It is through the operation of the law that human purpose expresses itself gradually, finally going far beyond the law which offers the suitable environment for the spiritual growth of the individual.

We may now sum up the answers obtained through the discussion made so far to some of the questions formulated in Section I.

1. There is no rigid dualism between man and nature. Man contains

nature within himself as does nature contain him.
1.1. Nature is purposive, even though it could be purely material in character. Nature might be called 'the vale of soul-making'.
2. The law of *karma* is a semi-natural moral law guaranteeing the conservation of moral pursuit.
2.1. Individuals are in a sense under the spell of destiny. But the destiny is his own creation. The individual is not a predetermined machine, but a free agent working under regulations.
2.2. Values are genuine, perfection being the highest value. Man's spiritual evolution starts with his breading through the physical and vital existence and gradually reaching the level of joyful existence in complete freedom.
3. The evolution goes on through an indefinite series of lives, with the probability of the soul being associated with different bodies. It is held to be the same individual with reinforced energies, so to say.
3.1. The notion of disembodied persons is not necessarily suggested; but the continuity of the soul in changing bodies or even without a body seems to be the traditional notion.
4. The question, then, is about the exact nature of the individual and his fulfillment.

IV

The highest value for the individual is *moksa* or liberation; but this is not the only value nor are all values a-social. The value-structure (*purusārtha*) commonly accepted in the Indian tradition appears unanimous in accepting perfection as the supreme value. It, however, cannot be attained all on a sudden. There are other wider though extrinsic values and they cannot be ignored. The other values are '*artha*', '*kāma*' and '*dharma*' standing for the economic values, the hedonic values and a proper harmony between all these ideals. The individual under normal circumstances is a social being enjoined to pursue the common values as a member of the society. It may be contended that an excessive emphasis on the spiritual values of the individual tends to undervalue or devalue the social aspect of man. The social values might be sacrificed at the altar of the individual values. This, however, is not the case. It cannot be contested that the highest good in the traditional value-scheme transcends the realm of social values as it does those of the individual in the common sense of the term. But the common social life of the average human beings seems never to have been neglected. The tradition on the other hand has attempted to construct the social pattern by codifying the conducts considered conducive to the realization of man's supreme end. The dignity associated with human existence, the purpose inherent in the continuity of life permeates both the natural and social conditions of existence and their interpretation.

The structure of the society and the position of the individual therein may be discussed with reference to the principal Hindu social institutions like *Varna* and *Āsrama*. The *Varnāsrama Dharma* has unfortunately degenerated into narrow casteism in later period whatever the historical justifications for it be. But the spirit in which it was originally conceived and followed for quite a few centuries in the early Hindu society can still be discerned from the way it works to-day. The Hindu social institutions are historically recognized to have been the few most stable ones. It must have succeeded in achieving social harmony and incalculating a proper sense of values in the individuals. This is most likely the source of the vitality of the Indian culture.

The institution of *Varna* (caste) emphasizes the social aspect of the individual and that of *Āsrama* deals with the different stages of the individual of his preparation for fulfilling the highest purpose. Both the institutions have their sanction in the Vedic tradition.[14] In the *Bhagavadgitā* the Lord (*Kṛsna*) says that the four castes are *created by* Him in accordance with the principle of *qualitative division of labour*.[15] The four *Varnas* are: (a) *Brāhman*, (b) *Kshatriya*, (c) *Vaiśya*, (d) *Sūdra*. The principle of division is the original quality of man and not any other extraneous consideration. It is rathter like a social division on the basis of the qualities of the soul as conceived by Plato.[16]

(a) A *Brāhman* as suggested by the term is one who knows the *Brahman*[17] – the infinite, ultimate reality. A *Brāhman* is the person having the highest intellectual qualities and is most advanced in the quest for perfection. He is the philosopher in Plato's society. He knows the truths of *Vedas* and *Upanisads* and it is his duty to inculcate the sense of righteousness and urge for perfection in others. He is to initiate people in the significance of life which is divine and eternal. *Brāhmans* are to be the advisers and ministers of the rulers and kings, but never kings themselves. In the Hindu society this

---

14. Reference may be made to *Manusamhitā* and the *Bhagavadgitā*.
15. *Bhagavadgita*.
16. Plato's Republic, any reliable translation.
17. *Brahman* indifferently mentioned in the early Vedas, is gradually developed as the concept standing for the Absolute, Ultimate Reality in the principal *Upaniṣads*. The notion reaches its fullest and most important development in the *Brahmasutra* of *Vyāsa* which was commented upon by *Sanakaracharyya*. A fuller discussion will be made in the next section.

class has supplied the teachers, priests, preceptors, ministers and advisers. Brahmans, as enjoined by *dharma*, have to enjoy the least of physical pleasures and comforts and set example by their own living of the deeper meaning of life which consists not in material enjoyment but in the realization of spirituality. All values are to be recognized and harmoniously organized for the fulfillment of man and a *brahmin* by his living must be a pointer to the practicality of such a life. The power this class would have enjoyed in the society, was not bestowed on them by any ecclesiastical authority or any political decree. They must have earned it by virtue of their qualities and spirituality. They were the spiritual leaders of the society. The value-orientation of the society is symbolized in the leadership allotted to this class for their spiritual superiority. It must have continued to be so for many centuries. But gradually the vitality of the principle based on qualitative division must have become a hereditary fact and degenerated into narrow casteism. A brahmin ??? is not one by birth but by the qualities of his soul. A substitution of this principle, as quite natural for man, has eaten into the vitals of the principle itself.

(b) The actual governance of the society and country, its defense from internal and external strifes, the whole range of military operation – all these have been left to the *Kshatrivas*. This class has supplied the kings, governors, military generals and personnel in general. They were to be the defenders of *dharma*, the dignity of women and the social order. In all their activities, the rulers would have to be advised by the spiritual leaders i.e., the Brahmins. This guaranteed the proper type of governance which was to be based on *dharma*, social harmony and justice. The best society is that which offers the maximum opportunity for the individual's multi-dimensional spiritual growth and the *Kshatrivas* were to seek for establishing or stabilizing such a society. This saved the society from pursuing economic and hedonic ends as the supreme values. The king was the protector of *dharma* which was not his creation. The balance between autocracy and democracy was maintained by the social value-structure which converged in individual perfection as the highest value. References may be made to the *Rāmāyana* and *Mahābhārata* which, in al allegorical way, present the social order and the nature of Hindu polity. The hierarchy of the society is designed on the assumption of spiritual hierarchy and not on any other factor exclusively.

(c) The class kown as the *Vaiśya* comprised of the merchants, traders, bankers and businessman in the society. The economic and commercial aspect of the social life was entrusted with this class. The material well-being of the society was taken care of by the *Vaiśya*. He must have possessed sufficient money; but the social code would not allow him to look upon riches as his own. The riches would have to be regarded as social property and the *Vaiśya* was merely keeping them on trust. In the heydays of Hinduism, the *Vaiśya* by and large would take care of the wealth of the society as care-takers on behalf of the society. He was never to use money as a lever of power to gain social supremacy. This ensured a form of social justice and helped checking economic disparity in the society. The basic point that emerges is that money corrupts only when it becomes an end in itself or it is used as a means for securing other things. But the moment the final end is regarded as something beyond the purchasing power of money and the entire social valuation is directed to it, money loses much of its charm. *Artha* (economic) is a value but only an extrinsic one; its instrumentality lies in its assisting man in the realization of perfection which cannot be bought for money, directly or indirectely. So, it is the scheme of telos and values and the success of its imprint on the common individual that accounts for the common norm of valuation.

(d) All the three classes mentioned so far – *Brāhmanas, Kshatriyas* and *Vaiśyas* were looked upon as twice born (*dwija*) – one the physiological birth and the other the spiritual birth after the initiation – and all of them would put on the sacred thread as a mark of initiation. The *Sudras* were a class apart. They were meant primarily for manual labour of the unskilled type. They were the class of workers and peasants. They, however, had their rightful place in the society. The Indian social order at that time seems to have been one based on the recognition of the fact that by natural potentialities human beings differ in their intellectual and practical skill. This difference also was sought to be explained through the law of *karma*. Not everybody is capable of everything; so, a coerced unity is arbitrary, artificial, and harmful to the harmonious social and individual life. Social harmony was established by admitting the reality and dignity of each man's station in the society and his duties. The entire system of class-division would work ideally so long as the basis of the distinction would be quality and the social dynamism of accepting anybody of a particular talent in the appropriate class moves on smoothly. The *Varna* (caste) system seems originally to have been based or designed to be based on the basis of qualitative distinction rather than on any other factor, though there might be other opinions. A *brāhmana* incapable of intellectual pursuit but expert in military activities was to have been regarded as a *kshatriya* and a *vaiśya* well-versed in the *Vedas* would have to be reckoned as a *brāhmana*. This interchange of castes must have been the original design. There are allegorical stories in the *Rāmāyana* and the *Mahābhārata* of *śudras* attaining liberation and regarded superior to *brāhmanas*.

In the course of history, however, the institution degenerated into a rigid hereditary caste system. The basis was still valuational but the dynamic core of it was missing. The flexibility of the social division must have been lost and the principal point for consideration was *jāti* (birth) rather than *guṅa*. A *brāhmaṇa* would then mean one born of brahmin parents and intellectual ability was associated with him in an essential way. It became his essential definition. As a matter of fact, many of the *brahmins* have been intellectually great but that is a different point. One might seek the historical reason of such a phenomenon in the advent of Islamic thought and its culture coupled with the hostility of the muslim rulers to the Hindus which contributed largely to the rigidity generated in the Hindu society. The society defended itself by entering into a protective shell which resulted in the loss of social dynamism which was the ideal. But the basic value-orientation of society saved it from complete ruination. Perfection and harmony, not material prosperity and military prowess, was still the highest value. There has always been a question of the conflicting demands of the essential values (*Svadharma*) of the individual and the changing social values (*Yugadharma*). But the individual has been urged to fulfill himself in all possible ways (*sarbabhāven*).

The rivalry among castes, if actual, was only peripheral. The individual has always been impressed by the meaning of human existence, its spiritual mission. There is no bar to any individual fulfilling himself through the social harmony which suggests unity in diversity. This is the meaning of life in general.

So, the caste system under ideal conditions is not to have been mainly an economic class division though it tends actually to degenerate into it. But the core of spirituality must have continued unabated for centuries. The truth that everybody is a potential *Brahman*[18] seems to have been a matter of common knowledge. Even the *śudra* could be a *Brahman* by his deeds,[19] as already pointed out. Some of the greatest sages universally admired by the Hindus are said to have been of a low origin.[20] Whatever the virtues or vices of the caste system and whatever the reasons of its present shape, a basic truth emerges from the ancient social system which must have been free from the type of economic competition one notices in the presentday societies. Human existence has a dignity of its own. The individual is poised for his fulfillment for his perfection by a harmonious play of his entire personality. He is a social being and has to abide by the social norms. But Supreme Value goes beyond the society and the individual in the ordinary sense of the term. All the social norms are preparations for the ideal. So society, just like nature, is the

18. *Mahābhārata, Sāntiparva,* p. 186, Sarvam brahman idam jagat.
19. Cp. Manusamhita, IX, 14.48.
20. *Vasistha* is said to have been born of a prostitute and *Parasara* of a *Sudra* girl.

appropriate background to prepare the individual for realizing his purpose.

The institution that has concerned the individual's life in society was known as *āśrama*. *Āśrama* refers to the different stages of the individual's life in its development. The four stages are: (a) *Brahmacharya*, the period of training through physical and mental restraint, (b) *Gārhasthya*, the period of all normal works as a householder in the society, (c) *Vānaprastha*, the period of voluntary retirement and retreat from the social bonds and obligations through withdrawal from the society, (d) *Sannyāsa*, the period of complete renunciation of the ordinary social duties and ties and single-minded application to the realization of freedom and perfection.

This fourfold scheme dividing life into four periods exhibits the way of preparing the individual to achieve his purpose in life. In the beginning the youth with plasticity of mind is moulded into a life of duty and temperance. A sense of restraint and of purposiveness is instilled in him so that the entire plan of life becomes orderly and oriented in the proper value-scheme. In this he has to be properly initiated and the success of the scheme depends on the quality of the man working as the preceptor (*guru*). The *guru* is to train him up about the worldly life and the significance of human existence. Only one who has the highest intellectual attainment and greatest integrity in character is to be a *guru* and generally the *Brāhmana*, as explained earlier, is to perform the function of the initiator. The youthful student is given lessons in the scale of priorities of values in life – *artha*, *kāma*, *dharma* and *mokṣa* and shape his life accordingly in the actual living. He has to learn it through great hardship living in the house of the preceptor as a preparation for the journey ahead.

After the successful completion of the period of training, the young student now maturing into full-bloom manhood, enters into actual life starting with the role of a householder. With the knowledge of the secrets of life he enters the society as a full partner and performs his duties to the society by marrying and begetting children in the process of continuation of the race, by contributing a substantial share of his earning to the benefit of the society, helping the poor and the sick, treating reverentially parents, women and old people. He has to the duties prescribed by the *sāstras* and live in the society as a normal, cultured, disciplined member. None of the basic instincts are overlooked; they are taken care of in a regulated way so that no one has an undue predominance over the others. Much importance is placed on this stage of *gārhasthya* as it is this stage which puts an individual to the acid test of life. There are detailed discussions regarding the types of marriage [21] and groups of girls[22] from whom to select the lifepartner. The role of the wife is quite

---

21. *Monusamhita*, iii, 34.

important. *Dharma* has to be performed along with her. She is like *prakṛti* helping the *puruṣa* in achieving his end. But she herself is also a conscious principle, unlike *prakṛti*, trying to fulfill herself through the proper discharge of duties and actions. Though marriage has been the accepted institution, living as bachelors or spinsters[23] has not been uncommon. There does not seem to have been any compulsion in this regard as the individual variation in the need and differing way of fulfillment has always been accepted. But the common practice has been to enter into marriage which has been regarded as sacred. This seems to have been the method of regulating the sex life of the individuals with religious and social sanctions. A marriage in which both the man and the woman are in perfect harmony is regarded as the ideal marriage. *Rāma* and *Sita* are taken as an ideal couple. Incidentally, the general sanction seems to have been for monogamy though polygamy was not uncommon. Broad rules and regulations are there, but not its detailed codification. So long as the spirit behind the regulations is considered supreme rigid formalization seems unnecessary. All individuals do not require the same code for achieving perfection. So, that being the point of unity, diversity has to be accepted as genuine and harmony becomes meaningless without this diversity.

The third stage is of voluntary retirement from the social position, power and enjoyment – it is *vānaprastha* – a stage for preparation for the final renunciation. After the life as a householder, there is a time to cry halt and giving up all responsibilities and powers to the next generation. The individual withdraws from the society which is symbolized by his going to the forest along with his wife, who is always a companion in *dharma*. This stage begins when the physical powers of the individual are on the decline and he has attained the age of a grandfather.[24] The man and the wife avoid the din and bustle of life and apply themselves exclusively to the meditation on the higher values of life which have been pursued all through in the other stages of life.

The last stage is of complete renunciation – the stage of *Sannyāsa* – where the individual is on the march to attain spirituality through freedom. He develops a sense of detachment and bears all suffering with calm and resignation. It is renunciation in action – *Karmasannyāsa* as spoken of in the *Gita*. This stage of life is indicative of the progressive transcendence of the stages of relative values and entering into the realm of the intrinsic value.

The institutions of *varṇa* and *āśrama* manifest the regulated character of the individual life both in the aspects of social as well as private living. It has

22. *Parāsara Samhitā* (Bombay Sanskrit Series), part II, p. 82.
23. Reference may be made to Gargi and mentioned in the *Brhadaranyakopanisad* and *Sabari* referred to in the *Rāmāyana*.
24. *Manusamhitā* in general is referred to for all the institutions.

been an attempt at achieving harmony in life in both the aspects with full recognition of difference between one individual and another. Life has been infused with a deeper meaning and human existence has been surcharged with a sense of dignity and purpose.

To some it might appear as an external imposition on the individual in his free actions and thinking. The value-orientation, it might be argues, cripples the expression of free life and leads to an excess of other-worldliness. It might in a subtle way deny the freedom of choice inasmuch as perfection as the highest value is sought to be impressed upon every individual. An obsession with purposiveness of life, it may be contended, tends to take away the zest of life and determine it in a particular way. Teleology might turn out to be an inverted mechanism.

To the observation that Indian traditional value-orientation makes man care more for something beyond the present world and less for the material prosperity of the present life, one has perhaps to admit it to some extent with some rejoinders. It is most likely historically true that Indian tradition has cared less for the ordinary values of life in the sense that they have not been regarded as ends in themselves. This might even have encouraged a sense of selflessness in a common understanding. None of the early thinkers has cared to keep any record of themselves and there is hardly any authentic bio-data available of the great thinkers, not even of the great *Advaitin* thinker *Sankarācharya* who was probably born as late as the eighth century A. D. Something else other than one's strong assertion of his present self has appeared as more worthwhile and the other aspects might have been counted less. But this is not the whole truth. The normal pursuits of material prosperity and healthy sense/sex life have been admitted and given due weightage. They, of course, have not been regarded as intrinsic except in the *nāstika Cārvāka* philosophy. This system stands out prominently as distinct from every other system in the complete rejection of spiritual values. The emergence of such a system shows the vitality and variety of the Indian mind. The general trend, however, has been for attaching greater importance to *dharma* i.e. harmonious living in accordance with one's own nature and the comomn codes of social, moral/religious life. All this is directed to the same end – perfection, liberation or *Mukti*. This determines the hierarchy of values and purposes of human life and living is regulated, both individually and socially, accordingly. Taking this into consideration, one perhaps has to admit some amount of other-worldliness in the traditional teaching though the transitional order always points out the need of other values.

This brings us to an important problem. The question of a choice among values is in the final analysis associated with the way of one's looking at life.

If human existence means only the present life and death of the body is regarded as the end of the individual, the scale of values seems to become one of a transitory nature. It may have a tendency to cling to the material values as the body becomes the principal determinant in the value-order. Physical values readily appeal to the senses and assures satisfaction through their intensity. In such a view human existence may not have any special dignity about itself as the purpose of such existence does not very much differ from that of the other forms of existence.

If however, human existence suggests any speciality, a meaning distinctive about itself, a totally different value-scheme may be worked out.

Does human existence possess a special significance? The answer of the tradition is strongly in the affirmative. And the logic of the admission of this purposiveness of man's being leads the tradition to the consequent acceptance of a continuous process, a progressive march to the achievement of the supreme value, which is spiritual in nature. It is spirit's fulfillment, realization of its own nature. But, does it not appear as an imposition on the free agent? The answer is equally strong in the negative. The tradition does not end merely with theorization about the meaning of life and establishing speculative metaphysics on the nature of the individual. It urges the end as practically attainable and makes a pointer to that direction. A man can answer demands of his being through all means (*mārga*) – knowledge, action and devotion (*jñana, karma, bhakti*. And there are people – the sages and seers – who have fulfilled themselves by all means (*sarvabhāvena*). They inspire faith in the methods and fact of realization.

But what is the individual and what does he become in perfection? Does the latter destroy the former? Is there any sense in which the same individual continues? These questions will engage us in the next section.

V

The main burden of the discussion made so far has been to show that the scheme of values accepted in the tradition puts the spiritual freedom of the individual on the apex and the natural and social order derive their meaning from this value-structure. Proper individuality is suggestive of harmony. Both in nature and in society diversity is the rule, but there is a deep sense of unity which pervades the shades of diversities. Difference between individuals is admitted, there is attempted explanation for this and the society does not intend to coerce all individuals into a pattern of living. To offer all possible assistance in man's quest for self-realization seems to be the basic theme behind the natural and social movement.

The notion of the individual may be taken both from the point of view of religion and philosophy. But it does not make much of a difference. There are many schools of thought or different sects and shades of Hinduism. But each philosophy is backed up by its practical application in actual living while each religion as a way of life has a sound philosophy behind it. So, the conflict between philosophy and religion is not the order. But there are different philosophies of life or religious shades each trying to understand the nature of the individual and the problems of its life. *Dharma*, the synonym for religion, has a much wider connotation. It is the way of living, it is that which keeps up the individual. *Dharma* is not necessarily tagged up with a personal goal, but a sense of deep spirituality must pervade it. It is quite possible to be *dhārmika* (religious or virtuous) without accepting a god. In the advanced stages of the spiritual progress it may not at all be necessary to take recourse to a medium like God, though it might be considered necessary to do so on the common plane. *Dharma* is righteousness, a dedication to the spiritual values.

Generally, however, people did (as many still do) believe in god/gods and for the ordinary individual the institution of *dharma* implies a belief in a supernormal being or beings. We may call this theism in the western sense (in a wide way implying belief in god) of the term and try to assess the position of the individual in theistic beliefs. We may next try to find out the philosophical position regarding the individual in the important philosophical systems. Of the different types of theism, special mention may be made of the following three: (a) *Vaiṣṇava*, (b) *Sākta*, (c) *Saiva*. The discussion here is by no means exhaustive for that does not fall within the main scope of this paper. Only the broad features will be examined to find out the status of the individual. Other minor sects will be ignored here as we shall also bypass Buddhism and Jainism as these religions do not accept any god. References to them may be made in the context of philosophical discussion.

Vaiṣṇava religion – as is suggested by the name, *Vaiṣṇava* religion centres round *Viṣṇu* – a Vedic deity. Though only a few hymns are addressed to him in the *Ṛg Veda*,[25] he gains in importance in the *Brāhmaṇas* and is regarded as the Supreme being in the *Purāāṇic* period. In the *Brahmanic* period *Viṣṇu is regarded as the highest god.*[26] We have it from a mythological story in the *Sāma Veda*[27] that in a mutual competition held among the gods for reaching

---

25. *Ṛg. Veda*, 1, 22, 20; Rv. 1, 154, 5.
26. *Atharva Veda*, 1.1.
27. *Sama Veda* XIV, 1.1.

the end of sacrifice directed to the achievement of greatest glory, *Viṡṅu* reached the end first and became the highest of all gods. *Viṡṅu* is identified with *Vāsudeva* who again has been identified with *Nāāyaṅa*[28] who has been regarded as the Supreme Lord. The idea of such a being is abundantly found in the different *Upaniṡads*.[29] All these diverse expressions might have been synthesized in the concept of *Puruṡottama* in the *Bhagavadgita*. The *Gita* is the earliest articulate exposition of the *Bhakti* system (religion of devotion to the Lord) known as *Bkāntika Dharma*. And in this sense, the *Gita* is one of the principal sources of *Vaiṡṅava* religion.

The *Gita* presents the *Bhagavat* (may be identified with *Nārāyaṅa*) speaking of three different ways for liberation: (i) *Jnāna-Yoga* or *Jnāna-mārga*, (ii) *Karma-Yoga* and (iii) *Bhakti-Yoga*. Each of these is capable of taking the individual to perfection. While the first two may not logically presuppose a personal god, for the third it is a logical necessity. *Vaiṡṅava* religion is a religion of *bhakti*, devotion being considered to be the path of one's union with God. From this point of view this religion represents Indian theism (in the ordinary sense) at its best.

The first six chapters of the *Gita* discuss *Karma Yoga* and the emphasis is put on renunciation in action (*Karma Sannyāsa* or *Niskāma Karma*). Such actions are based on proper knowledge and judicious discrimination between the right and the wrong. *Karma Yoga* appears to contain a core of theism as the injunction is to place all the actions at the disposal of the Lord. One may be a '*Karma Yogi*' or a '*Jnana Yogi*' – but these are not necessarily exclusive. It is a question of emphasis.

In the next six chapters, *Bhakti Yoga* (the path of devotion) is treated of. Mention has been made of two types of meditation with two types of objects – the *Akṡara Brahman* and the *Vāsudeva (Bhagavat)*. Here is probably the beginning of the cult of personal God and his worship in the form of *Vāsudeva*. But the other method of meditation on an impersonal being leads to the same end. It appears that the *Gita* is striving for harmony at two levels. At the philosophical level, it suggests the conception of *Aksara Brahman* as the Absolute, the ultimate reality. On the other hand, *Vāsudeva*, the personal God, is taken to be the highest deity. Both these conceptions are synthesized, one being regarded as the alternative for the other, finally both being identical. The other synthesis is in the attempt of treating *Jnāna, Karma* and

28. *Nārāyana* might have come from *Nādāyana* – the lord of sounds. It might also have been from the root Nr. Anyway, *Nārāyana* means the goal of men (*nara*).
29. Cp. *Svetāsvataropanisad*, Canto I, Slokas 3, 4. *Taittiriya Upanisad*, 2, Sayings 7. 8. *Mundaka Upanisad*, Canto 2, Sloka 1, 2, 5. *Prasna Upanisad*, Question 1, saying 4. *Isopanisad*, Sloka 1, Chapter 1. *Bṙhadaranyakopanisad* – Chapter 1, saying 1, 2, 3, 4.

Bhakti as alternative ways to perfection. How much success the *Gita* has achieved in this attempt at dual synthesis is an open (though secondary) question. One point appears to be clear, however. The *Gita* implicitly but unmistakably puts emphasis on *Bhakti Yoga* and the personal God as the object of *bhakti* (adoration and devotion). The entire discourse of *Bhagavat* to *Arjuna* is summed up by *Bhagavat* Himself when He asks *Arjuna* to surrender himself to Him,[30] with all the heart and promises eternal joy (*ānanda*) to him in the love of God. One who performs nothing but attaches himself to God with intense devotion and love, adores Him alone, is sure to realize perfection.

This is the beginning of *ekāntika dharma* (monotheistic religion) which is typically represented in *Vaiṣṇavism*. The *Gita* has its source in the *Upanisads* and some philosophical systems (like the *Samkhya-Yoga*). The *Gita* is the culmination of the progress of the religious and philosophic speculation that prevailed before the rise of Buddhism. And the conception of *bhakti* can also be traced to that of *Upāsanā mentioned in some of the Upanisads*.[31] It might be possible to show in this way that the different elements of the *ekāntika dharma* could be traced to earlier religious traditions.

The principal theme of *Vaiṣ.ṇava* religion is deep love of *Viṣṇu* (or *Vāsudeva, Kṛsna* or *Nārāyaṇa*). *Viṣṇu in the form of cowherd Kṛsna* or as the lover of *Rādhā* or as the benevolent lord of the universe is taken to be the only object of love and adoration and this deep personal love of the devotee (*bhakta*) for his god (*bhagawān*) marks out this religious sect from others. The devotee aims at complete union with God. What becomes of the individual in such a state or what he normally is, is our problem. And this can be brought out on the background of later *Vaiṣnava* thinkers like *Rāmānuja, Madhwa, Nimbārka* and *Vallabha* – the leaders of the four main sects of *Vaiṣṇavism*.

Of the two classes of *Vaiṣnava* teachers of the South, viz., *Alvārs* and *Achāryas*, the former has been concerned with the culture of love and devotion to *Viṣṇu* while the latter concerned more with the philosophical aspect of the religion in an attempt to prove its theoretical soundness on the face of opposition. *Rāmānuja*, a *vaiṣnava* fo the latter class flourishing most likely in the 12th century A. D., has engaged himself in answering the fundamental philosophical problems brought out primarily by *Samkarāchārya* in his commentary on *Bādārayana's Brahmasutra*. There have been challenges from Buddhism and Jainism too. *Rāmānuja's* principal philosophical concern is to find out the exact position of the individual (*jiva*) and its relation to God/Absolute.

30. *Bhagavatgita*, Chap. XVIII.
31. Reference may be made to the *Svetāsvataropanisad* and the *Bṛhadaranyakopanisad*.

It is rather difficult to give an adequate account of the philosophical position as developed by *Samkara* from *Gaudapāda*. This, however, is the background on the context of which *Rāmānuja*'s thesis can be understood. *Samkara*'s philosophy, famously known as *Advaita Vedanta*, presents an apparent paradox. From one point of view, it seems to suggest complete trivialization of the individual through illusionism. *Brahman* alone is stated to be real, everything else is treated as unreal making its appearance through cosmic illusion (*māyā* or *ajnāna*). *Samkara* does not claim to have established any new truths; he modestly professes only to illucidate the basic truth of the *Vedas* and the *Upaniṣads*.[32] He does his job with very subtle dialects and tries to clinch the issue in favour of non-dual (*advaita*) reality[33] which can be realized actually but only from the transcendental point of view (*pāramārthika dṛsti*). The multiplicity of the universe including the plurality of the individuals (*jiva*) is treated as false appearance on the substratum of *Brahman*. The things of common experience and the experiencing agents are less unreal than the contradictory things like sky-flower. They seem to possess a phenomenal reality. On closer inspection, however, all these multiple things are detected to be unreal as there is no genuine principle of individuation. Difference (*bheda*) in all its forms is unreal. Relation being unreal, the terms in relation also logically become unreal. The 'I' in its common sense is not identical with the self. It also is due to a false projection on the ultimate reality which is pure consciousness (*śuddha caitanya*). The change from one (*Brahman*) to many (*jagat* or world of many) is only apparent (*vivarta*); there cannot be any real change; such a theory negates the reality of the ordinary individual from the transcendental standpoint though some phenomenal plausibility (*vyāvahārika sattā*) is associated with it. Practical life is not impeded but the moment one crosses the frontiers of the world of practicality with superior knowledge, he starts understanding its unreality. Finally, when proper knowledge dawns on him, he realizes that the plurality is false and *Brahman* is the only reality. He realizes himself as identical with the *Brahman*.

This theory admits the practical necessity of religion and morality. But since both of them logically presuppose duality, they cannot be ultimately valid. Religion must admit a distinction between the worshipper (*bhakta*) and the worshipped (*bhagawān*) and as such it implies unreality. Morality presupposes

32. Samkara tries to explain the apparent paradox involved in such seemingly contradictory statements like: '*Brahma satya, jagat mithyā; Ekam syāt, bahudhā badanti; Naha nānā asti cincana*', etc.
33. For a fuller discussion of *Advaita* dialectics interested readers are referred to any good book on *Advaita* philosophy. Other than the *Samkara bhasya* on the *Brahmasutra*, *Citsukhi* and *Advaitasiddhi* may be consulted.

a duality between the ideal and the striving for it. Moral obligation suggests a duality between the agent and others to whom the agent owes obligation. This indicates invalidity. Any vestige of duality and plurality is shown to be born of ignorance or *Māyā*. *Māyā* is a potency in the *Brahman*, in a sense. But it itself being negative in character though appearing as positive (*bhāvarūpam ajnānam*) the question of its reality does not arise. It is nothing distinct from *Brahman*. *Māyā* functions in a dual capacity; in its cosmic aspect it makes the world-show of variety possible, while in the context of the individual it functions as *avidyā* over and above its being the apparent causal agency. *Māyā* acts in a twofold role in a more definite way. It covers up (*āvaraña*) the reality which is *Brahman* and distorts it (*vikṣepa*) into manyness. Plurality in all its senses is denied reality. So, things as well as individuals are unreal.

Considered from this point of view, *Advaita Vedanta* presents a clear example of the philosophical trivialization of the individual. It has a practical though apparent reality. And only from this angle of vision do its thoughts and actions, sentiments and passions gain any meaning. But this is an unstable position always sliding into falsity. The individual *qua* individual loses its significance and it may be pointless to speak of any purposiveness in the individual. But just in this simple manner *Advaita* position regarding the individual cannot be brushed aside. There is another equally legitimate viewpoint from which the entire philosophy could be judged as one ascertaining the highest dignity of the individual and equalling it with the fundamental reality not only ending in treating it as a necessary component of reality. In this sense, it is the negation of any reality other than the self. *Saṃkara* asserts not only that *Brahman* is the only reality, but also that it is identical with the self, with the 'I' (*Soham* – I am that *Brahman*).

The identity asserted between the 'I' and *Brahman* is unqualified total identity. The state of this assertion logically implies the supersession of the stage of phenomenal knowledge which necessarily involves a 'category-mistake' by assigning reality to what is not real. Ignorance (*avidyā*) is dispelled by proper knowledge and the false worldshow of plurality vanishes. Knowledge or pure consciousness as the only being shines forth in full glory (the concept of *satcidānandam* is being referred to). The individual devoid of the false locus of its ego turns out to be pure consciousness, which is nothing but *Brahman* – the non-dual reality. The 'I' freed from its 'ego-logical consciousness' realizes itself as consciousness *qua* consciousness. There is, however, a slightly different way of understanding the concept of *sat-cit-ānanda*.[34] The non-dual *Brahman* may be looked upon as having the three aspects of existence (*sat*), sentience, (*cit*) and bliss (*ānanda*) which might be analogically taken as the unity of the triad of values – *dharma, artha* and *kāma*. But the identity between the 'I' free from its ordinary apistemic and ontological association and the *Brahman* is asserted in all seriousness.

From such a transcendental point of view (*pāramārthika dṛisti*), the normal distinction of 'I-it and I-thou relationship' with the necessary background of all other things and individuals becomes completely transcended and so unreal. But to one who has not reached this level of existence, his world with his experiences appears to have a phenomenal reality. This is the ordinary level of existence with the reality of distinction between the experiences and the content of experience the devotee (*bhakta*) and his god (*bhagawān*) and the whole host of things with the distinction between subjectivity and objectivity. Even (.)*Saṁkara* himself does readily admit the necessity of this standpoint with common theism. One cannot rise all on a sudden to the supreme standpoint. But the possibility of the standpoint which could legitimately be called existential as it is beyond all subjectivity and objectivity cannot be denied, either by pure rational arguments or by actual realization.

It is difficult to sum up such a position like this. It emerges that there is a dual concept of the individual. The individual (*jiva*) as the ordinary agent with the normal environment, social and natural and his experiences stands for the normal level. The other is that of the individual becoming identical with existence itself in the very experience of the depths of being. The onion-skinning of the individual as conditioned is got rid of and experience as pure being stands out as the individual. This is pure being, pure freedom – limitless as free from possibilities, and absolute. The 'I' that is asserted is non-subjective since there is complete absence of any context through which the subjectivity could be asserted. This is pure, non-relational consciousness, free from contents and intention – identical with pure being or pure freedom which is complete joy (*ānanda*).

This concept of the individual as pure being goes beyond theism. One may try to work out the nature of the individual within the theistic scheme and *Rāmānuja* as a *Vaiṣṇava* tries to develop his theistic philosophy on the background of *Advaita Vedanta* notion of I as pure being. He tries to strike a balance between the extreme positons (viz., trivialization of the individual [in the ordinary sense] or trivialization of the absolute individual taken as supreme) into either of the ways in which *Saṁkara*'s philosophy could paradoxically be understood. For any religion to be possible, the duality of God and his devotee is a logical pre-requisite. In the theistic system the highest being one could philosophically talk about cannot be other than a personal

---

34. Tejobindupanisat, V i. 1–2; 20–31.

God which is regarded as identical with the philosophic absolute. The other aspect of such a system is the genuine reality of the individual which experiences its authentic living in union with its God. There may, however, be an apparent paradox even for theism. God (*Paramātma*) must be the supreme reality; but man (*jivātma*) also cannot be denied its reality for in its absence theism crumbles. One could, of course, speak of the individual as a part (*amśa*) of the Supreme Being; but the part can never be completely identified with the whole. Complete identity between the two must transcend and negate the level of religious experience. The identity between God and individual must be a qualified identity (*visitādvaita*) and *Rāmānuja* develops this standpoint in distinction from *Samkara*'s complete identity (*advaita*).

Rāmānuja's theism follows the pattern of the theistic logic. God (*Paramātma* or *Saguna Brahman* or *Iśvara*) is the highest being, the material and efficient cause of the universe. The two eternal principles of matter (*acit*) and sentience (*cit*) are constituent elements of God (*Isvara*) or one could view *Iśvara* as having these two necessary attributes (*cit-acit-viśista*). God as the all-inclusive principle includes within His nature both the individual (*jiva*) and the insensate world (*prakṛti*). But they exist as distinct entities within the whole. The *jiva* is subject to suffering while *Iśvara* is not. The *jiva* is controlled (*niyāmya*) while *Iśvara* is the controller (*niyāmaka*). The individual as a necessary part of God is never completely separated from Him.[35] Though the individual soul is variously spoken of either as a part or an attribute of *Brahman*, but the two are never identified as a part or an atttribute of *Brahman*, but the two are never identified in an unqualified way. The aphorism '*Tad tvam asi*' (That thou art) is not interpreted as the assertion of complete identity between 'that' and 'thou' (that is the *Samkarite* way). *Rāmānuja* understands it as implying a qualified identity between the part and the whole. They differ in their essential nature. In the state of liberation, the individuality of the soul is not lost, but the sense of separateness from *Brahman* (*Iśvara*) disappears. The liberated soul becomes free from the operation of the law of *karma* as all his activities are of detached nature (*niskāma*) which yield no potencies.

Rāmānuja recommends devotion and adoration of God (*bhakti*) as the principal path for the attainment of liberation. No more listening to the scriptures can do the trick; highest devotion to *Iśvara* can make one realize his self. Highest devotion is not unmixed with knowledge; it includes knowledge within it and the direct realization (*aporokṣa jnāna*) of *Iśvara* takes the form of devotion.[36] Devotion, however, is never exclusive of other elements of individual activity.

35. *Rāmāniya Bhāsya* on the *Brahmasutra* (*Sri Bhāsya*), II, iii, 45.

From *Rāmānuja*'s account, it seems clear that the individual has an obvious and distinct existence, though as a finite being it is included within the infinite. *Mokśa* or liberation, the highest value for the individual consists in its realizing the exact nature of itself as a part in the all-inclusive God. It does not lose its ego nor does it find itself completely identified with the unconditioned being. It is a concrete being though conditioned by the unconditioned being. Neither the individual nor the absolute is trivialized and a harmony between the two is sought to be attained. This presents the picture of reality as a unity containing genuine diversities. But the principal tune of unity can never be missed, though there are diverse tunes constituting the principal one.

The other principal exponents of different sects of *Vaiṡnavism* like *Madhva, Nimbārka, Vallabha* and *Caitanya* present similar philosophical views about the individual working within the same theistic framework. There are, however, important distinctions in details. These points of distinction generally centre round the problem of nature of God, his relation to nature and individual and the relative importance of *jñāna* and *karma* in the *bhaktimārga*. *Madhva*, also known as *Ānandatirtha*, opposes both *Saṁkara*'s unqualified non-dualism (*advaitavāda*) and *Rāmānuja*'s qualified non-dualism (*visistādvaitavāda*). He discards *Rāmānuja*'s theory regarding the relation between the inanimate world and God. *Rāmānuja* takes *prakŕti* as the body of God. In opposition to both the types of *advaita* theory he sets forth five types of distinction between (a) God and the individual spirit, (b) God and the inanimate world, (c) the individual spirit and the inanimate world, (d) one individual and another, (e) one inanimate object and another. *Paramātma* is the creator much in the sense of an efficient cause. *Prakŕti* is the primordial source with inherent equilibrium and God brings about the world of multiplicity out of *Prakŕti* by disturbing this equilibrium. Knowledge comes from God and knowledge might lead individuals either to cling to the worldly values or to aspire for *Moksa*. *Moksa*, however, requires more than mere knowledge. It is to be achieved through certain disciplines, performance or rituals and finally through devotion and love for God and prayer (*upāsanā*) to Him. The unmistakable implication of the theory is that individuals are real having genuine existence and *mokśa* is the highest value in individual life; it can be obtained primarily through love and devotion for God.

Nimbārka, another *Vaiṡnava* of the south (flourishing between the middle of the eleventh century and the middle of the thirteenth century), presents yet another version of the religion with a peculiar combination of monism and

---

36. *Sri Bhāsya*, 1, ii, 23.

pluralism. His philosophy has been presented by him in a summary way in a book of ten verses (*Daśaśloki*). He maintains that the individual soul is knowledge and is dependent on God (*Hari* or *Kṛṣṇa*). Individual soul and the inanimate world are distinct from each other but they are also in a way identical. They have no existence completely independent of God and in this way, they are identical with God. But still they exist either being separated from or being associated with God. The purpose of the individual is to realize union with God chiefly through self-surrender born of proper knowledge devotion and love for God. *Nimbārka*'s theory seems to have its basis on the philosophy of *Rāmānuja*. He has, however, made the reality of the individual more phenomenal in the spirit of the *advaita vedanta*. The other distinctions are more peripheral than real. While *Rāmānuja*'s object of worship is *Nārāyana* with his consort *Lakshmi*, *Nimbārka*'s is *Kṛṣṇa* with his beloved *Rādhā*. *Nimbārka* seems to have placed more emphasis on self-surrender as a means of liberation through the grace of God. This *bhakti* in the form of surrender is never without the elements of knowledge.

Vallabha, flourishing in the South in the sixteenth century recommends an exclusive cult of *Kṛṣṇa* of *Gokula* for *mukti* through divine grace (*pusti-mārga*). *Vallabha* thinks that the Supreme Soul feeling lonely has desired to be many and has become the inanimate world (*prakṛti*), the individual souls (*jiva*) and the controlling indwelling spirit (*antar-yāmin*). This suggests that *Vallabha* might have taken the Vedic saying '*ekaṁ syāt bahudhā bhavām*' literally and hence offered such an explanation of the world. The individual is regarded by him as identical with *Brahman* in so far as the soul is a part of it and it is atomic. The individual soul is not a product of *māyā*, but it is the same substance as the Supreme Soul with one attribute rendered imperceptible. The relation between the two may be compared to that existing between the sparks and fire, it is of identity of untransformed souls (*Suddhādvaita*). The souls are originally endowed with existence, consciousness and joy but because of delusion, they fail to realize this joy. Through love and devotion for God, liberation can be attained. His grace (*pusti* or *anugraha*) has to be obtained for final deliverance. When this grace is received the inner and outer life of the devotee becomes filled with *Kṛṣṇa*. The purpose of the individual is to obtain *pusti* of God for his self-realization.

At about the same time with *Vallabha*, *Sri Caitanya*, the leader of Bengal *Vaisnavism*, was preaching in Bengal. His religious view is distinct from the South *Vaisnavism* in its exclusive emphasis on *bhakti*, which could even dispense with any articulate knowledge. *Caitanya* lays stress on the emotional aspect of religion and disregards its ceremonial and ritualistic aspects. This might be a reaction to the intellectual formalism holding the philosophical stage in Bengal through the *Naiyāyikas* for some time. The School of Bengal *Vaisnavism* is famous for its devotional songs offered in the form of prayer. *Sri Caitanya*, also known as *Gourānga* or *Krsna Caitanya*, presents a philosophy close to that of *Nimbārka*. According to *Caitanya*, the individual soul is both identical with its distinction from the *Paramātma* so long as it does not drink the divine honey. Once it drinks it, it becomes full of it and forgets its distinct identity. It becomes absorbed in God (*Krsna*), the ecstatic state in which the individual becomes one with his God (*Krsnamoy*) though the two are really distinct. Through *bhakti* alone, can the devotee obtain the grace of God. He cuts off the shackles of ignorance (*māyā*) and allows the *jiva* to realize his own nature and his proper relation to God (regarded as the highest beloved). And in this consists the *summum bonum* of a *Vaisnava*.

The *Vaisnava* view in general of the individual and its relation to God may be expressed through that famous though dubious relation of the Hegelian philosophy – identity-in-difference. Individual existence is real but it gains its significance in the union with God to be obtained through love and surrender to Him. This conception has its origin in the Upanisads and has somehow permeated the thought of contemporary Indian philosophers. Rabindranath Tagore, the famous poet, in many of his lyrics has exquisitely brought out the theme of the interplay of the individual and the Supreme. In this thinking there is a sustained attempt to place importance on the conception of harmony, unity in diversity, as the key-concept of the Vedic tradition. *Vaisnava* theism[37] represents a dominant aspect of the Vedic line of thinking.

The other two principal types of theism – *Saivism* and *Sākta* faith – try to work out their theistic scheme in a slightly different way. But the status of the individual does not vary in any very significant manner. The origin of *Saivism*[38] cannot be very clearly pointed out; but the idea of the *Rudra-Siva*[39] is found in the *Rg-Veda* itself. *Rudra-Siva* is regarded more as an object of terror in the early conception. The god in some form might originally be an object of worship of the non-Aryan inhabitants of India; but quite early in the Vedic literature it finds its place in the Aryan worship. In the *Svetāsvatara Upanisad* the *Rudra-Siva* is elevated to the status of supreme god and considered from the religio-philosophic point of view. Whatever the historical origin, *Saiva* sects are found in India from quite an early period and there are a few sub-sects within the sect itself. One of these is famous as *Kāsmir*

---

37. One could also refer to the later period with *Nāmdev, Tukāram, Tulsidas* etc. giving the same philosophy with some variations.
38. One may consult *Vaisnavism Saivism* by Sri. R. G. Bhandarkar (Varanasi, 1965) in this connection.
39. *Rg. Veda* VII, 46, 3 & 1.114, 10.

Saivism. The main tenets of this religious faith in general seems to be that *Siva* (other names are *Maheśvara, Mahādeva, Paśupati* etc.) is the supreme god of creation and destruction. He creates and destroys being impelled by the potencies of actions (*karma*). The individual soul is atomic, eternal and all-pervading. It is both the agent and the subject (knower). Because of its fetters (*pāśa*) born out of ignorance it is incapable of boundless knowledge which is its original possession. When the fetters are removed, the individual becomes *Siva* and possesses infinite knowledge and indomitable power of action. For this perfection, one has to follow the prescribed course of *Sādhanā* and ultimately secure the favour of *Siva*. The individual attaining perfection (*mukta*) is identified with *Siva* himself. But this identification does not seem to be of the *advaitin* type. The *mukta* is dependent on *Siva* who is eternally free and independent. The individual when free is free within limits of its finitude and is never completely identical with the lord who is infinite. In this trend of thinking the *Saiva* school (and its later variant known as *lingāyat* school) appears to be close to *Rāmānuja*'s philosophy. The *Kāsmir Saivism* does not differ much in its theory of the individual and its relation to *Siva*, the Supreme being. But it suggests that the way of perception of identity between the individual and the lord is one of recognition rather than a new cognition. The identity has always been there, but because of fetters it could not be perceived. So, the individual attains to what is already his own. This is the concept of getting what it already is (*prāptasya prāpti*) a found in the main philosophical tradition, of the country.

This theme of identity of the individual with the Supreme being as an identity between the part and the whole is more clearly brought out in the *Virsaiva* or *Lingāyat* sect of *Saivism*. This sect regards *Siva* as the *Satcidānanda* and the creator of the individuals and the inanimate world. *Siva* has power (*sakti*) within Him and by the agitation of the innate power *Siva* (*sthala* – the static) becomes divided into two: (a) *Lingasthala*, and (b) *Angasthala*. *Lingasthala* is the lord himself, *Siva* as the object of love and worship. *Anga-sthala* is the individual soul who is the worshipper (*bhakta*) of the lord. *Bhakti* is the characteristic of the individual soul and through different (three) stages the individual soul attains perfection. The individual is never unconditionally identical with the absolute. It is the creation of the absolute but it is as eternal as the other inasmuch as it is in the supreme as a real existent. So, this presents a qualified non-dualism rather than an unqualified one. The reality of the individual is not denied, whether in fetters or free from them. The individual's highest goal consists in its realizing itself as eternal, free and sentient, in becoming *Siva*. Thus only can it fulfill itself. It knows no rest until it attains the knowledge of its proper nature which is to be an *anga* or *Siva*.

Along with the conception of the supreme being as a male god, there has always been an implied reference to some potency or power (*sakti*, sometimes called *prakrti*) through which the highest god creates the universe or sustains it. Both *Visnu* and *Siva* have been conceived on having their consorts in *Lakshmi* and *Umā* or *Durgā* or *Pārvati*. In a school of thinking the *Sakti* is regarded as the highest deity and it is conceived as a female deity excelling in power and glory all the other gods. It has been called in different names each suggesting a distinct motif. Names commonly used are: *Kāli, Durgā, Sivā, Sivāni, Rudrāni, Ramā, Rāmā, Karāli, Candi, Cāmundā, Umā, Pārvati* etc. But though they might have been conceived as different the inherent Hindu logic of thinking has ultimately united all of them in the conception of *Sakti* or *Durgā* or *Kāli*. The religious sect that takes this deity as the highest object of adoration and worship is known as the *Sāktas*. The deity in this faith is conceived not always as benevolent. It has a dreadful aspect also and it is the destroyer of all evils. But the devotee has nothing to fear from it. He is considered to be a part (*amsa*) of *Sakti* and his goal is to realize his proper nature as *Sakti*. The devotee is to offer himself to the mother goddess and realize his unity with her. But it does not appear that complete identity between the individual and the deity is asserted. It is a relation of the part to the whole and not of unqualified identity.

IV

The brief discussion of the different types of religious belief brings out the same truth as indicated by the philosophical systems. Whether it is a belief in *Viṡnu* or *Siva* or *Sakti* or it is unqualified non-dualism or monism or pluralism, the existence of the individual is surcharged with a deep significance. One is surprised to notice the amount of zeal and zest with which human living is looked upon in the earliest of the Vedas (*Rg-Veda*). The life there is taken quite often in a naturalistic sense to indicate the present life. A close study of the *Vedas* may lead one to conclude that there were all the rudiments of a clearly naturalistic-scientific explanation of the universe. But the prevalence of a belief in moral law can never be missed. This has conferred a special dignity on human existence. The conception of moral life and law has been taken to its philosophical culmination through the *Upanisads* and the philosophical systems. *Ātman* or the individual soul has been in the centre of philosophical and religious discourses and its teleology has been the principal determinant of the course of philosophical development.

Man's existence with its diverse experience is multi-dimensional. Its being cannot be looked upon in a compartmentalized fashion. Man has a normal, ordinary existence with common experiences. But that does not mark the end of his possibilities. He can transcend himself every moment in diverse directions and take a plunge into the depths of his being. The ordinary 'ego' in such moments yields to an expanding, deeper, freer ego. Man's seeming loss of normal individuality is more than compensated in his realization of freedom and emergence of a concrete, enriched individuality. If multi-dimensionality of human existence is a fact, levels of individuality is a logical consequent. The practical existence points to an alienation from fullness, but this alienation is not a phenomenological constituent of man. The philosophy that springs out from such a background cannot logically be one of despair; it is of robust optimism. Man, complex and expansive as he is, can fulfill himself in many ways (*sarvabhāven*). But fulfill himself he must, this is his purpose, this is the misison of philosophy to make him aware of the truth of his existence. Man cannot be negated, he can only awake to regain his full stature as *ānanda*. And to achieve this perfection, he has to move through harmony. Harmony of the different grades of meaning of life if a key-value in man's actual living. Man, fully realizing himself, is no other than God or *Brahman*. And in detailing out the means of such realization, one finds a unique unity in the Hindu *Sādhanā*.

This notion of man either as reality or as in reality is the message of Indian tradition. And reality is bliss, *ānanda*, perfection. It is full[40] from which nothing can be subtracted or to which nothing can be added; it remains the same under all conditions. The whole of man's life is dedicated to the realization of one value – realization of himself, his proper nature. This nature extends beyond the physical, psychical and epistemic existence. It is concreteness, fullness, perfection and bliss. Every little action of man is meaningful but in a transitive way. It points at the deeper intrinsic meaning from which every other meaning is derived. This is the truth of the divinity of the soul, immortality and perfection of its being. Free from its alienation as in bondage, it is in some sense identical with reality. But the stage of existence in bondage is not insignificant or valueless. It is because of its freedom that the soul is in bondage and it is because of the greater urge of freedom that the soul transcends its bondage to realize itself as pure freedom which is blissful. In the sojourn to perfection the soul is in association with different bodies, but that does not destroy the continuity of the individual.

This notion of an individual as either being without body or being

---

40. *Purnamadah* etc. referred in quite a few *Upanisads* (*Isa, Bṛhadāraṇyaka* etc.).

embodied but differently is what appears intriguing to the modern way of thinking of a individual as a person. But the Indian tradition seems to have accepted this at ease and realized the diverse meanings of the different levels of existence. Man can and does actually go beyond the fetters of his body and the physical existence and finds out the genuine meaning of his existence somewhere else. It is the realization of himself as pure being in and through all the levels of existence which seems to be the motto of human living. And this realization is realization of freedom itself which is blissful in its nature. This sense of human being as blissful harmonious existence constitutes the background of modern Indian thinking, however they might differ in developing the details of their thought. Realization of self through harmonious fulfillment by all means is conceived to be the purpose of man in traditional Indian thinking. The universe bears the message of divinity and man as divine is to work for regaining what is his by his very nature. He is *ānanda* and *amṛta*;[41] his alienation from it is real but not eternal. He has to work for that existence which transcends this ontological alienation. If the normal individual in alienation is the philosophical truth, the alienation-free existence is the meta-philosophical message, a practical urge and a programme for action.

---

41. *Bṛhadāraṇyakopaniṣad* – Canto V, 15, *Brāhman*.

CHAPTER 11

THE CONCEPTS OF MAN AND HUMAN PURPOSE IN CONTEMPORARY INDIAN THOUGHT

D. P. CHATTOPADHYAYA

I. Introduction

1. Whatever man does bears the imprint of his being. In the case of man what he is and what he is able to do cannot be neatly demarcated. Thought and action do not only interpenetrate but also interact in human situation: one influences and is influenced by the other. Philosophy is essentially a reflective activity partly expressing and partly concealing its author. The demand of the 'scientistic' philosopher that knowledge worth the name must be completely impersonal betrays his lack of understanding of the reflective character and anthropological root of knowledge. Complete impersonalization of knowledge (and action) is humanly impossible. For man can never get rid of himself either in knowing or in doing. The impossibility of knowledge without knower and doing without doer does not imply merely a linguistic relativity but a deeper conceptual interdependence of such pains of concepts as knowledge-knower, doing-doer, and action-agent. This is a very old but important view. The anthropological orientation of the Indian thinkers in general and the contemporary ones in particular are very clear indeed. The dualism between nature and man or that between pure reason and practical reason has never been a dominant feature of Indian philosophy, and in this respect its difference from European philosophy is noteworthy. Knowledge, whether it be of nature or of man, is regarded by most of the Indian philosophers as a necessary condition of human perfection. The axiological undertone of their ontologies is unmistakable.

1.1. Most if not all of the contemporary Indian philosophers and thinkers have been more or less influenced by the *Vedanta* system, Absolutism of Sankara, but it is interesting to note that none of them is prepared to accept its traditonal interpretations as ordinarily understood, viz., that the world is an illusion or *maya*, that human purpose is to be defined purely in terms of Divine purpose, and that from the ultimate point of view there is no purpose at all, Divine or human. Coming in contact with the western thought and civilization and impressed by the teachings of other religions like Islam and Christianity they realized the necessity and urgency of re-interpreting the pivotal concept of human purpose. Raja Rammohun Roy (1772–1833), the founder of modern India, showed the way. Having assimilated the teachings of Islam, Christianity, and Hinduism, he himself founded a new religion, *Brahma Dharma*. He did not accept Absolutism of Sankara without reservation. To him, Absolute is both qualified and unqualified, immanent and transcendent. Laws of nature are creation of God and as human beings we are subject to them. But by purifying our mind through meditation, contemplation, prayer and *samādhi* we can realize our unity with the Absolute. Before we realize the Highest we are to work and work selflessly (*niṣkāma Karma*) for our social and political upliftment and emancipation. Raja Rammohun believed in the underlying unity of all religions and preached universal fraternity. An apostle of reason and religiosity Rammohun had left behind some very influential ideas and ideals which were taken up and followed in right earnest by others in the nineteenth century.

1.2. In this paper I proopse to discuss the concepts of man and human purpose with particular reference to Tagore, Sri Aurobindo, and Gandhi. I would also briefly refer to Vivekananda and Radhakrishnan.

II

2. Rabindranath Tagore (1861–1941) was a poet-philosopher. Though great he is as a poet, but that is no reason why his philosophical position should not be properly and critically appreciated. Steeped in Upanisadic idealism, his philosophical views are full of creative insight, and remarkable for their consistency, clarity and beauty. Tagore does not use philosophical jargons, and that lends grace to his expressions and never makes his ideas obscure. The central theme of his thought is harmony, harmony between science and art, finite and infinite, life and death, god, nature and man. The key concept of his philosophy of harmony is man. 'Reality is the expression of personality, like a poem, like a work of art'.[1]

3. Tagore uses the term personality in a very philosophical sense. Person unrelated to the world, he says, is a mere abstraction. Real world is human world. Its true identity is not fully disclosed to our perceptual self but only to our emotional self. To the sense-mind world is a 'guest' and to the emotive mind a 'kinsman'. In sense-perception man is mainly passive and recipient, and cannot assimilate deeply all that he receives from the world around him. It is only in the depth of emotions and sentiments that the meanings of

---

1. Rabindranath Tagore, *Personality*, London, 1954, p. 69.

perception kindled by the outer world is beautifully assimilated. The outer world has its own 'juices', various qualities, exciting our emotional activities and thus making the secretion of inner 'juices' possible. Creative synthesis of the outer 'juices' and the inner 'juices' is called *rasa*, a very important concept in Sanskrit rhetoric. By *rasa* the world is transformed into a work of art. Without the world one ceases not only to be an artist but also to be a person. 'If this world were taken away, our personality would lose all its content'.[2]

3.1. Tagore attaches great significance to the artistic identity of man and takes immense pains to analyse it and show its relation with other identities of man – scientific, social etc. Man expresses himself in different ways, and for him existence without expression is impossible. To all forms of expression one characteristic is common: man cannot express the world without expressing himself *and* man cannot express himself without expressing the world. Man and world are indissolubly united. Neither man knows himself fully nor the world discloses all the levels of its existence to man at a time. In between his self and the world man is free to take different 'positions' – scientific, artistic etc., but he is never free enough either to ignore the world totally or to be completely indifferent to his own (originary) self. Man and the world are involved in an endless creative dialectic. The world is being incessantly created in man's perception and imagination. Deeply involved in his own personality the artist is 'apt to ignore the tyranny of facts'. The freest identity of man is artistic. Art 'is the response of man's creative soul to the call of the Real'.[3] Even in his freest moment the artistic consciousness of man remains constantly open to the call of the world and craves its touch, for it fears the dumb monotony of a dead world. When the world fails to evoke various and changing emotional reactions in the artist's mind, the artist becomes vague even to himself. In extreme loneliness man feels sick and fails to be creative. Underying creation there works an ineffable delight. Creative delight is causeless and endless. The primary commitment of the artist is neither to the natural world nor to the social world, Tagore strongly defends the 'art for art's sake' thesis; the artist, he says, forgets the 'claims of necessity' and the 'thrift of usefulness'. Artistic response is always 'disproportionate'; the feeling that is produced in us by an aesthetic object has a surplus in it and obviously this cannot be explained by the physical quantum of the object (and its force). Artistic feeling referred back to its producing object comes back to the artist's mind and makes him more and more deeply conscious by its 'return waves'. In art this efflux of the consciousness of the

2. *Ibid.*, p. 14.
3. Rabindranath Tagore, *The Religion of Man*, London, 1958, p. 139.

artist's personality finds an expression. While in science man 'has completely to conceal himself', in art he 'reveals himself and not his objects'. Rabindranath develops an expressionist view of art and an instrumentalist view of science, and encounters all the associated difficulties.

3.2. The distinciton between the artistic identity of man and the scientific identity of man may be indicated in various ways. First, one might say, as Rabindranath does, that science has use-value or that the only value of science is its use-value, but art has no use-value whatsoever. Science embodies man's knowledge of the world outside him – the world he has to know in his own interest and for purely practical purpose; and art, it is said, expresses the 'useless' surplus of human personality. One may *live* without art but not without science, provided, of course, we take the concept of living in a lower sense, e.g. biological. This way of drawing the line of distinction between art and science is perhaps slightly misleading. For in a sense science may also be characterized as 'useless' konwledge or disinterested pursuit of truth. Science should not be confused with its application or technological know-how. It has a theoretical core which is hardly verifiable or 'useful'. Like the artist the scientist is also engaged in discovering the harmony of the world. ging to discover the harmony of the world the scientist-man tries – tries his best – to forget himself and keep himself away from the world he studies and explains, but the artist-man in the course of discovering the harmony of the world discloses himself and realizes tat his personality and the world are the key notes of one and the same harmony. Secondly, the artist-man is like a player who plays the game without being aware of its rules, and the scientist-man tries to analyse and master the rules without being interested in playing the game.[4] The game *appears* differently to different persons: to some it is a means of earning, to some it is a sort of amusement, and so on. But in all cases the rules of the game hold good alike, no matter whether the persons concerned know it or not. Science deals with the world of *abstract* identity or sameness. The nature of the world or Reality *is* the variedness of the *unity* of its *appearances*. He 'knows' the game best who plays it with passion and interest and not who analyses it very carefully. The impersonal attitude of the scientist-man stands in his way to grasp the world in its *concrete* richness. Whatever the artist achieves he achieves by temporarily identifying himself with the object of his enjoyment (or suffering) and expression. Finally, the artist-man sees through the paradox of the infinite assuming finitude, but the scientist-man fails to see the paradox and pursues the knowledge of finite for its own sake. In this connection Rabindranath refers to two very significant verses of *Isopaniṣad*.

4. Rabindranath Tagore, *Personality*, p. 53.

They enter the region of the dark who are solely occupied with the knowledge of the finite, and they into a still greater darkness who are solely occupied with the knowledge of the infinite.

He who knows that the knowledge of the finite and the infinite is combined in one, crosses death by the help of the knowledge of the finite and achieves immortality by the help of the knowledge of the infinite.

'Solely occupied with the knowledge of the finite' the scientist-man, it is suggested, 'enter(s) the region of the dark', and 'solely occupied with the knowledge of the infinite' the philosopher-man 'enter(s) into a still greater darkness'. But it is the artist-man who avoids the errors of extremism, sees the unity of the finite and the infinite and how the latter is expressed in and through the former. It is to be noted that the Upanisadic poet is more opposed to infinitism (or absolutism) than to finitism. 'For the absolute infinite is emptiness. The finite is something'.[5] The philosopher takes a purely negative view of the world when he says that the world of space, time, colour and music turns out to be illusory (*māyā* in ultimate analysis. The more positive view which Rabindranath endorses is this: the mosaic of the empirical world is the *lilā* or manifest surplus of the creative delight of the infinite (God). Man communicates with God not necessarily through 'the world of extension in time and space' but also in 'the innermost solitude of consciousness'. To the artist-man the world of relation and the world of solitude are equally real.

3.3.1. The critic might feel that Tagore's view on the relation between the scientist-identify of man and the artist-identity of man is a rather oversimplification of the matter and, therefore, misleading. The scientist is not necessarily a finitist, engaged in a mere *fact*-finding mission and trying to *connect* the facts in terms of some *useful* laws or instruments. Like the artist he is also influenced, and at times even inspired, by the vision of the beyond. His theories are neither entirely based upon nor conclusively tastable by facts; scientific theories always contain some transcendental or metaphysical elements in their corpus. The scientist's primary concern is truth; his heuristic devices should not be taken too seriously. Like the poet he is also immensely impressed and feels drawn by the (macro- and micro-) structural harmony of the world. True that the artist's response to and expression of the harmony of the world differs vastly from the scientist's. But that does not mean that, what is often suggested, the scientist's picture of the world is impersonal while the artist's intimately personal. Either picture seems to be partly personal and partly impersonal. The artist's experience of the world is of course personal, but since it is communicable to and sharable by others it is also in a sense impersonal. The distinction between what is *private* and what is *personal* must

---

5. *Ibid.*, p. 56.

not be forgotten. In spite of its testable character the experience of the scientist is in a very important sense remains personal. Whatever might be its mode, artistic or scientific, experience has a personal (i.e. anthropological) presupposition. Absolute or impersonal experience is a philosophical abstraction. Experience is necessarily owned by this or that person: denial of this view betrays only conceptual incoherence. To say that the world of science is personal or human is not to suggest that scientific truth depends on human beings. On this point what Einstein, himself a scientist-artist, told Tagore is noteworthy indeed:

If there is a *reality* independent of man there is also truth relative to this reality; and in the same way the negation of the first engenders a negation of the existence of the latter.[6]

To show the *human* character of the objective world containing such objects as table and chair when Tagore says 'it [i.e., table] remains outside the individual mind, but not outside the universal mind',[7] he reminds us of Berkely, and we know how difficult it is to *disprove* universal solipsism. In terms of harmony, the key concept of Rabindranath's philosophy, the controversy over impersonal truth and personal realization or knowledge of that truth can be resolved and the poet himself has left behind several clues to that resolution. He says:[8]

In the apprehension of truth there is an eternal conflict between the universal human mind and the same mind confined in the individual. The perpetual process of reconciliation is being carried on in our science and philosophy, and in our ethics. In any case, if there be any truth absolutely unrelated to humanity then for us it is absoutely non-existing.

Individuated in space and time, man cannot know the world as a *totum simul*,. But whatever he *knows*, either as a scientist or as a philosopher, konws as a part of a bigger whole which he cannot immediately know but to which he *feels* irresistably (and intentionally) drawn. The limits encountered by the knowing-man are overcome by the feeling-man. The scientist tries to describe (the structures of) the world within a unified space-time framework. But the objects described or pictured in the world of art are free to appear unlike the objects perceived by us in the physical world. The scientist has to define first (in terms of class-properties) what he proposes to describe (structurally, *not* individually); the artist is not called upon to resort to this abstractionist strategy; he feels his object is free to create it, and need not know its space-

---

6. This point has been persuasively argued, among others, by P. F. Strawson. See his imaginative and careful book, *Individuals*, ch. 3.
7. Rabindranath Tagore, *The Religion of Man, p. 223.*
8. *Ibid.*, p. 225.

time address, if any. Yet the world of science and the world of art are somehow harmonious: one can hardly deny in good faith that the artistic identity of a flower, e.g., and the botanic identity of the same are consistent and form a unity. The underlying harmony of unity may be 'shown' in two different, but not entirely unrelated, ways. One way of 'showing' it is to postulate a Universal Mind and deduce the scientific and the aesthetic as two of its modes. And the other way of 'showing' it demands of us to start from the human end, reflect on different modes of human experience – aesthetic, scientific, moral etc., and discover their (covered or presupposed) anthropological unity. Tagore seems to favour the second approach to the unity (getting the got). Referring again to the *Isopaniṣad* (sixth verse) he says:[9]

We are hidden in ourselves ... when we know that this One in us is One in all, then our truth is revealed ... the unity of soul must not be an abstraction ... not that negative kind of universalism which belongs neither to one nor to another.

What is to be emphasized in this connection is this: *belonging to one* is not incompatible with *belonging to others*. For we must realize that one *is* always one-among-others despite one's creative solitude.

4. The ontology of man, rightly understood, shows how intimately the personal identity of man is related to his social identity, solitude to relation, and creation to tradition. Man is never completely given to himself. And his quest for knowledge of his own self never comes to an end. Ideally he is limitless. His actual limits are never complete and indicate always a beyond. The true unity of his self is beyond his actual reach.

Whatever else affects me ... is real for myself, and it inevitably attracts and occupies my attention for its own sake, blends itself with my personality, making it richer and larger and causing it delight. ... the world of our personality grows in its area with a large and deeper experience of our personal self in our own universe through sympathy and imagination.[10]

To man his own existence is 'a perpetual surprise'; and he can never fathom the depth of his existence. For the unfathomable depth of his existence his self is at times regarded as ideal. Life of man is continuous realization of this ideal. By personality Tagore means 'a self-conscious principle of transcendental unity within man which comprehends all the details of facts that are individually his own knowledge and feeling, wish and will and work'.[10] It is to this principle he attributes his poetic and creative powers, and

9. Rabindranath Tagore, *Personality*, p. 67.
10. Rabindranath Tagore, *The Religion of Man*, p. 131.
11. *Ibid.* p. 119; see also *Atmaparichay*, Collected Works (Centenary Govt. ed.), Vol. 10, p. 173. Rabindranath's position inevitably reminds us of Kant's. But Rabindranath is neither

also the unity of all that is *his*. Deep in his body but greater than it lies his humanity, says Tagore. This creative power in life is said to be his *dharma*, i.e. essence. And this essence – creativity – is his inmost truth. Whether this truth is expressed in art or in science the poet insists on regarding it as personal, not unrelated to his inmost essence. The paradigm existential statement for Rabindranath is 'I am', and *not* 'God is', or rather 'I-in-God am' but *not* 'God-in-I is'. From the beginning to the end human life is marked by freedom and creation. His physical 'capacity to stand erect' gave him manual freedom, enabling him to attain a posture of dignity, and use his hands for the purpose of producing what is useful and as well what is above use. This superior bodily organization made him a creative centre and 'as a centre he [found] his meaning in a wide perspective'. The physical freedom which man first started enjoying because of his manual skill was further expanded by his power of imagination. Man reaches and conquers the beyond by imagination. His hands and imagination thus enable man to exceed his biological existence and find his deeper meaning in a wider human perspective. Man is conscious of his 'inexhaustible abundance', the ontological mystery of his being, but fails to grasp it in its entirety. The deeper ideal unity of 'I am' 'is in his body, yet transcends his body; ... is in his mind, yet grows beyond his mind'. Tagore speaks of the paradox of human personality: 'it is more than itself; it is more than as it is seen, as it is known, as it is used'.[12] This paradox expresses what Merleau-Ponty calls 'the metaphysical in man'. Referring to 'this paradox of consciousness and truth' the French philosopher says:[13]

From the moment I recognize that my experience, precisely insofar as it is my own, makes me accessible to what is not myself, that I am sensitive to the world and to others, all the beings which objective thought placed at a distance draw singularly nearer to me. Or, conversely, I recognize, my affinity with them ... My life seems absolutely individual and absolutely universal to me.

Person is not pure consciousness, it is opaque, and the opacity is due to his embodiment and 'worldly' nature. In a sense he is of course *in* the world, but there is also sense in saying that he is *not* in the world. His being is prior to being-in-the-world and does not consist in its being perceived, but it is only in the world that he can be conscious of this priority. To a limited extent his being-in-the-world is preceded and succeeded by his being. His freedom is limited, and the limit, which is always changing, is set by *his* body and *his* world (containing *others*' bodies and others' worlds). Without using their

    a dualist nor a formalist like Kant.
12. Rabindranath Tagore, *Personality*, p. 38.
13. Maurice Merleau-Ponty, *Sense and Non-Sense*, North Western University Press, 1964, p. 94.

jargons, Rabindranath anticipated many ideas of the contemporary phenomenologists, existentialists, and philosophical anthropologists, and often he did it in details and as well as depth.

4.1. Man is born first in nature and then in society; his 'second birth' makes him painfully (and also joyfully) aware of his inherent 'paradox' and also of the power to solve the paradox. Not content with the world given to him, 'he is bent upon making it his own world'. He feels stifled 'to live in what *is*, for it is living in what is *not* ourselves'. [itals mine] It is his separation from nature to which he *originally* belonged and with which he is still in constant commerce that man becomes conscious of his creative freedom. Science and technology are said to be his instruments for extending the sphere of freedom. In his bid to be 'fully' free man cannot and should not try to snap his *originary* tie with nature. For it would be 'an ingratitude of deepest dye'. Man does not go to the opposite extreme either: he cannot totally identify himself with the Supreme Person. He cannot accept Him by rejecting or nihilating himself. 'The ultimate end of freedom is [not only the severance of relationship with nature but] also to know I am'.[14] Initially it is in the feeling of the separateness from all that I know that I am, but finally it is in the feeling of the unity with all that I identify my existence or personality. Human personality has levels within it, e.g. self-level and soul-level. Human self finds itself often caught in contradiction due to its dominant direction to the objects of deire. But when man succeeds in inwardizing his consciousness and turning 'his inward forces into the forward movement towards the infinite, from the contradiction of self in desire into the expansion of soul in love' he discovers his true identity and unity with others. Rabindranath speaks of 'a central personality' in relation to which 'this world is a real world' and without which 'it falls to pieces, becomes a heap of abstractions, matter and force, [and] logical symbols'.[15] It is in terms of this central personality, he insists, that the harmony not only between the objects but also that between the subjects are to be understood. In the deepest harmony, of course, both the subjective and the objective 'live' together; and that harmony is a living harmony. The harmony of the supreme personality is neither directly given to man nor an abstract principle postulated by him, it is for him a *lived* reality wherein the actual and the possible are gradually found to be compatible and compassible. Even the harmony of bones, limbs and cells in *a* human body, not to speak of other harmonies – cultural, national etc., is somehow related to this

14. Rabindranath Tagore, *Personality*, p. 95.
15. *Ibid.*, p. 98; see also Kant, *Critique of Pure Reason*, A 107–9. Husserl observes, 'Objects exist for me, and are for me what they are, only as objects of actual and possible consciousness'. *Cartesian Meditation*, (tr. Dorion Cairns), 1960, p. 65.

supreme harmony. The harmony or unity of the parts of a body is not achieved by the body but rather in the body, and, therefore, it is to be admitted that the 'principle' of the harmony is *relatively* independent of what is harmonized by it, i.e. subjects and objects. Subjects or persons are also relatively free from that central harmony of the infinite person and primarily *live* their own lives and do so in their own worlds.

4.2. The above point leads Tagore to raise a very fundamental question, and it seems to me that a correct understanding of the social identity of man is impossible without a satisfactory answer to this question.

> But these centres [i.e., human creatures] are innumerable. Each creature has its own little world related to its own personality. Therefore, the question naturally comes to our mind, – is the reality many, irreconcilably different each from the other?

Rabindranath has himself tried to answer this question in is own simple but profound way. Here again he notes the paradox between the individual (man) and the universal (man). Without egoism the individual is not conscious of its separation from other (individuals), without separation union makes no sense, and without union there is no love. But again in complete union there is no play-room for love. What man wants is a harmony of separation and union; separation must not destroy union and union must not devour separation. Man craves for that love wherein separation and union cohabit and do not quarrel.[16] But at times under the influence of passions and emotions man's sense of separation degenerates into a sense of isolation. Sense of isolation is oppressive and develops morbidity in us; sense of separation is supervened by consciousness of others from whom we are separated and towards whom we feel drawn and encourages our creative power. The moment of separation makes man all the more aware of the *lack* of harmony in him. He cannot live on bread alone, for *his* disharmony intends harmony with others, and his love for others starts supervening over his separation from them. It is basically this intention of harmony that explains human creativity – aesthetic, social and the rest. Individual man is never perfect; for perfection he intends union with others – union which does not mean negative separation. Union which leaves no room for separation is stifling and kills creative freedom. Rabindranath is strongly opposed to the negative concept of freedom; freedom, he says, is not relationlessness. Robinson Crusoe was not certainly the freest man *in the world*; one might even wonder whether he was man at all.

---

16. Rabindranath Tagore, *Collected Works*, Vol. 12, (Centenary Govt. ed.), pp. 135–7.

... in the social or political field, the lack of freedom is based upon the spirit of alienation ... There our bondage is in the tortured link of union. One may imagine that an individual who succeeds in dissociating himself from his fellows attains real freedom, inasmuch as all ties of relationship imply obligation to others. But we know that, though it may sound paradoxical, it is true that in the human world only a perfect arrangement of interdependence gives rise to freedom. The most individualistic of human beings who own no responsibility are the savages who fail to attain their fullness of manifestation.[17]

Man has two aspects of his being in him: he is both in himself and also for other selves. To be in his own self, paradoxically enough, he needs other selves and he cannot be in other selves without being in himself. His self-identification and (his) other-identification are contemporaneous and conceptually inseparable. He can neither 'erase' himself out of other selves and identify himself completely with the latter, nor can he 'expose' himself and other selves completely. He is always partly 'erased' and partly 'exposed'. This is the language of Gabriel Marcel. Rabindranath would say, man is partly 'hidden' and partly 'expressed'. It is to this 'expressed' aspect of man's being that his social identity is primarily due, but this *primary* identity is sustained, nourished or impoverished by the 'hidden' aspect of his being, his *basic* identity. Living amidst others man is obliged to live for others, but living for others does not prevent him from living in himself, and, therefore, in a basic sense man is always, or ontologically, free. Man can endlessly regress 'in' himself. However, at no (depth-) level of his *regress* can he hope to be *absolutely* free. Absolute freedom, i.e. the ideal freedom, cannot be achieved in the *progressive* direction either, for *he* cannot completely erase *himself* out. Human freedom is neither purely objective nor purely subjective. In the situation of freedom the subjective and the objective are compresent or, to use Tagore's term, interdependent. Freedom, according to Rabindranath, consists neither in total submission to nor in total withdrawal from *universal* necessity. The basic identity of the *individual* who is called upon either to submit or to withdraw cannot be presumed to be non-existent, for that makes no logical sense. Being what he is, i.e. free, man intends to become more and more free, and to fulfill this intention he has to explore continuously harmonious relation between himself and the world, the individual and the universal. An ideal society for Tagore is one in which harmony and not conflict between human beings is promoted. As man's egoism stands in the way of his true union with fellow human beings, national egoism or nationalism is detrimental to international co-operation and fraternity. Ideal unity should be tolerant and not totalitarian – tolerant of the individuality of

17. Rabindranath Tagore, *The Religion of Man*, p. 188; see also his *Collected Works*, Vol. 13, (Centenary Govt. ed.) p. 307.

its members. If the members of the national or international society lose their individuality, forget their soul-centres and try to live a life outside themselves, they would decay and die. The sign of change in life is expression and the sign of change in death decomposition, and, therefore, in a fast changing society if man fails in increasingly deepening his individual consciousness, going beyond his narrow egoism and *dis*covering his union with others, he would gradually annihilate himself and finally impoverish others. Perfection means expression and more expression, without freedom of expression man cannot be perfect, and expression is impossible without harmony between his ingoings and outgoings. Man expresses himself in different ways, abstract as well as concrete, in art, science, machine, mathematics, metaphysics, civilization etc., however different might be the ways of man's self-expression his identity is never lost. Human history is the story of man's quest for his hidden identity, getting the 'got' (but what seems to be lost), anad discovering the harmony between himself and the world.[18]

5. It cannot be denied that Tagore attaches great importance to man and that he is opposed to absolute monism of Sankara. But it seems equally undeniable to me that overimpressed by the *concept* of harmony he fails to take due note of the elements of *opposition* and *contingency* that we *perceptually* encounter *in* the world. Harmony may be approached from two different ends – from the end of creator (*not* Creator) and that of discoverer. If man is condemned to be a mere discoverer of harmony and is not credited with the ability to be its creator, his position in the world loses a definite meaning. If I am to remain content only with discovering what has already been created by the supreme creator, the same must be true of other persons as well, and then all our creations are reduced to mere imitations or dim analogies of the divine creation, and, what is more, the divine creator is to be regarded as the only creator. 'Man is true, where he feels his infinity, where he is divine, and', Tagore says,[19] 'the divine is the creator in him'. It is argued that the more we allow the divine in us to create through us the more beautiful and expressive become our creations. From this argument one gathers the impression that to be a 'true' man man should be a passive discoverer rather than an active creator. The question arises how the discoverer can *own* what is created by the divine *in him*? Tagore's answer seems to lie in the words *in*

18. That harmony is the key concept of Tagore's philosophy has been argued most persuasively by S. N. Ganguly, P. K. Roy and N. N. Banerjee in their book, *Rabindradarsan* (in Bengali), Visva-Bharati, 1969. So far as I am aware this is the best introduction to Tagore's philosophy. The insightful ideas of this rather small book, I hope, would be further developed.
19. Rabindranath Tagore, *Personality*, p. 31.

him. He speaks of a harmony between the 'world, whose soul seems to be aching for expression in its endless rhythm of lines and colours, music and movements, hints and whispers' and 'the ceaseless longing of the human heart', and man can be claimed to be creator only in this limited sense that he makes manifest what is suggested by the divine, i.e. plays second fiddle to the divine creation. Denial of human ultimacy in creation or authorship raises difficulties in theory of knowledge in general, and value discourse, e.g. art, in particular. To affirm human ultimacy is not to commit oneself to solipsism or to deny the relative independence of the world. Being idealist as he was Tagore construed the independence of the world as a sort of limit on the part of finite man to know (or be) the infinite. The harmony of the infinite is not a foregone conclusion, already achieved there eternally independent of my active participation in and contribution to it. Man is not a mere spectator of harmony, often he 'makes' what he 'sees'; but the primacy of seeing tends to conceal even from himself the ultimacy of making. Deeply involved in perception we are not aware at times except on later reflection what we do while we perceive. We aer 'having' and 'doing' at the same time. Harmony for man is more a matter of 'doing' than of 'having'. The artist and the revolutionary draw the elements of harmony – harmonious creation – out of chaos, confusion and disorder. Many of our lived harmonies are preceded and succeeded by *disorder* and *disharmony*. It is true that man is being constantly called upon to make meaning out of whatever he experiences. But the meanings he makes out some times turn out to be *unintelligible* or *absurd* before long. Intelligibility, order, and harmony not infrequently come to an *abrupt* end. When I say all this, of course, I do not propose to defend the irrationalist thesis that human world is an endless succession of contingency. What I do feel is this: perhaps because of his rather uncritical commitment to the concept of harmony Tagore has failed to appreciate properly the significance of *disorder, unintelligibility, absurdity* and *abruptness* in the world. Our finitude has put us under a difficult obligation, which we some time fail to discharge: we have to make sense out of non-sense. 'Non-sense' of our experience is not due to the 'cunning' of the Supreme Person; rather it betrays *positive lack* of harmony *in* our experience *of* the world. Harmony of 'sense' and 'non-sense' is our hope and not experience. No doubt man *is* guided by hope, and hope has its positive role in shaping our life. But undue allowance to hope tends to make us unfair to the facts of experience.

III

6. Sri Aurobindo (1872–1950) is an original thinker and like Tagore he always refers to the germinal philosophical ideas of the *Vedas* and the *Upaniṣads*. Although he got a thorough western education and went to Cambridge, it does not appear from his writings that he was much influenced by the philosophy that was very current there at that time. He is opposed to absolute monism of Sankar or to use this term, ilusionism, and builds up a very comprehensive system in which the importance of man, his scientific activities, and the world are 'duly' recognized; but it must be remembered that his standpoint is highly speculative and metaphysical. Sri Aurobindo's system of philosophy is known as integral monism (*purṇādvaitavāda*); god, nature and man being its three key concepts, which are shown to be integrally related in terms of evolutionary gradualism in a dynamic whole. While, according to Tagore, reality is harmonious, according to Sri Aurobindo, it is integral; the former lays emphasis on the concept of essential *harmony*, the latter on that of dynamic *integration*. Obviously these two concepts are very similar, but not without difference. In this section I propose to give an outline of Sri Aurobindo's concept of man with special reference to spiritual evolution.

7. Man is ambiguous: he can neither reject altogether his infra-mental past nor can he be completely aware of his supra-mental future. Caught in between the forces of nature and the spirit, man is evolving, moving towards a definite goal. He is 'nature's unnatural', a mental being (*manomaya puruṣa*) placed in, purposively related to and influenced but not guided by, nature (*prakṛti*). Nature is said to be the executrix-force *of* consciousness and, therefore, natural phenomena must not be explained in terms of mechanical causation. Sri Aurobindo says that nature is 'the principle of deliberation and liberation'. In this respect his position is free from the shortcomings of dualism as advocated by the *Sānkhya* and Kant, for instance.[20] To be ethical or spiritual man does not really encounter what Kant calls a step-motherly nature. There is definitely something in nature which kindles the spirit in him. Nature poses a sort of spirtual challenge to man and does it with a purpose, which she only partly reveals and mainly conceals, and of which man is peculiarly equipped to be conscious on reflection.

7.1. Sri Aurobindo's evolutionary gradualism is evident in his view on the relation between man and nature. Unless nature is deemed to be spiritual it is not easy to explain how man, 'in spite' of his place in nature, can at all

---

20. Sri Aurobindo, *The Life Divine*, New York 1949, pp. 295–98. See especially 9. 317, where he argues that duality is apparent.

aspire to the divine. Nature is in-spired by the divine so that she can a-spire to it. To say, as Sri Aurobindo does, that 'apparent Nature is secret God' or that 'what Nature does is really done by the Spirit' is unmistakably intended to smooth over the body-mind, matter-spirit, and similar other dichotomies. In the scale of the evolutionary ascent of the divine man stands in between matter and spirit. Man is the latest but certainly not the last evolute of nature; the spirit in him has not yet been fully realized by him. According to Sri Aurobindo, man is supramental (*atimānasa*) being in the making.[21] To quote his own words, 'mind is not native dynamism of consciousness of the spirit; supermind, the light of gnosis, is its native dynamism'.

7.2. Sri Aurobindo thinks that man's subjection to the laws of matter (in motion) and life does not and in fact cannot negative his supramental aspirations. The inframental 'push' of matter and life, on the one hand, and supramental pull of (overmiind and) supermind, on the other have got peculiarly mixed up in the mental plane of man. The mental equilibrium of the supramental and the inframental is dynamic. And it may be viewed from two different ends – from below and from above: while the former is called ascent, the latter descent. The human or mental equilibrium of the natural and the spiritual is, as has been indicated before, always unsteady, and this unsteadiness is mainly attributed to a spiritual urge for creation. The essential dynamism of the human cycle is spiritual. But ist 'deliberating and liberating' power is rather inarticulate in the sub-human plane. The distinction between different planes of existence and consciousness is said to be one of degree and not of kind; and every plane exhibits continuously graded sub-planes within it. This reminds one of Leibniz's law of continuity, a sort of gradualism, which obviously clashes with Kantian dualism. It seems that neither Kan's as-if teleological affinity of body and mind nor Leibniz's view of pre-established harmony between body and mind will be quite acceptable to Sri Aurobindo. He holds that body is not alien to mind, rather it is oriented by mind; in other words, one might say, body is already mentalized, of course in an obscure way. This may sound Leibnizian, but Leibniz does not make use of the concept of evolution. His ontology is classificatory and not evolutionary. When it is said that body is mentalized this is particularly true of human body which occupies a position of privilege in the world of bodies. This privileged position of human body is due to its superior *organ*ization and *deliberate* orientation, which taken together make relatively distinct – relative to other sub-human bodies – 'liberation' of mental powers in it possible. It is not easy

21. *Ibid.*, Book Two, ch. XXIII. Sri Aurobindo writes, 'mind is only a middle term of consciousness ... a transitional being ... opening to what exceeds it ... super-mind and supermanhood', p. 754.

to find out a European counterpart of Sri Aurobindo. For his pronounced bias towards monism and dynamism, one might think, his position is near-Hegelian; but Sri Aurobindo is sure to reject at least a very important part of Hegel's theory of knowledge on the ground of its alleged intellectualism.[22] He is almost equally distant from the absolutist like Sankar or Hegel and the personal idealist like, say, Pringle-Pattison. In Indian tradition his system stands very close to Ramanuja's; but while Ramanuja defends the cult of *bhakti* or devotion, Sri Aurobindo upholds primarily that of *sakti* or power; but, he admits, *bhakti* and *sakti* may go together. Viewed from this end the latter may be regarded as a continuer of the occult *tāntrika* tradition of Bengal. This partly explains the importance he attaches to body in his discipline of integral or *purṇa yoga*. In order to be perfect, to realize the spirit in him, man should avoid the extremes of hedonism and asceticism. Sri Aurobindo whole-heartedly endorses the Hellenic ideal of a sound mind in a sound body. He is opposed to those who like the *haṭa yogī* speak of the necessity of mortifying the body and foregoing the pleasures of life for self-realization. Self – self in the higher sense – he reminds us quoting the *Upaniṣads*, is there slumberously operative not only in human body but also in the inconscient matter. Body, he reminds us, 'is an incident in the progress of the soul' – 'a symbol of our real being'. Man's spiritual journey is not being impeded by his body, it is rather 'a support and instrument for the action' of his spiritual consciousness.[23]

7.3. In the philosophy of integralism one finds a very adequate description of man in depth and also in details, clearly indicating his multilateral relations with what have gone in making him what he is now, the forces and promises which sustain him now, and, above all, what he will be, i.e. his possibilities. Some existentialist philosophers have defined man exclusively in terms of his possibilities; some theologians have said too much of man's fall and too little of his promise and significance in the scheme of things and beings of this world; but Sri Aurobindo is one of those few insightful thinkers who going to emphasize the immense *possibilities* of man never fail to point out the importance of his *actualities* and *past*. Sri Aurobindo's description of man seems to be adequate because we find it not only (a pre-view of) his

22. *Ibid.*, pp. 489–90. Sri Aurobindo is for dialectical intellect only so far as it helps us to clarify and order our knowledge and not prepared to allow the rigid frame of its logic to govern our intuitive and germinal conceptions.
23. Max Scheler, *Philosophische Weltanschauung*, München, 1954, p. 62. Quoted from Dr. J. N. Mohanty's 'Integralism and Modern Philosophical Anthropology' in *The Integral Philosophy of Sri Aurobindo*, Haridas Chaudhuri and Frederic Spiegelberg (eds.), London, 1960, p. 156.

possibilities but also (a re-view of) his actualities – a description given not merely from a horizontal (or metaphysical-evolutionary) standpoint but also from a vertical (or socio-cultural) one. Sri Aurobindo reminds one of Max Scheler's proposed philosophical-anthropological description of man.[24]

Philosophical anthropology is a fundamental science of the essence and essential structure of man; of his relation to the realms of Nature (the inorganic, plants and animals), as well as to the basis of all things; of his metaphysical origin as well as his physical, psychical and spiritual beginning in the world, of the forces and powers that move him and which he sets in motion, of the basic directions and laws of his biological, psychical, cultural-historical and social development, of their essential possibilities as much as of their actualities.

In this section we would try to follow Sri Aurobindo's account of man, how 'pushed' by nature and 'pulled' by supermind man first 'affirms himself in the universe' and then 'exceed(s) himself' to fulfill himself, to realize his supramental possibilities.

8.1. The lowest plane of man is physical and, Sri Aurobindo thinks that, humanity as a whole has arrived at no higher plane than the physical-mental – the lowest sub-plane of the intelligence. The physical man works only with the physical brain, the physical sense-mind, the physical sense organs, and is therefore said to be incapable of acquiring anything other than a mere physical sense of reality. He has a vital part which is predominantly instinctive and impulsive. These impulses and instincts are hereditary and in most cases customary and form no disciplined order. True discipline comes from within and not from without. But sensations, desires, hopes, feelings, satisfactions and all impulsive formations of life-consciousness are dependent upon or occasioned by external things, contacts or stimuli. Engrossed in the practical, the immediately realizable and possible, the common average mode of life, the vital man misses the spiritual sense of reality, cannot discover the secret unity underlying the forces operative in the surface of nature, raises a mass of reactions against himself and is finally found to be caught in the paradox of hedonism. He is so much concerned with self-affirmation, self-aggrandisement, and self-enlargement, the immediate claims of his vital ego, domination, power, excitement, battle and struggle, inner and outer adventure, that he has no time or mind to think over where all these will lead him to. The main element of the vital man being air, he is mobile, active, turbulent and even chaotic. He does not have that material poise and balance that one finds in the physical man, whose main element is earth. But if the vital man succeeds in enlisting the support of reasoning intelligence in his

24. Sri Aurobindo, *The Life Divine*, p. 643; see also pp. 799–800.

favour then can he only hope to influence his time and place. Sri Aurobindo thinks that the success or influence of the vital man is bound to be shortlived, and he is definitely against 'colossalizing' this sort of human creature – 'a Nietzschean supermanhood'. The vital man tends to identify himself with his bodily existence and the resulting way of life becomes hedonic. But unlike the physical man he is not satisfied only with the actual and the physical facts; he is 'a dealer in possibilities' and guided by the passion for novelty trying always to go beyond the limits set by physical sense-organs and mind, and persistently questions the validity of the findings of the different natural sciences.

> Physical Science is a vast extension of this mentality: it corrects the errors of the sense and pushes beyond the first limitations of the sense-mind by discovering means of bringing facts and objects not seizable by our corporeal organs into the fields of objectivity; but it has the same standard of reality, the objective, the physical actuality; its test of the real is *possibility of verification by positive reason* and objective evidence.[25] (my emphasis)

8.2. The mental part of the physical man is concerned mainly with the physical nature and its images. To the physical man images are more spatial and less ideal, i.e. he fails to grasp the deeper *meanings* of those *images*. It is for this limitation of the physical-vital mind, Sri Aurobindo argues, that it cannot get at the truths which the poet-philosophers of the *Vedas* and the *Upanisads* have expressed in their intriguing and inimitable language through symbols, metaphors and imageries. The ideas of the physical man are either derived from sensible objects or at least confirmable by the same, i.e. *objective*; his ideals customary, practical or traditional; and values for him are nothing more than helpful adjuncts to life. What he is incapable of is to rely upon self-evident ideas – ideas which are not objective or verifiable – and self-authenticated ideals – ideals which are not borrowed from this or that tradition or society. Whatever is spiritual seems to him unsubstantial, unreal, and he feels uneasy with it. He cannot ignore it altogether; nor can he accept it in its given form – unverifiable form. He does not know what to do with it. The creative unrest of the vital mind not only constantly interrogates the conclusions of science and philosophy but also 'brings about ... an incessant drive towards an exceeding of the bounds of circumstance and a self-exceeding'. Above the physical mind appears the vital mind. The vital man (*prāṇapuruṣa*) stands in between the physical man (*jaḍapuruṣa*), on the one hand, and the mental man (*manomaya puruṣa*), on the other. Partly free from

25. *Ibid.*, p. 372; see also *Sri Aurobindo International Centre of Education Collection* [AICEC], Vol. IX (which contains three books – The Human Cycle [*HC*], *The Ideal of Human Unity* [*IHU*], and *War and Self-Determination* [*WSD*], Pondicherry, 1962, p. 157.

the bondage of the blind physical necessity the vital man can partly understand the inner life of nature without the help of 'the body and of the symbols of the physical world'. Sri Aurobindo writes:[26]

Above physical mind and deeper within physical sensation, there is what we may call the intelligence of the life-mind, dynamic, vital, nervous, more open, though still obscurely to the psychic, capable of a first soul-formation, though only of an obscurer life-soul not the psychic being, but a frontal formation of the vital Purusha.

As the physical plane of human evolution has some sub-planes in it, the vital plane too has its several sub-planes. The first sub-plane is a 'dumb inconscient drive or urge', an imprisoned will, incapable of foreseeing its consequences, and completely under the influence of the Universal Will. It is in this plane that the seed of individuality makes itself felt for the first time, of course in a very obscure way. The second sub-plane is the ground of blind desire and possessive instinets. In the third sub-plane desires and possessive instincts remain no longer dumb and blind but develop the power of love in order to be successful in realizing their objects. 'The bud of the third is Love' – says Sri Aurobindo. The bud blossoms into a flower of perfection in the fourth plane where the original will of Life becomes more articulately conscious of its objects of desires and aspirations. The vital man does not know as yet what light – what message – he is carrying within him. Matter for its own 'apparent-inherent inconscience' and Life for its own 'apparent-inherent ignorance' confuse their restricted autonomy with the sovereignty which is enjoyed truly by the spirit alone. The movement in every plane has double significance: it not only realises the potentialities peculiar to the plane but also those which lie beyond its surface-limits. Self-fulfillment of every plane entails self-exceeding. From the standpoint of sovereign Spirit all potentialities of different planes and sub-planes are His own and integrally related in Him, and the process of their actualization is spread over all the conceivable planes and sub-planes of evolution. Nature is realizing the spiritual significance which is dumb or dormant in Matter and only partially expressed in Life, and thus paving the way for man's self-affirmation. Man exceeds himself in true self-affirmation. This constitutes the only rationale of the wohle evolution of nature– sub-human, human, and super-human.

8.3. Man is the 'thinking instrument' of nature – comparatively free from the rigidity and inflexibility of the vital and physical laws, more or less able to grasp the modes of working of these laws and thus vary their modes of working to a certain extent so that the *deliberate* variation might help him to be liberated from the pulls of the infra-mental planes. What man is after is

26. Sri Aurobindo, *The Life Divine*, p. 640.

nature's natural, but from his finite point of view seems to be un-natural or super-natural. To him the spiritual goal of nature is not open in its entirety and complexity. His intellectual ways of harmonizing the workings of the different laws of nature *sub specie temporis* ultimately turn out to be inadequate and dispensable. Man – the mental being – is only the middle term of Nature's evolution. Sri Aurobindo says:

> In mind itself there are grades of the series and each grade again is a series in itself; there are successive elevations which we may conveniently call planes and sub-planes of the mental consciousness and the mental being.

Above the level of vital mentality there is 'a midplane of pure thought and intelligence' to which things are the most important realities. Mental intelligence is said to have three functions – primarily the function of understanding, then critical and finally organizing, controlling and formative.[27] The philosopher, thinker, scientist, intellectual creator, the idealist and the dreamer are at the top of the midplane of pure thought. At this stage man has mostly, but not completely, overcome the struggles and conflicts of the physical and vital levels and is engaged mainly in solving the problems of the intellectual level. Man has not yet discovered his own natural truth: he is still 'the abnormal in the normalcy of Nature' and wandering in the twilight region of reason. Man is still an imperfect apostle of an absolute ideal, of which he has had only occasional glimpses and towards which he feels irresistably drawn. 'This imperfection', says Sri Aurobindo,[28] 'is not a thing to be at all deplored, but rather a privilege and promise, for it opens out to us an immense vista of self-developing and self-exceeding'. Man's struggle is more or less self-conscious; matter and life are almost blindly engaged in asserting their own nature, and as a result of that the twilight region of mental-rational activities often becomes obscure and dark, but mind is trying to mentalize (i.e. to illuminate the relatively dark chambers of) matter and life. It is rather easy for mind to understand the simple organization and workings of matter and overcome its opposition. But from life it receives stiff opposition which refuses to surrender without a fierce fight. In this fight against the lower nature man's final victory is said to be assured by the Divine; but this victory becomes smooth and its pace accelerated if mind keeps itself continuously open to the supramental light and power.*Exclusive* self-affirmation of mind only delays the spiritual evolution of higher nature. Sri Aurobindo states it very clearly that reason cannot take us to 'the ultimates

27. *Ibid.*, p. 718.
28. Sri Aurobindo, *Sri Aurobindo International Centre of Education Collection*, Vol. IX, [*HC*], p. 315.

of life'. For its business is 'intermediate': it is parasitical, conservative, and practical – even the worth of theory it weighs in terms of practical use. Reason arranges, organizes and criticizes what is given to it; in any case it has to depend upon the given. In the level of thought the limits of reason do not pose a big problem. It can bring and hold together opposite view-points by introducing modification, shifting emphasis, or resorting to other *ad hoc* devices. But when the reason leaves the level of thought and comes down to practice and seeks to govern life its *ad hoc* approaches prove unsuccessful and even perilous. To the reason 'the integral truth of things' is never clearly revealed. Its dependence upon the given and tendency to fix its partial viewpoint and crystallize its system make it hopelessly inadequate for the purpose of grasping and expressing 'the fluidity of things'. To look freely and flexibly at the facts of existence, Sri Aurobindo says, man must dissolve the rigid constructions of the ignorant and self-willed intellect.

There we say, not the intellect and will, but that supreme thing in us yet higher than the Reason, the spirit, here concealed behind the coatings of our lower nature, is the secret seed of the divinity and will be, when discovered and delivered, luminous above the mind, the wide ground upon which a divine life of the human being can be with security founded.[29]

The more man deepens his inlook into himself and broadens his outlook on the world the more he realizes the imperfections of his rigid intellectual and self-willed constructions. First, his inlook persuades him of his *separate identity* – separated from the world and at the same time takes him to the world; then thrown in the world he discovers a new identity of his own – *identity in relation with* the rest of the world, based upon its indirect knowledge of other things and beings, and always unsure of its base; and finally a creative and explorative scepticism brings him back to his own deeper self, and he discovers his *spiritual identity* on which his previous and separate identity and the world together with its individual things and beings acquire an *integral meaning*. It should be remembered that man's inward journey knows no end, in other words, he cannot completely discover his own spiritual identity without ceasing to be what he is. He is indeed a dealer in endless possibilities.

8.4. A relentless critic of rationalism Sri Aurobindo does not fail to indicate its limited but undeniable importance in the integral scheme of life and reality. First, human reason is said to be built upon things which are finite – individuated in space and time, experience of the finite operations of physical

---

29. *Ibid.*, p. 314; see also *The Life Divine*, pp. 612–3.

nature; although unsure of its own foundation, it always seeks to make its fallible concepts general and universal and whatever departs or proves inconsistent with these concepts is regarded as irrational, false or inexplicable. There is a pronounced reductionist bias in it.[30] Secondly, Sri Aurobindo places reason in between the subconscient, what lies behind mind in the course of evolution, or Life and the superconscient, what lies ahead, or Light. And he speaks of triple errors inherent in the operations of normal or human reason. It takes the gulf between the Absolute and the relative to be unbridgable, makes extravagent use of the law of contradiction and does so very rigidly, and conceives 'in terms of Time the genesis of things which have their origin and first habital in the Eternal'. Lastly, whatever might be its limitations the aim and essence of reason is pursuit of Knowledge or Truth by the elimination of error. It can progressively eliminate error because its very essence is Knowledge and it can gradually overcome the dualities of right knowledge and wrong knowledge. Human ignorance is never entire; it is a limiting, a separative, very largely, a falsifying knowledge. There is no clear-cut demarcation between knowledge and ignorance.

8.5. In knowledge it is not easy to separate the knower from the knowing. The knower is partly identified with the knowing process but not entirely lost in it. He can watch his knowings in their origination and development, step back into the mental self judging and evaluating them, and be simultaneously conscious of his witnessing self and the operation and direction of the mind's action. Sri Aurobindo speaks of four different – yet not quite different – methods of knowing: (i) knowledge by identity, (ii) knowledge by intimate direct contact, (iii) knowledge by separative direct contact, and (iv) wholly separative knowledge by indirect contact. The difference between different cognitive methods is one of degree, and it is indicated in terms of knower-knowing identity and separateness. The knower can know by being what he knows, i.e. he becomes one with the content of knowledge, and at this stage subject-object and object-content distinctions disappear – do not simply exist. In knowledge by identity our essential existence is disclosed to ourselves – we *know* what we are. This supreme form of identification is possible but rare. The second way of knowing, although rooted in a secret knowledge by identity, is actually separated from its root. As this separation is not complete this mode of cognition continues to be very powerful and has a double tendency in it, that is to get back to the 'got' – its root and also to go out to the object snapping its connection with the root. In case the latter tendency

---

30. *Ibid.*, p. 297; see also p. 62. Sri Aurobindo's argument at this stage (pp. 338–47) seems to be addressed to such philosophers as F. H. Bradley.

prevails over the former the object we get is abstract, mutilated and appears as not-self. Paradoxically enough, mind in its eagerness to get to object separates itself from its own root – self – and as a result of that becomes separated from its object of knowledge as well. Sri Aurobindo believes in the foundational identity and unity of the subject and the object. Even in the third way of knowing, he says, mind is partly supported, may be very weakly, by the self. But in the fourth method of knowledge, when we know external things, our knowledge assumes an entirely separative character. Sparated from the object of perception and unsupported by the self we know object merely by deciphering the physical symbols of sense-mind. Consequently our knowledge of the world needs constant filling up, correction, addition and co-ordination.

Even so our knowledge of the world ... is narrow and imperfect, our interpretations of its significance doubtful: imagination, speculation ... measurement, testing, a further correction and amplification of sense evidence by Science, – all this apparatus had to be called in to complete the incompleteness. After all that the result still remains a half-certain, half-dubious accumulation of acquired indirect knowledge, a mass of significant images and ideative representations; abstract thought counters hypotheses, theories, generalisations, but also with all that a mass of doubts and a never-ending debate and inquiry.[31]

It is clear that Sri Aurobindo does not recognize science as a superior mode of cognition, but, as we have said before, he admits its limited significance and necessity. Unless we know our true self lying deep within our 'apparent phenomenal self' and grasp 'the true meaning of our existence', the power that we have gathered from our 'meagre and pitifully insufficient' knowledge is open to the risk of being misused and abused by ourselves. True knowledge, which alone can give us true power, takes us deep within our soul-consciousness, breaks the boundaries between our inner self and our ignorant surface self and the boundaries between that surface self and the external world, and enables us to realize the cosmic spirit and makes us entirely open to the universal energy, which brings about a profound change in our mind, life, and body, and also in our mental individuality. 'It is then', says Sri Aurobindo, 'that the existence of the cosmic Being becomes a certitude and a reality and is no longer an ideative perception'. True knowledge is claimed to be direct and intuitive and not obtained through interpretation of what is given in sense-perception and does not require any external test. It is self-verified and unfalsifiable. The question of fallibility does not arise in the case of knowledge by identity.

9. Sri Aurobindo thinks that man's true identity, although in essence

31. *Ibid.*, p. 473. For different types of knowledge see pp. 469–71.

unchanging and eternal, is disclosed in time; man's essential eternity and temporal individuality are two halves of one and the same necessary truth. His individuality is a vehicle of progressive evolutionary manifestation of the divine unity. But how the universal unity of the divine is individuated in finite human beings like ourselves is a very difficult question to 'the logical reason' and its correct answer is to be found in 'a larger and more catholic enlightened reason', in an 'inward and upward self-unfolding'. Being-in-time is progressive and individuated self-realization of the Being-eternal. That is how Sri Aurobindo puts the matter. 'Eternity', he says, 'is the common term between Time and Timeless Spirit', and the latter is not to be construed 'necessarily a blank'.

What is in the Timeless unmanifestd, implied, essential, appears in Time in movement, or at least in design and relation, in result and circumstance. These two then are the same Eternity or the same Eternal in a double status; they are a twofold status of being and consciousness, one an eternity of immobile status, the other an eternity of motion in status.[32]

Sri Aurobindo uses the concept of eternity in a special sense: to him it means neither *absolute* timelessness nor *absolute* everlastingness. Eternity in one of its asepcts is temporal – manifests in time – and in another remains unmanifest. The true identity of man is not to be found in the unchanging witnessing self, who witnesses all change without being involved in or subject to it. He is not the stream of *his* consciousness either. But divorced from his becoming his being is an inconceivable blank. Human becoming has its definite rhythms and that again may be studied in two different ways. Some 'objectivists' think that man's true identity is to be discovered from some external data, laws, institutions, rites, customs, economic factors and developments. Opposed to this 'narrow' scientific way of looking at the thing Sri Aurobindo speaks of the necessity of 'emancipation from the obsession of physical science', and welcomes 'the beginning of a perception that behind the economic motives and causes of social and historical development there are profound psychological, even perhaps soul-factors'.[33] In one of his major works, *The Human Cycle*, he tries to establish the view that different stages and forms of human civilization and culture are being influenced and shaped by certain deep-rooted subjective forces or soul-factors. In other words it is suggested that the 'objective' approach to the study of socio-political institutions and organizations is bound to be superficial unless it is suitably supplemented by and seen as an integral part of a deeper 'subjective' process. In the spiritual depth of man the distinction between the subjective and the

32. *Ibid.*, p. 324; see also pp. 331–33.
33. Sri Aurobindo, [*AICEC*] Vol. IX, *The Human Cycle*, p. 2.

objective loses the significance ordinarily attached to it. This is not a new view nor does Sri Aurobindo claim to be its original author. But it is undeniable that drawing heavily upon European and Indian history he gives flesh and blood to this otherwise highly speculative hypothesis. The human cycle, according to Sri Aurobindo, begins at the fourth stage of natural evolution, when mind assumes the capacity to be simultaneously conscious of itself and the other three previous planes of existence, Matter, Life and Mind. Self-conscious man holds the key to the proves of natural evolution, but it must be realized that he himself is unable to know all that he stands for. Sri Aurobindo defends a teleological account of the evolution of man in the world against two other plausible accounts, one is scientific and the other metaphysical. First, the scientist contends that human evolution is 'the work of an inconscient energy which acts automatically by mechanical processes and can have no element of purpose in it'. Sri Aurobindo rejects this naturalistic theory of human evolution on the ground that it concentrates exclusively on the working machinery and surface process of the evolution and totally fails to take note of the purpose working there under a thick veil. Secondly, the metaphysician says 'that the Infinite and Universal has everything in it already, that it cannot have something unaccomplished to accomplish, something to add to itself, to work out, to realize, and there can therefore be in it no element of progress, no original or emergent purose'.[34] Sri Aurobindo dismisses the anti-teleological objection of the metaphysician by pointing out that teleology means only the realization of the totality in the part and does not bring in any factor that does not belong to the totality. Totality and individuality are said to be two inseparable aspects of one and the same reality. The individual has no purpose of his own which could be regarded as quite independent of the divine purpose. The liberation of the individual is the keynote of divine action and it is the pivot on which all else turns. Different forms of society at different stages of the human cycle provide various opportunities, conditions and fields for expression and development of human personality.

9.1. The early stage of every civilization is pervaded by a strong symbolic mentality. At that time man had an intuitive and imaginative outlook, and it enabled him to enter into the nature of things and feel its mysterious depth and spiritual significance. Deeply conscious of the indwelling spirit in the world around him, man tried to utilize it in shaping all his life personal as well as social. Human society of the period was a free and fluid association not restrained by the iron yoke of the collectivity. Guided by natural instinct or

---

34. Sri Aurobindo, *The Life Divine*, pp. 742-3.

free knowledge man shaped and developed his life properly and harmoniously having in him a constant touch with the rest of the world. If we forget the symbolic mental make-up of the authors of ancient cultures most of their ideas, customs, rituals, institutions etc. would appear irrational to us. To support his theory of primitive symbolism Sri Aurobindo refers, among others, to the religious institution of sacrifice, the social institution of marriage and four-fold order (*caturvarna*), and the highly metaphoric, picturesque and allegoric language of the poets and philosophers of the *Vedas* and the *Upaniṣads* and brings out their inner significance. The *Ṛg Vedic* hymn of marriage was originally purported to express the successive marriage of *Surva*, daughter of the sun, with different gods, but now it is supposed to be a mere marriage hymn for the union of a human couple.

9.2. The symbolic period of the human cycle is succeeded by the typal or conventional period. In this period what is admired most is the power of reason. The typal-rational man concentrates exclusively on symbols, steadily loses sight of the living reality standing behind, and to him finally the symbols turn out to be dead ideas. A tendency to intellectualize the intuitive, impulsive and subliminal modes of understanding and action is noticed in every sphere of life. Mental intelligence surveys only the outer features of the objects of study and remains content with discovering or formulating their superficial laws of operation. Types replace truths. Typal mind does not feel at home with intuitive truths and always tries to typify or standardize them. Life and conduct tend to become more and more formal and empty. 'A complete denial of religion, occultism and all that is supraphysical is the last outcome of this stage, a hard dry paroxysm of the superficial intellect hacking away the sheltering structures that are refuges for the deeper parts of our nature'.[35]

9.3. Typal period ripens into conventional period. Old types are new conventions. The typal-conventional period does not stifle to death all that it receives from the symbolic past. In their eagerness to preserve the valuable experience of the symbolic period the people of the typal-conventional period resort to systematization, formalization and codification. The ideal of liberty is superseded by that of order. The process of crystallization and stabilization is indeed necessary to impart a definite and durable character to the highly plastic culture and constitutions of the symbolic age. For the spiritual basis of life is found not broad and strong enough to support the increasing pressure and forces of many-sided practical and rational life of man in the second stage of the human cycle. But too much of stabilization and formalization instead of being and aid to social and intellectual progress proves to be its fetter in practice.

35. *Ibid.*, p. 771.

9.4. Due to the steady decline of the psychological basis of society and growing pressure of the outer structure the gulf between truth and convention becomes too wide to be bridged over by the materials available in the period itself. To get rid of this intolerable state of affairs man in spite of his natural conservatism begins to seek a new opening – a way out of the conventional shell of his society. The corruption and failure of the conventional age gives rise to an individualistic age of human society. Completely convinced of the uselessness and worthlessness of the petrified types and conventions the individual man is obliged to fall back upon his own understanding, intuition and idealism. In the light of his own *svadharma* he starts questioning the rationale of the *yugadharma*. The dawn of individualism is marked by restlessness, scepticism and denial. In the typal-conventional society true science and kowledge are either banned or forced to rely on fixed authorities, the politics of divine rights, vested interests, and serfdom is deemed to be very natural and rational, and man is told to believe that fixed privileges of the rich, the fixed disabilities of the poor and the blind prostration of the low are all traditionally obligatory and morally sound. In the age of individualism and reason man rises in revolt against all these outdated ideas and dark forces of reaction, irrational authority and useless tradition. This age is generally piloted by new and protesting religious spirit and it culminates in marvellous progress of physical sciences. The leaders of the movement of religious freedom in Europe took their stand on the right of the individual illumination and reason to determine the true meaning of Scripture, the true Christian ritual and order of the Church. To the defenders of the old order the champions of the new are nothing but destructive agents threatening social security, political order or religious tradition. Although Sri Aurobindo does not share this unduly pessimistic view about the age of individualism, he admits that 'the unrestrained use of individual illumination or judgment without any outer standard or any generally recognisable source of truth is a perilous experiment for our imperfect race ...[and] is likely to lead rather to a continual fluctuation and disorder of opinion than to a progressive unfolding of the truth of things'.[36] Consequently the search for supreme desiderata – a freely acceptable general standard of truth and a principle of social order founded on a universally recognizable truth of things – became imperative for man in this age. It is in verifiable science that he found what he had been seeking for so long, a norm of true knowledge and a rational basis for social life. Paradoxically enough the fulfillment and triumph of the individualistic age sounded its death knell. By allowing the mechanical laws

---

36. Sri Aurobindo, [*AICEC*] Vol. IX. *The Human Cycle*, p. 21.

of science discovered by his own free understanding to govern his living and thinking he started losing his place of pride in the scheme of things. Setting out to discover the law of his own individual being man discovered a law of collectivity. Experimental science and socialism are two of the most important results of the age of individualism.

9.5. This age first appeared in the West and in the course of its self-expansion over the world the West has awakened India and other eastern countries from their 'long contented slumber in the cramping bonds of a mechanical conventionalism'. When at the end of a long and lingering typal-conventional period India was groping in the darkness trying to realize its own inner truth, other influence of the West supplied the necessary light. The Indian response to the Western challenge found its expressions in several religious, social, and political movements of the nineteenth century. The Young Bengal Movement under the leadership of D'rozio was deeply influenced, almost overwhelmed, by the Western culture, ways of living and thinking. The leaders of the Brahma Movement, Raja Rammohun Roy, Devendra Nath Tagore, Keshab Chandra Sen and others, made a serious attempt to incorporate the liberal and rational elements of the West into the native mould, but perhaps because of the unmistakable intellectual undertone of their spiritual message it did not reach the masses of the country and they did not feel drawn into the movement. Despite its revivalist character the Dakshineshwar Movement under the spiritual leadership of Ramkrishna displayed the broad, catholic and liberal features of the Hindu religion and culture. The cause of true orthodoxy and revivalism was championed by Dayanand Saraswati and other leaders of the Arya Samaj Movement. Although its underlying motive force was communal, the Aligarh Movement undeniably contributed to the nineteenth century Renaissance of India. The same may be said, at least to a certain extent, of the Wahabi Movement as well. As the result of all these movements the Indian people re-discovered their lost identity, got the necessary courage and light to strike a new and progressive balance between their *svadharma* (own nature) and *yugadharma* (time-spirit). This marked the end of the typal-conventional period and the beginning of the period of individualism and reason in Indian history. But it seems highly doubtful if India would be able to travel in her own way the full length of this new age. For a new force has appeared on the Indien scene and this is the force of Socialism, and this force too is western in its origin. Sri Aurobindo is in favour of selective assimilation, subordination and transformation of foreign influences, and warns us that if we 'attempt to remain exactly what we were before the European invasion or to ignore in future the claims of a modern environment and necessity' we will surely fail.

Cultural integration presupposes true self-identification.

the man who most finds and lives from the inner self, can most embrace the universal and become one with it ... it is one of the greatest secrets of the old Indian spiritual knowledge ... to live in one's self, determining one's self-expression from one's own centre of being in accordance with one's own law of being, *svadharma*, is the first necessity.[37]

9.6. The instruments and institutions of modern society are growing rapidly in number and complexity. Under the increasing pressure of lifeless and mechanical society man is becoming more and more conscious of the inadequacy of intellectual reason for the purpose of tackling the external problems of life and the growing necessity of discovering a deeper subjective identity. This is the beginning of the coming of the subjective age. Unless man returns to his own self and discovers new powers and means within himself he is sure to be overwhelmed by the forces around him. He must go deep within himself and enter into conscious harmony with what lies below the surface mind and behind the sensible outside. Under the insufficient light of reason he should not be a fumbling seeker of truth; he must enlighten his reason and make dynamic his action through the newly discovered light and power. The subjective age made its appearance felt first in the field of art and literature. The subjectivist tendency is evident also in the field of education. It is being increasingly realized that true education consists not in imposing some foreign ideas or skill on the student but in bringing out of his own intellectual and moral capacities to their highest possible excellence. but it can hardly be denied that emergent subjectivism has shown itself mainly in the new collective self-consciousness of man, national or communal, and not so much in the relations of individuals. The error of individualistic egoism of the passing phase of the human cycle is going to be transformed into the more momentous error of a great communal or national egoism. Body was being confused with soul, ego with self: the ugly face of false subjectivism started appearing in different parts of the world, most conspicuously in Germany. False subjectivism encourages certain pernicious tendencies, such as stateism, racism, national egoism and international egoism, each of which proves detrimental to the fulfillment of individual human purpose. True subjectivism helps man to realize that 'there is one self of all and the soul is a portion of ... universal Divinity' and 'that he is not only himself, but is in solidarity with all of his kind', i.e. the individual and the universal are two inseparable aspects of the one and the same Divine. Human purpose is integral to the Divine purpose.

37. Sri Aurobindo, *The Foundations of Indian Culture*, New York, 1953, pp. 438–39; see also p. 440.

9.7. There is no doubt that Sri Aurobindo is a holist and historicist. Man by his very nature 'belongs' to the whole of reality and human society, although because of insufficient self-realization he may not be aware of this deeper truth. And it is further said that human history is governed by some definite and inexorable law, and that the role of an individual in history is ultimately determined (horizontally) by the social whole(s) to which he 'belongs' and (vertically) by the forces collectively designated as the law of history. If these arguments prove valid, the importance of human purpose and freedom does not get its due recognition. But Sri Aurobindo seems to be clear on these points and not prepared to accept the criticisms of the anti-holist and anti-historicist thinkers. Sri Aurobindo points out that whatever man does he does primarily following his *svabhava* and *svadharma*, the law of his own being, but this law forms an integral part of the law of the human type. What man has done up till now is to act within the circle of his *svabhava*, to move in a spiral, sometimes descending, sometimes ascending – but always following the same or constantly similar curves of direction. It is through supramental transformation of man, Sri Aurobindo believes, a new age is coming – a new age in which the promise of the subjective age will be fulfilled, the harmony between man, community and humanity will be freely realized.

IV

10. Gandhi is generally known as a politician. Many people think that he is a saint. But the few people who have taken the rewarding trouble of going through his numerous writings, political, religious, autobiographical etc., cannot fail to be impressed by the striking consistency of his ideas, consistency between his profession and practice, and the definite *Weltanschauung* underlying all his utterances, ideas and actions. He lived an intensely spiritual life and the harmony of his life as a whole is an unmistakable proof and expression of it.

10.1. The basic idea of Gandhi, the votary of non-violence (*ahimsa*), is very simple. According to him, man is essentially, i.e. by his very nature (*svabhava*), non-violent (*ahimsa*). Although the term non-violence sounds negative, its meaning is supremely positive.

In its positive form, *ahimsa* means the largest love, greatest charity. If I am a follower of *ahimsa*, I *must love* my enemy ... This active *ahimsa* necessarily includes truth and fearlessness ... The practice of *ahimsa* calls forth the greatest courage.[38]

38. *Speeches and Writings of Mahatma Gandhi,* Madras Quoted from *Selections From Gandhi*

To *be* truly non-violent it is not enough to refrain from killing or injuring other being. That is only the negative part of the thing. Without being violent in overaction one may be violent in one's attitude and disposition towards others. Non-violence in its Gandhian sense is really a question of *being*. And it is not at all an easy thing to root out violence from the very core of our heart. Unless and until one becomes utterly selfless, i.e. completely free from a regard for one's body, one cannot *be* non-violent. For Gandhi to *be* non-violent is to realize one's own self, i.e. Truth, and its distinction from body. That Gandhi regards the issue of non-violence as a metaphysical issue becomes further evident when he says that so long as we exist physically or are inhabiting the body we cannot be perfectly non-violent.[39] What Gandhi means is this: Truth of our being is spiritual and disembodied. Perfect non-violence is a theory like Euclid's point or straight line, i.e. a regulative ideal, which we cannot fully realize in our life but we have to endeavour every moment to realize it for 'it is our supreme duty'. '*Ahimsa* is the means'; and, says Gandhi, 'Truth is the end'.[40]

10.2. One must not fail to note the special sense in which Gandhi uses the concept of Truth. Its metaphysical implication is unmistakable. Like other people he first says 'God is Truth' but then unlike other people he goes 'a step further' and says 'Truth is God'. And then he asks us to 'see the fine distinction between the two statements'. One may not accept God as the embodiment of highest value, but as regards Truth, Gandhi thinks, there is hardly any room for such controversy. Every man, be he a scientist or metaphysician, theist or atheist, wants to know what exists, i.e. *sat* – what is true. It has been said in Hindu philosophy that God alone *is* and nothing else *exists*. Elucidating this point Gandhi says that whoever wants to know what is *sat* is seeker of God. Truth may be approached from different ends. For Truth is manysided (*anekānta*). In his own way gandhi accepted the Jaina doctrines of *anekāntavāda* and *svyadvāda*. One and the same reality or object may be affirmed and negated, severally and jointly, in seven different ways (*saptabhangi*) without self-contradiction. This shows, Gandhi says, endless complexity, impossibility of (one and only one) definite predication, and dynamic character of Truth or Reality. Truth is not something theoretical and abstract; the nearest approach to it is through love. The love for Truth must be pure – free from all bodily passion. Man's search after truth as God, Gandhi insists, 'must go through several vows ... the vow of truth, the vow

    by Nirmal Kumar Bose, Ahmedabad, 1968, pp. 157–58. All subsequent quotations, unless otherwise mentioned, are taken from this well-known book by Bose.
39. *Young India*, 4–11–1926, pp. 154–55.
40. *From Yerveda Mandir*, pp. 13–4.

of *brahmacharva* (purity) ... the vow of non-violence, of poverty and non-possession'. Truth is self-evident and as soon as we remove the cobwebs of ignorance that surround it we see its shine clearly. To know Truth what man needs most is *satyāgraha* or soul-force. Soul-force sustains him in his patient endeavour and silent prayer, and develops a sense of humility in him. 'Constant endeavour and silent prayer are always my two trusty companions along the weary but beautiful path that all seekers [of Truth or God] must tread'. Truth-consciousness is ineffable and mystic, and in it 'reason and intellect, and the body' are 'completely subordinate'. In a mystic vein Gandhi says, 'If you would swim on the bosom of the ocean of Truth you must reduce yourselves to a zero. Further than this I cannot go along this fascinating path'.[41]

10.3. To Gandhi God is not only Truth but also Law. God as Law rules our actions from within. The more we deepen our consciousness and realize His will *within* us the more we understand what God as Law means. Gandhi 'literally' believes 'that not a blade of grass grows or moves without His will', but, he thinks, this is not inconsistent with human freedom. To the question 'Do you feel a sense of freedom in your communion with God?' his answer is noteworthy.

> I do. I do not feel cramped as I would on a boat full of passengers. Although I know that my freedom is less than that of a passenger, I appreciate that freedom as I have imbibed through and through the central teaching of the *Gita* that man is the maker of his own destiny in the sense that he has the freedom of choice as to the manner in wihch he uses that freedom. But he is no controller of results. The moment he thinks he is, he comes to grief.[42]

Being an *advaitin* (non-dualist) in his philosophical persuasion Gandhi believes 'in the essential unity of man' and 'that if one man gains spiritually, the whole world gains with him and, if one man falls, the whole world falls to that extent'. When Gandhi says that God 'overrides all our intentions, all our plans and carries out His own plans' one might think he is a holist and determinist but we are to revise our opinion when he declares clearly that 'the individual is the one supreme consideration' or that non-violence implies decentralization and supreme importance of *Swaraj*, self-rule. To Gandhi national liberation is a help towards self-liberation and the latter is more important than the former. 'Government over self is the truest *Swaraj*'. The truly liberated man realizes his essential unity with other things, beings and God. It is through self-surrender, surrendering to God all that he has and

---

41. *Young India*, 31–12–1931, p. 6; see also *Collected Works*, Vol. 21, pp. 472–78.
42. *Harijan*, 23-3-1940, p. 6; see also *Young India*, 4-12-1924, p. 25; see also, *Collected Works*, Vol. 29, p. 410–12.

possesses that man can realize God and achieve emancipation, *moksa*. It seems that Gandhi has been very much influenced by the christian doctrines of confession and grace. 'Perfection', he says, 'comes only from grace'. And perfection necessitates self-rule or self-control. By sincerely confessing his limitations and imperfections man has nothing to lose but a lot to gain instead; he can thus lighten his spiritual burden and move quicker along the path of Truth for attaining perfection. Practice of non-violence in thought and action enables man to be really free, realize the Truth of his being, and discover the essential unity of mankind apparently separated by space and time, or class, caste and religion. Non-violence is not a cloistered virtue. It is a force to be reckoned with in every sphere of life – personal, national and even international.

I believe that true democracy can only be an outcome of non-violence. The structure of a world federation can be raised only on a foundation of non-violence, and violence will have to be totally given up in world affairs.

When man realizes Truth as Law he knows the inner bond that connects him with all other human beings, the spiritual force which polices them all alike from within. This realization develops in him deep love for fellow human beings. Gandhi makes no distinction between loving man and loving God. 'My creed is service of God and therefore of humanity', he says. God is sun and we, human beings, are His rays. Sun shines even when its rays are not visible to us on the earth. In a true *advaita* vein he observes: 'We are *not*, He alone *is*'.

10.4. Gandhi is a profoundly religious man. But his religious outlook and attitude are very unorthodox and liberal. True that he is proud of being a Hindu, yet what *he* means by religion 'transcends Hinduism'. For him religion and morality are absolutely inseparable. He rejects any religious doctrine that does not appeal to reason and proves inconsistent with morality. Scriptures and tradition must not be accepted uncritically. 'Scriptures cannot transcend reason and truth', observes Gandhi. He is uncompromisingly against untouchability and child marriage, for instance, even though these are backed by the tradition of the land. 'Any tradition, however ancient, if inconsistent with morality, is fit to be banished from the land'. Like Sri Aurobindo Gandhi is also very much opposed to typal-conventional morality and religion. True religion and true morality must be 'creative' and cannot consist in 'following the beaten track'. He is definitely against 'slavishly copying the past' and 'multiplying past errors'. To Gandhi there is no religion higher than Truth and Righteousness. Religious quest is quest for what is true and what is right. Religious life is very comprehensive; politics is an integral part of this life. He says –

I cannot conceive politics as divorced from religion. Indeed religion should pervade every one of our actions. Here religion does not mean sectarianism. It means a belief in ordered moral government of the universe. It is not less real because it is unseen. This religion transcends Hinduism, Islam, Christianity, etc. It does not supersede them. It harmonizes them and gives them reality.[43]

Religious life is a life of progressive self-realization. The more one realizes one's self the more one realizes one's spiritual unity and harmony with other selves. Too much of institutionalization of a religion is a very bad thing indeed, for it stifles its inner growth. To start with religion is a personal affair, but in its depth it is universal. 'There are as many religions as there are individuals', but all religions ultimately 'converge to the same point'. A truly religious man loves not only his friend but also his enemy. 'To a good man the whole world is good'. The politics of *ahmisa* is based upon the religion of Truth and Right. True politics is inseparable from religion and morality.

10.5. Gandhi's approach to religion, as I have already pointed out, is very liberal and unconventional. Throughout his life he went on experimenting with Truth. The name of his autobiography, *My Experiments with Truth*, is very sugestive indeed. He is extremely humble as regards his knowledge of Truth. He is an *anekāntavadī)*, a believer in the manysidedness of Truth. Sometimes he says, 'God is not a person', but sometimes he says, 'He is a personal God to those who need His personal touch'. From some of his writings he seems to be a *mayavadi*, an absolute monist, but from some other writings one gathers the impression that he is a *līlāvādī*, qualified monist. According to *māyāvād*, the world is an illusion; those who advocate the doctrine of *līlā* accord attributive, i.e. limited, reality to the world. Gos is creative and as well as non-creative. In His creative aspect God may be said to have created all of us, i.e. human beings; but He may be thought of as non-creative as well. From one point of view Gandhi feels justified in saying, 'We are *not*, He alone Is'; from another point of view he confesses, 'I know I cannot find Him apart from humanity'. Gandhi explains his religious, political and philosophical catholicity in terms of his own interpretation of *anekāntavāda*, the Jaina doctrine of the manysidedness of Reality. 'My *anekāntavāda*', he says, 'is the result of the twin doctrine of *satya* (truth) and *ahimsā* (non-violence)'.[44] The main two moving forces behind Gandhi's politics are truth and non-violence. To love Truth is difficult unless one realizes Truth *as* God and knows human beings *are* expressions of God. Deeply moved by the *Gītā* Gandhi observes, 'The path of *bhakti* [devotion],

43. *Harijan*, 10-2-1940, p. 256; see also, *Collected Works*, Vol. 22, pp. 194, 271.
44. *Young India*, 21-1-1926, Quoted from M. K. Gandhi, *Hindu Dharma*, Ahmedabad, 1958, p. 55; see also sections 2 and 9.

karma [action], love ... leaves no room for the despising of man by man'. Love for man liberates man, takes him nearer to God, and gradually fulfills his purpose. He invites us to join him in his prayer with Newman:

> Lead, kindly Light, amid the encircling gloom
> Lead Thou me on:
> The night is dark and I am far from home,
> Lead Thou me on.
> Keep Thou my feet, I do not ask to see
> The distant scene; one step enough for me.

Human purpose is to realize the purpose of God in every sphere of life, in politics, ethics and religion.

10.6. The ideas about God and Man that we find in the writings of Tagore, Sri Aurobindo and Gandhi may be found also in the writings of Vivekananda (1863–1902) whose *Vedantic* bias is unmistakable. In the early years of his spiritual journey Sri Aurobindo was very much influenced by Vivekananda. Both Vivekananda and Gandhi are practical Vedantists, bring religion very close to practical and even political affairs. Vivekananda's mission was spiritual, and not political in the ordinary sense. But to him as it is to Gandhi spiritual life is sovereign and all-comprehensive and nothing falls outside its scope. All human endeavours, theoretical and practical, individual and collective, are directed towards God. All religions are 'forces in the economy of God, working for the good of mankind'. In spite of their surface differences all religions have a common spiritual core and common spiritual end; 'they are not contradictory, they are supplementary'. Vivekananda assures us that the universal religion about which philosophers and thinkers have dreamed in every country and in every age is not a dream at all, but already exists. The religion of *Vedanta*, rightly understood, is a truly universal religion. The priests and preachers who claim exclusiveness in favour of their respective religion are conservative in their outlook and superficial in their inlook. The Vedantist says:

> As so many rivers, having their sources in different mountains, roll down, crooked or straight and at last come into the ocan, so all these various creeds and religions, taking their start from various standpoints and running through crooked or straight courses, at last come unto Thee.

Vivekananda preached the Vedantic message of universal brotherhood based upon the spiritual unity of mankind. We are alll seeking God, some knowingly and some unknowingly, some in a straight course and some in a crooked course. Vivekananda says:[45]

45. Swami Vivekananda, *What Religion Is*, John Yale (ed.), London, 1962 p. 10.

No search has been dearer to the human heart than that which brings us light from God ... Man has wanted to look beyond, wanted to expand himself; and all that we call progress, evolution, has always been measured by that one search – the search for human destiny, the search for God.

God is the universal existence. He is the ultimate Unity in the universe without destroying its diversity. True that in God we are all one, but allows our difference to remain in Him. There are two types of unity – unity in difference and unity of sameness. The latter, according to Vivekananda, is not only destructive but also dangerous. The ideal of universal religion is not incompatible with the existence of different religions '... God is the centre of all religions, and ... each of us is moving towards him along one of these radii, ... it is certain that all of us *must* reeach the centre'. In God we are one, and at the centre all our differences will cease. There are different paths leading to the ideal centre. We may get to God either through selfless action (*karmayoga*), or dispassionate love or devotion (*bhaktiyoga*), or knowledge (*jñāna yoga*). Karma Yoga teaches to work selflessly, to do our duty for the sake of duty, without caring in the least for the possible results of our work. Bhakti yoga teaches us to love God, to love all beings as the manifestations of God as Love. Love itself is the highest recompense of love. The jñāna yogi endeavours to realize God through meditation and contemplation. To him, God is the soul of his soul. Knowing himself he knows God. 'God is his own Self'. Every man seeks God according to his own nature and there is no general and universally accepted way of God-realization. Vivekananda, who is otherwise a devout Hindu, is very liberal in his attitude towards all other religions. He always speaks of 'harmony of different religions'. He who has realized his true self knows what harmony – social, religious and cosmic – really means.

10.7. In recent time it is Radhakrishnan, the statesman-philosopher, who has emphasized the spiritual unity of mankind and the harmony of different religions. He feels 'fairly certain' that the Hindu solution of the problem of the conflict of religions will be accepted in the future.

God wills a rich harmony and not a colourless uniformity. The comprehensive and synthetic spirit of Hinduism has made it a mighty forest with a thousand waving arms each fulfilling its function and all directed by the spirit of God. Each thing in its place and all associated in the divine concert making with their various voices and even dissonances ... the most exquisite harmony should be our ideal.[46]

This ideal is the key-note of the Hindu view of life and thought. This ideal harmonizes *Puruṣa* (Person or Man) with *Prakṛti* (Nature), and both with the Divine (*Isvara*). Everything in the world is of use *and* value for the self-

---

46. Radhakrishnan, *The Hindu View of Life*, London, 1962, p. 43; see also p. 58.

realization of self. Nothing is purposeless. Every detail of this universe is not decreed. 'We are partly free to change its course, for together with God we ourselves are *in* this very course. 'God is not somewhere above us and beyond us, he is also in us'. God being our *karmādhyakṣah* (supervisor of our *karma*), He regulates our *karma* from within. The doctrine of *karma* does not imply denial of human freedom: it only implies that our actions are *ultimately* regulated by an inner spiritual necessity, by God as Law (*Ṛta*). Dharma (Religion) and *Ṛta* (Law or Order) are very intimately related concepts, the former liberally means that which holds a thing and maintains it in being, and the connotation of the latter comprehends both the natural and the spiritual orders. Life of *dharma* or virtue consists in continuous conformity with the truth of things. Irreligiosity or immorality is 'disharmony with the truth which encompasses and controls the world'. Man must live to work, but not to work alone. He has to earn his bread, but he does not live by bread alone. He must affirm himself by exceeding himself. His end is self-emancipation, *Mokṣa*, and 'all [his] activities are directed to the realization of this end'.

11. 'Unity in diversity' is the foundation of Indian culture and the key concept of the Indian view of life. Man is here in the world to fulfill himself. His body, life, and mind, his history and society provide him with all that he needs to fulfill himself by exceeding himself. His economic (*artha*) and hedonic (*kāma*) needs must also be fulfilled, but the ways of fulfillment must be consistent with *dharma*, and ultimately leading to the end of *mokṣa*. It has been very clearly observed in the *Gita* that man must seek the Divine in every way of his being, *sarvabhavena*. This old and undying truth of the Indian concept of human purpose has been re-affirmed by all contemporary Indian thinkers. In his individuality and as well as universality man seeks to realize and express himself. He wants to live and grow in harmony with the rest of the world, natural and human.

INDEX

Biblical Reformation language 165
Buddhism 45

Comprehensively meaningful 28
Concept of intentionality 32
Concept of the sacred 43
Contemporary Indian Thought 271

Darkness around the meaning-of-life questions 26
Drive for wholeness 204

Empirical naturalism 66
Epoche 34
Eschatological verification 187

Freedom of man 127

God 35
God as Being-itself 84
God's purpose 169
God's purposiveness 179
Ground of Being 81

Happiness and satisfaction 64
Hinduism 303
Human purpose 61

Indian Religion 233
Intentional discourse 34

Judaic-Christian tradition 44
Judaism 115, 122
Justification for our existence 8

Kabbalistic thought 118

Liberal Judaism 123
Liberation 251
Limiting questions 21
Linguistic philosophers 29

Man 28, 41, 63
Man and the sacred 44
Man of the Ground 84
Meaning of Life 4
Myths 42

Naturalistic humanist perspective 50
Neo-Reformation 176
Nirvăna 41
Notion of power 38
Notion of the holy 38

Organism's well-being 63
Orthodox Judaism 105
Other-wordliness of the religious attitude 37

Phenomenology of religious experience 33
Phenomenology of the religious moment 37
Primordial totality 216

Reformation thought 165
Reformation view of Purpose 166
Religion and secularism 69
Religious holism 197

Sacred history 42
Scientific humanism 50

Theological doctrine of happiness 162
Theological theory of man's ultimate end 143
Theory of man's natural ultimate end 143
Torah 109
Totality 206

Ultimacy 72
Ultimate in secular experience 199